ACCA

ADVANCED TAXATION (ATX – UK)

FA 2017

P
R
A
C
T
I
C
E

&

R
E
V
I
S
I
O
N

K
I
T

FOR EXAMS IN JUNE 2018, SEPTEMBER 2018, DECEMBER 2018 AND MARCH 2019

BPP
LEARNING MEDIA

First edition 2007
Twelfth edition October 2017

ISBN 9781 5097 1539 8
(previous ISBN 9781 5097 0839 0)

e-ISBN 9781 5097 1543 5

British Library Cataloguing-in-Publication Data
A catalogue record for this book
is available from the British Library

Published by

BPP Learning Media Ltd
BPP House, Aldine Place
London W12 8AA

www.bpp.com/learningmedia

Printed in the United Kingdom

Your learning materials, published by BPP Learning Media Ltd,
are printed on paper obtained from traceable, sustainable sources.

We are grateful to the Association of Chartered Certified
Accountants for permission to reproduce past examination
questions. The suggested solutions in the Practice & Revision Kit
have been prepared by BPP Learning Media Ltd, except where
otherwise stated.

Contents

BPP
LEARNING MEDIA

Question index

The headings in this checklist/index indicate the main topics of questions, but questions are expected to cover several different topics.

Mock exam 1 (ACCA September/December 2016 Sample questions)

Mock exam 2 (Specimen Exam)

Mock exam 3 (ACCA March/June 2017 Sample questions)

Topic index

Listed below are the key Advanced Taxation (ATX – UK) syllabus topics and the numbers of the questions in this Kit (excluding the Mock exams) covering those topics.

If you need to concentrate your practice and revision on certain topics or if you want to attempt all available questions that refer to a particular subject, you will find this index useful.

Syllabus topic	Question numbers
Administration of tax – individuals	10, 16, 20
Administration of tax – companies	21, 22
Capital allowances	8, 22, 25, 26, 28, 29, 35, 37
Chargeable gains – companies	23, 24, 25, 26, 29, 30, 31, 32, 39, 40
Chargeable gains – computation for individuals	4, 6, 10, 11, 15, 16, 17, 18, 19, 37, 38
Chargeable gains – shares/securities for individuals	13, 17
Chargeable gains – reliefs for individuals	4, 5, 6, 10, 15, 17, 18, 19, 20, 28, 31, 37, 38
Chargeable gains – additional aspects	4, 7, 10, 11, 15, 18, 19, 20, 35
Companies – administration, winding up	30
Companies – corporation tax computation	22, 24, 25, 26, 27, 31, 32, 33, 34, 36, 37
Companies – close and investment	28, 35
Companies – groups and consortia	22, 23, 24, 25, 26, 29, 31, 39
Companies – losses	35, 37, 38
Companies – overseas aspects	21, 30, 34, 36
Companies – personal service	7
Companies – repurchase of shares	38
Ethics	15, 16, 23, 24, 26, 41
Income tax computation	1, 2, 5, 6, 7, 9, 18, 28, 31, 35, 37, 41
Individuals – employment income	5, 7, 9, 21, 25, 33, 40, 41
Individuals – property and other investment income	6, 38, 40
Individuals – trading income	3, 5, 7, 18, 33, 41
Individuals – losses	4, 5, 8, 16, 18, 37, 41
Individuals – overseas aspects of income tax	3, 4, 9, 12, 18
Inheritance tax – introduction	2, 5, 11, 13, 14, 15, 16, 17, 19, 37, 38
Inheritance tax – valuation, reliefs and death estate	11, 14, 15, 17, 19, 37, 38, 41
Inheritance tax – additional aspects	4, 12, 14, 15, 17, 18, 19, 38
National insurance contributions	7, 28
Partnerships	8
Stamp taxes	11, 15, 24
Tax efficient investments	2, 9, 13, 17
Tax planning and impact of taxes	33, 36, 37, 38, 39, 40, 41
Value added tax	4, 10, 16, 25, 26, 27, 28, 29, 31, 33, 34, 35, 37, 40

Helping you with your revision

As an ACCA **Approved Content Provider**, BPP Learning Media gives you the **opportunity** to use revision materials reviewed by the ACCA examining team. By incorporating the ACCA examining team's comments and suggestions regarding the depth and breadth of syllabus coverage, the BPP Learning Media Practice & Revision Kit provides excellent, **ACCA-approved** support for your revision.

Tackling revision and the exam

Using feedback obtained from the ACCA examining team review:

- We look at the dos and don'ts of revising for, and taking, ACCA exams

- We focus on Advanced Taxation (ATX – UK); we discuss revising the syllabus, what to do (and what not to do) in the exam, how to approach different types of question and ways of obtaining easy marks

Selecting questions

We provide signposts to help you plan your revision.

- A full **question index**

- A **topic index** listing all the questions that cover key topics, so that you can locate the questions that provide practice on these topics, and see the different ways in which they might be examined

Making the most of question practice

At BPP Learning Media we realise that you need more than just questions and model answers to get the most from your question practice.

- Our **Top tips** included for certain questions provide essential advice on tackling questions, presenting answers and the key points that answers need to include

- We show you how you can pick up **Easy marks** on some questions, as we know that picking up all readily available marks often can make the difference between passing and failing

- We include **marking guides** to show you what the examining team rewards

- We include **comments from the examining team** to show you where students struggled or performed well in the actual exam

- We refer to the **Finance Act 2017 BPP Study Text** for exams in June 2018, September 2018, December 2018 and March 2019 for detailed coverage of the topics covered in questions

Attempting mock exams

There are three mock exams that provide practice at coping with the pressures of the exam day. We strongly recommend that you attempt them under exam conditions.

Mock exam 2 is the Specimen exam paper. **Mock exam 1** and **Mock exam 3** are compiled from questions selected by the examining team from the September and December 2016 exams and from the March and June 2017 exams respectively. They do not reflect the entire exams but contain questions most appropriate for students to practice. You should note that the selection of questions in Mock exam 1 and Mock exam 3 reflects the change in the Advanced Taxation exam format from June 2018 to two compulsory Section B questions rather than three optional Section B questions as when these exams were originally set.

Revising Advanced Taxation (ATX – UK)

Firstly we must emphasise that you will need a good knowledge of the **whole syllabus**. This means **learning/memorising the rules** in order to be able to answer questions. The examining team has commented that it is a **lack of precise knowledge** that causes many candidates problems in the exam.

All the questions in Section A and Section B are compulsory and any part of the syllabus can be examined in any question. However, there are certain topics which are **particularly important**:

- The **calculation of income tax payable**, including the **restriction of the personal allowance** and **tax reducers**

- **Personal pension schemes**, in particular the **annual allowance** and the **annual allowance charge**

- The **basis of assessment for unincorporated businesses**, including rules on commencement and cessation. Don't neglect the **impact of losses** in these situations

- The **calculation of benefits from employment** so that you can make sensible comparisons between **remuneration packages**. Make sure you can advise on **tax free benefits** too. The rules for **share schemes** and on **termination payments** should be known very well

- The **structure and mechanics** of **inheritance tax** (eg types of transfer, nil rate band, seven year cumulation, residence nil rate band)

- The **exemptions** and **reliefs available for the different taxes**, in particular **for capital gains tax** (eg entrepreneurs' relief, gift relief, rollover relief) and **inheritance tax** (eg spouse exemption, business property relief). **Exemptions and reliefs** are the **foundation of any tax planning**

- The **computation of corporation tax**, including dealing with **loan relationships**, **intangible assets**, and **research and development expenditure**

- **Close companies** including the position of **participators**

- All aspects of **corporation tax groups** including the impact of loss relief, chargeable gains groups, the effect of group VAT registration and stamp taxes groups. You should pay particular attention to the impact on **corporate restructuring**

- For **value added tax**, the **rules on land and buildings**, the **capital goods scheme**, **special VAT schemes** available for small businesses so that you can advise if and when they might be appropriate, and the **partial exemption rules**

- **Overseas aspects** of income tax, CGT, IHT, corporation tax and VAT

- **Tax administration**, including filing dates, penalties and interest for all taxes

- **Ethical considerations** when acting for clients

You should use the Passcards and any brief notes you have to revise these topics, but you mustn't spend all your revision time passively reading. **Question practice is vital**; doing as many questions as you can in full will help develop your ability to analyse scenarios and produce relevant discussion and recommendations.

You should make sure you leave yourself enough time during your revision to practise Section A questions as the scenarios and requirements of Section A case-study questions are more complex than Section B questions. You should also leave yourself enough time to do the three mock exams.

Passing the Advanced Taxation (ATX – UK) exam

Displaying the right qualities

The examining team expects students to display the following qualities.

Qualities required	
Knowledge development	Basic knowledge of the core taxes from Taxation (TX – UK) is key, extended to encompass further overseas aspects of taxation, additional aspects of CGT and IHT, trusts, stamp taxes and additional exemptions and reliefs.
Knowledge application	You must be able to apply your knowledge to the issues commonly encountered by individuals and businesses. You will be expected to consider more than one tax at any one time and to identify planning issues and areas of interaction of the taxes.
Skill development	Advanced Taxation (ATX – UK) seeks to develop the skills of analysis and interpretation. You must be able to interpret and analyse the information provided in the question, keeping your answers focused and as accurate as possible, while avoiding waffle.
Communication skills	Advanced Taxation (ATX – UK) also seeks to develop the skill of communication. It is no good having the knowledge but not being able to communicate it effectively, so ensure you keep your communication appropriate to the intended audience. Practise using the appropriate terminology in your answers: you will need to be more technical when communicating with a tax manager (eg using technical terms for loss relief) and less so when speaking to a client (who may not understand 'early years loss relief'!)
Keeping current	The examining team expects you to advise using established tax planning methods in the exam. Fortunately they do not expect you to invent new ones. However, you must be aware of current issues in taxation.
Computation skills	Computations are not the main focus of the Advanced Taxation (ATX – UK) exam. However, they may be required in relation to new topics such as partial exemption for value added tax and also in support of explanations. It is therefore essential that you can complete calculations of tax liabilities speedily.

You will not always produce the exact same solution as we have in our answer section. This does not necessarily mean that you have failed the question, as marks are often available for any other relevant key points you make.

Avoiding weaknesses

We give details of the examining team's comments and criticisms at various points throughout this Kit. These reports always emphasise the need to demonstrate a fairly wide syllabus knowledge, but also to identify and justify the availability (or non-availability) of particular reliefs and exemptions. There are various things you can do on the day of the exam to enhance your chances. Although these all sound basic, the examining team has commented that scripts show:

- A failure to read the question and requirements properly and answer the question set, instead churning out irrelevant 'set pieces'
- Clear evidence of poor time management
- Tendency to confuse CGT and IHT and even personal and corporation tax issues

Start each question on a new page, clearly labelled.

Finally, never ever cross your workings out. These may be correct and you will not be given credit if you have crossed the working out.

Choosing which questions to answer first

You will need to answer the two compulsory questions in Section A and two compulsory questions in Section B, with a larger number of marks awarded for the Section A questions (60 marks in total).

- We recommend that you spend time at the beginning of your exam carefully reading through all of the questions in the paper, and each of their requirements. Once you feel familiar with your exam paper we then recommend that you attempt Section B questions first.

- The Section B questions will be for 20 marks each covering both business and personal tax issues. Answer the question on your most comfortable topic first but be strict with timing. It is all too tempting to write everything you know about your favourite topic. Don't!

- The reason for attempting the Section B questions first is, in the examining team's words:

  'The majority of…candidates appeared to attempt the Section A questions first, and overrun the time allocation, which they may have regretted later when they reached some relatively straightforward areas in the Section B questions, but didn't have time to have a reasonable attempt at them.'

- Doing the Section B questions first should mean that you can manage your time more effectively and not run out of time answering the longer Section A questions. Attempting the easier questions first means that you will have been generating ideas and remembering facts for the more difficult questions.

- In Section A there will be 35 marks for question 1 and 25 marks for question 2. Many students prefer to answer question 1 with the larger number of allocated marks first. Others again prefer to answer a question on their most comfortable topic. There will also be four professional marks and five marks for ethics. Usually one question will be a personal tax question and one question a business tax question.

- Whatever the order, make sure you leave yourself **sufficient time** to tackle all the questions. Don't get bogged down in the more difficult areas, or re-write your answer two or three times. Instead move on and try the rest of the question as there may be an easier part. You do not want to be in a position where you have to rush the rest of the paper.

- Allocate your time carefully between different question parts. If a question is split into a number of requirements, use the number of marks available for each to allocate your time effectively. Remember also that small overruns of time during the first half of the exam can add up to leave you very short of time towards the end.

Tackling questions

You'll improve your chances by following a step-by-step approach along the following lines.

Step 1   Identify the requirements of the question

Identify the knowledge areas being tested and see precisely what the examining team wants you to do. This will help you focus on what's important in the question.

In Section B questions, this means reading the requirement of the question. However, in Section A questions, you will usually need to look also at the more detailed instructions within the body of the question to find out exactly what is required. Look for key phrases in the question such as 'I need the following ….' or 'Please prepare the following for me…'.

Step 2   Check the mark allocation

This helps you allocate time.

Step 3   Read the question actively

You will already know which knowledge area(s) are being tested from having identified the requirements so whilst you read through the question underline or highlight key words and figures as you read. This will mean you are thinking about the question rather than just looking at the words blankly, and will allow you to identify relevant information for use in your advice and supporting calculations.

Step 4   Plan your answer

You may only spend five minutes planning your answer but it will be five minutes well spent. Identify the supporting calculations (and appropriate proformas) you will need to do, if any. Plan the structure of your written answer, even if it is only a series of bullet points, or maybe a spider diagram, using suitable headings and sub headings. Determine whether you can you use bullet points in your answer or if you need a more formal format.

Step 5   Write your answer

Stick carefully to the time allocation for each question, and for each part of each question.

Gaining the easy marks

There are two main ways to obtain easy marks in the Advanced Taxation (ATX – UK) exam.

Providing supporting computations

Although computations will not always be required in isolation in Advanced Taxation (ATX – UK) as the main focus is on written explanations and advice, there will always be marks available for calculating figures which will support your recommendations. Often you cannot provide any sensible advice until you know the tax cost of a course of action so make sure you can readily set out proformas and fill in the numbers from the question. Make it easy for yourself to pick up the easy marks.

Answering the question

If you need to consider alternative planning strategies in a question and provide advice on which is the most suitable, do exactly that. If you do not advise on the most suitable plan you'll be losing easy marks. Similarly, if you are asked to consider CGT and IHT in a requirement, don't think that by including some income tax considerations you will pick up extra marks – you won't. Show the examining team you have read the question and requirements carefully and have attempted to answer them as expected – not how you would like to.

Exam information

Format of the exam

The **time allowed** for the paper is 3 hours and 15 minutes.

Advanced Taxation (ATX – UK) consists of two sections:

Section A consists of two compulsory case-study questions. Question 1 has 35 marks and question 2 has 25 marks. There will be five ethics marks and four professional skills marks available in this section. Professional marks are awarded for aspects such as adopting a logical approach to problem solving, clarity of calculations, the effectiveness with which information is communicated and the overall presentation of the required memorandum, notes or letter. There are no set topics for Section A questions, but you should expect to see coverage of technical taxation topics new in Advanced Taxation (ATX – UK), such as international aspects, and tax planning and interaction of taxes as well as application of technical aspects from Taxation (TX – UK).

Section B consists of two compulsory 20 mark questions, covering both business and personal tax issues. Again, there are no set topics, but you might expect to find more specialist questions concentrating on such areas as advanced corporation tax (for example, dealing with close companies or advising on the tax effects of purchase of own shares by a company), advanced personal tax (for example, advising on tax advantaged share schemes) or advanced capital taxes (for example, dealing with trusts).

You will be expected to undertake both calculation and narrative work. The questions will be scenario based and may involve consideration of more than one tax, together with some elements of planning and the interaction of taxes.

Tax rates, allowances and information on certain reliefs will be provided in the examination paper.

Examining team's general comments

If you are preparing to sit Advanced Taxation (ATX – UK) you should pay particular attention to the following in order to maximise your chances of success.

1   *Know your stuff*

- Successful candidates are able to demonstrate sufficient, precise knowledge of the UK tax system. This knowledge must be up to date. Candidates sitting the exam in June 2018, December 2018, September 2018 and March 2019 must familiarise themselves with changes introduced by Finance Act 2017 as summarised in the Finance Act article published in Student Accountant magazine and on the ACCA website.

- This includes knowledge brought forward from the Taxation (TX – UK) syllabus, which remains very important.

2   *Question practice*

- Candidates who perform well in the exam have clearly practised questions from past exams. By doing so, they have become familiar with what to expect in the exam in terms of the style and content of the questions. This is particularly relevant to the often more intellectually demanding Section A style questions. The candidates who have practised past exam questions also improve their ability to adopt the style of the model answers, such that their answers are specific, direct and concise.

3   *Address the requirement*

- You must read the requirement carefully – in the Section A questions the detailed tasks that you are to perform will be set out in one of the documents. It may be helpful to tick off the tasks as you address them. Marks are awarded for satisfying the requirements and not for other information even if it is technically correct.

- The requirements of each question are carefully worded in order to provide you with guidance as regards the style and content of your answers. You should note the command words (calculate, explain, etc), any matters which are not to be covered, and the precise issues you have been asked to address.

- You should also note any guidance given in the question or in any notes following the requirement regarding the approach you should take when answering the question.

- Pay attention to the number of marks available – this provides you with a clear indication of the amount of time you should spend on each question part.

4   *Don't provide general explanations or long introductions*

- If you are asked to calculate, there is no need to explain what you are going to do before you do it; just get on with it – only provide explanations when you are asked to.

- Think before you write. Then write whatever is necessary to satisfy the requirement.

- Apply your knowledge to the facts by reference to the requirement. Remember that in Advanced Taxation (ATX – UK) you will be asked to apply your knowledge, rather than just reproduce information you have learned.

5   *Think before you start and manage your time*

- Ensure that you allow the correct amount of time for each question.

- Before you start writing, think about the issues and identify all of the points you intend to address and/or any strategy you intend to adopt to satisfy the requirement.

Resitting Advanced Taxation (ATX – UK)

If you are preparing to resit the exam, think about the number of additional marks you need and identify a strategy to earn them. For example:

- Identify those areas of the syllabus where you are weakest and work to improve your knowledge in those areas. This should include any technical areas brought forward from Taxation (TX – UK) where necessary.

- Practise past exam questions in order to familiarise yourself with the style of questions that you will have to deal with.

- Ask yourself whether you could improve the way you manage your time in the exam and whether you address all of the parts of all four questions or whether you waste time addressing issues which have not been asked for.

- Make sure that you earn the professional skills marks and that you are prepared to address the ethical issues that may be examined.

Marks available in respect of professional skills

In order to earn marks for professional skills such as report writing, candidates first have to satisfy the requirement in relation to the format of the document requested. Further marks are then available for the clarity of the answer, including the ease with which it can be marked and the degree to which the conclusions reached follow logically from the explanations and calculations provided. These latter marks are more likely to be earned by those candidates who think about the manner in which they intend to satisfy the requirement such that there is a sense of purpose and a coherency to their answers.

Analysis of past papers

The table below provides details of when each element of the syllabus has been examined in the ten most recent sittings and the question number and section in which each element was examined.

Since September 2015 ACCA have been issuing two "sample" exams each year, after the December and June exam sessions. These exams are compiled from questions selected from the two preceding sessions eg in December 2016, the sample exam questions were compiled from September 2016 and December 2016 exams.

Covered in Text chapter		Mar/ Jun 2017	Sep/ Dec 2016	Mar/ Jun 2016	Sep/ Dec 2015	June 2015	Dec 2014	June 2014	Dec 2013	June 2013	Dec 2012
	INCOME TAX										
1	Principles of income tax	1(a)		2(b), 5(a), 5(b)	1(a), 2(b), 5(a)	3(b), 5(a)	1(b)	1(a), 4(a), 5(c)	5(a)	3(a)	2(a)
2	Pensions and other tax efficient investment products	1(c)			5(a), 5(b)				3(b)	3(a)	
3	Property and other investment income				4(b)	4(b)		4(a)	5(a)		
4	Employment income	1(a)	4(b)	2(b), 3(c)	1(a), 4(a)	5(a)		3(a), 5(c)	4(c)	3(a), 5(b)	2(a)
5	Employment income: additional aspects	4(a)	4(a)	5(b)			5(b)	3(b), 3(c)	5(b)	5(b)	1(a), 2(a)
6	Trade profits	1(a)	2(a), 3(b)	1(a), 5(a)	1(a)	5(b)	4(a)	1(a)			2(a)
7	Capital allowances	1(a)	3(b)	1(a)		3(a)	2(a)	1(a), 5(b)	1(b)	4(b)	1(a)
8	Trading losses	1(a)			1(a)	1(b)	1(b)			5(a)	2(a)
9	Partnerships and limited liability partnerships			5(a)							
10	Overseas aspects of income tax	3(b)	2(b), 4(c)			1(a)	4(b)			3(b)	
	CAPITAL GAINS TAX										
11	Chargeable gains: an outline	4(b)	2(a)	1(b), 3(a)		4(a)	1(a), 3(d)	1(a)	1(b), 3(b), 5(a)	2(b)	4(a)
12	Shares and securities			1(b)					3(b)		
13	Chargeable gains: reliefs	1(c), 3(b), 4(b)	2(a)	3(a), 4(a)	2(b)	1(c), 4(b)	3(c)	1(a), 5(b)	1(b), 3(b), 5(a)	2(b)	2(b), 4(a)
14	Chargeable gains: additional aspects	3(b), 5(c)	2(a), 2(c)	1(b), 3(a)		1(c), 3(a), 5(c)	3(d)	4(b)		2(a)	4(a)
	TAX ADMINISTRATION FOR INDIVIDUALS										
15	Self assessment for individuals and partnerships			1(a)			1(b)				4(c), 5(a), 5(b)

Covered in Text chapter		Mar/ Jun 2017	Sep/ Dec 2016	Mar/ Jun 2016	Sep/ Dec 2015	June 2015	Dec 2014	June 2014	Dec 2013	June 2013	Dec 2012
	INHERITANCE TAX										
16	An introduction to inheritance tax	1(b), 3(a)		1(b), 3(b)	5(b)	4(b)	1(a), 3(a)	1(b)	1(b), 3(a)	2(b)	2(b), 5(c)
17	Inheritance tax: valuation, reliefs and the death estate	3(a)	3(a)	3(b)	1(b)	4(c)	3(b)	1(b)	3(a)	2(b)	5(c)
18	Inheritance tax: additional aspects	1(b), 3(a)	2(c)			1(d), 4(c)	3(c)	4(c)	1(b), 3(c)		5(c)
	STAMP TAXES										
19	Stamp taxes	2(b)			2(a)					2(b)	
	CORPORATION TAX										
20	Corporation tax computation	5(a)		2(a), 4(b)	2(a), 3(a), 4(a)	2(b)	2(a), 2(b)		2(a), 2(b)		1(a)
21	Chargeable gains for companies	5(c)	1(a), 5(a)	2(a)	2(b), 3(b)	2(a), 2(c)	2(a)	2(b)	2(a)	4(a)	1(a)
22	Corporation tax administration	2(a)	1(a)	2(a)	2(a)		5(a)		2(a)	1(a)	
23	Administration, winding up, purchase of own shares	4(b)	5(a)	4(a)						1(c)	3(a)
24	Losses and deficits on non-trading loan relationships		5(b)	4(b)		2(b)	2(a)				
25	Close companies and investment companies		4(b)			3(a)		5(c)	2(b)		3(a), 3(b)
26	Groups and consortia	2(a), 2(b), 5(c)	1(a)	2(a)	2(b), 3(a), 3(c)	2(a), 2(c)	2(a)	2(a)	2(a)	1(a)	1(a)
27	Overseas aspects of corporate tax						5(c)		4(b)		3(b)
	VALUE ADDED TAX										
28	Value added tax 1	2(c), 5(d)	1(b), 5(b)	1(a), 4(c)	2(b), 2(c)	1(d)	1(d)			4(c)	4(b)
29	Value added tax 2	5(d)		4(c)	4(c)	3(c)	2(c)	1(a), 5(a)	2(c), 4(a)	1(b)	1(a)
	IMPACT OF TAXES AND TAX PLANNING										
30	Impact of taxes and tax planning	1(a), 2(d), 4(c)	1(c)	2(b), 2(c)	1(a)	2(d)	1(c)	1(a), 2(c)	1(a), 5(a)	1(a), 1(c), 1(d), 3(a)	1(b)

IMPORTANT!

The table above gives a broad idea of how frequently major topics in the syllabus are examined. It should not be used to question spot and predict for example that Topic X will not be examined because it came up two sittings ago. The examining team's reports indicate that the examining team is well aware some students try to question spot. Examining teams avoid predictable patterns and may, for example, examine the same topic two sittings in a row, particularly if there has been a recent change in legislation.

Additional information

The study guide provides more detailed guidance on the syllabus and can be found by visiting the exam resource finder on the ACCA website: www.accaglobal.com/uk/en/student/exam-support-resources.htm

Useful websites

The websites below provide additional sources of information of relevance to your studies for *Advanced Taxation (ATX – UK)*.

- www.accaglobal.com

  ACCA's website. The students' section of the website is invaluable for detailed information about the qualification, past issues of *Student Accountant* (including technical articles) and even interviews with the examining team.

- www.bpp.com

  Our website provides information about BPP products and services, with a link to the ACCA website.

- www.gov.uk/government/organisations/hm-revenue-customs

  HM Revenue & Customs official site. The section for tax agents and advisors is particularly relevant.

Note on exam name (P6 UK)

This text is valid for exams from June 2018 to March 2019. In June 2018, the first session of a new exam year for tax, a new format will be introduced for the P6 Advanced Taxation (UK) exam, to align with the formats that will be introduced in all of the Options exams from September 2018. From the September session, a new naming convention is being introduced for all of the exams in the ACCA Qualification, so from that session, the name of the exam will be Advanced Taxation (ATX – UK). Since this name change takes place during the validity of this text, both the old and new names have been used.

Questions

PART A: INCOME TAX AND NATIONAL INSURANCE CONTRIBUTIONS

Questions 1 to 9 focus on income tax and national insurance contributions. These are the subject of Chapters 1 to 10 in the BPP Study Text.

1 The Bale Family (practice question)   25 mins

You should assume that today's date is 15 March 2018.

You have recently been approached to act as an accountant for Frank Bale and other members of his family. The following information has been obtained in a meeting with members of the Bale family.

Frank:

- Has employment income of £47,000, building society interest of £1,500 and dividends of £10,000 in the tax year 2017/18

- Expects to receive the same amounts of income in the tax year 2018/19

Frank's wife, Deborah:

- Has employment income of £15,500 in the tax year 2017/18
- Expects to receive the same amount of employment income in the tax year 2018/19
- Does not own any bank or building society deposits nor any shares

Frank's daughter, Emily:

- Has trading income of £5,500, bank interest of £6,200 and dividends of £25,000 in the tax year 2017/18

Frank's father, Harvey:

- Has pension income of £8,500 and dividends of £5,000 in the tax year 2017/18

- Expects to receive the same amounts of income in the tax year 2018/19

- Would like to increase his pension income for 2018/19 under flex-access drawdown but would only do so if he did not have to pay any income tax on the additional pension income

Required

(a) Calculate the income tax liability of Frank for the tax year 2017/18.   **(4 marks)**

(b) Advise Frank and Deborah how they could reduce their overall income tax liabilities for the tax year 2018/19.
                                                                                          (3 marks)

(c) Calculate the income tax liability of Emily for the tax year 2017/18.   **(3 marks)**

(d) Advise Harvey about the extent to which he could increase his pension income for the tax year 2018/19 without paying any income tax on the additional pension income.   **(3 marks)**

                                                                          (Total = 13 marks)

2 Stella and Maris (Sep/Dec 15) (amended)   39 mins

Your firm has been asked to provide advice to two unrelated clients, Stella and Maris. Stella requires advice on the tax implications of making an increased contribution to her personal pension scheme. Maris requires advice regarding the lump sum payment she has received from her pension scheme and the inheritance tax exemptions available on her proposed lifetime gifts.

(a) **Stella:**

- Is resident and domiciled in the UK

- Receives a gross salary of £80,000 each year

- Started investing in unfurnished residential properties in 2018/19 which were financed with her own capital and interest-only mortgages

- Has the following property income and expenses (no accruals at 5 April 2019):

	£
Rents received	90,000
Less: Mortgage interest paid in year	(20,000)
Other expenses (all allowable)	(11,000)
Net income	59,000

- Has no other source of taxable income

- Wishes to make an increased contribution to her personal pension scheme in the tax year 2018/19

Personal pension scheme contributions:

- Stella started making pension provision by joining a personal pension scheme in August 2017.
- Stella contributed £30,000 (gross) to her personal pension scheme in August 2017.
- Stella wishes to make an increased contribution of £90,000 (gross) in the tax year 2018/19.

Required

Calculate Stella's income after tax and pension contributions for the tax year 2018/19 if she does pay £90,000 (gross) into her personal pension scheme.

You should assume that the tax rates and allowances for the tax year 2017/18 will continue to apply for the foreseeable future. **(10 marks)**

(b) **Maris:**

- Is resident and domiciled in the UK and is widowed
- Has 3 married children and 5 grandchildren under the age of 12
- Attained the age of 68 on 30 January 2018 and decided to vest her pension benefits on that date
- Wishes to make regular gifts to her family in order to reduce inheritance tax on her death

Personal pension fund:

- Maris had a money purchase pension scheme which was valued at £1,300,000 on 30 January 2018.

- Maris followed advice to reinvest £750,000 of the fund to provide taxable pension income for the future and to take the remainder of the fund as a lump sum.

- Maris does not understand why the amount of cash she received as the lump sum was £385,000.

Assets and income:

- In addition to pension income and savings income totalling around £60,000, Maris receives dividends from shareholdings in quoted companies of around £45,000 each year.

- The shareholdings in quoted companies are currently valued at £980,000.

- Maris wishes to gift some of the shares or the dividend income to her children and grandchildren on their birthdays each year.

- Maris already makes gifts each year to use her annual exemption for inheritance tax purposes.

Required

(i) Explain how the cash of £385,000 received by Maris as a lump sum from her pension scheme was calculated. **(4 marks)**

(ii) Advise Maris of **TWO** relevant exemptions from inheritance tax which she will be able to use when making the birthday gifts, together with any conditions she will need to comply with in order to obtain them. **(6 marks)**

You should assume that the tax rates and allowances for the tax year 2017/18 will continue to apply for the foreseeable future.

(Total = 20 marks)

3 Piquet and Buraco (12/14)

Your firm has been asked to provide advice to two unrelated clients, Piquet and Buraco. Piquet, an unincorporated sole trader, requires advice on a proposed change to the date to which he prepares his accounts. Buraco requires advice on his residence status and the remittance basis.

(a) **Piquet:**

- Began trading as an unincorporated sole trader on 1 January 2011
- Has always prepared accounts to 31 October
- Has overlap profits of £15,000 for a 5-month overlap period
- Is planning to change his accounting date to 28 February 2019

Actual and budgeted tax adjusted trading profit of Piquet's business:

	Profit per month	Profit for the period
	£	£
Year ended 31 October 2017	4,500	54,000
16 months ending 28 February 2019	5,875	94,000
Year ending 28 February 2020	7,333	88,000
Year ending 28 February 2021	9,000	108,000

Alternative choice of accounting date:

- Piquet is also considering a year end of 30 April.

- To achieve this, Piquet would prepare accounts for the 18 months ending 30 April 2019 and annually thereafter.

Required

(i) On the assumption that Piquet changes his accounting date to 28 February, state the date by which he should notify HM Revenue & Customs of the change, and calculate the taxable trading profit for each of the tax years 2018/19 and 2019/20. **(3 marks)**

(ii) On the assumption that Piquet changes his accounting date to 30 April, state the basis periods for the tax years 2018/19 and 2019/20 and the effect of this change on Piquet's overlap profits. **(3 marks)**

(iii) Identify and explain **TWO** advantages for Piquet of using a year end of 30 April rather than 28 February. **(4 marks)**

(b) **Buraco's links with the country of Canasta:**

- Buraco is domiciled in Canasta.
- Buraco owns a home in the country of Canasta.
- Buraco's only income is in respect of investment properties in Canasta.
- Buraco frequently buys and sells properties in Canasta.

Buraco's links with the UK:

- Buraco's ex-wife and their 12 year old daughter moved to the UK on 1 May 2017.
- Buraco first visited the UK in the tax year 2017/18 but was not UK resident in that year.
- Buraco did not own a house in the UK until he purchased one on 6 April 2018.
- Buraco expects to live in the UK house for between 100 and 150 days in the tax year 2018/19.

Required

(i) Explain why Buraco will not satisfy any of the automatic overseas residence tests for the tax year 2018/19 and, on the assumption that he does not satisfy any of the automatic UK residence tests, explain how his residence status will be determined for that tax year. **(7 marks)**

(ii) On the assumption that Buraco is resident in the UK in the tax year 2018/19, state the tax implications for him of claiming the remittance basis for that year and explain whether or not there would be a remittance basis charge. **(3 marks)**

(Total = 20 marks)

4 Jodie (06/15)

Your manager has received a letter from Jodie in connection with her proposed emigration from the UK. Extracts from the letter and from an email from your manager are set out below.

Extract from the letter from Jodie

I have always lived in the UK. I plan to leave the UK and move to the country of Riviera on 5 April 2019. My intention is to move to Riviera permanently and acquire a new home there. However, if my children are not happy there after four years, we will return to the UK.

My husband died three years ago. My brother lives in Riviera and is the only close family I have apart from my children. I will not have any sources of income in the UK after 5 April 2019.

I intend to work part time in Riviera so that I can look after my children. In the tax year 2019/20, I will return to the UK for a holiday and stay with friends for 60 days; for the rest of the tax year I will live in my new home in Riviera.

My unincorporated business

I prepared accounts to 31 December every year until 31 December 2017. I then ceased trading on 31 May 2018. I made a tax adjusted trading loss in my final period of trading of £18,000.

I attach an appendix setting out the information you requested in relation to the business.

I was unable to sell my business as a going concern due to the decline in its profitability. Accordingly, on 31 May 2018 I sold my business premises for £190,000. I paid £135,000 for these premises on 1 June 2004. I also sold various items of computer equipment, which I had used in my business, for a total of £2,000. This equipment cost me a total of £5,000. I retained the remaining inventory, valued at £3,500, for my own personal use.

My sources of income for the last five tax years are set out below. There is no property income in the 2018/19 tax year because I sold my rental property in May 2017.

	2014/15	2015/16	2016/17	2017/18	2018/19
	£	£	£	£	£
Trading income	64,000	67,000	2,000	3,000	Nil
Property income	15,000	13,000	17,000	2,500	Nil
Bank interest	2,000	2,000	3,000	3,500	8,000 (est.)

Other matters

On 30 April 2018 I sold my house, which is built on a 1 hectare plot, for £400,000. I purchased the house for £140,000 in March 1996 and lived in it throughout my period of ownership. I have been living in a rented house in the UK since 1 May 2018. My tenancy of this rented house will end on 5 April 2019.

When we spoke, you mentioned that you wanted details of any gifts I have received. The only item of significance is 2,000 ordinary shares in Butterfly Ltd which my mother gave to me on 14 May 2016 when the shares were worth £60,000. Butterfly Ltd is a UK resident trading company.

My mother and I submitted a joint claim for capital gains tax holdover relief on the gift of these Butterfly Ltd shares, such that no capital gains tax was payable. I recently received an offer of £68,000 for these shares, but I decided not to sell them. My mother had inherited the shares from her brother on 18 December 2003 when they were worth £37,000. Neither I nor my mother have ever worked for Butterfly Ltd.

Extract from an email from your manager

Additional information

(i) Jodie's business has always been registered for the purposes of value added tax (VAT). The sales proceeds in respect of the business assets are stated net of VAT.

• Jodie has overlap profits from the commencement of her business of £6,500.

Please prepare paragraphs for inclusion in a letter from me to Jodie addressing the following issues.

(a) **UK tax residence status and liability to UK income tax**

   (i) Assuming Jodie leaves the UK in accordance with her plans, explain how her residence status for the tax year 2019/20 will be determined and conclude on her likely residence status for that year. To help, I have already concluded that Jodie will **not** be regarded as non-UK resident using the automatic overseas tests so there is no need to consider these tests.

   (ii) State how becoming non-UK resident will affect Jodie's liability to UK income tax.

(b) **Relief available in respect of the trading loss**

   (i) Calculate the income tax relief which Jodie would obtain if she were to claim terminal loss relief in respect of her trading loss. You should **not** consider any other ways in which the loss could be relieved.

   (ii) There is no need to calculate Jodie's tax liabilities for each of the years concerned; just calculate the tax which will be saved due to the offset of the loss and explain how you have determined this figure.

(c) **Capital gains tax**

Assuming that Jodie becomes non-UK resident from 6 April 2019 and does not return to the UK for at least four tax years:

   (i) Explain how this will affect her liability to UK capital gains tax in the tax year 2019/20 and future years and in 2018/19 (the tax year prior to departure); and

   (ii) Calculate her capital gains tax liability for the tax year 2018/19. You should include explanations of the chargeable gains which have arisen or may arise in that year and the tax rate(s) which will be charged.

(d) **Other matters**

   (i) Explain how leaving the UK will affect the UK inheritance tax liability on any gifts Jodie may make in the future.

   (ii) Explain the matters which Jodie should be aware of in relation to VAT in respect of the cessation of her business. I have already checked that Jodie charged the correct amount of VAT when she sold the business premises and the computer equipment.

Tax manager

Required

Prepare the paragraphs for inclusion in a letter from your manager to Jodie as requested in the email from your manager. The following marks are available:

(a)	UK tax residence status and liability to UK income tax	**(7 marks)**
(b)	Relief available in respect of the trading loss	**(8 marks)**
(c)	Capital gains tax	**(11 marks)**
(d)	Other matters	**(5 marks)**

Professional marks will be awarded for following the manager's instructions, the clarity of the explanations and calculations, the effectiveness with which the information is communicated, and the overall presentation. **(4 marks)**

Notes

1 You should assume that the tax rates and allowances for the tax year 2017/18 apply to all tax years.

2 Ignore national insurance contributions throughout this question.

(Total = 35 marks)

5 Dana (12/12)

Your manager has received a letter from Dana, a new client of your firm. Extracts from the letter and from an email from your manager are set out below.

Extract from the letter from Dana

Relief available in respect of a trading loss

I resigned from my job on 31 December 2015, having earned an annual salary of £40,000 for the previous 3 years. I spent the whole of 2016 planning my new business and began trading on 1 January 2017. The business was profitable initially but I made a loss in the year ended 30 September 2018.

The results of the business have been:

Period ended 30 September 2017 – a profit of £14,900
Year ended 30 September 2018 – a loss of £30,000

I own a number of residential rental properties that are let on long-term tenancies. On 1 February 2018, I sold one of these properties for £310,000. I paid £250,000 for this property on 1 December 2016.

My taxable property business profits in recent tax years have been:

	£
2014/15	15,520
2015/16	17,700
2016/17	30,025
2017/18	36,000
2018/19 (estimated)	46,600

Please let me know how much tax I can save by relieving my trading loss for the year ended 30 September 2018.

Transfer of a residential rental property to a trust on 1 September 2018

On 1 September 2018, I transferred a residential rental property worth £270,000 to a trust for the benefit of my brother's children. I assume that there will be no tax liabilities for me or the trustees in respect of this gift. I also transferred a residential rental property to a trust in December 2013 and I am sure that no tax was paid in respect of that gift. I have never made any other gifts apart from gifts of cash to members of my family; none of these gifts exceeded £2,000.

Email from your manager

Dana is unmarried and has no children. She is resident and domiciled in the UK.

I have just spoken to Dana and she has provided me with the following additional information:

(a)   Dana received a bonus of £2,000 from her employer when she left her job in December 2015. The bonus was to thank her for all of the work she had done over the years.

(b)   The results Dana has provided in respect of her unincorporated business have been adjusted for tax purposes but do not take account of expenditure she incurred during 2016. During that year, Dana spent £1,400 on petrol as she travelled around the UK visiting potential customers.

Dana had no income or capital gains in the tax years concerned other than those referred to in her letter and in the additional information set out above.

Work required:

Please prepare the following for me for my next meeting with Dana.

(a)   **Relief available in respect of the trading loss**

A reasoned explanation, with supporting calculations, of the most tax-efficient manner in which Dana's trading loss can be relieved, together with a calculation of the total tax relief obtained by following the most tax-efficient strategy. I want you to consider all of the ways in which Dana could relieve the loss with the exception of carry forward for relief in the future. You should assume that gift relief will be claimed in respect of the transfer of the rental property to the trust on 1 September 2018 when carrying out this work.

Your explanation should include:

(i) A brief summary of the other reliefs available for relieving the loss, together with your reasons for rejecting them

(ii) The implications of the additional information provided by Dana

(b) **Transfer of the rental property to the trust on 1 September 2018**

   (i) **Capital gains tax**

   An explanation as to whether or not gift relief is available in respect of the transfer of the residential rental property on 1 September 2018 and, on the assumption that it is available, the action required in order to submit a valid claim.

   (ii) **Inheritance tax**

   In relation to Dana's gifts prior to 1 September 2018:

   (1) A list of the precise information we need to request from Dana in order to enable us to determine whether the gifts to her family members were exempt and to calculate the inheritance tax due on the transfer to the trust on 1 September 2018

   (2) An explanation of why the information is required

Tax manager

Required

Carry out the work required as requested in the email from your manager. The following marks are available.

(a) Relief available in respect of the trading loss

In respect of part (a) of this question you should:

(i) Ignore national insurance contributions

(ii) Assume that the tax rates and allowances for the tax year 2017/18 apply to all years **(18 marks)**

(b) Transfer of the rental property to the trust on 1 September 2018

(i) Capital gains tax **(2 marks)**

(ii) Inheritance tax **(5 marks)**

(Total = 25 marks)

6 Monisha and Horner (12/13) (amended)   39 mins

Your firm has been asked to advise two unrelated clients, Monisha and Horner. The advice relates to tax planning for a married couple and the personal service company (IR35) rules.

(a) **Monisha:**

   - Is married to Asmat
   - Earns a salary of £80,000 per year and realises chargeable gains of £6,000 per year
   - Owns a UK investment residential property, which is let to short-term tenants

   Asmat:

   - Looks after the couple's children and has no income or chargeable gains
   - Expects to return to work on 6 April 2024 on an annual salary of £18,000

   The UK investment property owned by Monisha:

   - The property cost £270,000 and is currently worth £300,000.

   - The property was purchased using an interest-only mortgage.

   - The letting does not qualify as a commercial letting of furnished holiday accommodation.

- Annual income and expenditure:

	£
Rental income	24,000
Repairs and maintenance	1,600
Mortgage interest	5,400
Agent's fees	2,000

- Monisha spends £1,800 a year on replacement furniture.

- The property will be sold on 5 April 2025 and is expected to create a chargeable gain of £100,000.

Proposals to reduce the couple's total tax liability:

- Monisha will give a 20% interest in the investment property to Asmat on 1 April 2019.

- The couple will ensure that, from 6 April 2019, the letting of the investment property will qualify as a commercial letting of furnished holiday accommodation.

- From the tax year 2019/20 onwards, Monisha will claim annual capital allowances equal to the expenditure on replacement furniture.

Required

Calculate the total tax saving in the six tax years 2019/20 to 2024/25 if **ALL** of the proposals to reduce the couple's tax liabilities are carried out. In respect of the second proposal, you should assume that the letting will qualify as a commercial letting of furnished holiday accommodation for the whole of the period of joint ownership and that all beneficial reliefs are claimed.

Notes

1   You should assume that the tax rates and allowances for the tax year 2017/18 apply to all tax years.
2   You should ignore inheritance tax.   **(13 marks)**

(b)   **Horner:**

- Horner owns all of the shares of Otmar Ltd.

- Horner is the sole employee and director of Otmar Ltd.

- All of the income of Otmar Ltd is subject to the personal service company (IR35) rules.

- Budgeted figures for Otmar Ltd for the year ending 5 April 2019 are set out below. Where applicable, these amounts are stated exclusive of value added tax (VAT).

	£
Income in respect of relevant engagements carried out by Horner	85,000
Costs of administering the company	3,900
Horner's annual salary	50,000
Dividend paid to Horner	15,000
Contributions paid into an occupational pension scheme in respect of Horner	2,000

Required

(i)   Outline the circumstances in which the personal service company (IR35) rules apply.   **(3 marks)**
(ii) Calculate the deemed employment income of Horner for the year ending 5 April 2019.   **(4 marks)**

(Total = 20 marks)

7 Cate and Ravi (06/15)

Cate requires advice on the after-tax cost of taking on a part-time employee and the tax implications of starting to sell items via the internet. Cate's husband, Ravi, requires advice in relation to capital gains tax on the disposal of an overseas asset.

Cate:

- Is resident and domiciled in the UK
- Is married to Ravi
- Runs a successful unincorporated business, D-Designs
- Receives dividends of £33,000 each year
- Wants to sell some secondhand books online

D-Designs business:

- Was set up by Cate in 2011
- Is now making a taxable profit of £90,000 per annum
- Operates a number of dress shops and already employs six full-time staff
- Requires an additional part-time employee

Part-time employee – proposed remuneration package:

- Salary of £12,000 per annum.

- Qualifying childcare vouchers of £25 per week for 52 weeks a year.

- Mileage allowance of 50 pence per mile for the 62-mile round trip required each week to redistribute stock between the shops. This will be for 48 weeks in the year.

- This employment will be the employee's only source of taxable income.

Sale of secondhand books:

- Cate inherited a collection of books from her mother in December 2016.
- Cate intends to sell these books via the internet.
- Some of the books are in a damaged state and Cate will get them rebound before selling them.

Ravi:

- Is domiciled in the country of Goland

- Has been resident in the UK since his marriage to Cate in February 2010

- Has UK taxable income of £125,000 in the tax year 2017/18

- Realises chargeable gains each year from disposals of UK residential property equal to the capital gains tax annual exempt amount

- Sold an investment residential property in Goland in February 2018 for £130,000, realising a chargeable gain of £70,000; none of the proceeds from the sale of this property have been remitted to the UK

Required

(a) Calculate the annual cost for Cate, after income tax and national insurance contributions, of D-Designs employing the part-time employee. **(9 marks)**

(b) Discuss whether the profit from Cate's proposed sale of books via the internet will be liable to either income tax or capital gains tax. **(5 marks)**

(c) Advise Ravi on the options available to him for calculating his UK capital gains for 2017/18. Provide supporting calculations of the tax payable by him in each case. **(6 marks)**

(Total = 20 marks)

8 Simone (06/09) (amended)

39 mins

You should assume that today's date is 15 March 2019.

Simone is a partner in the firm Ellington and Co. She is seeking advice on the tax-efficient use of her share of the partnership's loss for the year ended 5 April 2019. Simone intends to establish a new business and is considering the need to register for the purposes of value added tax (VAT).

The following information has been obtained from a meeting with Simone.

Simone's income:

- Dividends received of £14,000 in the tax year 2017/18, £4,800 in the tax year 2018/19 and £Nil in subsequent years
- Share of profits from Ellington and Co for the year ended 5 April 2018 of £51,230

Simone's capital gains:

- Simone disposed of 8,000 shares in Duke plc, a quoted company, for proceeds of £190,000 in February 2019.
- Simone had acquired 12,000 Duke plc shares for £146,500 in July 2011.
- Duke plc made a rights issue in August 2013 and Simone sold her rights nil paid for proceeds of £2,500.

Ellington and Co:

- Has been trading for many years
- Has two partners, Ellington and Simone; a third partner, Basie, retired on 28 February 2019
- Made a loss in the year ended 5 April 2019
- Is budgeted to make tax adjusted trading profits of no more than £25,000 per year for the next few years
- Is registered for the purposes of VAT

Ellington and Co – results for the year ended 5 April 2019:

- The firm made a tax adjusted trading loss, before deduction of capital allowances, of £90,000.
- The firm purchased office equipment on 1 December 2018 for £21,200 exclusive of VAT.
- The balance on the capital allowances main pool as at 5 April 2018 was £700.

Ellington and Co – profit sharing arrangements:

- From 6 April 2018 until 28 February 2019

	Ellington	Simone	Basie
Annual salaries	£15,000	£11,500	£13,000
Profit sharing ratio	3 :	2 :	2

- From 1 March 2019

	Ellington	Simone
Annual salaries	£14,000	£14,000
Profit sharing ratio	1 :	1

Simone's new business:

- Simone intends to start trading on 1 September 2019.
- Taxable trading profit is budgeted to be approximately £1,550 per month.
- Taxable supplies are expected to be between £80,000 and £100,000 in the first year.
- Simone does not wish to register voluntarily for VAT.

Required

(a) (i) Calculate Simone's share of the tax adjusted trading loss for the year ended 5 April 2019. **(5 marks)**

     (ii) State the alternative strategies available to Simone in respect of her share of the taxable trading loss for the year ended 5 April 2019. **(3 marks)**

(iii) Explain, using supporting calculations where necessary, which of the strategies will save the most tax and calculate the total tax saved via the operation of this strategy.

Note. Your calculations should be based on the assumption that the tax rates and allowances for the year 2017/18 apply to all relevant years. **(9 marks)**

(b) Explain when Simone would be required to register and to start charging her customers VAT and, in relation to this, comment on the relevance of Ellington and Co being VAT registered.

Note. You are not required to prepare calculations for part (b) of this question. **(3 marks)**

(Total = 20 marks)

9 Shuttelle (06/13) (amended)   39 mins

Your firm has been asked to provide advice to Shuttelle in connection with personal pension contributions and to three non-UK domiciled individuals in connection with the remittance basis of taxation for overseas income and gains.

(a) **Personal pension contributions:**

- Shuttelle has been the production director of Din Ltd since 1 February 2005.
- Shuttelle joined a registered personal pension scheme on 6 April 2015.

Shuttelle's tax position for the tax year 2017/18:

- Shuttelle's only source of income is her remuneration from Din Ltd.
- Shuttelle's annual salary for the tax year is £204,000.
- Shuttelle lived in a house owned by Din Ltd for a period of time during the tax year 2017/18.

The house provided by Din Ltd for Shuttelle's use:

- Was purchased by Din Ltd on 1 January 2005 for £635,000 and has an annual value of £10,000
- Was lived in by Shuttelle from 1 February 2005 until 30 June 207
- Had a market value of £870,000 on 6 April 2017

Contributions to Shuttelle's personal pension scheme:

- Shuttelle has made the following gross contributions.

  6 April 2015 – £9,000
  6 April 2016 – £38,000
  6 April 2017 – £120,000

- Din Ltd contributes £4,000 to the scheme in each tax year.

- Shuttelle was entitled to an annual allowance of £40,000 in each of the tax years 2015/16 and 2016/17.

Required

(i) Calculate Shuttelle's income tax liability for the tax year 2017/18. **(8 marks)**

(ii) Calculate the amount of tax relief obtained by Shuttelle as a consequence of the gross personal pension contributions of £120,000 she made on 6 April 2017. **(3 marks)**

(b) The remittance basis of taxation:

- Advice is to be provided to 3 non-UK domiciled individuals.
- Each of the 3 individuals is more than 18 years old.

Details of the three individuals:

Name	Lin	Nan	Yu
Tax year in which the individual became UK resident	2007/08	2002/03	2007/08
Tax year in which the individual ceased to be UK resident	Still resident	2015/16	Still resident
Overseas income and gains for the tax year 2017/18	£39,200	£68,300	£130,700
Overseas income and gains remitted to the UK for the tax year 2017/18	£38,500	Nil	£1,400

Required

(i)   In respect of each of the three individuals for the tax year 2017/18:

    (1)   Explain whether or not the remittance basis is available

    (2)   On the assumption that the remittance basis is available to **ALL** three individuals, state, with reasons, the remittance basis charge (if any) that they would have to pay in order for their overseas income and gains to be taxed on the remittance basis

    The following mark allocation is provided as guidance for this requirement:

    (1)   3 marks
    (2)   4 marks   **(7 marks)**

(ii)   Give **TWO** examples of actions that would be regarded as remittances other than simply bringing cash into the UK.   **(2 marks)**

                                                      (Total = 20 marks)

PART B: CAPITAL GAINS TAX, TAX ADMINISTRATION FOR INDIVIDUALS, INHERITANCE TAX AND STAMP TAXES

Questions 10 to 20 focus on capital gains tax, tax administration for individuals, inheritance tax and stamp taxes. These are the subject of Chapters 11 to 19 in the BPP Study Text.

10 Ash (12/12)   39 mins

Ash requires a calculation of his capital gains tax liability for the tax year 2017/18, together with advice in connection with entrepreneurs' relief, registration for the purposes of value added tax (VAT) and the payment of income tax.

Ash:

- Is resident in the UK

- Had taxable income of £29,000 in the tax year 2017/18

- Was the owner and managing director of Lava Ltd until 1 May 2017, when he resigned and sold the company

- Is a partner in the Vulcan Partnership

Ash – disposals of capital assets in the tax year 2017/18:

- The sale of the shares in Lava Ltd resulted in a capital gain of £235,000, which qualified for entrepreneurs' relief.

- Ash assigned a 37-year lease on a property for £110,000 on 1 May 2017.

- Ash sold 2 acres of land (not residential property) on 1 October 2017 for £30,000.

- Ash sold quoted shares and made a capital loss of £17,300 on 1 November 2017.

The lease:

- The lease was previously assigned to Ash for £31,800 when it had 46 years remaining.
- The property has always been used by Lava Ltd for trading purposes.
- Lava Ltd paid Ash rent, equivalent to 40% of the market rate, in respect of the use of the property.

The sale of the two acres of land:

- Ash purchased 8 acres of land for £27,400 on 1 June 2008.
- Ash sold 6 acres of the land for £42,000 on 1 August 2017.
- The remaining 2 acres of land were worth £18,000 on 1 August 2011.

Vulcan Partnership (Vulcan):

- Vulcan has a 31 March year end.

- Vulcan has monthly turnover of:

Standard rated supplies	£400
Exempt supplies	£200
Zero rated supplies	£5,600

- Its turnover is expected to increase slightly in 2019.

- None of its customers is registered for the purposes of VAT.

- Ash expects to receive less profit from Vulcan for the tax year 2018/19 than he did in 2017/18.

Required

(a)   (i)   State the conditions that must be satisfied for Ash's assignment of the lease to be an associated disposal for the purposes of entrepreneurs' relief.   **(3 marks)**

(ii)   Calculate Ash's capital gains tax liability for the tax year 2017/18 on the assumption that the assignment of the lease does qualify as an associated disposal and that entrepreneurs' relief will be claimed where possible.

Note. The following lease percentages should be used, where necessary.

37 years 93.497
46 years 98.490   **(7 marks)**

(b)   Discuss in detail whether the Vulcan Partnership may be required to register for VAT and the advantages and disadvantages for the business of registration.   **(7 marks)**

(c)   Set out the matters that Ash should consider when deciding whether or not to make a claim to reduce the payment on account of income tax due on 31 January 2019.   **(3 marks)**

(Total = 20 marks)

11 Brad (06/13)   49 mins

Your manager has had a meeting with Brad, a client of your firm. Extracts from your manager's meeting notes together with an email from your manager are set out below.

Extracts from meeting notes

Personal details

Brad is 69 years old. He is married to Laura and they have a daughter, Dani, who is 38 years old.

Brad had lived in the UK for the whole of his life until he moved with his wife to the country of Keirinia on 1 January 2015. He returned to live permanently in the UK on 30 April 2018. Therefore, he was non-UK resident for the years 2015/16 to 2017/18 inclusive but otherwise UK resident. The split year treatment did not apply in either 2015/16 or 2018/19. He has always been domiciled in the UK. Brad has significant investment income and has been a higher rate taxpayer for many years.

Capital gains

Whilst living in the country of Keirinia, Brad sold various assets as set out below. He has not made any other disposals since 5 April 2014.

Asset	Date of sale	Proceeds £	Date of purchase	Cost £
Quoted shares	1 February 2015	18,900	1 October 2013	14,000
Painting	1 June 2017	36,600	1 May 2013	15,000
Antique bed	1 March 2018	9,400	1 May 2015	7,300
Motor car	1 April 2018	11,000	1 February 2014	8,500

I explained that, although Brad was non-UK resident for several tax years, these disposals may still be subject to UK capital gains tax because he will be regarded as only temporarily non-UK resident. There is no capital gains tax in the country of Keirinia.

Inheritance tax planning

Brad's estate is worth approximately £5 million so the residence nil rate band will not be applicable on his death. He has not made any lifetime gifts and, in his will, he intends to leave half of his estate to his daughter, Dani, and the other half to his wife, Laura. I pointed out that it may be advantageous to make a lifetime gift to Dani of assets other than his main residence. Brad agreed to consider giving Dani 1,500 of his shares in Omnium Ltd and has asked for a general summary of the inheritance tax advantages of making lifetime gifts to individuals.

Omnium Ltd is an unquoted manufacturing company which also owns a number of investment properties. Brad was given his shares in the company by his wife on 1 January 2014. The ownership of the share capital of Omnium Ltd is set out below.

	Shares
Laura (Brad's wife)	4,500
Brad	3,000
Vic (Laura's brother)	1,500
Christine (friend of Laura)	1,000
	10,000

The current estimated value of a share in Omnium Ltd is set out below.

Shareholding	Value per share
	£
Up to 25%	190
26% to 50%	205
51% to 60%	240
61% to 74%	255
75% to 80%	290
More than 80%	300

Email from your manager

In preparation for my next meeting with Brad, please prepare the following:

(a) **Capital gains tax**

An explanation, with supporting calculations, of the UK capital gains tax liability in respect of the disposals made by Brad whilst living in the country of Keirinia. Your explanation should include the precise reasons for Brad being regarded as only temporarily non-UK resident and a statement of when the tax was/will be payable.

(b) **Inheritance tax**

(i) An explanation of the inheritance tax advantages of making lifetime gifts to individuals, in general.

(ii) In respect of the possible gift of 1,500 shares in Omnium Ltd to Dani:

(1) A calculation of the fall in value of Brad's estate which will result from the gift

(2) A detailed explanation of whether or not business property relief would be available in respect of the gift and, on the assumption that it would be available, the manner in which it would be calculated

(3) A **brief** statement of any other tax issues arising from the gift, which will need to be considered at a later date

Tax manager

Required

Carry out the work required as requested in the email from your manager. The following marks are available.

(a) Capital gains tax **(8 marks)**

(b) Inheritance tax

(i) Explanation of the inheritance tax advantages of making lifetime gifts to individuals **(7 marks)**

(ii) In respect of the possible gift of 1,500 shares in Omnium Ltd to Dani **(10 marks)**

You should assume that the 2017/18 tax rates and allowances apply in all years.

(Total = 25 marks)

12 Sushi (12/10) (amended)   49 mins

An extract from an email from your manager regarding a meeting with a client, Sushi, together with an email from Sushi are set out below.

Email from your manager

I have just had a meeting with Sushi who has been a client of the firm since she moved to the UK from the country of Zakuskia in May 2004. Sushi was born in the country of Zakuskia in 1961 and I am satisfied that she has retained her domicile of origin in Zakuskia as she intends to return there permanently in the future, but not before 2023. Her father died in 2011 and, as you will see from her email, her mother died in October 2018. Her father and mother were both domiciled and resident in the country of Zakuskia throughout their lives. Zakuskian inheritance tax is charged at the rate of 24% on all land and buildings situated within the country that are owned by an individual at the time of death. There is no capital gains tax in the country of Zakuskia. There is no double tax treaty between the UK and the country of Zakuskia.

Until the death of her mother, Sushi's only assets consisted of a number of investment properties situated in the UK, and cash in UK non-interest bearing bank accounts. She does not own a main residence in the UK as she lives in a rented house. Her total UK assets are worth approximately £3 million. Sushi has taxable income (all non-savings income) of £33,500 each year and realises taxable capital gains on the disposal of shares of more than £20,000 each year. She has made significant cash gifts to her son in the past and, therefore, does not require an explanation of the taxation of potentially exempt transfers or the accumulation principle. Sushi is resident in the UK.

I want you to write a letter to Sushi addressing the points below:

(a)   **UK inheritance tax and the statue**

An explanation of:

(i)   The UK inheritance tax implications of the death of Sushi's mother

(ii)   Which of Sushi's assets will be subject to UK inheritance tax on her death assuming that she continues to be UK resident until at least 2023 and dies whilst being UK resident

(iii)   The manner in which UK inheritance tax would be calculated, if due, on any land and buildings situated in the country of Zakuskia that are owned by Sushi when she dies if she leaves her estate to her son

(iv)   Why the gift of the statue to her son, as referred to in her email, will be a potentially exempt transfer, and how this treatment could be avoided

The statue has not increased in value since the death of Sushi's mother. Accordingly, the proposed gift of the statue to Sushi's son will not give rise to a capital gain.

(b)   **The Zakuskian income**

The Zakuskian income will be subject to tax in the UK because Sushi is UK resident. Accordingly, we need to think about whether or not Sushi should claim the remittance basis. In order to do this I want you to prepare calculations of the increase in her UK tax liability due to the Zakuskian income on the assumption that the remittance basis is not available and then on the assumption that it is available. You should assume that Sushi remits £30,000 (gross) to the UK each year in accordance with her plans.

In relation to the taxation of the Zakuskian income, the letter should include explanations of the meaning of the terms 'remittance basis' and 'remittance', and whether or not the remittance basis is available to Sushi, together with your conclusions based on your calculations but no other narrative. You should include brief footnotes to your calculations where necessary to aid understanding of the figures.

There is no need to consider the implication of capital gains on overseas assets as Sushi does not intend to dispose of any of her Zakuskian assets, apart from the statue, for the time being.

Thank you

Tax manager

Email from Sushi

My mother died on 1 October 2018 and left me the whole of her estate. I inherited the following assets:

- The family home in the country of Zakuskia which is my main residence
- Investment properties in the country of Zakuskia
- Cash in Zakuskian bank accounts
- Paintings and other works of art in the country of Zakuskia

The works of art include a statue that has been owned by my family for many years. I intend to bring the statue to the UK in December 2018 and give it to my son on his birthday on 1 July 2019. The statue was valued recently at £390,000.

The assets inherited from my mother will generate gross annual income of up to £55,000 before tax of which £50,000 relates to the investment properties and the remaining £5,000 relates to the bank accounts, all of which is subject to 10% Zakuskian income tax. I intend to bring £30,000 (gross) of this income into the UK each year. The balance will remain in a bank account in Zakuskia.

I would like to meet with you to discuss these matters.

Thank you for your help.

Sushi

Required

Prepare the letter to Sushi requested in the email from your manager. The following marks are available.

(a)	UK inheritance tax and the statue	**(10 marks)**
(b)	The Zakuskian income	**(12 marks)**

Professional marks will be awarded in this question for the appropriateness of the format of the letter, the degree to which the calculations are approached in a logical manner, and the effectiveness with which the information is communicated. **(3 marks)**

You should assume that the tax rates and allowances of the tax year 2017/18 will continue to apply for the foreseeable future. **(Total = 25 marks)**

13 Capstan (06/11)   39 mins

Capstan requires advice on the transfer of a property to a trust, the sale of shares in respect of which relief has been received under the Enterprise Investment Scheme (EIS), and the sale of shares and qualifying corporate bonds following a takeover.

The following information was obtained from a meeting with Capstan.

Capstan:

- Expects to have taxable income in the tax year 2018/19 of £80,000
- Transferred a UK property to a discretionary trust on 1 May 2018
- Plans to sell ordinary shares in Agraffe Ltd and loan stock and ordinary shares in Pinblock plc
- Will make all available claims to reduce the tax due in respect of his planned disposals
- Entrepreneurs' relief is not available in respect of any of these disposals

Transfer of a UK property to a discretionary trust:

- Capstan acquired the property in May 2009 for £285,000.
- The market value of the property on 1 May 2018 was £425,000.
- Capstan had used the property as a second home throughout his period of ownership.
- Capstan will pay any inheritance tax due on the gift of the property to the trust.

Sale of ordinary shares in Agraffe Ltd:

- Capstan subscribed for 18,000 shares in Agraffe Ltd for £32,000 on 1 February 2016.
- He obtained EIS relief of £9,600 against his income tax liability.

- Capstan intends to sell all of the shares for £20,000 on 1 July 2018.
- Capstan will relieve the loss arising on the shares in the most tax-efficient manner.

Sale of loan stock and ordinary shares in Pinblock plc:

- Capstan will sell £8,000 7% Pinblock plc non-convertible loan stock for £10,600.
- Capstan will also sell 12,000 shares in Pinblock plc for £69,000.
- The sales will take place on 1 August 2018.

Capstan's acquisition of loan stock and ordinary shares in Pinblock plc:

- Capstan purchased 15,000 shares in Wippen plc for £26,000 on 1 May 2010.

- Pinblock plc acquired 100% of the ordinary share capital of Wippen plc on 1 October 2013.

- The takeover was for *bona fide* commercial reasons and was not for the avoidance of tax.

- Capstan received £8,000 Pinblock plc non-convertible loan stock (a qualifying corporate bond) and 20,000 ordinary shares in Pinblock plc in exchange for his shares in Wippen plc.

- The loan stock and the shares were worth £9,000 and £40,000 respectively as at 1 October 2013.

Required

(a) Set out, together with supporting calculations, the inheritance tax and capital gains tax implications of the transfer of the UK property to the trust and the date(s) on which any tax due will be payable. **(7 marks)**

(b) Explain, with supporting calculations, in connection with the sale of shares in Agraffe Ltd:

    (i)   The tax implications of selling them on 1 July 2018
    (ii) Any advantages and disadvantages to Capstan of delaying the sale **(8 marks)**

(c) Calculate Capstan's taxable capital gains for the tax year 2018/19. **(5 marks)**

    Note. In parts (a) and (b) you should clearly state any assumptions you have made together with any additional information that you would need to confirm with Capstan before finalising your calculations.

You should assume that the tax rates and allowances of the tax year 2017/18 will continue to apply for the foreseeable future.

(Total = 20 marks)

14 Surfe (12/11) (amended)   39 mins

Surfe has requested advice on the tax implications of the creation of a discretionary trust and a calculation of the estimated inheritance tax liability on her death. The following information was obtained at a meeting with Surfe.

Surfe:

- Is a 63 year old widow who has 2 adult children
- Intends to create a trust on 1 January 2019

Death of Surfe's husband:

- Surfe's husband, Flud, died on 1 February 2008 leaving net estate for inheritance tax valued at £1,500,000.
- Flud had made no gifts during his lifetime.
- In his will, Flud left £148,000 in cash to his sister and the remainder of his estate to Surfe.

The trust:

- The trust will be a discretionary (relevant property) trust for the benefit of Surfe's two children.

- Surfe will give 200 of her ordinary shares in Leat Ltd and £100,000 in cash to the trustees of the trust on 1 January 2019.

- The inheritance tax due on the gift will be paid by Surfe.

- The trustees will invest the cash in quoted shares.

Leat Ltd:

- Leat Ltd has an issued share capital of 1,000 ordinary shares.
- Surfe owns 650 of the company's ordinary shares.
- The remaining 350 of its ordinary shares are owned by 'Kanal', a UK registered charity.
- Leat Ltd is a property investment company such that business property relief is not available.

Leat Ltd – value of an ordinary share:

- As at:

	1 January 2019 £	1 July 2021 £
As part of a holding of 75% or more	2,000	2,400
As part of a holding of more than 50% but less than 75%	1,000	1,200
As part of a holding of 50% or less	800	1,000

Surfe – lifetime gifts:

- 1 February 2007: Surfe gave 350 ordinary shares in Leat Ltd to 'Kanal', a UK registered charity.
- 1 October 2018: Surfe gave £85,000 in cash to each of her two children.

Surfe's death:

- It should be assumed that Surfe will die on 1 July 2021 and that the residence nil rate band at that date will be £100,000.

- Her death estate will consist of her main residence worth £800,000, quoted shares worth £200,000 and her remaining shares in Leat Ltd.

- Her will divides her entire estate between her two children.

Required

(a) Outline **BRIEFLY**:

   (i) The capital gains tax implications of:

   (1) The proposed gift of shares to the trustees of the discretionary trust
   (2) Any future sale of the quoted shares by the trustees
   (3) The future transfer of trust assets to Surfe's children

   (ii) The inheritance tax charges that may be payable in the by the trustees of the discretionary trust

   Note. You are not required to prepare calculations for part (a) of this question.

   The following mark allocation is provided as guidance for this requirement:

   (i) 4 marks
   (ii) 2 marks   **(6 marks)**

(b) Calculate the inheritance tax liabilities arising as a result of Surfe's death on 1 July 2021 assuming any relevant claims are made.   **(14 marks)**

You should assume that the tax rates and allowances for 2017/18 will continue to apply for the foreseeable future.

(Total = 20 marks)

15 Una (06/12)

Your manager has sent you an email, together with an attachment in respect of a new client called Una. The email and the attachment are set out below.

Email from your manager

I have had a meeting with Una, a new client of the firm. Una was born in 1944 and is a widow. She has a son, Won, who was born in 1969.

Una is resident and domiciled in the UK. Her annual taxable income is approximately £90,000. She makes sufficient capital gains every year to use her annual exempt amount.

Una made a gift of cash of £40,000 to Won in May 2014. This is the only transfer she has made for the purposes of inheritance tax in the last seven years.

Una has left the whole of her estate to Won in her will. Her estate is expected to be worth more than £3 million at the time of her death.

For the purposes of this work I want you to assume that Una will die on 31 December 2023.

Gift to son

Una is considering making a gift to Won of either some farmland situated in England or a residential villa situated in the country of Soloria which has always been rented out. Una has prepared a schedule setting out the details of the farmland and the villa. The schedule is attached to this email. Una will make the gift to Won on his birthday on 18 November 2018; she is not prepared to delay the gift, even if it would be advantageous to do so.

The tax system in the country of Soloria

Capital gains tax	There is no capital gains tax in Soloria.
Inheritance tax	If Una still owns the villa at her death on 31 December 2023, the inheritance tax liability in Soloria would be £170,000.
	If Una gifts the villa to Won on 18 November 2018 and dies on 31 December 2023, the inheritance tax liability in Soloria would be £34,000, all of which would be payable following Una's death.

The Double Taxation Agreement between the UK and the country of Soloria includes an exemption clause whereby assets situated in one of the countries that is party to the agreement are subject to inheritance tax in that country only and not in the other country.

Gift to granddaughter

Una's granddaughter, Alona, will begin a three-year university course in September 2018. Una has agreed to pay Alona's rent of £450 per month while she is at university.

Undeclared income

Una purchased a luxury motor car for her own use in 2014, but found that many of her friends wanted to borrow it for weddings. In June 2015, she began charging £200 per day for the use of the car but is of the opinion that the income received cannot be subject to income tax as she only charges a fee 'to help cover the car's running costs'. However, I have considered the situation and concluded that the hiring out of the car has resulted in taxable profits.

I want you to prepare the following:

(a) **Gifts to son and granddaughter**

A **memorandum** for the client file that addresses the following issues.

(i) In respect of the gift to Won:

(1) Calculations of the potential reduction in the inheritance tax payable on Una's death as a result of each of the possible gifts to Won. The farmland will not qualify for business property relief, but you will need to consider the availability of agricultural property relief.

(2) Calculations of the capital gains tax liability in respect of each of the possible gifts.

(3) Explanations where the calculations are not self-explanatory, particularly in relation to the availability of reliefs, and a note of any assumptions made.

(4) A concise summary of your calculations in relation to these capital taxes in order to assist Una in making her decision as to which asset to give to Won.

(5) Any other tax and financial implications in respect of the gifts of which Una should be aware before she makes her decision.

(ii) In respect of the payment of Alona's rent:

(1) The conditions that would need to be satisfied in order for the payments to be exempt for the purposes of inheritance tax.

(b) **Undeclared income**

A **brief letter** to be sent from me to Una in relation to the luxury motor car.

The letter should explain the implications for Una and our firm of failing to declare the income to HM Revenue & Customs and the implications for Una of not having declared the income sooner.

Tax manager

Attachment – Schedule from Una – Details of the farmland and villa

	Notes	Date acquired	Cost £	Estimated value 18 November 2018 £	Estimated value 31 December 2023 £
Farmland	1	September 2015	720,000	900,000	1,100,000
Villa	2	August 2004	510,000	745,000	920,000

Notes

1 The agricultural value of the farmland is approximately 35% of its market value. The farmland has always been rented out to tenant farmers.

2 I inherited the villa when my husband died on 14 January 2008. Its market value at that date was £600,000. The villa has never been my principal private residence. It is situated in the country of Soloria and rented out to long-term tenants. The income is subject to Solorian tax at the rate of 50%. I do not own any other assets situated in Soloria.

3 The whole of my husband's nil rate band was used at the time of his death.

Required

(a) Prepare the memorandum requested in the email from your manager.

Note. For guidance, the calculations in part (a) of this question are worth no more than half of the total marks available. **(23 marks)**

Professional marks will be awarded in part (a) for the overall presentation of the memorandum and the effectiveness with which the information is communicated. **(3 marks)**

(b) Prepare the letter requested in the email from your manager. **(8 marks)**

A professional mark will be awarded in part (b) for the overall presentation of the letter. **(1 mark)**

You should assume that the tax rates and allowances for the tax year 2017/18 will continue to apply for the foreseeable future. **(Total = 35 marks)**

16 Kantar (12/14) 68 mins

Your manager has had a meeting with Kantar. Kantar recently appointed your firm to be his tax advisers. Extracts from the memorandum recording the matters discussed at the meeting and from an email from your manager are set out below.

Extract from the memorandum

Kantar is resident and domiciled in the UK.

Kantar has owned and operated his unincorporated business since 2005. In February 2018 Kantar disposed of some land. He used the proceeds to purchase equipment and vans on 1 May 2018 in order to expand his business.

Kantar's only other income consists of UK property business income of £5,000 per year. He does not have any financial costs in relation to his property business income.

Capital transactions

1 November 2016	Kantar inherited eight acres of land from his uncle. Kantar's uncle had purchased the land for £70,000 in 1999. At the time of the uncle's death, the land was worth £200,000. The land does not include any residential property.
5 November 2016	Kantar gave £400 to each of his 3 nephews.
1 February 2018	On this date, when the 8 acres of land were worth £290,000, Kantar gave 2 acres, valued by an independent expert at £100,000, to his son. Capital gains tax gift relief was not available in respect of this gift.
2 February 2018	Kantar sold the remaining 6 acres of land at auction for £170,000.

Kantar has not made any disposals for the purposes of capital gains tax other than those set out above.

Kantar has not made any transfers of value for the purposes of inheritance tax other than those set out above.

Kantar's business

Kantar's business provides delivery services. The majority of its customers are members of the public. Kantar is not registered for the purposes of value added tax (VAT).

The recent actual and budgeted results of the business are set out below.

	Actual 2017 £	Actual 2018 £	Budgeted 2019 £
	Year ended 31 March		
Sales	48,000	67,000	98,000
Expenses	(6,000)	(8,000)	(13,000)
Profit per the accounts	42,000	59,000	85,000
Adjustment for tax purposes	2,000	1,000	4,000
Capital allowances	(1,000)	(1,000)	(157,000)
Tax adjusted profit/(loss)	43,000	59,000	(68,000)
Income tax liability for the tax year	8,400	14,300	Nil

In the year ending 31 March 2020, no capital allowances will be available to Kantar. With the exception of capital allowances, the results for the year ending 31 March 2020 are expected to be the same as those for the year ended 31 March 2019.

Extract from an email from your manager

Additional information

- The income tax liabilities in the memorandum take account of Kantar's UK property business income as well as his trading income and are correct.

- Kantar pays all of his tax liabilities on or before the due dates.

Please prepare notes for use in a meeting with Kantar. The notes should address the following issues:

(a) **Capital transactions**

    (i) **Inheritance tax**

        (1) The availability of the small gifts exemption in respect of Kantar's gifts to his nephews

        (2) A calculation of the potentially exempt transfer on 1 February 2018 after deduction of any available exemptions

    (ii) A calculation of Kantar's chargeable gains and capital gains tax liability for the tax year 2017/18

(b) **Budgeted trading loss for the year ending 31 March 2019**

    (i) Calculations, with **brief** supporting explanations where necessary, of the tax which would be saved in respect of the offset of the trading loss for the tax year 2018/19 if:

        (1) The loss is relieved as soon as possible
        (2) The loss is carried forward for relief in the future

    A brief evaluation of your findings and the relevance to Kantar of the £50,000 restriction on the offset of trading losses.

    (ii) On the assumptions that the trading loss is carried forward and that Kantar wishes to maximise his cash flow position, prepare a schedule of the dates and amounts of the payments on account and balancing payments Kantar would expect to make, post 1 January 2019, in respect of his tax liabilities for 2017/18, 2018/19 and 2019/20. Include brief explanations of the payments on account amounts.

(c) **Reporting of chargeable gains**

    Kantar does not intend to report his chargeable gains on his income tax return as he believes that the tax authorities should be able to obtain this information from other sources. Explain the implications for Kantar, and our firm, of Kantar failing to report the chargeable gains to HM Revenue & Customs.

Required

Prepare the meeting notes requested in the email from your manager. The following marks are available:

(a)   Capital transactions

   (i)   Inheritance tax   **(4 marks)**
   (ii)   Capital gains tax   **(4 marks)**

(b)   Budgeted trading loss for the year ending 31 March 2019

   (i)   Offset of the trading loss   **(10 marks)**
   (ii)   Further tax payments if the loss is carried forward

          Note. Ignore national insurance contributions and VAT.   **(5 marks)**

(c)   Reporting of chargeable gains   **(4 marks)**

(d)   VAT   **(4 marks)**

Professional marks will be awarded for the clarity of the calculations, analysis of the situation, the effectiveness with which the information is communicated, and the quality of the overall presentation.   **(4 marks)**

(Total = 35 marks)

17 Pescara (12/13)   **39 mins**

Pescara requires advice on the inheritance tax payable on death and on the gift of a property, and on the capital gains tax due on a disposal of shares, together with the relief available in respect of the purchase of enterprise investment scheme shares.

Pescara and her parents:

- Pescara is a higher rate taxpayer who is resident and domiciled in the UK.
- Pescara's father, Galvez, died on 1 June 2007.
- Pescara's mother, Marina, died on 1 October 2018.
- Both Galvez and Marina were resident and domiciled in the UK.

Galvez – lifetime gifts and gifts on death:

- Galvez had not made any lifetime gifts.
- In his will, Galvez left cash of £80,000 to Pescara and a further £80,000 to Pescara's brother.
- Galvez left the remainder of his estate to his wife, Marina.

Marina – lifetime gifts:

- On 1 February 2014, Marina gave Pescara 375,000 shares in Sepang plc.
- Marina had made no other lifetime gifts.

Marina – gift of 375,000 shares in Sepang plc to Pescara:

- 1 January 2011:   Marina purchased 375,000 shares for £420,000.

- 1 February 2014:   Marina gave all of the shares to Pescara.
                     The shares were quoted at £1.84 – £1.96.
                     The highest and lowest marked bargains were £1.80 and £1.92.
                     Assume that the valuation rules for gifts of quoted shares applicable in the tax year
                     2017/18 also applied in the tax year 2013/14.

- The shares did not qualify for business property relief or capital gains tax gift relief.

Acquisition of Sepang plc by Zolder plc and subsequent bonus issue:

- 1 January 2016:   Zolder plc acquired the whole of the ordinary share capital of Sepang plc. Pescara received 30 pence and 2 ordinary shares in Zolder plc, worth £1 each, for each share in Sepang plc.

    The takeover was for genuine commercial reasons and not for the avoidance of tax.

- 1 July 2017:   Zolder plc declared a 2 for 1 bonus issue.

Pescara's actual and intended capital transactions in the tax year 2018/19:

			£
15 November 2018	Sale	1,000,000 shares in Zolder plc	445,000
1 April 2019	Purchase	Qualifying enterprise investment scheme (EIS) shares	50,000

Pescara – gift of a UK property:

- Pescara intends to give her UK main residence to her son on 1 October 2019.
- Pescara intends to continue to use this property, rent-free, such that this gift will be a gift with reservation.

Required

(a)   Calculate the inheritance tax payable in respect of Marina's gift of the shares in Sepang plc, as a result of her death.   **(7 marks)**

(b)   (i)   Calculate Pescara's capital gains tax liability for the tax year 2018/19 on the assumption that EIS relief is claimed in respect of the shares to be purchased on 1 April 2019 and that entrepreneurs' relief is not available.   **(6 marks)**

    (ii)   State the capital gains tax implications of Pescara selling the EIS shares at some point in the future.   **(3 marks)**

(c)   Explain how the proposed gift of the UK main residence will be treated for the purposes of calculating the inheritance tax due on Pescara's death.   **(4 marks)**

(Total = 20 marks)

18 Mirtoon (12/11)   68 mins

Your manager has sent you an email, together with an attachment, in respect of a client called Mirtoon. The email and the attachment are set out below.

Email from your manager

Mirtoon intends to leave the UK on 15 January 2019 in order to live in the country of Koro. He has entered into a full-time contract of employment for a fixed term of four years starting on that date but he may stay in Koro for as long as ten years. He will buy a house in Koro and will not make any return trips to the UK whilst he is living in Koro.

Mirtoon will sell his house in the UK and cease his business prior to his departure. Details of these proposals, together with information regarding agricultural land owned by Mirtoon, are set out in the attached extract from his email.

Background information

Mirtoon is divorced. He has always been resident and domiciled in the UK. He will continue to be UK domiciled whilst living in the country of Koro.

He does not own any buildings other than his home. He receives bank interest in respect of UK bank deposits of £34,775 per year. He will continue to hold these bank deposits whilst living in the country of Koro and this will be his only UK source of income.

Mirtoon has not made any disposals for the purposes of capital gains tax in the tax year 2018/19. He has capital losses brought forward as at 5 April 2018 of £4,000.

Mirtoon is self-employed. He has overlap profits brought forward in respect of his business of £7,600. He is registered for value added tax (VAT) and makes standard rated supplies only. He has never made any claims in respect of entrepreneurs' relief.

I want you to prepare the following:

(a) **Mirtoon's financial position**

Mirtoon wants to know how his plans to dispose of assets and his departure from the UK will affect his financial position. The details of his plans are in the following attachment. He has asked us to prepare a calculation of the total of the following amounts:

(i) The after-tax proceeds from the sale of his home and business assets

(ii) The tax saving in respect of the offset of his trading losses

The trading losses should be offset against the total income of the tax year 2017/18; there is no need to consider any other loss reliefs.

In order to accurately determine the tax effect of the relief available, you should prepare calculations of Mirtoon's income tax liability for 2017/18 both before and after the offset of the losses.

(iii) Any other tax liabilities arising as a result of Mirtoon's plans to leave the UK

You should include explanatory notes where this is necessary to assist Mirtoon's understanding of the calculations. This may be particularly useful in relation to the availability of any reliefs and allowances and the tax relief available in respect of the offset of the trading losses.

(b) **A letter to be sent from me to Mirtoon that addresses the following matters**

(i) VAT: The VAT implications of the cessation of the business and the sale of the business assets.

(ii) Income tax and capital gains tax: Whether or not Mirtoon will be liable to UK income tax and capital gains tax whilst he is living in the country of Koro by reference to his residence and domicile status. You should include specific reference to the capital gains tax implications of the proposed sale of the agricultural land in June 2020. There is no double tax treaty between the UK and the country of Koro.

(iii) Inheritance tax: Mirtoon has asked me to discuss some ideas he has had in relation to reducing the potential inheritance tax liability on his death. To help me with this, please include a summary of the rules relating to associated operations and gifts with reservation in the letter.

Tax manager

Attachment – Extract from an email from Mirtoon

Sale of house

I will sell my house on 31 December 2018 for £850,000. I purchased the house for £540,000 on 1 July 2008 and I have lived there ever since that date. Two rooms, representing 20% of the property, have always been used exclusively for the purposes of my business.

Sale of business assets

My business made a tax adjusted profit in the year ended 30 June 2017 of £90,000. However, in the year ended 30 June 2018 it made a tax adjusted loss of £20,000. I have not been able to find a buyer for the business and will therefore cease trading on 31 December 2018. I will then sell any remaining business assets.

I expect to be able to sell the business assets, consisting of machinery and inventory, for £14,000, with no asset being sold for more than cost. The business will make a tax adjusted loss of £17,000 in the 6 months ending 31 December 2018 after taking account of the sale of the business assets.

Agricultural land

In May 2014 my father gave me 230 acres of agricultural land situated in the UK. A capital gain of £72,900 arose in respect of this gift and my father and I submitted a joint claim for gift relief. I expect the value of the land to increase considerably in 2019 and I intend to sell it in June 2020.

Required

(a)   Prepare calculations showing how Mirtoon's disposal of assets and subsequent departure from the UK will affect his financial position as requested in the email from your manager.

Note. Ignore national insurance contributions.   **(17 marks)**

(b)   Prepare the letter to Mirtoon requested in the email from your manager. The following marks are available.

     (i)   VAT   **(3 marks)**
     (ii)   Income tax and capital gains tax   **(6 marks)**
     (iii)   Inheritance tax   **(6 marks)**

Professional marks will be awarded in this question for the extent to which the calculations are approached in a logical manner in part (a) and the effectiveness with which the information is communicated in part (b).   **(3 marks)**

You should assume that the tax rates and allowances for 2017/18 will continue to apply for the foreseeable future.

(Total = 35 marks)

19 Cada (12/14)   **39 mins**

Your firm has been asked to provide advice in connection with inheritance tax and capital gains tax following the death of Cada. The advice relates to the implications of making lifetime gifts, making gifts to charity, varying the terms of a will and other aspects of capital gains tax planning.

Cada and her family:

*   Cada, who was UK domiciled, died on 20 November 2018.
*   Cada is survived by two daughters: Raymer and Yang.
*   Raymer has an adult son.
*   Yang has no children.

Cada – lifetime gifts and available nil rate band:

*   Cada had not made any lifetime gifts since 30 November 2014.
*   Cada's nil rate band available at the date of her death was £220,000.

Cada's death estate and the details of her will:

*   Cada owned assets valued at £1,000,000 at the time of her death.
*   Cada left her main residence, valued at £500,000, to Raymer.
*   Cada left cash of £60,000 to a UK national charity.
*   Cada left her remaining assets (including a portfolio of shares) valued at £440,000 to Yang.
*   None of the remaining assets qualified for any inheritance tax reliefs.

Raymer:

*   Is not an accountant, but has some knowledge of the UK tax system
*   Has made four observations regarding her mother's estate and her inheritance

Raymer's four observations:

*   'My mother should have made additional gifts in her lifetime.'

*   'The tax rate on the chargeable estate should be less than 40% due to the gift to charity.'

*   'I do not intend to live in the house but will give it to my son on 1 July 2019.'

*   'My mother paid capital gains tax every year. However, when she died, some of her shareholdings had a value of less than cost.'

Cada's shareholdings at the time of her death:

*   Quoted shares in JW plc valued at more than cost
*   Quoted shares in FR plc valued at less than cost
*   Unquoted shares in KZ Ltd valued at £Nil

Required

(a) Explain the inheritance tax advantages, other than lifetime exemptions, which could have been obtained if Cada had made additional lifetime gifts of quoted shares between 1 December 2014 and her death.

(4 marks)

(b) Calculate the increase in the legacy to the charity which would be necessary in order for the reduced rate of inheritance tax to apply and quantify the reduction in the inheritance tax liability which would result.

(5 marks)

(c) Explain the capital gains tax and inheritance tax advantages which could be obtained by varying the terms of Cada's will and set out the procedures required in order to achieve a tax-effective variation. **(6 marks)**

(d) In relation to capital gains tax, explain what beneficial actions Cada could have carried out in the tax year of her death in respect of her shareholdings. **(5 marks)**

(Total = 20 marks)

20 Meredith and Adrian (practice question) 27 mins

Meredith:

- Has always been UK resident
- Recently inherited assets situated outside the UK
- Has not yet reported income arising from those assets to HM Revenue & Customs (HMRC)
- Is considering deliberately not informing HMRC of the income arising from the assets
- Has used a number of tax avoidance schemes, one of which has been defeated in the courts in May 2017

Adrian:

- Has run his sole trader business for five years

- Has decided to incorporate his trading business by selling the assets of his business to a new company, Better Ltd, in exchange for loan notes (so incorporation relief is not available)

- Will be the sole director and shareholder of Better Ltd

- Has no intention of selling his shares in Better Ltd in the near future

- Will sell 2 chargeable assets to Better Ltd which are a freehold shop (gain on sale £50,000) and goodwill (gain on sale £42,000)

- Has no other chargeable assets and is a higher rate taxpayer

Required

(a) (i) Outline the penalty for error that might be imposed on Meredith if she deliberately omits to inform HMRC of the offshore income and the circumstances in which a further penalty might be imposed. You should assume that the error will be treated as deliberate but not concealed. **(5 marks)**

(ii) Outline how HMRC will deal with Meredith if she is classed as serial tax avoider. **(4 marks)**

(b) Advise Adrian of the capital gains tax liability that will arise on the sale of his business to Better Ltd.

(5 marks)

(Total = 14 marks)

PART C: CORPORATION TAX

Questions 21 to 32 cover the taxation of companies. This is the subject of Chapters 20 to 27 of the BPP Study Text.

21 Klubb plc (12/14)   39 mins

Klubb plc, a client of your firm, requires advice on the penalty in respect of the late filing of a corporation tax return, the establishment of a tax-advantaged share scheme, and its shareholding in an overseas-resident company.

Klubb plc:

- Is a UK resident trading company
- Has been charged a penalty in respect of the late filing of corporation tax return
- Intends to establish a tax-advantaged share plan
- Purchased 30% of the ordinary share capital of Hartz Co from Mr Deck on 1 April 2018

Late filing of corporation tax returns:

- Klubb plc prepared accounts for the 16-month period ended 31 March 2017.
- The corporation tax returns for this period were filed on 31 May 2018.

Tax-advantaged share plan:

- The plan will be either a Schedule 2 share incentive plan (SIP) or a Schedule 4 company share option plan (CSOP).

- If a SIP, the shares would be held within the plan for five years.

- If a SIP, members will not be permitted to reinvest dividends in order to purchase further shares.

- If a CSOP, the options would be exercised within five years of being granted.

- In both cases it can be assumed that the plan members would sell the shares immediately after acquiring them.

Klubb plc wants the share plan to be flexible in terms of:

- The employees who can be included in the plan
- The number or value of shares which can be acquired by each plan member

Hartz Co:

- Hartz Co is resident in the country of Suta.
- Mr Deck continues to own 25% of the company's ordinary share capital.
- Kort Co, a company resident in the country of Suta, owns the remaining 45%.

Budgeted results of Hartz Co for the year ending 31 March 2019:

- Hartz Co has trading profits of £330,000.
- Hartz Co has chargeable gains of £70,000.
- All of Hartz Co's profits have been artificially diverted from the UK.
- Hartz Co will pay corporation tax at the rate of 10% in the country of Suta.
- Hartz Co will not pay a dividend for the year ending 31 March 2019.

Required

(a) State the corporation tax returns required from Klubb plc in respect of the 16-month period ended 31 March 2017 and the due dates for filing them. Explain the penalties which may be charged in respect of the late filing of these returns.   **(4 marks)**

(b)   Compare and contrast a Schedule 2 share incentive plan with a Schedule 4 company share option plan in relation to:

   (i)   The flexibility desired by Klubb plc regarding the employees included in the plan and the number or value of shares which can be acquired by each plan member

   (ii) The income tax and capital gains tax implications of acquiring and selling the shares under each plan

(9 marks)

(c)   (i)   Explain whether or not Hartz Co will be regarded as a controlled foreign company (CFC) for the year ending 31 March 2019 and the availability or otherwise of the low profits exemption.   **(4 marks)**

   (ii) On the assumption that Hartz Co is a CFC, and that no CFC exemptions are available, calculate the budgeted CFC charge for Klubb plc based on the budgeted results of Hartz Co for the year ending 31 March 2019.   **(3 marks)**

You should assume that the tax rates and allowances for the financial year to 31 March 2018 will continue to apply for the foreseeable future.

(Total = 20 marks)

22 Sank Ltd and Kurt Ltd (06/12)   39 mins

Sank Ltd and Kurt Ltd are two unrelated clients of your firm. Sank Ltd requires advice in connection with the payment of its corporation tax liability and the validity of a compliance check enquiry it has received from HM Revenue & Customs. Kurt Ltd requires advice in connection with the purchase of machinery and expenditure on research and development.

(a)   **Sank Ltd:**

   - Has been a large company for the purposes of payment of corporation tax for many years
   - Has had 2 related 51% group companies for many years
   - Will prepare its next accounts for the 11 months ending 30 September 2018
   - Has received a compliance check notice from HM Revenue & Customs

   Taxable total profits for the 11 months ending 30 September 2018:

   - Figures prepared on 31 March 2018 indicated taxable total profits for this 11-month period of £640,000.
   - As at 1 June 2018, taxable total profits for this 11-month period are expected to be £750,000.

   The compliance check notice from HM Revenue & Customs:

   - HM Revenue & Customs gave notice of the compliance check on 31 May 2018.
   - It relates to Sank Ltd's corporation tax return for the year ended 31 October 2015.
   - No amendments have been made to the corporation tax return since it was submitted.

   Required

   In relation to Sank Ltd:

   (i)   Explain, with supporting calculations, the payment(s) required in respect of the company's corporation tax liability for the 11 months ended 30 September 2018 and the implications of the increase in the expected taxable total profits.   **(9 marks)**

   (ii) In relation to the date on which the compliance check into the corporation tax computation for the year ended 31 October 2015 was notified, explain the circumstances necessary for the notice to be regarded as valid. You should assume that Sank Ltd has not been fraudulent or negligent.   **(3 marks)**

(b) **Kurt Ltd:**

- Was incorporated and began to trade on 1 August 2017
- Is owned by Mr Quinn, who also owns three other trading companies
- Has made a tax adjusted trading loss in the eight months ending 31 March 2018
- Has no other income or chargeable gains in the eight months ending 31 March 2018
- Is expected to be profitable in future years
- Is a small enterprise for the purposes of research and development

Expenditure in the period ending 31 March 2018:

- Machinery for use in its manufacturing activities – £210,000
- The cost of staff carrying out qualifying scientific research in connection with its business – £28,000

Required

In relation to Kurt Ltd, explain the tax deductions and/or credits available in the period ending 31 March 2018 in respect of the expenditure on machinery and scientific research and comment on any choices available to the company. **(8 marks)**

You should assume that the tax rates and allowances for the financial year to 31 March 2018 will continue to apply for the foreseeable future.

(Total = 20 marks)

23 Opus Ltd group (06/14) 49 mins

Your manager is due to attend a meeting with the finance director of Opus Ltd. A schedule of information obtained from the client files and an email from your manager in connection with the Opus Ltd group are set out below.

Schedule of information

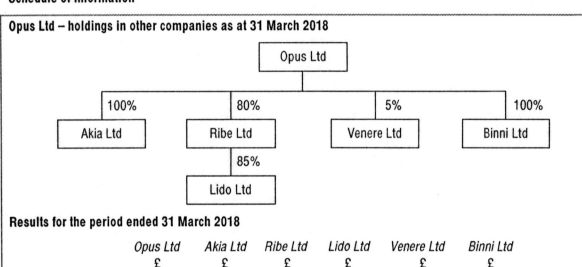

Opus Ltd – holdings in other companies as at 31 March 2018

Results for the period ended 31 March 2018

	Opus Ltd £	Akia Ltd £	Ribe Ltd £	Lido Ltd £	Venere Ltd £	Binni Ltd £
Trading profit/(loss)	10,000	(93,000)	41,000	75,000	160,000	78,000
Property income	8,000	–	–	–	–	–
Chargeable gain	Note 3	6,000	–	21,000	–	–

Notes

Holdings in other companies

1   All of the companies are UK resident trading companies.

2   All of the companies, including Binni Ltd, have always paid corporation tax by instalments.

3	Opus Ltd – acquisition of the holdings in other companies:

- Opus Ltd acquired Akia Ltd and the shareholding in Ribe Ltd (together with its subsidiary Lido Ltd) on 1 January 2003.

- Venere Ltd has an issued share capital of 1,000,000 ordinary shares. Opus Ltd acquired 170,000 ordinary shares in Venere Ltd on 1 July 2008 for £65,000. It sold 120,000 of these shares on 1 October 2017 for £150,000. Assume the indexation factor from July 2008 to October 2017 is 0.261.

- Opus Ltd acquired Binni Ltd on 1 December 2017.

4	The minority interests in Ribe Ltd and Lido Ltd are owned by individuals.
5	Venere Ltd is a 75% subsidiary of Jarrah Ltd, a company with no connections to the Opus Ltd group.

Results for the period ended 31 March 2018

6	All of the companies, with the exception of Binni Ltd, have prepared accounts for the year ended 31 March 2018. Binni Ltd has prepared accounts for the ten months ended 31 March 2018.
7	Where necessary, the results shown above have been adjusted for tax purposes.
8	Akia Ltd's trading loss includes writing down allowances in the main pool of £35,000.
9	Akia Ltd is not expected to return to profitability for a number of years.
10	Ribe Ltd has trading losses brought forward of £68,000 as at 1 April 2017.

Email from your manager

Please carry out the following work in preparation for the Opus Ltd meeting.

(a) **Relieving the trading losses of Akia Ltd and Ribe Ltd**

The objective of the group is to relieve all losses as soon as possible.

Prepare calculations, together with supporting explanations, to show how the group's objective can best be achieved, clearly identifying any losses to be carried forward as at 31 March 2018 and any further information which may need to be obtained.

There may be some interesting planning possibilities here; you should think carefully about the tax position of each company.

(b) **Sale of the shares in Venere Ltd**

Opus Ltd has received an offer of £80,000 for its remaining 50,000 ordinary shares in Venere Ltd. If the sale were to go ahead, it would take place on 30 June 2018. However, the management of Opus Ltd are of the opinion that the results of Venere Ltd for the year ending 31 March 2019 will be such that the shares could be worth as much as £100,000 if the sale were to be delayed until 30 April 2019.

Set out the matters which the management of Opus Ltd should consider in order to decide on which of the two dates it would be more financially advantageous to sell the shares in Venere Ltd. When calculating the indexation allowance, use an approximate indexation factor of 0.400 for the period from 1 July 2008 until the date of sale.

(c) **Error in the corporation tax return of Binni Ltd**

A detailed review of the results of Binni Ltd for the year ended 31 May 2016 has revealed that no adjustment was made in respect of an amount of disallowable expenditure. As a result of this, the company's corporation tax liability for the year was understated by £8,660. I have told the company that there may be interest and penalties in respect of this error.

Explain how the interest on the underpaid tax will be calculated and state the matters which would need to be considered if the company were unwilling to disclose the error to HM Revenue & Customs.

Tax manager

Required

Carry out the work required as set out in the email from your manager. The following marks are available:

(a)   Relieving the trading losses of Akia Ltd and Ribe Ltd   **(14 marks)**

(b)   Sale of the shares in Venere Ltd   **(5 marks)**

(c)   Error in the corporation tax return of Binni Ltd

     Note. You are not required to calculate the amount of interest payable or to consider any penalty which may be charged.   **(6 marks)**

                                                                          (Total = 25 marks)

24 Helm Ltd group (06/15)   **49 mins**

Your manager has had a number of telephone conversations with Gomez, a potential new client. Gomez owns the whole of the ordinary share capital of Helm Ltd. Extracts from the memorandum prepared by your manager setting out the matters discussed and an email from your manager in connection with the Helm Ltd group are set out below.

Extracts from the memorandum

Helm Ltd

The past and present members of the Helm Ltd group are set out below.

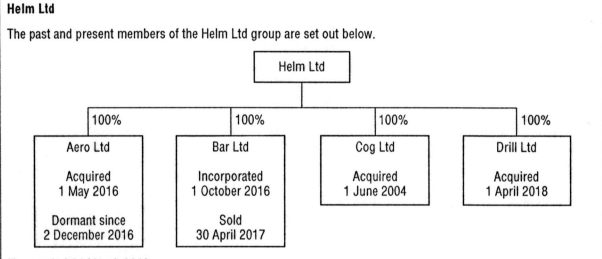

Year ended 31 March 2018

Sale of Bar Ltd

The whole of the ordinary share capital of Bar Ltd was sold to an unconnected party on 30 April 2017 for £1,200,000. Bar Ltd was incorporated on 1 October 2016, when Helm Ltd subscribed £1,000,000 for 200,000 ordinary shares.

Bar Ltd was formed to purchase the entire trade and assets of Aero Ltd for £1,000,000. This purchase occurred on 1 December 2016. The assets consisted of a building located in England valued at £830,000, inventory and receivables. The building had cost Aero Ltd £425,000 on 1 July 1997 and was valued at £880,000 on 30 April 2017 when it was still owned by Bar Ltd.

Year ended 31 March 2019

Purchase of Drill Ltd

Helm Ltd purchased the whole of the ordinary share capital of Drill Ltd on 1 April 2018. Drill Ltd has capital losses to carry forward as at 31 March 2018 of £74,000.

The business of Drill Ltd is to be expanded in the year ending 31 March 2019.

(a) Drill Ltd intends to borrow £1,350,000 in order to finance the purchase of a building and to provide additional working capital. Drill Ltd will be required to pay an arrangement fee of £35,000 in order to obtain this loan.

(b) The building will cost Drill Ltd £1,200,000. To begin with, this building will be larger than Drill Ltd requires. One-quarter of the building will be rented out to a third party until Drill Ltd needs the additional space.

Cog Ltd

On 1 May 2018, Cog Ltd sold a warehouse for £470,000. Cog Ltd had owned the warehouse for almost two years and had rented it to a tenant throughout this period. Cog Ltd had always intended to bring the warehouse into use in its trade at some point in the future but, before this could happen, it sold the warehouse and realised a chargeable gain of £82,000.

Email from your manager

Additional information

(1) All of the companies are UK resident trading companies.
(2) All of the companies are profitable and prepare accounts to 31 March each year.

Please carry out the following work in preparation for a meeting with Gomez.

(a) **Sale of Bar Ltd**

 (i) Calculate the chargeable gain resulting from the sale of the shareholding in Bar Ltd assuming the substantial shareholding exemption is not available. Explain any significant matter(s) which affect this calculation.

 (ii) Explain whether or not the substantial shareholding exemption will be available.

 (iii) Explain the implications of the sale in relation to stamp duty land tax. You should assume that the rules and rates of stamp duty land tax at the date of sale also applied in relation to any earlier transaction.

(b) **Drill Ltd**

 Explain how tax relief may be obtained in respect of the arrangement fee and the interest payable on the loan of £1,350,000 (you should be aware that Drill Ltd receives less than £50 of interest income each year).

(c) **Cog Ltd – chargeable gain on the sale of the warehouse**

 Explain:

 (i) Whether or not the chargeable gain on the sale of the warehouse can be relieved by rollover relief; and

 (ii) How Drill Ltd's capital losses can be relieved; in particular, whether or not they can be offset against the chargeable gain made on the sale of the warehouse by Cog Ltd.

(d) **Becoming tax advisers to Gomez and the Helm Ltd group of companies**

 Prepare a summary of the information we require, and any actions which we should take before we agree to become tax advisers to Gomez and the Helm Ltd group of companies.

Tax manager

Required

Carry out the work required as requested in the email from your manager. The following marks are available:

(a) Sale of Bar Ltd **(11 marks)**

   Note. The following figures from the Retail Prices Index should be used, where necessary.

July 1997	157.5
October 2016	264.8
December 2016	267.1
April 2017	269.6

(b) Drill Ltd **(5 marks)**

(c) Cog Ltd – chargeable gain on the sale of the warehouse **(4 marks)**

(d) Becoming tax advisers to Gomez and the Helm Ltd group of companies **(5 marks)**

(Total = 25 marks)

25 Flame plc group (12/12) 68 mins

Your manager has had a meeting with Gordon, the Group Finance Director of the Flame plc group of companies. Flame plc is quoted on the UK Stock Exchange. An extract from the memorandum prepared by your manager after the meeting, together with an email from him detailing the tasks for you to perform, is set out below.

Extract from the memorandum prepared by your manager

Background

Flame plc is a UK resident company, which has annual taxable profits of more than £200,000. It owns the whole of the ordinary share capital of Inferno Ltd, Bon Ltd and six other companies. All of the companies in the Flame plc group are UK resident companies with a 31 March year end.

Flame plc – sale of Inferno Ltd

Flame plc purchased the whole of the ordinary share capital of Inferno Ltd on 1 March 2014 for £600,000. The value of Inferno Ltd has increased and Gordon has decided to sell the company. For the purposes of our work, we are to assume that the sale will take place on 1 January 2019. The budgeted taxable profits of Inferno Ltd for the 9 months ending 31 December 2018 are £160,000.

The sale will be carried out in one of two ways:

(a) A sale by Flame plc of the whole of the ordinary share capital of Inferno Ltd for £1 million; or
(b) A sale by Inferno Ltd of its trade and assets for their market value.

Gordon needs to know the tax cost for the Flame plc group of each of these options to help him in his negotiations.

Inferno Ltd owns the following assets.

	Notes	Cost £	Current market value £
Equipment	1, 3	100,000	60,000
Milling machine	2, 3	95,000	80,000
Goodwill	4	Nil	530,000
Building – business premises	5	300,000	490,000

Notes

1   No item of equipment will be sold for more than cost.

2   The milling machine is an item of fixed plant and machinery that was purchased on 1 June 2015. Inferno Ltd claimed rollover relief in respect of the purchase of this machine to defer a chargeable gain of £8,500 made on 1 May 2014.

---

3   Capital allowances have been claimed in respect of the equipment and the milling machine. The tax written down value of the main pool of Inferno Ltd as at 1 April 2018 was zero. There have been no additions or disposals since that date.

4   The goodwill has been generated internally by Inferno Ltd since it began trading on 1 May 2009.

5   Inferno Ltd purchased the building from Flame plc on 15 March 2014 for its market value at that time of £300,000. Flame plc had purchased the building on 1 January 2010 for £240,000.

Flame plc – employee share scheme

Gordon is planning to introduce a share option scheme in order to reward the senior managers of Flame plc.

Bon Ltd – the grant of a lease

Part of the trading premises of Bon Ltd, a subsidiary of Flame plc, is surplus to requirements. Bon Ltd intends to grant a lease to an independent third-party company in respect of that part of its premises.

Bon Ltd – refund of corporation tax

Bon Ltd received a refund of corporation tax from HM Revenue & Customs on 1 June 2018. The company has not been able to identify any reason for this refund.

Email from your manager

(a)   I want you to draft a report to the Group Finance Director that addresses the following:

   (i)   **Flame plc – sale of Inferno Ltd**

   The tax cost of each of the two possible ways of carrying out the sale. Please note that I have already considered the availability of the substantial shareholding exemption and concluded that it will not be available in respect of the sale of Inferno Ltd because the Flame plc group is not a trading group.

   The report should include concise explanations of matters where the calculations are not self-explanatory.

   (ii)   **Flame plc – employee share scheme**

   (1)   The tax advantages for the employees of introducing a Schedule 4 company share option plan (CSOP) as opposed to a non tax advantaged share option scheme

   (2)   Why a CSOP would be a suitable tax-advantaged scheme for Gordon to choose

   (3)   The restrictions within the CSOP rules in respect of the following:

   ○   The number of share options that can be granted to each employee
   ○   The price at which the shares can be sold to the employees

   (iii)   **Bon Ltd – the grant of a lease**

   The value added tax (VAT) implications for the lessee if Bon Ltd were to opt to tax the building prior to granting the lease.

(b)   **Bon Ltd – refund of corporation tax**

   Prepare a summary of the actions that we should take and any matters of which Bon Ltd should be aware in respect of the refund of corporation tax.

Tax manager

Required

(a)   Draft the report to the Group Finance Director requested in the email from your manager. The following marks are available.

   (i)   Flame plc – sale of Inferno Ltd

   Notes for part (a)(i)

   1   For guidance, approximately equal marks are available for calculations and explanations.

The following indexation factors should be used, where necessary.

January 2010 to March 2014	0.169
January 2010 to January 2019	0.287 (assumed)
March 2014 to January 2019	0.100 (assumed) **(15 marks)**

(ii) Flame plc – employee share scheme **(8 marks)**

(iii) Bon Ltd – the grant of a lease **(3 marks)**

Professional marks will be awarded in part (a) for the overall presentation of the report, the provision of relevant advice and the effectiveness with which the information is communicated. **(4 marks)**

(b) Prepare the summary requested in the email from your manager. **(5 marks)**

(Total = 35 marks)

26 Bond Ltd group (12/14)   49 mins

You have received an email with an attachment from your manager relating to a new client of your firm.

The attachment is a memorandum prepared by the client, Mr Stone, who owns the whole of the ordinary share capital of Bond Ltd. The email from your manager contains further information in relation to the Bond Ltd group of companies and sets out the work you are to perform. The attachment and the email are set out below.

Attachment – Memorandum from Mr Stone

Bond Ltd group of companies

Formation of the group

The Bond Ltd group consists of Bond Ltd, Ungar Ltd and Madison Ltd.

1 April 2016	I purchased the whole of the ordinary share capital of Bond Ltd.
1 December 2016	Bond Ltd purchased the whole of the ordinary share capital of Ungar Ltd.
1 October 2018	Madison Ltd was incorporated on 1 October 2018. Bond Ltd acquired 65% of the ordinary share capital of Madison Ltd on that date.

Bond Ltd – results for the six months ended 30 September 2018

	£	Notes
Trading losses brought forward	(20,000)	1
Tax adjusted trading income for the period	470,000	2, 3
Chargeable gain	180,000	4

Notes

1   On 31 March 2016, Bond Ltd had trading losses to carry forward of £170,000. The company's total taxable trading income for the 2 years ended 31 March 2018 was only £150,000, such that on 31 March 2018 it had trading losses to carry forward of £20,000.

2   Bond Ltd's trade consists of baking and selling bread and other baked products. Up to 31 March 2018, its main product had always been low-cost bread which was sold to schools, hospitals and prisons. In April 2018, Bond Ltd introduced a new range of high-quality breads and cakes. This new range is sold to supermarkets and independent retailers and, for the 6 months ended 30 September 2018, represents 65% of the company's turnover and 90% of its profits.

3   In order to produce the new product range, Bond Ltd invested £180,000 in plant and machinery in April 2018. The tax adjusted trading income is after deducting capital allowances of £180,000, ie 100% of the cost of the plant and machinery.

The tax written down value brought forward on the company's main pool as at 1 April 2018 was zero and there were no other additions or disposals of plant and machinery in the period.

| 4 | The chargeable gain arose on the sale of a plot of land on 1 May 2018 for proceeds of £350,000. The land had always been used in the company's business but was no longer required. |

Ungar Ltd

The trade of Ungar Ltd consists of baking high-quality cakes. Ungar Ltd trades from premises purchased on 1 July 2017 for £310,000.

Ungar Ltd also develops new baking processes and techniques which it has patented. It uses these processes and techniques itself and licenses the patents to other manufacturers.

Madison Ltd

Madison Ltd purchased a building for £400,000 (plus 20% value added tax (VAT)) and machinery for £300,000 (plus 20% VAT) and began to trade on 1 October 2018.

Madison Ltd is partially exempt for the purposes of VAT. In the year ending 30 September 2019, its VAT recovery percentage is expected to be 80%. However, I expect this percentage to fall slightly in future years.

Email from your manager

Additional information

- Bond Ltd, Ungar Ltd and Madison Ltd are all resident in the UK.

- Bond Ltd and Ungar Ltd had always prepared accounts to 31 March. However, in 2018 it was decided to change the group's year end to 30 September and accounts have been prepared for the six months ended 30 September 2018.

- The original cost of the land sold by Bond Ltd on 1 May 2018 was £150,000. The chargeable gain of £180,000 is after the deduction of indexation allowance and is correct.

Please carry out the following work:

(a) **Corporation tax liability of Bond Ltd**

Calculate the corporation tax liability of Bond Ltd for the six months ended 30 September 2018 based on the information provided by Mr Stone. You should review Mr Stone's capital allowances figure of £180,000 and assume the company will claim the maximum possible rollover relief.

Include notes on the following matters:

(i) The capital allowances available

(ii) The use of Bond Ltd's trading losses brought forward bearing in mind that Mr Stone only recently acquired the company

(iii) The availability of rollover relief in respect of the chargeable gain on the land

You should **ignore VAT** when carrying out this work.

We will need to do further work in order to finalise this computation. In the meantime, make a note of any assumptions you have made in order to complete the computation as far as possible for now.

(b) **Ungar Ltd – patent box regime**

State, giving reasons, whether or not the patent box regime is available to Ungar Ltd and briefly describe the operation of the regime.

(c) **Madison Ltd – recovery of input tax**

Explain how much of the input tax in respect of the purchase of the building and machinery can be recovered by Madison Ltd in the year ending 30 September 2019 and how this may be adjusted in future years. Include an example of a possible adjustment in the year ending 30 September 2020.

Tax manager

Required

Carry out the work required as requested in the email from your manager. The following marks are available:

(a) Corporation tax liability of Bond Ltd

Note. For guidance, approximately two-thirds of the available marks relate to the written notes. **(16 marks)**

(b) Ungar Ltd – Patent box regime **(4 marks)**

(c) Madison Ltd – Recovery of input tax **(5 marks)**

(Total = 25 marks)

27 Maria and Granada Ltd (Mar/Jun 16) (amended)   39 mins

Your firm has been asked to provide advice to Granada Ltd and one of its shareholders, Maria. Maria wants advice on the tax consequences of selling some of her shares back to Granada Ltd. Granada Ltd wants advice on the corporation tax and value added tax (VAT) implications of the recent acquisition of an unincorporated business.

Maria:

- Is resident and domiciled in the UK
- Is a higher rate taxpayer and will remain so in the future
- Has dividend income of £6,000 in the tax year 2018/19
- Has already realised chargeable gains of £15,000 in the tax year 2018/19

Shares in Granada Ltd:

- Maria subscribed for 10,000 £1 ordinary shares in Granada Ltd at par in June 2009.

- Maria is one of four equal shareholders and directors of Granada Ltd.

- Maria intends to sell either 2,700 or 3,200 shares back to the company on 31 March 2019 at their current market value of £12.80 per share.

- All of the conditions for capital treatment are satisfied except for, potentially, the condition relating to the reduction in the level of shareholding.

Granada Ltd:

- Is a UK resident trading company which manufactures knitwear
- Prepares accounts to 31 December each year
- Is registered for VAT
- Acquired the trade and assets of an unincorporated business, Starling Partners, on 1 January 2019

Starling Partners:

- Had been trading as a partnership for many years as a wholesaler of handbags within the UK

- Starling Partners' main assets comprise a freehold commercial building and a patent for a process used in making handbags, which were valued on acquisition by Granada Ltd at £105,000 and £40,000 respectively

- Is registered for VAT

- The transfer of its trade and assets to Granada Ltd qualified as a transfer of a going concern (TOGC) for VAT purposes

- The business is forecast to make a trading loss of £130,000 in the year ended 31 December 2019

Granada Ltd – results and proposed expansion:

- The knitwear business is expected to continue making a taxable trading profit of around £100,000 each year.

- Granada Ltd has no non-trading income but realised a chargeable gain of £10,000 on 1 March 2019.

- Granada Ltd is considering expanding the wholesale handbag trade acquired from Starling Partners into the export market from 1 January 2020.

- Granada Ltd anticipates that this expansion will result in the wholesale handbag trade returning a profit of £15,000 in the year ended 31 December 2020.

(a)   (i)   Explain, with the aid of calculations, why the capital treatment **WILL NOT** apply if Maria sells 2,700 of her shares back to Granada Ltd, but **WILL** apply if, alternatively, she sells back 3,200 shares.

(4 marks)

      (ii)   Calculate Maria's after-tax proceeds per share if she sells:

         (1)   2,700 shares back to Granada Ltd; and, alternatively
         (2)   3,200 shares back to Granada Ltd.   **(4 marks)**

(b)   (i)   Describe the corporation tax treatment of the acquisition of the patent by Granada Ltd if no charge for amortisation was required in its statement of profit or loss.   **(3 marks)**

      (ii)   Discuss how Granada Ltd could obtain relief for the trading loss expected to be incurred by the trade acquired from Starling Partners, if it does not wish to carry any of the loss back.   **(5 marks)**

(c)   Explain the VAT implications for Granada Ltd in respect of the acquisition of the business of Starling Partners, and the additional information needed in relation to the building to fully clarify the VAT position.

(4 marks)

You should assume that the tax rates and allowances of the tax year 2017/18 and financial year 2017 will continue to apply for the foreseeable future.   **(Total = 20 marks)**

28 Bamburg Ltd (06/14)   39 mins

Charlotte is the owner of Bamburg Ltd. She requires advice on the value added tax (VAT) flat rate scheme, the sale of a substantial item of machinery, and the alternative methods by which she can extract additional funds from the company.

Charlotte:

- Is UK resident and UK domiciled
- Owns 100% of the ordinary share capital of Bamburg Ltd
- Earns an annual salary from Bamburg Ltd of £46,000 and has no other income
- Has two ideas to generate additional cash in Bamburg Ltd
- Wants to receive an additional £14,000 (after the payment of all personal taxes) from Bamburg Ltd on 30 June 2018

Bamburg Ltd:

- Is a UK resident trading company
- Is registered for VAT
- Has budgeted sales revenue for the year ending 31 March 2019 of £120,000 excluding VAT
- Makes wholly standard rated supplies apart from £6,000 of exempt supplies
- Has a nil tax written down value on its main pool as at 31 March 2018
- Will not purchase any plant and machinery in the year ending 31 March 2019

Charlotte's ideas to generate additional cash in Bamburg Ltd:

- 'Bamburg Ltd should join the VAT flat rate scheme in order to save money.'
- 'Bamburg Ltd should sell the 'Cara' machine and offset the resulting loss against its profits.'

The 'Cara' machine:

- The 'Cara' machine was purchased on 1 January 2016 for £94,000.
- Rollover relief was claimed in respect of this purchase to defer a chargeable gain of £13,000.
- The 'Cara' machine is currently worth £80,000.
- Following the sale of the 'Cara' machine, Bamburg Ltd will rent a replacement machine.

Alternative methods of extracting an additional £14,000 from Bamburg Ltd:

- Bamburg Ltd to pay Charlotte a bonus
- Bamburg Ltd to pay Charlotte a dividend
- Bamburg Ltd to make an interest-free loan of £14,000 to Charlotte

Required

(a) Explain, with reference to the information provided, whether or not Bamburg Ltd would be permitted to join the value added tax (VAT) flat rate scheme and set out the matters which would need to be considered in order to determine whether or not it would be financially beneficial for the company to do so. **(5 marks)**

(b) Explain the tax and financial implications of Bamburg Ltd selling the 'Cara' machine during the year ending 31 March 2019. **(5 marks)**

(c) (i) Prepare calculations to determine whether it would be cheaper for Bamburg Ltd to pay Charlotte a bonus or a dividend, such that she would receive £14,000 after the payment of all personal taxes. You should assume that the employment allowance has already been used against other employee wages. **(5 marks)**

   (ii) Explain the immediate tax implications for Bamburg Ltd and Charlotte of Bamburg Ltd making an interest-free loan of £14,000 to Charlotte. **(5 marks)**

(Total = 20 marks)

29 Liza (06/13)   39 mins

Liza requires detailed advice on rollover relief, capital allowances and group registration for the purposes of value added tax (VAT).

Liza's business interests:

- Liza's business interests, which have not changed for many years, are set out below.

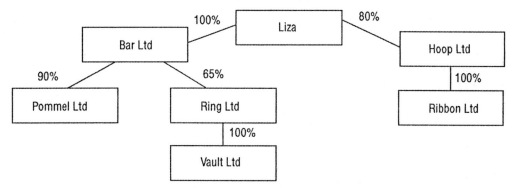

- All six companies are UK resident trading companies with a 31 March year end.

- All of the minority holdings are owned by individuals, none of whom is connected with Liza or with each other.

A building ('Building I') sold by Bar Ltd:

- Bar Ltd sold Building I on 31 May 2018 for £860,000.

- Bar Ltd had purchased the building on 1 June 2012 for £315,000 plus legal fees of £9,000.

- On 5 June 2012, Bar Ltd had carried out work on the building's roof at a cost of £38,000 in order to make the building fit for use.

- On 1 July 2017, Bar Ltd spent £14,000 repainting the building.

- Bar Ltd used Building I for trading purposes apart from the period from 1 January 2014 to 30 June 2015.

- It is intended that the chargeable gain on the sale will be rolled over to the extent that this is possible.

A replacement building ('Building II') purchased by Bar Ltd:

- Bar Ltd purchased Building II, new and unused, for £720,000 on 1 May 2018.
- Bar Ltd uses two-thirds of this building for trading purposes; the remaining one-third is rented out.

The trading activities of the Bar Ltd and Hoop Ltd groups of companies:

- The number of transactions between the Bar Ltd group and the Hoop Ltd group is increasing.
- Vault Ltd makes zero rated supplies; all of the other five companies make standard rated supplies.

Required

(a)   (i)   Calculate the chargeable gain on the sale of Building I, ignoring any potential claim for rollover relief.

(3 marks)

(ii)   In relation to claiming rollover relief in respect of the disposal of Building I, explain which of the companies in the Bar Ltd and Hoop Ltd groups are, and are not, able to purchase qualifying replacement assets, and state the period within which such assets must be acquired.   **(4 marks)**

(iii)   Explain, with the aid of supporting calculations, the additional amount that would need to be spent on qualifying assets in order for the maximum amount of the gain on Building I to be relieved by rollover relief.

(4 marks)

Notes

1   You should ignore VAT when answering part (a) of this question.

2   The following figures from the Retail Prices Index should be used, where necessary.

June 2012   241.8
July 2017   271.0 (assumed)
May 2018   277.2 (assumed)

(b)   Explain the capital allowances that are available in respect of the electrical, water and heating systems that were acquired as part of Building II.   **(2 marks)**

(c)   Explain which of the companies in the Bar Ltd and Hoop Ltd groups would be able to register as a single group for the purposes of VAT and discuss the potential advantages and disadvantages of registering them as a single VAT group.   **(7 marks)**

You should assume that the tax rates and allowances of the tax year 2017/18 and for the financial year to 31 March 2018 will continue to apply for the foreseeable future.   **(Total = 20 marks)**

30 Banger Ltd and Candle Ltd (12/12)   39 mins

Banger Ltd and Candle Ltd are two unrelated companies.

The management of Banger Ltd requires advice on the implications for one of the company's shareholders of the use of a motor car owned by the company and the proposed liquidation of the company.

The management of Candle Ltd has asked for a calculation of the company's corporation tax liability. Candle Ltd is an investment holding company.

(a)   **Banger Ltd:**

- Banger Ltd is a UK resident trading company.
- 65% of the company's share capital is owned by its managing director, Katherine.
- The remaining shares are owned by a number of individuals who do not work for the company.
- None of the shares have been acquired under the Enterprise Management Investment scheme.

Motor car provided to minority shareholder throughout the year ended 31 March 2018:

- Banger Ltd paid £17,400 for the motor car, which had a list price when new of £22,900.
- The car has a petrol engine and has CO_2 emissions of 107 grams per kilometre.

Liquidation of Banger Ltd:

- It is intended that a liquidator will be appointed on 31 January 2019 to wind up the company.

Distributions of company assets to shareholders being considered by Banger Ltd:

- A total distribution of £280,000 in cash to the shareholders prior to 31 January 2019

- The distribution of a commercial building with a market value of £720,000 to Katherine after 31 January 2019

Required

(i) Explain, with supporting calculations, the amount of the minority shareholder's taxable income in respect of the use of the motor car. **(3 marks)**

(ii) Explain in detail the tax implications for Banger Ltd, the minority shareholders and Katherine of the distributions that the company is considering. **(7 marks)**

(b) **Candle Ltd:**

- Is a UK resident investment holding company

The results of Candle Ltd for the year ended 31 March 2018:

	£
Interest receivable	41,100
Chargeable gains realised in the country of Sisaria, net of 17% Sisarian tax	15,770
Chargeable gains realised in the UK, excluding the sale of shares in Rockette plc	83,700
Fees charged by a financial institution in respect of an issue of loan stock	14,000
Interest payable on loan stock	52,900
General expenses of management	38,300

Sale of shares in Rockette plc on 1 January 2018:

- Candle Ltd purchased a 2.2% holding of the shares in Rockette plc for £31,400 in 2004.

- Piro plc acquired 100% of the ordinary share capital of Rockette plc on 1 January 2018.

- Candle Ltd received shares in Piro plc worth £147,100 and cash of £7,200 in exchange for its shares in Rockette plc.

- Piro plc's acquisition of Rockette plc was a commercial transaction and was not part of a scheme to avoid tax.

- The relevant indexation factor is 0.505.

Required

Calculate the corporation tax liability of Candle Ltd for the year ended 31 March 2018, giving explanations of your treatment of the disposal of the shares in Rockette plc. You should assume that Candle Ltd will claim all reliefs available to reduce its tax liability and you should state any further assumptions you consider necessary. **(10 marks)**

(Total = 20 marks)

31 Christina (Sep/Dec 15)

49 mins

Your manager has received a letter from Christina. Christina is the managing director of Sprint Ltd and owns the whole of that company's ordinary share capital. Sprint Ltd is a client of your firm. Extracts from the letter from Christina and an email from your manager are set out below.

Extract from the letter from Christina

I intend to purchase the whole of the ordinary share capital of Iron Ltd on 1 November 2018. My company, Sprint Ltd, purchases components from Iron Ltd, so the two companies will fit together well. I hope to increase the value of Iron Ltd over the next three to five years and then to sell it at a profit.

I need your advice on the following matters:

Corporation tax payable

Iron Ltd has not been managed particularly well. It has had significant bad debts and, as a result, is in need of more cash. To help determine its financial requirements, I need to know how much corporation tax Iron Ltd will have to pay in respect of its results for the 16-month period ending 30 June 2019. Iron Ltd's tax adjusted trading income for this period is budgeted to be only £30,000. In fact, if we discover further problems, it is quite possible that Iron Ltd will make a trading loss for this period; but please base your calculations on the budgeted profit figure of £30,000.

Iron Ltd has no income other than trading income. Following the acquisition, Iron Ltd will sell a small industrial building for £160,000 and an item of fixed machinery for £14,000 on 1 December 2018. The industrial building and the item of fixed machinery were both purchased on 1 June 2015 for £100,000 and £13,700 respectively. At that time, rollover relief of £31,800 was claimed against the acquisition of the industrial building and £3,200 against the acquisition of the item of fixed machinery.

Ownership of Iron Ltd

I need to decide whether I should purchase the shares in Iron Ltd personally or whether the shares should be purchased by Sprint Ltd. I will be the managing director of Iron Ltd regardless of who purchases the shares.

My preference would be to own Iron Ltd personally. However, I would be interested to learn of any advantages to the company being owned by Sprint Ltd. When Iron Ltd is eventually sold, I intend to use the proceeds to purchase a holiday home in Italy.

Value added tax (VAT)

Iron Ltd is not registered for the purposes of VAT. The current management of the company has told me that the level of bad debts is keeping the company's cash receipts in a 12-month period below the registration limit of £85,000. However, I suspect that when I have the opportunity to look at the figures in more detail, it will become apparent that the company should be registered.

Extract from the email from your manager

Additional information

(a) Sprint Ltd owns the whole of the ordinary share capital of Olympic Ltd. Both these companies are profitable and prepare accounts to 30 June each year. Both companies are registered for the purposes of VAT.

(b) Sprint Ltd, Olympic Ltd and Iron Ltd are all UK resident trading companies.

(c) Sprint Ltd will sell a warehouse on 1 February 2019. This will result in a capital loss of £38,000.

(d) Iron Ltd currently makes up its accounts to 28 February each year. Following its acquisition, however, its next set of accounts will be for the 16 months ending 30 June 2019.

(e) Iron Ltd currently has no related 51% group companies.

Please carry out the work set out below.

There will be quite a few points to draw to Christina's attention, so keep each one fairly brief.

(a) **Iron Ltd – corporation tax payable**

Assuming the entire ordinary share capital of Iron Ltd is purchased by Christina personally on 1 November 2018, calculate the corporation tax payable by Iron Ltd in respect of the 16-month period ending 30 June 2019, and state when this tax will be due for payment.

(b) **Ownership of Iron Ltd**

Explain the tax matters which Christina needs to be aware of in order to decide whether the ordinary share capital of Iron Ltd should be purchased by herself, personally, or by Sprint Ltd. You should assume that Iron Ltd will be required to register for VAT. You should consider the tax implications of both:

- The ownership of Iron Ltd
- The eventual sale of Iron Ltd (by either Christina or Sprint Ltd)

You should recognise, regardless of who purchases and subsequently sells Iron Ltd, that Christina intends to use the proceeds for personal purposes and that she is a higher rate taxpayer.

(c) **VAT registration**

Set out the matters which Christina should be aware of in relation to the need for Iron Ltd to register for VAT and the implications for that company of registering late.

Tax manager

Required

Carry out the work required as requested in the email from your manager. The following marks are available:

(a) Iron Ltd – corporation tax payable

Note. The following figures from the Retail Prices Index should be used, where necessary.

June 2015	258.9
December 2018	280.0

(9 marks)

(b) Ownership of Iron Ltd **(13 marks)**

(c) Value added tax (VAT) registration **(3 marks)**

You should assume that the tax rates and allowances for the tax year 2017/18 and the financial year to 31 March 2018 will continue to apply for the foreseeable future. **(Total = 25 marks)**

32 Drake Ltd, Gosling plc and Mallard Ltd (practice question)
35 mins

Drake Ltd, Gosling plc and Mallard Ltd are three unrelated clients of your firm. Drake Ltd requires advice in connection with goodwill. Gosling plc requires advice in connection with expenditure on research and development. Mallard Ltd requires advice in connection with disincorporation.

(a) **Drake Ltd:**

- Acquired the assets of the business of another company, including goodwill, on 1 September 2017
- Will amortise the goodwill in the company's accounts
- May sell the goodwill in a few years' time

Required

Explain the tax treatment of the goodwill while owned by Drake Ltd and on sale. **(4 marks)**

(b) **Gosling plc:**

  - Is a large company for the purposes of research and development (R&D)
  - In the year to 31 March 2018 spent £500,000 on qualifying R&D
  - Has taxable total profits, before taking into account R&D expenditure, of £4,500,000

  Required

  Calculate the corporation tax payable by Gosling plc for the year ended 31 March 2018.   **(3 marks)**

(c) **Mallard Ltd:**

  - Carries on a trade of computer repairs
  - Owns a freehold shop and a motor car
  - Has goodwill built up since incorporation in 2007
  - Has inventory of computer spare parts

  Nathan:

  - Is the sole shareholder of Mallard Ltd, acquiring his shares on incorporation

  - Wishes to disincorporate Mallard Ltd in February 2018, acquiring ownership of all its assets, and thereafter will carry on the computer repair business as a sole trade

  Required

  In relation to Mallard Ltd:

  (i) Explain the conditions for an election for disincorporation relief to be made, identifying any further information required.   **(4 marks)**

  (ii) State who must enter into the election for disincorporation relief and the date by which it must be submitted to HM Revenue & Customs.   **(2 marks)**

  (iii) Outline the effect of disincorporation relief.   **(3 marks)**

  (iv) Explain the effect of any other reliefs which may be relevant on the disincorporation of Mallard Ltd.   **(2 marks)**

  (Total = 18 marks)

PART D: VALUE ADDED TAX

Questions 33 to 35 cover value added tax (VAT). This is the subject of Chapters 28 and 29 in the BPP Study Text.

33 Jerome (06/12)   39 mins

Jerome is an unincorporated sole trader who is about to sell his business to a company. He requires advice on the value added tax (VAT) implications of the sale of the business, on whether a new lease in respect of a motor car for use by him should be entered into by him or by the company and on the payment of travel expenses in respect of the family of an employee working overseas.

Jerome's business:

- Jerome's business has annual taxable profits of £85,000 and is growing.

- Jerome's business is registered for the purposes of VAT.

- Jerome leases a motor car in which he drives 20,000 miles per year of which 14,000 miles are on business. He anticipates that this level and pattern of mileage will continue in the future.

- The assets of the business include a building that was completed in 2016 and purchased by Jerome in April 2016 for £320,000.

The sale of Jerome's business to Tricycle Ltd:

- The business will be sold to Tricycle Ltd on 1 August 2018.

- Jerome will own the whole of the share capital of Tricycle Ltd.

- Tricycle Ltd will not change the nature of the business but will look to expand it by exporting its products to Italy.

The lease of the motor car:

- The existing lease will end on 31 July 2018.
- A new lease will be entered into on 1 August 2018 by either Jerome or Tricycle Ltd.
- The annual leasing costs of the new car will be £4,400.

The motor car to be leased on 1 August 2018:

- Will be diesel powered and have a list price when new of £31,000
- Will have CO_2 emissions of 137 grams per kilometre
- Will have annual running costs, including fuel, of £5,000 in addition to the leasing costs

Remuneration to be paid by Tricycle Ltd to Jerome:

- Jerome will be paid a salary of £4,000 per month.

- If Tricycle Ltd leases the motor car, Jerome will use it for business and private purposes and will be provided with fuel for all his motoring.

- If Jerome leases the motor car, he will be paid 50 pence per mile for driving it on business journeys.

Expansion into Europe:

- An employee of Tricycle Ltd will work for up to three months in Italy between April and July 2019.

- The employee will continue to be resident and domiciled in the UK.

- Tricycle Ltd will pay the travel costs of the employee's wife and three year old child when they visit him in June 2019.

- The travel costs will be taxable in the hands of the employee as employment income.

Required

(a) Explain the VAT implications of the sale of Jerome's business to Tricycle Ltd. **(7 marks)**

(b) Prepare calculations for the 12-month period to show the total tax cost, for Tricycle Ltd and Jerome, of the car being leased by:

    (i)   Tricycle Ltd
    (ii)   Jerome

    Note. Ignore VAT for part (b) of this question. **(11 marks)**

(c) State the conditions that must be satisfied for a deduction for the travel costs paid by Tricycle Ltd to be given against the employee's total employment income. **(2 marks)**

You should assume that the tax rates and allowances for the tax year 2017/18 and for the financial year to 31 March 2018 will continue to apply for the foreseeable future. **(Total = 20 marks)**

34 Spetz Ltd group (12/13)　　　　　39 mins

The management of the Spetz Ltd group requires advice on the value added tax (VAT) annual adjustment for a partially exempt company, the tax position of a company incorporated and trading overseas, and the income tax treatment of the costs relating to an employee working abroad.

Spetz Ltd group of companies:

- Novak Ltd and Kraus Co are two 100% subsidiaries of Spetz Ltd.
- Novak Ltd has a VAT year end of 30 September.
- Spetz Ltd acquired Kraus Co on 1 October 2017.
- Meyer, an employee of Spetz Ltd, has been seconded to work for Kraus Co.

Novak Ltd – figures for the year ended 30 September 2018:

		£
Taxable supplies (excluding VAT)		1,190,000
Exempt supplies		430,000
Input tax:	Attributed to taxable supplies	12,200
	Attributed to exempt supplies	4,900
	Unattributed	16,100
	Recovered on the four quarterly returns prior to the annual adjustment	23,200

Kraus Co:

- Is incorporated in, and trades through, a permanent establishment in the country of Mersano

- Has no taxable income or chargeable gains apart from trading profits

- Has taxable trading profits for the year ended 30 September 2018 of £520,000, all of which arose in Mersano

- It has been determined that no charge would arise within the controlled foreign company (CFC) regime in respect of Kraus Co

- Has not made an election to exempt its overseas trading profits from UK tax

The tax system in the country of Mersano:

- It can be assumed that the tax system in the country of Mersano is the same as that in the UK.
- However, the rate of corporation tax is 16%.
- There is no double tax treaty between the UK and Mersano.

Meyer:

- Will work for Kraus Co in the country of Mersano from 15 December 2018 to 31 March 2019
- Will continue to be employed by Spetz Ltd
- Will continue to be resident and domiciled in the UK

The costs relating to Meyer's secondment to Kraus Co:

- Meyer will be reimbursed for the cost of the flights at the start and end of the contract.
- Meyer will return to the UK for a holiday in February 2019, and will pay his own transport costs.
- Meyer will be reimbursed for the cost of laundry and telephone calls home.

Required

(a) Calculate the value added tax (VAT) partial exemption annual adjustment for Novak Ltd for the year ended 30 September 2018 and state when it must be reported to HM Revenue & Customs. You should state, with reasons, whether or not each of the three *de minimis* tests is satisfied. **(7 marks)**

(b) (i) Explain how to determine whether or not Kraus Co is resident in the UK. **(3 marks)**

    (ii) Explain, with supporting calculations, the UK corporation tax liability of Kraus Co for the year ended 30 September 2018 on the assumption that it is resident in the UK, and discuss the advantages and disadvantages of making an election to exempt its overseas profits from UK tax. **(5 marks)**

(c) Explain the UK income tax implications for Meyer of the costs relating to his secondment to Kraus Co. **(5 marks)**

(Total = 20 marks)

35 Nocturne Ltd (06/15)   39 mins

Nocturne Ltd, a partially exempt company for the purposes of value added tax (VAT), requires advice on the corporation tax implications of providing an asset to one of its shareholders; the income tax implications for another shareholder of making a loan to the company; and simplifying the way in which it accounts for VAT.

Nocturne Ltd:

- Is a UK resident trading company
- Prepares accounts to 31 March annually
- Has 4 shareholders, each of whom owns 25% of the company's ordinary share capital
- Owns a laptop computer, which it purchased in October 2015 for £1,200, and which has a current market value of £150
- Has purchased no other plant and machinery for several years and the tax written down value of its main pool at 31 March 2018 was £Nil

Provision of a laptop computer to one of Nocturne Ltd's shareholders:

- Nocturne Ltd is considering two alternative ways of providing a laptop computer in the year ending 31 March 2019 for the personal use of one of its shareholders, Jed.
- Jed is neither a director nor an employee of Nocturne Ltd.
- Option 1: Nocturne Ltd will buy a new laptop computer for £1,800 and loan it immediately to Jed.
- Option 2: Nocturne Ltd will gift its existing laptop to Jed and will purchase a replacement for use in the company for £1,800.

Loan from Siglio:

- Siglio will loan £60,000 to Nocturne Ltd on 1 October 2018 to facilitate the purchase of new equipment.
- Siglio is both a shareholder of Nocturne Ltd and the company's managing director.
- Nocturne Ltd will pay interest at a commercial rate on the loan from Siglio.
- Siglio will borrow the full amount of the loan from his bank on normal commercial terms.

VAT – partial exemption:

- Nocturne Ltd is partially exempt for the purposes of VAT.

- Nocturne Ltd's turnover for the year ended 31 March 2018 was £240,000 (VAT exclusive).

- Nocturne Ltd's turnover for the year as a whole for VAT purposes comprised 86% taxable supplies and 14% exempt supplies.

- The input VAT suffered by Nocturne Ltd on expenditure during the year ended 31 March 2018 was:

	£
Wholly attributable to taxable supplies	7,920
Wholly attributable to exempt supplies	1,062
Unattributable	4,150

- Nocturne Ltd expects its turnover and expenditure figures to increase by approximately 25% next year.

- Siglio has heard about an annual test for computing the amount of recoverable input VAT during an accounting period and would like more information about this.

Required

(a) Explain, with the aid of supporting calculations, which of the two proposed methods of providing the laptop computer to Jed would result in the lower after-tax cost for Nocturne Ltd.

Note. You should ignore VAT for part (a) of this question. **(7 marks)**

(b) Explain the income tax implications for Siglio of providing the loan to Nocturne Ltd. **(4 marks)**

(c) (i) Determine, by reference to the *de minimis* tests 1 and 2, Nocturne Ltd's recoverable input VAT for the year ended 31 March 2018. **(4 marks)**

(ii) Advise Siglio of Nocturne Ltd's eligibility for the annual test for computing the amount of recoverable input VAT for the year ending 31 March 2019 and the potential benefits to be gained from its use. **(5 marks)**

(Total = 20 marks)

PART E: IMPACT OF TAXES AND TAX PLANNING

Questions 36 to 41 cover impact of taxes and tax planning. These are the subject of Chapter 30 in the BPP Study Text.

36 Loriod plc group (06/11)

39 mins

The Loriod plc group intends to acquire an overseas business. It requires advice on the relief available in respect of any initial losses made by the business, the use of foreign tax credits, and transfer pricing. The following information has been obtained from the management of the Loriod plc group.

Loriod plc group:

- Loriod plc is a UK resident trading company.
- Loriod plc has a large number of wholly owned UK resident trading subsidiary companies.
- Elivar Ltd, one of the Loriod plc group subsidiaries, is to acquire the 'Frager' business.
- The purchase of the 'Frager' business will follow either Strategy A or Strategy B.

Elivar Ltd:

- Makes qualifying charitable donations of £2,000 each year
- Has taxable total profits of approximately £90,000 per year

The 'Frager' business:

- Is carried on in the country of Kuwata and is owned by Syme Inc, a company resident in Kuwata
- Manufactures components used by Elivar Ltd and other Loriod plc group companies
- Carries on the same trade as Elivar Ltd
- Is expected to make a loss in the year following its acquisition by Elivar Ltd
- Is expected to have taxable profits of £120,000 per year following the year of acquisition

Strategy A:

- Elivar Ltd will purchase the trade and all of the assets of Syme Inc such that Elivar Ltd will be carrying on the 'Frager' business through a permanent establishment in Kuwata.
- The permanent establishment will be controlled from the UK.

Strategy B:

- Elivar Ltd will purchase the whole of the share capital of Syme Inc such that Syme Inc will be a subsidiary of Elivar Ltd resident in Kuwata.
- It has been determined that no charge would arise within the controlled foreign company (CFC) regime in respect of Syme Inc.

The tax system in the country of Kuwata:

- The tax system is broadly the same as that in the UK with a corporation tax rate of 16%.
- Trading losses may only be utilised by companies resident in Kuwata.
- Kuwata is not a member of the European Union and there is no double tax treaty between the UK and Kuwata.

Required

(a) Provide a detailed explanation of the relief available in respect of the expected loss to be made by the 'Frager' business depending on whether the purchase follows Strategy A or Strategy B. **(8 marks)**

(b) For this part of the question it should be assumed that the purchase has followed Strategy A, that the 'Frager' business is now profitable and that no election has been made in respect of the profits of the business.

Explain, with supporting calculations, how to determine the maximum loss that can be surrendered to Elivar Ltd by the Loriod plc group companies if relief in respect of the tax suffered in Kuwata is not to be wasted. **(6 marks)**

(c)   For this part of the question it should be assumed that the purchase has followed Strategy B.

        Explain the effect of the prices charged by the subsidiary in Kuwata to other companies in the Loriod plc group on the total tax paid by the group and the implications of the transfer pricing legislation.   **(6 marks)**

You should assume that the tax rates and allowances of the financial year to 31 March 2018 will continue to apply for the foreseeable future.   **(Total = 20 marks)**

37 Ziti (06/14)   **68 mins**

Your manager has received a letter from Ziti. Ziti owns and runs an unincorporated business which was given to him by his father, Ravi. Extracts from the letter and from an email from your manager are set out below.

Extract from the letter from Ziti

I have decided that, due to my father's serious illness, I want to be able to look after him on a full-time basis. Accordingly, I am going to sell my business and use the proceeds to buy a house nearer to where he lives.

My father started the business in 2003 when he purchased the building referred to in the business assets below. He gave the business (consisting of the goodwill, the building and the equipment) to me on 1 July 2014 and we submitted a joint claim for gift relief, such that no capital gains tax was payable. I have no sources of income other than this business.

I have identified two possible methods of disposal.

(a)   My preferred approach would be to close the business down. I would do this by selling the building and the equipment on 31 January 2019 at which point I would cease trading.

(b)   My father would like to see the business carry on after I sell it. For this to occur, I would have to continue trading until 30 April 2019 and then sell the business to someone who would continue to operate it.

In each case I would prepare accounts for the year ending 30 April 2018 and then to the date of cessation or disposal.

I attach an appendix setting out the information you requested in relation to the business.

Sadly, I have been told that my father is unlikely to live for more than three years. Please let me know whether his death could result in an inheritance tax liability for me in respect of the gift of the business.

My father's only lifetime gift, apart from the business given to me, was of quoted shares to a discretionary (relevant property) trust on 1 May 2010. The shares had a market value of £190,000 at the date of the gift and did not qualify for business property relief.

Appendix

Business assets (all figures exclude value added tax (VAT))

	Goodwill £	Building £	Equipment £
Original cost of the business assets	Nil	60,000	18,000
Market value at the time of my father's gift on 1 July 2014	40,000	300,000	9,000
Expected market value as at 31 January 2019 and 30 April 2019	40,000	330,000	10,000

Financial position of the business

The tax adjusted trading profits for the year ended 30 April 2017 were £55,000.

From 1 May 2017, it can be assumed that the business generates trading profits of £5,000 per month. The only tax adjustment required to this figure is in respect of capital allowances.

The tax written down value of the main pool as at 30 April 2017 was nil. I purchased business equipment for £6,000 on 1 August 2017. There have been no disposals of equipment since 30 April 2017.

Additional background information

- Ziti and Ravi are both resident and domiciled in the UK.
- Ziti has overlap profits from when he took over the business of £9,000.
- All of the equipment is moveable and no item has a cost or market value of more than £6,000.
- The business is registered for the purposes of VAT.
- No election has been made in respect of the building in relation to VAT.

Please prepare notes, which we can use in a meeting with Ziti, which address the following issues:

(a) **Sale of the business**

    (i)   Calculations to enable Ziti to compare the financial implications of the two possible methods of disposal

        You will need to calculate:

        (1)   Ziti's taxable trading profits from 1 May 2017 onwards and the income tax thereon
        (2)   Any capital gains tax (CGT) payable

        You should include:

        (1)   Explanations of the availability of any CGT reliefs
        (2)   A summary of the post-tax cash position
        (3)   Any necessary assumptions

    (ii)   Explanations of whether or not VAT would need to be charged on either or both of the alternative disposals

(b) **Inheritance tax**

Calculations of the amount of inheritance tax which would be payable by Ziti for all possible dates of his father's death between 7 June 2018 and 30 June 2021. You should include an explanation of the availability of any inheritance tax reliefs.

When calculating these potential inheritance tax liabilities you should assume that Ziti will sell the business on 30 April 2019.

The best way for you to approach this is to identify the particular dates on which the inheritance tax liability will change.

Tax manager

Required

Prepare the meeting notes requested in the email from your manager. The following marks are available.

(a)   Sale of the business

    (i)   Comparison of the financial implications of the alternative methods for disposing of the business.
        Note. Ignore national insurance contributions. **(17 marks)**

    (ii)   VAT. **(5 marks)**

(b)   Inheritance tax **(9 marks)**

Professional marks will be awarded for adopting a logical approach to problem solving, the clarity of the calculations, the effectiveness with which the information is communicated, and the overall presentation of the notes. **(4 marks)**

(Total = 35 marks)

38 King (06/15)

39 mins

King, a wealthy client of your firm with a significant property portfolio, requires advice on the sale of some unquoted shares and on the capital gains tax and inheritance tax implications of transferring assets to a trust and to his two children.

King:

- Is resident and domiciled in the UK
- Is an additional rate taxpayer
- Has used his capital gains tax annual exempt amount for the tax year 2018/19
- Has made one previous lifetime gift of £25,000 to his daughter, Florentyna, on 1 June 2017
- It should be assumed that King will die on 1 May 2020

King's family:

- King's daughter, Florentyna, is 34 years old and has 2 young children.

- Florentyna will have income from part-time employment of £11,500 in the tax year 2018/19. This is her only source of taxable income.

- King's son, Axel, is 40 years old and has an 18 year old daughter, who is a university student.

King's plans:

- On 1 September 2018, King will sell some of his shares in Wye Ltd.

- On 1 October 2018, King will put a cottage he owns in Newtown and the after-tax cash proceeds from the sale of the shares in Wye Ltd into an interest in possession trust for Florentyna and her children.

- On 1 March 2019, King will gift his share of a flat in Unicity to Axel.

Sale of shares in Wye Ltd:

- Wye Ltd is an unquoted investment company.
- King acquired 5,000 shares in Wye Ltd on 1 June 2005 at a cost of £5 each.
- These shares will be worth £45 each on 1 September 2018.
- King will sell sufficient shares to generate after-tax proceeds of £30,000.

Cottage in Newtown:

- This property is wholly owned by King.
- It is expected to have a value of £315,000 on 1 October 2018.

Creation of the interest in possession trust:

- King will pay any inheritance tax arising as a result of the gifts made to the trust.

- Florentyna will be the life tenant and her two young children will be the remaindermen of the trust.

- Florentyna will live in the cottage in Newtown and the trustees will invest the cash in quoted shares which will generate annual dividends of £3,000.

Flat in Unicity:

- The flat in Unicity is jointly owned by King and his wife, Joy, in the proportions: King 75% and Joy 25%.

- King and Joy have recently signed a contract with Axel's daughter to rent the flat to her for three years starting on 1 September 2018.

- The rental agreement is on a commercial basis.

- King has obtained the following expected valuations for the flat as at 1 March 2019:

	With vacant possession £	Without vacant possession £
Value of a 25% share	60,000	40,000
Value of a 75% share	220,000	160,000
Value of the whole property	340,000	250,000

Required

(a) Calculate the minimum number of shares in Wye Ltd which King must sell to generate after-tax proceeds of £30,000. **(3 marks)**

(b) (i) Advise King, with the aid of supporting calculations, of the capital gains tax and immediate inheritance tax implications of the proposed gift of assets into the interest in possession trust on 1 October 2018. **(6 marks)**

    (ii) Explain how Florentyna will be taxed on the income arising in the trust and calculate the additional income tax, if any, payable by her in respect of this income for the tax year 2018/19. **(3 marks)**

(c) Explain, with the aid of supporting calculations, why the disposal of the flat in Unicity may be caught by the associated operations rules and the increase in the inheritance tax liability which would arise on King's death on 1 May 2020 if these rules were to apply. **(8 marks)**

(Total = 20 marks)

39 Cinnabar Ltd (Sep/Dec 15)   39 mins

Cinnabar Ltd requires advice on the corporation tax treatment of expenditure on research and development, the sale of an intangible asset, and a proposed sale of shares. Cinnabar Ltd has also requested advice on the potential to claim relief for losses incurred in a new joint venture.

Cinnabar Ltd:

- Is a UK resident trading company

- Has one wholly owned UK subsidiary, Lapis Ltd

- Is a small enterprise for the purposes of research and development expenditure

- Prepares accounts to 31 March each year

- Expects to pay corporation tax by instalments for all relevant accounting periods

- Intends to enter into a joint venture with another UK company, Amber Ltd; this joint venture will be undertaken by a newly incorporated company, Beryl Ltd

Research and development expenditure – year ended 31 March 2018:

- The expenditure on research and development activities was made up as follows:

	£
Computer hardware	44,000
Software and consumables	18,000
Staff costs	136,000
Rent	30,000
	228,000

- The staff costs include a fee of £10,000 paid to an external contractor, who was provided by an unconnected company.

- The remainder of the staff costs relates to Cinnabar Ltd's employees, who are wholly engaged in research and development activities.

- The rent is an appropriate allocation of the rent payable for Cinnabar Ltd's premises for the year.

Sale of an intangible asset to Lapis Ltd:

- The intangible asset was acquired by Cinnabar Ltd in May 2013 for £82,000.

- The asset was sold to Lapis Ltd on 1 November 2017 for its market value on that date of £72,000, when its tax written down value was £65,600.

Sale of shares in Garnet Ltd:

- Cinnabar Ltd acquired a 12% shareholding in Garnet Ltd, a UK resident trading company, in July 2012 for £120,000.

- Cinnabar Ltd sold one-third of this shareholding on 20 October 2017.

- Cinnabar Ltd intends to sell the remaining two-thirds of this shareholding on 30 November 2018 for £148,000.

- It would be possible to bring forward this sale to October 2018 if it is beneficial to do so.

Beryl Ltd:

- Will be incorporated in the UK and will commence trading on 1 January 2019
- Is anticipated to generate a trading loss of £80,000 in its first accounting period ending 31 December 2019
- Will have no sources of income other than trading income

Alternative capital structures for Beryl Ltd:

- Two alternative structures have been proposed for the shareholdings in Beryl Ltd:

  - **Structure 1**: 76% of the shares in Beryl Ltd will be held by Amber Ltd, with the remaining 24% held by Cinnabar Ltd.

  - **Structure 2**: 70% of the shares will be held by Amber Ltd, 24% by Cinnabar Ltd and the remaining 6% held personally by Mr Varis, the managing director of Amber Ltd.

Required

(a) (i) Explain, with supporting calculations, the treatment for corporation tax purposes of the items included in Cinnabar Ltd's research and development expenditure for the year ended 31 March 2018.
(5 marks)

(ii) Explain the corporation tax implications for Cinnabar Ltd of the sale of the intangible asset to Lapis Ltd.
(2 marks)

(b) Calculate the after-tax proceeds which would be received on the proposed sale of the Garnet Ltd shares on 30 November 2018 and explain the potential advantage of bringing forward this sale to October 2018.

Note. The following indexation factor should be used where necessary:

July 2012 – November 2018 – 0.1549
(5 marks)

(c) Explain, with supporting calculations, the extent to which Cinnabar Ltd can claim relief for Beryl Ltd's trading loss under each of the proposed alternative capital structures.
(8 marks)

You should assume that the tax rates and allowances for financial year to 31 March 2018 will continue to apply for the foreseeable future.
(Total = 20 marks)

40 Hyssop Ltd (Sep/Dec 15)

39 mins

Hyssop Ltd wishes to provide assistance with home to work travel costs for Corin, who is an employee, and also requires advice on the corporation tax implications of the purchase of a short lease and the value added tax (VAT) implications of the sale of a warehouse.

Hyssop Ltd:

- Is a UK resident trading company
- Prepares accounts to 31 December each year
- Is registered for VAT
- Leased a factory on 1 February 2018

Corin:

- Is resident and domiciled in the UK
- Is an employee of Hyssop Ltd, who works only at the company's head office
- Earns an annual salary of £55,000 from Hyssop Ltd and has no other source of income

Hyssop Ltd – assistance with home to work travel costs:

- Hyssop Ltd is considering two alternatives to provide assistance with Corin's home to work travel costs.

  Alternative 1 – provision of a motorcycle:

  - Hyssop Ltd will provide Corin with a leased motorcycle for travelling from home to work.
  - Provision of the leased motorcycle, including fuel, will cost Hyssop Ltd £3,160 per annum. This will give rise to an annual taxable benefit of £3,160 for Corin.
  - Corin will incur no additional travel or parking costs in respect of his home to work travel.

  Alternative 2 – payment towards the cost of driving and provision of parking place:

  - Hyssop Ltd will reimburse Corin for the cost of driving his own car to work up to an amount of £2,240 each year.
  - Corin estimates that his annual cost for driving from home to work is £2,820.
  - Additionally, Hyssop Ltd will pay AB Parking Ltd £920 per year for a car parking space for Corin near the head office.

Acquisition of a factory:

- Hyssop Ltd acquired a 40-year lease on a factory on 1 February 2018 for which it paid a premium of £260,000.
- The factory is used in Hyssop Ltd's trade.

Disposal of a warehouse:

- Hyssop Ltd has agreed to sell a warehouse on 31 December 2018 for £315,000, which will give rise to a chargeable gain of £16,520.
- Hyssop Ltd had purchased the warehouse when it was newly constructed on 1 January 2015 for £270,000 (excluding VAT).
- The warehouse was used by Hyssop Ltd in its trade until 31 December 2017, since when it has been rented to an unconnected party.
- Until 1 January 2018, Hyssop Ltd made only standard rated supplies for VAT purposes.
- Hyssop Ltd has not opted to tax the warehouse for VAT purposes.
- The capital goods scheme for VAT applies to the warehouse.

Required

Note. You should ignore value added tax (VAT) for parts (a) and (b).

(a) Explain, with the aid of calculations, which of the two alternatives for providing financial assistance for home to work travel is most cost efficient for:

     (i)   Corin   **(5 marks)**
     (ii)   Hyssop Ltd   **(3 marks)**

(b) Explain, with the aid of calculations, the corporation tax implications for Hyssop Ltd of the acquisition of the leasehold premises on 1 February 2018, in relation to the company's tax adjusted trading profits for the year ended 31 December 2018 and its ability to roll over the gain on the sale of the warehouse. **(8 marks)**

(c) Explain, with the aid of calculations, the VAT implications of the disposal of the warehouse on 31 December 2018. **(4 marks)**

You should assume that the tax rates and allowances for financial year to 31 March 2018 will continue to apply for the foreseeable future.

(Total = 20 marks)

41 Jonny (Sep/Dec 15)

69 mins

Your manager has had a meeting with Jonny who is establishing a new business. An extract from an email from your manager, a schedule and a computation are set out below.

Extract from the email from your manager

> Jonny's new business will begin trading on 1 November 2018. Jonny will use an inheritance he received following the death of his mother to finance this new venture.
>
> We have been asked to advise Jonny on his business and his inheritance. Some of the work has already been done; I want you to complete it.
>
> **Please prepare a memorandum for Jonny's client file addressing the following issues:**
>
> (a)   **Unincorporated business**
>
>   I attach a schedule which sets out Jonny's recent employment income and his plans for the new business. I think you will find it useful to read the schedule before you go through the rest of this email.
>
>   You should assume that Jonny does not have any other sources of income or any taxable gains in any of the relevant tax years.
>
>   (i)   **Jonny's post-tax income**
>
>   Jonny has asked for an approximation of his post-tax income position for the first two trading periods. I want you to prepare calculations in order to complete the following table, assuming that any available trading loss reliefs will be claimed in the most beneficial manner. You should include explanations of the options available to relieve the loss, clearly identifying the method which will maximise the tax saved (you do not need to consider carrying the loss forward).
>
>   **Table to be completed**
>
> | | Strong demand £ | Weak demand £ |
> |---|---|---|
> | Aggregate budgeted net profit of the first two trading periods | 39,200 | 2,800 |
> | Aggregate income tax (payable)/refundable in respect of the profit/loss for the first two tax years | ? | ? |
> | Budgeted post-tax income | ? | ? |
>
>   Include a brief explanation as to why these calculations are only an approximation of Jonny's budgeted post-tax income.
>
>   (ii)   **Salesmen**
>
>   Jonny intends to hire two salesmen to get the business started. Their proposed contractual arrangements are as set out in the attached schedule.
>
>   Explain which of the proposed contractual arrangements with the salesmen indicate that they would be self-employed and state any changes which should be made to the other arrangements in order to maximise the likelihood of the salesmen being treated as self-employed.

(iii)   New contracts for the business

Jonny is hoping to obtain contracts with local educational establishments and has asked us to help. One of our clients is a college and an ex-client of ours provided services to a number of schools and colleges. Accordingly, we have knowledge and experience in this area.

Explain the extent to which it is acceptable for us to use the knowledge we have gained in respect of our existing client and ex-client to assist Jonny.

(b)   Jonny's inheritance from his mother

Jonny's mother died on 31 July 2018. She left the whole of her estate, with the exception of a gift to charity, to Jonny. I attach a computation of the inheritance tax due; this was prepared by a junior member of staff and has not yet been reviewed. I can confirm, however, that all of the arithmetic, dates and valuations are correct. In addition, there were no other lifetime gifts, and none of the assets qualified for business property relief.

I want you to review the computation and identify any errors. You should explain each of the errors you find and calculate the value of the inheritance which Jonny will receive after inheritance tax has been paid.

Tax manager

Schedule – Employment income and plans for the new business

Jonny's income

Jonny worked full time for many years until 30 June 2016 earning a salary of £6,000 per calendar month. From 1 July 2016, he worked part time earning a salary of £2,000 per calendar month until he ceased employment on 31 March 2018.

Two budgets have been prepared for Jonny's business based on customer demand being either strong or weak. You should assume that no tax adjustments are required to Jonny's budgeted profit/loss figures for the first two trading periods.

For strong demand, the taxable trading profit for the first two tax years has been computed; these figures are correct and you do not need to check them. You will, however, need to calculate the equivalent figures for weak demand.

	Strong demand £	Weak demand £
Budgeted net profit/(loss):		
Eight months ending 30 June 2019	9,200	(15,200)
Year ending 30 June 2020	30,000	18,000
Aggregate budgeted net profit of the first two trading periods	39,200	2,800
Taxable trading profit/(loss):		
2018/19	5,750	?
2019/20	19,200	?

Salesmen

Jonny is proposing to enter into the following contractual arrangements with two part-time salesmen:

- They will work on Tuesday and Wednesday mornings each week for a two-month period.
- They will be paid a fee of £300 for each new sales contract obtained. No other payments will be made.
- They will use their own cars.
- Jonny will lend each of them a laptop computer.

Computation – Inheritance tax payable on the death of Jonny's mother

Mother's lifetime gift

	£
1 June 2014 – Gift of cash to Jonny	30,000

Mother's chargeable estate at death on 31 July 2018

	£	£
Freehold property – Mother's main residence		530,000
UK quoted shares		400,000
Chattels – furniture, paintings and jewellery	40,000	
Less items individually worth less than £6,000	(25,000)	
		15,000
Cash		20,000
		965,000
Less gift to charity		(70,000)
Annual exemption		(3,000)
Chargeable estate		892,000
Less nil rate band	325,000	
Gift in the 7 years prior to death (£30,000 – £6,000)	(24,000)	
		(301,000)
		591,000
Inheritance tax (£591,000 × 40%)		236,400

Required

Prepare the memorandum as requested in the email from your manager. The following marks are available:

(a) Unincorporated business:

    (i)   Jonny's post-tax income   **(15 marks)**

    (ii)   Salesmen   **(4 marks)**

    (iii) New contracts for the business   **(4 marks)**

(b) Jonny's inheritance from his mother   **(8 marks)**

Professional marks will be awarded for following the manager's instructions, the clarity of the explanations and calculations, problem solving, and the overall presentation of the memorandum.   **(4 marks)**

Notes

1   Assume that the tax rates and allowances for the tax year 2017/18 apply to all tax years.

2   Ignore national insurance contributions throughout this question.

(Total = 35 marks)

Answers

1 The Bale Family

Marking scheme

		Marks	
(a)	Taxable income	1½	
	Income tax liability	2½	
			4
(b)	Current waste of nil rate bands	1	
	Transfer of assets by Frank to Deborah	1	
	Reduction in income tax liabilities	1	
			3
(c)	Taxable income	1½	
	Income tax liability	1½	
			3
(d)	Income tax position 2017/18	2	
	Increase in pension without income tax for 2018/19	1	
			3
			13

(a) **Frank – income tax liability 2017/18**

	Non-savings income £	Savings income £	Dividend income £	Total £
Employment income	47,000			
BSI		1,500		
Dividends			10,000	
Net income	47,000	1,500	10,000	58,500
Less personal allowance	(11,500)			
Taxable income	35,500	1,500	10,000	47,000

Income tax

	£
Non-savings income	
£33,500 × 20%	6,700
£2,000 (35,500 – 33,500) × 40%	800
Savings income	
£500 × 0% (savings income nil rate band – higher rate taxpayer)	0
£1,000 (1,500 – 500) × 40%	400
Dividend income	
£5,000 × 0% (dividend nil rate band)	0
£5,000 (10,000 – 5,000) × 32.5%	1,625
Tax liability	9,525

(b) Frank and Deborah – reduction in overall tax liabilities

In the tax year 2017/18, Deborah is a basic rate taxpayer as she has taxable income of £(15,500 – 11,500) = £4,000. She is therefore entitled to a savings income nil rate band of £1,000 which she is not using since she does not have any relevant investments. She is also not using her dividend nil rate band of £5,000.

At the start of the tax year 2018/19, Frank should transfer to Deborah building society funds which will generate interest of £1,000 and shares which will generate dividends of £5,000. This means that all of the savings and dividend income will be covered by nil rate bands as the remaining £500 of interest and £5,000 of dividends will fall within Frank's nil rate bands.

Deborah's income tax liability in 2018/19 will remain the same as in 2017/18. Frank's income tax liability for 2018/19 will be reduced by £(400 + 1,625) = £2,025 in comparison to 2017/18.

(c) Emily – income tax liability 2017/18

	Non-savings income £	Savings income £	Dividend income £	Total £
Trading income	5,500			
BI		6,200		
Dividends			25,000	
Net income	5,500	6,200	25,000	36,700
Less personal allowance	(5,500)	(200)	(5,800)	
Taxable income	0	6,000	19,200	25,200

Tutorial note

The personal allowance is always set against non-savings income first. The savings income starting rate of £5,000 and the savings income nil rate band of £1,000 should be preserved by only setting the personal allowance against savings income to reduce that income of £6,000. The remainder of the personal allowance is then set against dividend income. Note that this is not a matter of tax planning nor a claim but just the correct way to set off the personal allowance to minimise Emily's income tax liability.

Income tax

	£
Savings income	
£5,000 × 0% (savings income starting rate band)	0
£1,000 × 0% (savings income nil rate band – basic rate taxpayer)	0
Dividend income	
£5,000 × 0% (dividend nil rate band)	0
£14,200 (19,200 – 5,000) × 7.5%	1,065
Tax liability	1,065

(d) Harvey – increasing pension income without additional tax liability

In the tax year 2017/18, Harvey has nil income tax liability as follows:

	Non-savings income £	Dividend income £	Total £
Pension income	8,500		
Dividends		5,000	
Net income	8,500	5,000	13,500
Less personal allowance	(8,500)	(3,000)	
Taxable income	0	2,000	2,000

Income tax
Dividend income

£2,000 × 0% (dividend nil rate band)	0

However, it will be seen that £3,000 of the personal allowance is wasted because it is being set against dividend income which would be covered by the dividend nil rate band.

In the tax year 2018/19, Harvey could therefore increase his pension income by £3,000 so that the whole of his personal allowance is set against his pension income. The dividend nil rate band of £5,000 will then be fully utilised so that Harvey's income tax liability remains nil.

2 Stella and Maris (Sep/Dec 15)

Text references. The income tax computation is dealt with in Chapter 1. Pensions are covered in Chapter 2. Property income is covered in Chapter 3. Inheritance tax exemptions are dealt with in Chapter 16.

Top tips. In part (a) you need to consider the impact of the pension contribution on the personal allowance. You also need to think about how the basic rate and higher rate limits are increased.

Easy marks. There were some easy marks in part (a) for a basic income tax computation. The inheritance tax exemptions in part (b)(ii) should have been well known.

Examining team's comments. Part (a) required a calculation of an individual's income after the deduction of tax and pension contributions. In order to do this well, candidates had to pay attention to detail and to think before writing. This part of the question was done reasonably well. The question highlighted the following technical issues.

(a)   In order to determine any reduction in the level of the personal allowance, it is necessary to compare adjusted net income (income after deduction of qualifying pension contributions) with the £100,000 limit.

(b)   The basic and higher rate bands must be extended by the gross amount of the qualifying pension contributions.

(c)   There were excess contributions made. This required consideration of the contributions made and the annual allowance for [the current year and the preceding year].

Well-prepared candidates dealt with all three of these issues accurately. A final technical point, which was missed by the majority of candidates, was the need to consider relevant earnings in order to determine qualifying pension contributions. (**BPP note.** The restriction on finance costs was not relevant when this question was originally set.)

(**BPP note.** Part (b)(i) has been rewritten and the examining team's comments are no longer relevant.)

Part (b)(ii), the final part of the question, required candidates to identify two inheritance tax exemptions that were relevant to the facts given (other than the annual exemption). This was not a difficult requirement, but most candidates did not perform as well as they could have done because they started to write before they had identified the two exemptions. Many candidates wrote about potentially exempt transfers and the fact that no tax would be due if the donor survived the gift for seven years, which is nothing to do with exemptions. However, there were some satisfactory answers to this part. The two exemptions that candidates were expected to write about were the small gifts exemption and the exemption in respect of regular gifts out of income. These exemptions then needed to be addressed in relation to the particular gifts referred to in the question (cash or shares) and not to gifts generally. The conditions relating to the small gifts exemption are very easy to state but those relating to regular gifts out of income require more care if marks are to be maximised.

Marking scheme

			Marks
(a)	Qualifying pension contributions	1½	
	Taxable income	3	
	Excess pension contribution	1	
	Income tax liability	3½	
	Net income after tax and pension contributions	2	
	Max		10

					Marks
(b)	(i)	Tax-free amount		1½	
		Taxed amount		2½	
					4
	(ii)	Small gift exemption		3	
		Exemption for normal expenditure out of income		4	
			Max		6
					20

(a) **Stella – income after tax and pension contributions 2018/19**

	£
Employment income	80,000
Property business income (W1)	64,000
Net income	144,000
Less personal allowance (W2)	(11,500)
Taxable income	132,500

Income tax liability (W3)

	£
£113,500 × 20%	22,700
£19,000 × 40%	7,600
£132,500	30,300
Less: Finance costs tax reducer £20,000 × 25% × 20%	(1,000)
Add: Pension contribution additional charge £30,000 × 40% (W4)	12,000
Income tax liability	41,300

Income after tax and pension contributions is as follows:

	£
Employment income	80,000
Property income after full mortgage interest deduction	59,000
Income before tax and pension contributions	139,000
Less: Income tax liability	(41,300)
Pension contribution (W5)	(74,000)
Income after tax and pension contributions	23,700

Workings

1   *Property business income*

	£
Rents received	90,000
Less: Mortgage interest paid in year × 75%	(15,000)
Other expenses (all allowable)	(11,000)
Property business income	64,000

2   *Personal allowance*

The pension contributions qualifying for tax relief cannot exceed Stella's net relevant earnings, which are £80,000. Adjusted net income is £(144,000 – 80,000) = £64,000 so there is no restriction of the personal allowance.

3   *Increasing the basic and higher rate band thresholds*

The basic rate band threshold is increased to £113,500 (£33,500 + £80,000).

The higher rate band threshold is increased to £230,000 (£150,000 + £80,000).

4   *Excess qualifying pension contribution*

	£
Annual allowance for 2018/19	40,000
Unused annual allowance for previous tax year:	
2017/18 £(40,000 − 30,000)	10,000
Maximum gross pension contribution in 2018/19	50,000

Excess pension contribution is £(80,000 − 50,000) = £30,000.

The annual allowance is not reduced in 2017/18 or 2018/19 as Stella's adjusted income is equal to her net income which does not exceed the threshold of £150,000 in either year.

Stella is not entitled to annual allowances for 2015/16 or 2016/17 since she was not a member of a pension scheme in those years.

5   *Pension contributions paid*

The amount actually paid in respect of the pension contribution by Stella is £74,000 (£64,000 (£80,000 × 80%) (qualifying pension contribution) + £10,000 (non-qualifying pension contribution)).

(b)   (i)   **Maris – maximum receivable as a lump sum**

The value of Maris's pension fund exceeds the lifetime allowance of £1,000,000.

The maximum lump sum which she could take tax free was restricted to £250,000 (25% × £1,000,000).

The excess of the fund over the lifetime allowance was also taken as a lump sum, subject to an income tax charge at 55% on the value of this excess. Maris therefore received an additional £135,000 (45% × (£1,300,000 − £1,000,000)).

Maris's total receipt was therefore £385,000 (£250,000 + £135,000).

Tutorial note. The amount reinvested of £750,000 was equal to the remainder of the lifetime allowance (£1,000,000 − £250,000) after taking the tax-free lump sum.

(ii)   **Inheritance tax – lifetime exemptions available**

Small gift exemption

Maris can make exempt gifts valued at up to £250 each tax year to any number of recipients. If the total value of the gifts to any one recipient exceeds £250, the full value of the gifts will be taxable. The gifts can comprise either cash or shares.

Exemption for normal expenditure out of income

The following conditions must be satisfied for the gifts to be exempt:

(1)   The gift is made as part of Maris's normal expenditure. As she is intending to make regular gifts to her family on their birthdays, she should be able to establish a regular pattern of giving.

(2)   The gift is made out of income, not capital. Maris must therefore give cash from the dividend income, not part of her shareholdings.

(3)   Maris is left with sufficient income to maintain her usual standard of living. As she appears to have fairly significant pension and savings income, this condition should be satisfied.

There is no monetary limit on the amount of this exemption.

3 Piquet and Buraco (12/14)

Marking scheme

			Marks	
(a)	(i)	Date for notification to HMRC	1	
		Calculations of taxable trading profits	2	
				3
	(ii)	Basis periods for two tax years	1½	
		Creation of overlap profits	1½	
				3
	(iii)	Identification of issue – one mark each	2	
		Explanation of issue – one mark each	2	
				4

				Marks
(b)	(i)	Automatic overseas tests	1	
		Days in UK and UK ties	2½	
		Work, family and available accommodation ties	3	
		90 day tie	1½	
		Conclusion	1	
		Max		7
	(ii)	UK tax on overseas income and gains	1	
		Personal allowance and annual exempt amount	1	
		No remittance basis charge	2	
		Max		3
				20

(a) (i) Accounting date changed to 28 February

If Piquet changes his accounting date to 28 February, the year of change is 2018/19 so he must notify HMRC of the change by 31 January following the end of the tax year (ie 31 January 2020).

Taxable trading profits

	£
2018/19 (year of change)	
16 months ended 28 February 2019 (long period of account ending in year)	94,000
Less relief for overlap profits £15,000 × 4/5	(12,000)
Taxable trading profits	82,000
2019/20	
Year ended 28 February 2020 (current year basis)	88,000

(ii) 30 April year end – basis periods and overlap profits

The basis period for 2018/19 is the 12 months to the new accounting date which would have fallen in that tax year which is 30 April 2018.

This will create additional overlap profits as profits for the period 1 May 2017 to 31 October 2017 have already been taxed in the tax year 2017/18. These overlap profits are £4,500 × 6 = £27,000.

The basis period for the tax year 2019/20 is the 12 months ended 30 April 2019.

Tutorial note. If accounts are prepared for the 18-month period to 30 April 2019, there will be no period of account ending in the tax year 2018/19. A basis period for 2018/19 must be manufactured by taking the actual new accounting date of 30 April 2019 and deducting one year.

(iii) Advantages of 30 April year end

As Piquet's profits are rising, a date early in the tax year, such as 30 April, delays the time when rising accounts profits feed through into rising taxable profits, whereas a date late in the tax year, such as 28 February, accelerates the taxation of rising profits. This is because with an accounting date of 30 April, the taxable profits for each tax year are mainly the profits earned in the previous tax year. With an accounting date of 28 February the taxable profits are almost entirely profits earned in the current year.

An accounting date of 30 April gives the maximum interval between earning profits and paying the related tax liability. For example, if Piquet prepares accounts to 30 April 2020, this falls into the tax year 2020/21 with payments on account being due on 31 January 2021 and 31 July 2021, and a balancing payment due on 31 January 2022. If he prepares accounts to 28 February 2020, this falls in the tax year 2019/20 and the payments will be due one year earlier (ie on 31 January 2020, 31 July 2020 and 31 January 2021).

Knowing profits well in advance of the end of the tax year makes tax planning much easier. For example, if Piquet wants to make personal pension contributions and prepares accounts to 30 April 2020 (2020/21), he can make contributions up to 5 April 2021 based on those relevant earnings. If he prepares accounts to 28 February 2020, he will probably not know the amount of his relevant earnings until after the end of the tax year 2019/20, too late to adjust his pension contributions for that tax year.

Note. Only **two** advantages were required.

Tutorial note. Credit would also be given to students who explained the effect of a trader's year end on the basis period in the tax year of cessation (although this may be a disadvantage since, with an accounting date of 30 April, the assessment for the year of cessation could be based on up to 23 months of profits).

(b)   (i)   **Residence status for the tax year 2018/19**

Automatic overseas residence tests

Buraco does not satisfy the only relevant automatic overseas residence test for the tax year 2018/19 as he will spend 46 days or more in the UK in that tax year.

Tutorial note. As Buraco does not work full time overseas, the spending less than 91 days in the UK test is not relevant.

Residence status for tax year 2018/19

As Buraco meets none of the automatic overseas tests and (as stated in the question) none of the automatic UK tests, the 'sufficient ties' test must be considered to decide if he is UK resident for the tax year 2018/19.

As Buraco was not UK resident in any of the previous three tax years, the relevant ties are:

(1)   UK resident close family: Buraco has a minor child who is UK resident so this is a tie.

(2)   Substantive UK work: Buraco does not work in the UK so this is not a tie.

(3)   Available UK accommodation: Buraco has accommodation available to him for a consecutive period of 91 days or more in the tax year and in which he spends one or more nights during the tax year so this is a tie.

(4)   90 day tie: If Buraco spent more than 90 days in the UK in either or both of the previous 2 tax years (in this case only 2017/18 is relevant based on the information in the question) this would be a tie. More information is needed on this point.

Buraco therefore has two definite UK ties and one possible UK tie.

As Buraco was not previously resident in the UK in any of the previous three tax years, if he has two ties he will be UK resident for the tax year 2018/19 if he spends between 121 days and 150 days in the UK, but not UK resident if he spends between 100 days and 120 days in the UK.

If, however, it is found that Buraco has three UK ties, he will be UK resident for the tax year 2018/19 based on any number of his expected days in the UK since the minimum number of days for this test is 91 days.

(ii)   **Tax implications of claiming remittance basis**

If Buraco claims the remittance basis for the tax year 2018/19, he will be liable to UK tax on overseas income and gains arising in that tax year only to the extent that they are remitted to the UK.

Buraco would not be entitled to the personal allowance for income tax or the annual exempt amount for capital gains tax for the tax year 2018/19.

The remittance basis charge would not apply in the tax year 2018/19 as Buraco has not been UK resident for at least seven of the nine tax years preceding that tax year.

4 Jodie (06/15)

Text references. Overseas aspects of income tax are dealt with in Chapter 10. Trading losses are covered in Chapter 8. The calculation of gains and capital gains tax liability are dealt with in Chapter 11. Gift relief and principal private residence relief will be found in Chapter 13 and overseas aspects of capital gains tax in Chapter 14. Overseas aspects of inheritance tax are covered in Chapter 18. Value added tax (VAT) deregistration is dealt with in Chapter 28.

Top tips. It is really important to attempt all the requirements of the question. For example, in part (d) you needed to discuss both the inheritance tax aspects of Jodie leaving the UK and the value added tax aspects of ceasing to trade.

Easy marks. There were some easy marks in part (a) for explaining the statutory residence tests. However, it was important to apply the rules to the particular scenario rather than just state all the tests.

Examining team's comments. Part (a) was generally answered well, with many candidates demonstrating a strong knowledge of these aspects of the syllabus. In particular, candidates knew how to determine the number of ties that needed to be satisfied and were able to describe the ties and relate them to the facts of the question. Unfortunately, many candidates failed to consider the automatic UK residence tests and were unable to state clearly the income tax implications of being non-UK resident, ie not being subject to UK income tax on overseas income. This latter point was part of an overall lack of clarity among many candidates in relation to the overseas aspects of personal tax. Candidates were vague about the implications or wasted time providing significant amounts of information on the remittance basis.

Part (b) was generally answered well. This was a marked change in the performance in this area when compared with that in recent exams. In particular, many candidates were able to calculate the terminal loss reasonably accurately and to calculate the tax saving at the margin without preparing detailed income tax computations. Those candidates who performed less strongly had two main problems. Firstly, they did not know the detailed process necessary to calculate a terminal loss, such that they simply used the loss of the final trading period. Secondly, they prepared various detailed income tax computations in the hope that this would eventually lead to the tax saving required by the question. The problem with this approach was that it was very time consuming and, on the whole, it did not produce an acceptable answer. Well-prepared candidates scored well in this part and were able to do so in a sensible amount of time.

Part (c) was perhaps more challenging than part (b), but there were still plenty of very accessible marks, such that a well-prepared candidate should have no issue achieving a reasonable number of marks. The first requirement was the more challenging aspect of this part of the question and required candidates to state the basic rule in relation to residency and capital gains tax and to highlight the possible issue of temporary non-residence. The temporary non-resident rule was relevant due to the statement in the question that Jodie would return to the UK after four years (ie within five years) if her children were not happy overseas. This was only answered well by a minority of candidates. The main problem related to something which came up throughout this exam which was a lack of clarity as regards the overseas aspects of personal taxation. Some candidates thought that being non-resident was only relevant in relation to assets situated overseas whilst others wrote at length about the remittance basis and the importance of either remitting or not remitting gains made but did so by reference to Jodie's non-resident status as opposed to her domicile status.

There were a number of tasks to carry out in order to satisfy the second requirement of part (c) and those candidates who kept moving and tried to address all of the aspects of the question were able to score well. The gains on the business assets and the availability of entrepreneurs' relief were tackled well by the majority of candidates. The availability of the relief in respect of the principal private residence was identified by most candidates but only a minority considered the relevance of the size of the plot of land on which the property stood. The more challenging aspect of the question related to the charging of the heldover gain on the Butterfly Ltd shares as a result of Jodie leaving the UK within six years of the gift. This was, perhaps not surprisingly, missed by many candidates, although it was picked up by some.

BPP LEARNING MEDIA

The final part of the question related to other aspects of Jodie leaving the UK and concerned inheritance tax and VAT. The inheritance tax aspects were not done particularly well, with only a minority of candidates stating clearly the implications of Jodie's departure from the point of view of inheritance tax. In particular, candidates should have stated the relevance of domicile to inheritance tax and referred to the relevance of deemed domicile. The VAT aspects were handled better but still very few candidates were able to pick up all of the available marks here.

Marking scheme

				Marks
(a)	Automatic UK residence test		2	
	Sufficient ties test			
	Number of ties relevant for 60 day period		1	
	Consideration of each tie (1 mark each – maximum 4 marks)		4	
	Conclusion		1	
	Tax implications		1	
		Max		7
(b)	Calculation of terminal loss		4	
	Relief available			
	Calculation		2	
	Explanations		3	
		Max		8
(c)	Becoming non-UK resident			
	Future liability to capital gains tax		3	
	Shares in Butterfly Ltd		3	
	Disposals			
	Business assets		3	
	Home		2	
	Liability		2	
		Max		11
(d)	Inheritance tax			
	Cessation of UK domicile		1	
	Deemed domicile		1	
	Liability to UK inheritance tax		1	
	Value added tax			
	Notify HM Revenue & Customs		1	
	Business assets retained		2	
		Max		5
	Followed instructions		1	
	Clarity of explanations and calculations		1	
	Effectiveness of communication		1	
	Overall presentation and style		1	
				4
				35

Notes for meeting

Client: Jodie
Prepared by: Tax senior
Date: 5 June 2018

(a) UK tax residence and liability to UK income tax

It has already been concluded that you will not be non-UK resident in the tax year 2019/20 under the automatic overseas residence tests.

It is therefore necessary to consider whether you will be UK resident in the tax year 2019/20 under the automatic UK residence tests. You will be UK resident under the automatic UK resident tests if, during 2019/20:

(i)   You spend **183 days or more in the UK**;

(ii)   You have a **home in the UK** and **no home overseas**; or

(iii)   You **work full time in the UK**.

Since none of these tests will be met during 2019/20, you will not be UK resident under the automatic UK resident tests.

There is a further set of tests which will be used to determine whether you are UK resident in the tax year 2019/20. These are the 'sufficient ties' tests which consider the number of days you spend in the UK and the number of connection factors or 'ties' you have to the UK. Since you have been UK resident in at least one of the previous 3 tax years and want to spend between 46 and 90 days in the UK during 2019/20, you will be UK resident for that year if you have 3 or more ties.

The ties are as follows:

(i)   You have **UK resident close family** (spouse/civil partner, child under the age of 18) during the tax year.

(ii)   You do **substantive UK work** (40 days or more) during the tax year.

(iii)   There is **UK accommodation available to you** for a consecutive period of 91 days or more during the tax year.

(iv)   You spent **90 days or more in the UK** in either or both of the previous 2 tax years.

(v)   You are **in the UK for the same or more days in that tax year than in any other country**.

Since the only tie that you have with the UK for 2019/20 is the 90 day tie, you will not be UK resident for that tax year under your current plans. However, if you change your plans, for example you spend more days in the UK during that tax year, it will be necessary to reconsider your residence status.

As a non-UK resident, you will only be liable to UK income tax on your UK source income and not on your overseas income, even if you remit that income to the UK.

(b)   **Terminal loss relief**

Your terminal trading loss for the final 12 months of trading is £22,750 (see Appendix 1). This loss can be relieved against your taxable trading profits for tax year of cessation (2018/19 – but in your case there are no trading profits in that year) and the preceding three tax years, relieving later years before earlier years.

The total income tax saved is £7,500 (see Appendix 1).

(c)   **Capital gains tax**

Non-UK residence in the tax year 2019/20

You will not be subject to UK capital gains tax in 2019/20 under general rules if you are non-UK resident in that tax year nor in any subsequent year when you are non-UK resident.

However, if you are non-UK resident for a temporary period (five years or less), there is a special charging rule which applies to you because you were UK resident for at least four out of the seven tax years immediately preceding 2019/20. This rule states that gains made by you in the non-UK resident period on assets which you owned before you became non-resident, such as the shares in Butterfly Ltd, will be chargeable in the tax year you become UK resident again.

Withdrawal of holdover (gift) relief on shares in Butterfly Ltd

Since you will become non-UK resident within six tax years following the year of the transfer of the shares in Butterfly Ltd to you and you still own those shares, the gain held over will become chargeable on you as if it arose immediately before you become non-UK resident (ie on 5 April 2019 so taxable in 2018/19). The gain is £(60,000 − 37,000) = £23,000. It will be taxable at the rate of 20%.

Sale of business

The gain of the sale of your business premises is £(190,000 – 135,000) = £55,000. You can claim entrepreneurs' relief on this disposal so the gain will be taxable at the rate of 10%. This is because the premises were in use for the purposes of a business at the time when the business ceased to be carried on, you carried on the business throughout the period of one year ending with the date of cessation and that cessation date is within three years before the date of the disposal.

There is no chargeable gain on the computer equipment because this is a chattel which was sold for gross proceeds of £6,000 or less. Inventory is not a chargeable asset for capital gains tax.

Sale of your home

The gain arising on the sale of your only or main private residence is exempt from capital gains tax. The exemption covers total grounds of up to half a hectare. The total grounds can exceed half a hectare if the house is large enough to warrant it but, if not, the gain on the excess grounds is taxable.

Since your house stood on a one hectare plot, it will be necessary to investigate whether the extended exemption applies. If it is decided that part of the gain is chargeable, it will be subject to capital gains tax at the rate of 28% since it is residential property.

Capital gains tax liability 2018/19

Your capital gains tax liability for 2018/19 will be at least £7,840 (see Appendix 2). It may be larger if it is determined that part of the gain on the sale of your home is chargeable to capital gains tax.

(d) **Other matters**

Inheritance tax

If you are UK domiciled, or deemed to be UK domiciled, transfers of all your assets, wherever situated, are subject to inheritance tax. Under general law, you are domiciled in the country which you regard as your permanent home. You will be deemed to be UK domiciled for inheritance tax purposes for 36 months after ceasing to be domiciled in the UK under general law. If you are not UK domiciled nor UK deemed domiciled, only transfers of your UK assets are subject to inheritance tax.

You can become non-UK domiciled under general law by severing your ties to the UK and settling permanently in another country. Given your current plans, since you may return to the UK if your children are not happy in Riviera, it is likely that you will still be domiciled in the UK under the general law until it is clear that you have settled permanently in Riviera.

Value added tax (VAT)

You will be subject to compulsory deregistration from VAT because you are no longer making taxable supplies and you must notify HM Revenue & Customs accordingly. Failure to notify within 30 days may lead to a penalty.

On deregistration, VAT is chargeable on all assets on which input tax was claimed and you have retained, since you are making a taxable supply to yourself as a newly unregistered trader. However, if the VAT chargeable does not exceed £1,000, it need not be paid. Since the only asset retained is the inventory of £3,500, no payment is required.

APPENDIX 1

Terminal loss relief

Calculation of terminal trading loss

	£	£
2018/19 (6 April 2018 to 31 May 2018)		
Loss £18,000 × 2/5		7,200
Overlap relief		6,500
2017/18 (1 June 2017 to 5 April 2018)		
1 June 2017 to 31 December 2017		
Profit £3,000 × 7/12	(1,750)	
1 January 2018 to 5 April 2018		
Loss £18,000 × 3/5	10,800	
		9,050
Terminal loss		22,750

Tax saving using terminal loss relief

	2015/16	2016/17	2017/18	Total
	£	£	£	£
Trading income	67,000	2,000	3,000	
Loss relief	17,750	2,000	3,000	22,750
Tax saving				
2017/18 (N1)			3,000 @ 0%	0
2016/17 (N2)		2,000 @ 20%		400
2015/16 (N3)	17,750 @ 40%			7,100
Total				7,500

Notes

1   Your income in the tax year 2017/18 will be covered by your personal allowance so no income tax will be saved for that tax year since there was no tax liability.

2   You paid income tax at the basic rate of 20% in the tax year 2016/17 and so the trading loss will save tax at 20%.

3   You paid income tax at the higher rate of 40% in the tax year 2015/16 on your taxable income in excess of the basic rate threshold and so the trading loss will save 40% tax since you had at least £17,750 taxable at the higher rate.

APPENDIX 2

Capital gains tax liability 2018/19

	Qualifying for entrepreneurs' relief	Not qualifying for entrepreneurs' relief
	£	£
Business premises	55,000	
Heldover gain on Butterfly Ltd shares		23,000
Less annual exempt amount		(11,300)
		11,700
Capital gains tax at 10%/20%	5,500	2,340
Total liability £(5,500 + 2,340)		7,840

1   The annual exempt amount will be deducted from the heldover gain as this gain is taxed at a higher rate than that on the business premises.

2   The heldover gain will be taxable at the rate of 20% because the gain on the sale of the business premises will be treated as using up Jodie's basic rate band.

5 Dana (12/12)

Text references. Trading losses for individuals are covered in Chapter 8 and the income tax computation in Chapter 1. Employment income generally is covered in Chapter 4 and terminal bonuses are dealt with in Chapter 5. Pre-trading expenditure and the basis of assessment for trading profits are covered in Chapter 6. Gift relief for capital gains tax is one of the topics in Chapter 13. Inheritance tax on lifetime transfers will be found in Chapter 16.

Top tips. When thinking about the use of trade loss relief, the three key aspects are the rate of relief, the timing of the relief and the loss of personal allowances.

Easy marks. Nearly all of the marks in this question were for knowledge from Taxation (TX – UK). You should have been able to gain easy marks for working out the trading profit for the period to 30 September 2017 and the opening years assessments in part (a). The technical information in part (b) was not difficult but you needed to keep your answer succinct and to the points required.

Examining team's comments. In part (a), the first task was to determine the trading profit/loss for each of the tax years. This required candidates to deduct the pre-trading expenditure from the profit of the first trading period and then to apply the opening years rules. They also needed to know that losses are only recognised once in the opening years. The treatment of the pre-trading expenditure was done well by only a minority of candidates. Other candidates either missed it out altogether or deducted it from the taxable profit for the tax year 2016/17 rather than the profit of the first trading period. The opening year rules and the treatment of the loss within those rules were done well by the majority of candidates. This was a significant improvement over the performance in recent exams.

Once the profits and losses had been determined, candidates needed to consider the reliefs available in respect of the loss. There were two aspects to this. First, candidates needed to know all of the available reliefs for the losses. This was done very well by the vast majority of candidates.

Secondly, candidates needed to compare the different reliefs and then calculate the total tax relief obtained by the most efficient strategy. Performance of this second task was mixed with some candidates calmly and efficiently calculating the tax due before and after claiming relief in order to determine the tax saving, whilst others wrote about how to do it in general terms without actually doing it. This is perhaps a confidence issue; candidates should ensure that they have practised as many questions as possible prior to sitting the exam and, once in the exam, should have the self-belief to address the figures and come up with specific advice.

Part (b)(i) concerned the availability of gift relief on the transfer of a rental property to a trust and was not done particularly well. The issue here was that gift relief would be available because the transfer was immediately subject to inheritance tax. This is true regardless of the nature of the asset, such that those candidates who focused on whether or not the property was a business asset had missed the point. This was not too great a problem as there were only two marks available. However, a minority of candidates made things worse by ignoring the fact that this question part needed to be answered in approximately four minutes and wrote about gift relief at length, thus wasting time.

Part (b)(ii) concerned Dana's inheritance tax position. Those candidates who made a genuine attempt to answer the question here did well. The technical issues in this question were:

(a)   The transfer of the rental property in December 2013 was a chargeable lifetime transfer, such that we needed a value for the property in order to determine the nil band available for the transfer in September 2018.

(b)   The gifts of cash to family members were potentially exempt transfers, such that they would not affect the nil band whilst Dana is alive.

(c) The cash gifts may be exempt depending on the amount given, the date of the gift and the reason for the gift. Exempt gifts would not use Dana's annual exemptions, such that they may be available for relief against the transfer to the trust.

This question was different from past inheritance tax questions and required some thought before it could be answered. It was not technically difficult but required candidates to address the specific question; the minority of candidates who wrote about inheritance tax in general terms and ignored the specifics of the question did poorly, as did those who tried to calculate inheritance tax liabilities. Some candidates let themselves down by writing that they needed 'the details of the gifts' without specifying what those details were and why they needed them.

Marking scheme

			Marks
(a)	Identification of years in which relief available	4	
	Employment income	1	
	Trading income	4	
	Income taxable at the higher rate	4	
	Capital gains taxable at the higher rate	1½	
	Tax savings	5	
	Notes in respect of additional information	2	
		Max	18
(b)	(i) Capital gains tax		2
	(ii) *Inheritance tax*		
	Gift in December 2013	1½	
	Gifts to family members		
	Information required	1½	
	Relevance of information	3	
		Max	5
			25

(a) Relief available in respect of trading loss

A trading loss for tax purposes of £22,500 (W2) has arisen in the tax year 2018/19.

It can be relieved against Dana's total general income of 2018/19, the year of the loss, and/or 2017/18.

Alternatively, because the loss has arisen in one of the first four tax years of trading, it can be relieved against Dana's total general income of the three years prior to the year of the loss starting with the earliest year, ie 2015/16.

The income taxable at the higher rate in each of the tax years is set out below.

	2015/16 £	2016/17 £	2017/18 £	2018/19 £
Employment income (W1)	32,000	0	0	0
Trading income (W2)	0	4,500	6,000	0
Property business income	17,700	30,025	36,000	46,600
Less personal allowance	(11,500)	(11,500)	(11,500)	(11,500)
Taxable income	38,200	23,025	30,500	35,100
Less basic rate band	(33,500)	(33,500)	(33,500)	(33,500)
Income taxable at higher rate/(basic rate band remaining)	4,700	(10,475)	(3,000)	1,600
Taxable gain: £([310,000 – 250,000] – 11,300)			48,700	
Gains taxable at the higher rate			45,700	

The claims against general income are 'all or nothing' claims. This means that the trading loss will be offset in full in one of 2015/16 or 2017/18 or 2018/19, depending on which relief is claimed. Because an early years trading loss relief claim would relieve the loss in full in 2015/16, it is not possible to relieve the loss in 2016/17.

The year with the most income taxable at the higher rate is 2015/16. Relieving the loss of £22,500 in that year would save income tax as follows:

	£
£4,700 × 40%	1,880
£(22,500 − 4,700) = £17,800 × 20%	3,560
Tax saving	5,440

Relieving the loss in 2018/19 would clearly save less tax, as there is less income taxable at the higher rate in that year than there is in 2015/16.

There is no income taxable at the higher rate in 2017/18 but there is a capital gain. Relieving the loss against the general income in the basic rate band would allow an equivalent amount of the capital gain to be taxed in the basic rate band (18% as residential property gain) rather than the higher rate band (28%).

Accordingly, relieving the loss in 2017/18 would save tax as follows:

	£
Income tax	
£22,500 × 20%	4,500
Capital gains tax	
£22,500 × (28% − 18%)	2,250
Tax saving	6,750

The most beneficial claim is to relieve the loss in 2017/18 in order to save tax of £6,750.

Notes in respect of the additional information provided by Dana

1   The bonus is in respect of work carried out by Dana for her employer. Accordingly, it is taxable in full in the year of receipt.

2   The cost of travelling around the UK in 2016 would have been allowable had it been incurred after Dana began to trade. Accordingly, because it was incurred in the seven years prior to commencing to trade, it is treated as if it had been incurred on the first day of trading.

Workings

1   *Employment income in 2015/16*

	£
Salary for 9 months £40,000 × 9/12	30,000
Bonus	2,000
	32,000

2   *Trading income*

	£
2016/17 (1 January 2017 to 5 April 2017)	
£13,500 (W3) × 3/9	4,500
2017/18 (1 January 2017 to 31 December 2017)	
£13,500 − 7,500 (£30,000 × 3/12)	6,000
2018/19 (Year ended 30 September 2018)	
Loss £(30,000 − 7,500)	(22,500)

The trading loss of £7,500 deducted in arriving at the taxable profit for the tax year 2017/18 is excluded from the loss available for relief in respect of the tax year 2018/19.

3   *Trading profit for the nine months ended 30 September 2017*

	£
Original figure	14,900
Less pre-trading expenditure	(1,400)
	13,500

(b)   **Transfer of the rental property to the trust on 1 September 2018**

(i)   *Capital gains tax*

Dana can claim gift relief in respect of the transfer of the property to the trustees because a lifetime transfer to any trust is a chargeable lifetime transfer for inheritance tax. The election must be signed by Dana and submitted by 5 April 2023 (ie four years after the end of the tax year in which the gift was made).

(ii)   *Inheritance tax*

Information required in respect of the transfer to the trust in December 2013

(1)   The value of the property at the time of the gift: the gift in December 2013 is within the seven-year period prior to the gift on 1 September 2018, and so will reduce the nil rate band available for the latter gift.

Information required in respect of the gifts to family members

(2)   Date, value, recipient and occasion of each gift: this information is required in order to determine whether the gifts to family members are exempt or not. This will affect the annual exemptions available in respect of each of the gifts to the trusts.

In addition to the annual exemption, the following lifetime gifts are exempt:

(1)   Gifts of less than £250 in total to any individual in a tax year
(2)   Gifts of no more than £1,000, made on the occasion of a marriage or civil partnership
(3)   Normal (regular) gifts made out of income that do not affect Dana's standard of living

6 Monisha and Horner (12/13) (amended)

Text references. The principles of income tax, including jointly held property, will be found in Chapter 1. Property income is covered in Chapter 3. The basics of chargeable gains are dealt with in Chapter 11 and reliefs in Chapter 13. Personal service companies are covered in Chapter 4.

Top tips. You might want to start with part (b) of this question as it was self-contained and would have taken less time to achieve the available marks than part (a) which needed a bit more thought.

Easy marks. The computation of the deemed employment income in part (b) was relatively straightforward.

Examining team's comments.

BPP note. Part (a) has been rewritten and the examining team's comments are no longer relevant.

Part (b)(i) required an outline of the circumstances in which the personal service company rules (IR35) apply. The majority of candidates struggled to satisfy this requirement despite a reasonable knowledge of the rules. It was generally recognised that the rules were in place in order to prevent the avoidance of tax but there was some confusion as to exactly where tax was being avoided. Very few candidates were able to state the commercial relationship between the taxpayer, the personal service company and the client in a clear manner.

Part (ii) required a calculation of the deemed employment income under the rules. This was done well or very well by the majority of candidates. The only common error was a failure to calculate employer's national insurance contributions in respect of the salary paid.

			Marks
(a)	Income tax		
	Property business income tax liability of Monisha	3½	
	Property business income tax liability of Asmat	3	
	First five tax years tax saving	1½	
	Final tax year tax saving	1	
	Capital gains tax		
	No gain, no loss disposal	1	
	CGT if proposals not carried out	1½	
	CGT if proposals are carried out	2½	
	Total tax saving	½	
	Max		13
(b) (i)	Conditions for IR35 – 1 mark each	4	
	Employment/self-employment test reference	1	
	Max		3
(ii)	95% of income	1½	
	Deductions:		
	Salary and pension contributions	1	
	Employer's NIC on actual salary	1½	
	Employer's NIC on deemed employment income	1	
	Max		4
			20

(a) **Monisha**

Total tax saving for six years ending 5 April 2025

Income tax

	£
Income tax saved in first 5 tax years £((5,550 (W1) × ½) – 0 (W2)) × 5	13,875
Income tax saved in final tax year £((5,550 (W1) × ½) – 1,320 (W2))	1,455
Total income tax saved	15,330

Workings

1   *Property business income liability of Monisha if proposals **not** carried out*

	£
Rental income	24,000
Less: Allowable expenses £(1,600 + (5,400 × 75%) + 2,000)	(7,650)
Replacement furniture relief	(1,800)
Property business income	14,550
Tax on property business income	
£14,550 × 40%	5,820
Less: Finance costs tax reducer £5,400 × 25% × 20%	(270)
	5,550

2   *Property business income liability of Asmat if proposals **are** carried out*

	£
Rental income	24,000
Less: Allowable expenses £(1,600 + 5,400 + 2,000)	(9,000)
Capital allowances	(1,800)
Property business income	13,200
Property business income taxable on Asmat £13,200 × ½	6,600

For the first five tax years, Asmat will not have any other income so that his share of the property income will be covered by his personal allowance and his income tax liability will be £0. In the final tax year, Asmat will have employment income so that the property income will be taxed at 20% so his liability will be £6,600 × 20% = £1,320.

Tutorial notes

1   Only 75% of the finance costs are allowable (using the 2017/18 tax rates and allowances as directed in the question) when computing property business income for Monisha if the property is not let as furnished holiday accommodation. The remaining 25% of the finance costs will be eligible for a tax reducer at 20%. If the property is let as furnished holiday accommodation there is no restriction on the finance costs.

2   The income of a jointly held asset is automatically split equally between a married couple, regardless of their actual interests in the property. (Monisha and Asmat could elect to split the income between them in the ratio 80:20, but to do so would not be beneficial in their particular circumstances.) Accordingly, property income of £6,600 will be subject to income tax on Asmat.

Capital gains tax

The gift of the 20% interest in the property will take place on a no gain, no loss basis because Monisha and Asmat are a married couple. The gain on the sale of the property will therefore be allocated between Monisha and Asmat in the ratio 80:20. A gain on the sale of furnished holiday accommodation qualifies for entrepreneurs' relief.

	£
Capital gains tax on sale of property if proposals **not** carried out	
Monisha: £(100,000 − £[11,300 − 6,000]) × 28%	26,516
Capital gains tax on sale of property if proposals **are** carried out	
Monisha: £(80,000 − £[11,300 − 6,000]) × 10% (entrepreneurs' relief)	7,470
Asmat: £(20,000 − 11,300) × 10% (entrepreneurs' relief)	870
Total capital gains tax on sale	8,340
Capital gains tax saved £(26,516 − 8,340)	18,176

Total tax saving

	£
Income tax saving	15,330
Capital gains tax saving	18,176
Total tax saving	33,506

(b)   **Horner**

    (i)   **Circumstances in which personal service company (IR35) rules apply**

        (1)   An individual ('the worker') performs, or has an obligation to perform, services for 'a client'.

        (2)   The performance of those services is referable to arrangements involving a third party (eg the personal service company), rather than referable to a contract between the client and the worker.

        (3)   If the services were to be performed by the worker under a contract between himself and the client, the worker would be regarded as employed by the client (using the usual tests which distinguish between employment and self-employment).

        (4)   The worker (alone or with associates) controls more than 5% of the ordinary share capital of the company, or is entitled to receive more than 5% of any dividends from the company, or the worker receives, or could receive, payments or benefits from the company which are not salary, but could reasonably be taken to represent payment for the services he provides to clients.

(ii) **Deemed employment income for the year ending 5 April 2019**

		£
Otmar Ltd – 95% of income from relevant engagements		
£85,000 × 95%		80,750
Less:	Salary paid to Horner	(50,000)
	Pension contributions	(2,000)
	Employer's NIC on actual salary	
	£(50,000 – 8,164) = £41,836 × 13.8%	(5,773)
		22,977
Less:	Employer's NIC on deemed payment	
	£22,977 × 13.8/113.8	(2,786)
Deemed employment income		20,191

Tutorial notes

1   The employment allowance is not available as Horner is the sole employee of Otmar Ltd and is a director of the company.

2   The dividend paid to Horner will be treated as exempt to avoid a double charge to tax on the same income.

7 Cate and Ravi (06/15)

Text references. Employment income, including national insurance aspects, is the subject of Chapter 4. The income tax computation is covered in Chapter 1. The badges of trade are dealt with in Chapter 6. The chattels exemption and overseas aspects of capital gains tax are covered in Chapter 14.

Top tips. In part (a) it is important to work out the marginal cost of Cate employing the new employee. The key points are that Cate is a higher rate taxpayer and pays some of her Class 4 NICs at 2%. As a result she will save tax and Class 4 NICs of 42% of these costs.

Easy marks. The badges of trade in part (b) should have been familiar from Taxation (TX – UK). However, it was important to apply the tests to the specific situation given in the question.

Examining team's comments. Part (a) concerned an individual, Cate, running a successful unincorporated business that required an additional part-time employee. The requirement was to calculate the annual cost of employing the part-time employee. The first thing candidates had to do was determine all of the costs that were going to be incurred. On the whole this was done reasonably well, although some candidates confused cost with tax deductibility, and some simply prepared tax computations for Cate, which was not what they had been asked to do. In addition, many candidates failed to consider the employer national insurance contributions aspects which were a key part of the question. Once the costs had been determined, it was simply a case of recognising that Cate was a higher rate taxpayer, such that she would save income tax at 40% and Class 4 national insurance contributions at 2% as a result of the increased costs. This was not tackled well by the majority of candidates who tried to do before and after calculations rather than working at the margin. In addition, many failed to consider the Class 4 national insurance contribution implications altogether. There was a more subtle point in the question in relation to the income tax personal allowance. The reduction in Cate's taxable trading income due to the costs relating to the part-time employee meant that part of her personal allowance would be reinstated, thus reducing the after-tax cost to her of taking on the new employee.

Part (b) required a discussion of the tax treatment of the profit derived from the sale of books on the internet. This required candidates to consider the badges of trade in relation to the specific transactions taking place. This part of the question was done well by many candidates. However, some candidates did not give themselves sufficient thinking time, such that they failed to realise what the question was testing. It was important that candidates tried to reach a conclusion based on the information provided and that they thought about the capital gains tax implications as well as the income tax implications. There was no right answer as such, just a need to think about the relevant issues and to express the implications in a clear manner.

The final part of the question was arguably more challenging. It concerned the capital gains tax position of an individual, Ravi, who was resident in the UK but domiciled overseas and focused principally on the remittance basis. Although some candidates did reasonably well here, almost all candidates could have scored more marks if they had organised their thoughts before they began writing. There was a mark for making the point that Ravi was liable to UK capital gains tax because he was UK resident and a further mark for recognising that the remittance basis was available because he was domiciled overseas. In order to score these two marks, candidates had to make it clear that the liability to capital gains tax was due to his residence status and the remittance basis was due to his domicile status. Many candidates did not make these two points clearly, such that they only scored one of the two available marks. Candidates were then expected to address the remittance basis charge and the loss of the annual exempt amount. This was done well by the majority of candidates.

Marking scheme

				Marks
(a)	Total additional expenditure		5	
	Income tax and Class 4 NIC saving		2	
	Saving due to personal allowance		2½	
		Max		9
(b)	Trading income or capital gain issue		1	
	Relevant badges of trade factors		3	
	Any reasonable conclusion		1	
	Chattels exemption		1	
		Max		5
(c)	CGT on arising basis as UK resident		2	
	Optional remittance basis as non-UK domiciled		1	
	CGT implications if remittance basis used		2	
	Remittance basis charge		1½	
	Conclusion		½	
		Max		6
				20

(a) Cate – after-tax cost of taking on part-time employee

	£
Salary	12,000
Childcare vouchers £25 × 52	1,300
Mileage allowance £0.50 × 62 × 48	1,488
Class 1 NI employer's contributions (W1)	550
Total additional expenditure	15,338
Less: Income tax higher rate tax saving £15,338 × 40%	(6,135)
Class 4 NIC saving £15,338 × 2%	(307)
Income tax personal allowance saving £7,669 (W2) × 40%	(3,068)
After-tax cost	5,828

Workings

1 *Class 1 NI employer's contributions*

	£
Salary £(12,000 – 8,164) = £3,836 × 13.8%	529
Mileage allowance £(0.50 – 0.45) = £0.05 × 62 × 48 × 13.8%	21
	550

Tutorial note. The employment allowance would have already been fully used against the Class 1 employer's NI contributions payable in respect of D-Designs' existing employees.

2   *Personal allowance*

	Before £	*After* £
Basic personal allowance	11,500	11,500
Less: [£90,000 + £33,000 = £(123,000 – 100,000) = £23,000 × ½	(11,500)	
Less: £(123,000 – 15,338 – 100,000) = £7,662 × ½		(3,831)
Personal allowance available	0	7,669

Tutorial notes

1   Only the excess mileage over 45p per mile is liable to Class 1 NIC.

2   Childcare vouchers up to £55 per week for a basic rate taxpayer are exempt from Class 1 NIC.

3   Cate's (adjusted) net income before taking on the part-time employee was £123,000 so her personal allowance was reduced to nil.

Cate's (adjusted) net income after taking on the part-time employee would be reduced by the total additional expenditure of £15,338 to £107,662. She will therefore be entitled to a personal allowance of £7,669.

(b)   **Cate – sale of secondhand books**

The tax treatment of the profit from the sale of the books will depend on whether Cate is carrying on the trade of selling books or whether she is selling them as capital assets. If she is carrying on a trade, her profit will be trading income (in the same way as her profit from D-Designs) and subject to income tax. If she is selling the books as capital assets (chattels), she may be liable to capital gains tax on the gains.

In order to ascertain whether or not a trade is being carried on, a number of factors known as 'the badges of trade' must be considered. The most relevant factors in this case are:

(i)   **Frequency of transactions**: Transactions which may, in isolation, be of a capital nature will be interpreted as trading transactions where their frequency indicates the carrying on of a trade. Cate only intends to sell the books she has inherited from her mother and so this appears to be an isolated transaction and so not a trading transaction.

(ii)   **Existence of similar trading transactions or interests**: If there is an existing trade, then a similarity to the transaction which is being considered may point to that transaction having a trading character. Cate's existing trade of running dress shops is not similar to selling books online and again this suggests there is not a trading transaction.

(iii)   **Way in which the assets sold were acquired**: If goods are acquired deliberately, trading may be indicated. If goods are acquired unintentionally, for example by gift or inheritance as in this case, their later sale is unlikely to be trading.

(iv)   **Supplementary work and marketing**: When work is done to make an asset more marketable, or steps are taken to find purchasers, the courts will be more ready to ascribe a trading motive. Cate will be carrying on supplementary work by having some of the books rebound and this could be considered to point to a trading transaction.

Overall, a consideration of these factors suggests that Cate will not be carrying on a trade by selling the books. She will therefore be making disposals of the books as chattels but these are likely to be exempt disposals as both cost and deemed proceeds are likely to be less than £6,000.

Tutorial note. Marks are available for discussion of **any** relevant factors and for reaching a **sensible** conclusion.

(c) **Ravi – capital gains tax on overseas property gain**

As Ravi is UK resident, under general principles he will be liable to UK capital gains tax on gains arising from assets situated anywhere in the world.

On the arising basis, the overseas residential property gain will be subject to CGT at the rate of 28% since Ravi has already used his annual exempt amount for 2017/18 against disposals of UK residential property and his income exceeds the basic rate threshold in that year. The CGT payable is therefore £70,000 × 28% = £19,600. If Ravi has paid tax on the gain in Goland, UK double taxation relief will be available under either treaty relief or unilateral credit relief.

Since Ravi is not UK domiciled, he can make a claim for the remittance basis to apply so that his overseas property gain is taxable only to the extent that the proceeds of the disposal are remitted to the UK. As none of the proceeds have been remitted, there will be no liability to CGT on this gain.

If Ravi makes a remittance basis claim, he will not be entitled to annual exempt amount and so he will have an additional CGT liability of £11,300 × 28% = £3,164. In addition, since Ravi has been resident in the UK since February 2010 (at least seven out of the previous nine tax years prior to 2017/18), he will be subject to a remittance basis charge of £30,000. The total amount payable as a result of claiming the remittance basis would therefore be £(30,000 + 3,164) = £33,164.

Ravi should therefore not make a remittance basis claim for 2017/18.

Tutorial note. If Ravi makes a remittance basis claim, he would also not be entitled to the personal allowance for income tax. However, since Ravi is not entitled to a personal allowance for income tax in 2017/18 as his income exceeds £123,000, this is not a factor in deciding whether a remittance basis claim should be made.

8 Simone (06/09) (amended)

Text references. Capital allowances are covered in Chapter 7, trading losses in Chapter 8 and partnerships in Chapter 9. Shares are covered in Chapter 12. Value added tax (VAT) registration is covered in Chapter 28.

Top tips. Use a proforma to calculate the share of the loss for each partner.

Easy marks. The calculation of capital allowances should have been easy marks.

Examining team's comments. In part (a) the calculation of the capital allowances was done well. However, the allocation of the loss between the partners was done poorly with the majority of candidates treating the salaries as employment income rather than as a share of the trading loss. The use of the loss was also problematic. Weaker candidates were confused as to corporate and personal loss offset rules.

Even many stronger candidates lacked the precise knowledge required to score well; a statement of how losses can be used must describe precisely the income against which the loss can be offset, for example, 'against future profits of the same trade' in order to earn all of the marks available. Many candidates ignored the requirement to calculate the total tax saved and simply prepared various income tax computations.

In part (b) weaker candidates wasted time describing the future test in detail despite it not being relevant to this particular question. In addition, many candidates lacked precise knowledge (for example in relation to the date registration comes into effect) such that they did not score as well as would have been expected.

				Marks
(a)	(i)	Capital allowances	1½	
		6 April 2018 to 28 February 2019	2	
		1 March 2019 to 5 April 2019	2	
		Max		5
	(ii)	Against general income of 2018/19 and/or 2017/18	1	
		Against capital gain in 2018/19	1	
		Against future profits of the same trade	1	
				3
	(iii)	Evaluation of offset against future profits of the same trade	2	
		Evaluation of offset against general income and gain in 2018/19	4	
		Evaluation of offset against general income in 2017/18	3	
		Calculation of maximum tax saving	½	
		Max		9
(b)		Taxable supplies exceed limit in the previous 12 months	1	
		Exclude capital assets	½	
		Notify within 30 days	½	
		Date of effective registration	1	
		Relevance of Ellington and Co being VAT registered	1	
		Max		3
				20

(a) (i) **Share of the taxable trading loss for the year ended 5 April 2019**

	Total £	Ellington £	Simone £	Basie £
Tax adjusted trading loss	(90,000)			
Capital allowances				
Additions in the year within AIA limit	(21,200)			
Writing down allowance (Note)	(700)			
Loss available for relief	(111,900)			
6 April 2018 – 28 February 2019				
Loss £(111,900) × 11/12	(102,575)			
Salaries				
£15,000/£11,500/£13,000 × 11/12	(36,209)	13,750	10,542	11,917
Balance 3:2:2	(138,784)	(59,478)	(39,653)	(39,653)
1 March 2019 – 5 April 2019				
£(111,900) × 1/12	(9,325)			
Salaries £14,000 × 1/12	(2,334)	1,167	1,167	0
Balance 1:1	(11,659)	(5,830)	(5,829)	(0)
	(111,900)	(50,391)	(33,773)	(27,736)

Note. As the unrelieved expenditure on the main pool is less than £1,000, a writing down allowance (WDA) can be claimed equal to this amount.

(ii) **Alternative strategies**

The following alternative strategies are available to Simone in respect of her share of the taxable trading loss.

Offset against her general income for the current year (2018/19) and/or the previous year (2017/18).

Following a claim against her general income in 2018/19, the remaining loss could be offset against her capital gain of that year.

Any losses not used as set out above will be carried forward for offset against her share of the taxable trading profits of Ellington and Co in the future.

(iii) **Advice**

Offset against future profits of the same trade

Assuming an annual taxable trading profit of £25,000, Simone's share of the budgeted profit of Ellington and Co in 2019/20 and future years will be £12,500 (£25,000 × 1/2). The profit from her new business is budgeted to be £10,850 (£1,550 × 7) in 2019/20 and £18,600 (£1,550 × 12) in future years. Accordingly, Simone will be a basic rate taxpayer and the total tax saved via the offset of the loss will be £6,755 (£33,773 @ 20%). The tax saved in 2019/20 and 2020/21 will be £2,500 (£12,500 @ 20%) and the balance of £1,755 (£6,755 – (2 × £2,500)) will be saved in 2021/22.

Offset against general income and capital gains in 2018/19

Simone's only income in 2018/19 is dividend income of £4,800. Offsetting her loss against this income will not save any tax as this income is covered by the dividend nil rate band.

However, having offset the loss against her general income in 2018/19, Simone would then be able to offset the remaining loss of £28,973 (£33,773 – £4,800) against her chargeable gain of £94,000 (W). The capital gains tax saved would be £5,795 (£28,973 @ 20% – this is Simone's highest marginal rate on her gains). However, this is not as beneficial as using the loss in 2017/18 (see below) considering both the rate at which tax is saved and the time at which it is saved.

Working: Gain on Duke plc shares

Share pool

	No. of shares	Cost £
7.11 Acquisition	12,000	146,500
8.13 Rights issue proceeds (small disposal)		(2,500)
		144,000
2.19 Sale	(8,000)	(96,000)
c/f	4,000	48,000

Gain

	£
Proceeds	190,000
Less cost	(96,000)
Gain	94,000

Offset against general income in 2017/18

Simone's original income tax liability in 2017/18 is set out below.

	Non-savings income £	Dividend income £	Total £
Trading income	51,230		
Dividend income		14,000	
Net income	51,230	14,000	65,230
Less personal allowance	(11,500)		
Taxable income	39,730	14,000	53,730

	£
Tax on non-savings income	
£33,500 @ 20%	6,700
£6,230 (39,730 – 33,500) @ 40%	2,492
Tax on dividend income	
£5,000 × 0%	0
£9,000 (14,000 – 5,000) × 32.5%	2,925
Tax liability/tax payable	12,117

Simone's liability in 2017/18 following the offset of the trading loss is:

	Non-savings income £	Dividend income £	Total £
Trading income	51,230		
Dividend income		14,000	
Total income	51,230	14,000	65,230
Less trading loss	(33,773)		
Net income	17,457	14,000	31,457
Less personal allowance	(11,500)		
Taxable income	5,957	14,000	19,957

	£
Tax on trading income	
£5,957 @ 20%	1,191
Tax on dividend income	
£5,000 @ 0%	0
£9,000 (14,000 – 5,000) @ 7.5%	675
Tax liability/tax payable	1,866

The tax saved via the offset of the trading loss would be £10,251 (£12,117 – 1,866).

Conclusion

Simone will save the most tax by offsetting the loss against her general income in 2017/18. This claim saves some tax at the higher rate and saves tax at the basic rate at the earliest time.

Note. The use of the loss would also have resulted in a saving of Class 4 NICs which could also have been mentioned.

(b)   Value added tax **(VAT registration)**

Simone is required to register for VAT when her cumulative taxable supplies (standard and zero rated), excluding supplies of capital assets, exceed £85,000 in the previous 12 months.

Simone must notify HM Revenue & Customs (HMRC) within 30 days of the end of the month in which the limit is exceeded.

Simone will be registered and must charge VAT from the end of the month following the month in which the limit is exceeded, or from an earlier date if she and HMRC agree.

As Simone and Ellington and Co are separate taxable persons, the fact that Ellington and Co is VAT registered is irrelevant when considering Simone's position.

9 Shuttelle (06/13) (amended)

Text references. Employment income is covered in Chapter 4 and pensions in Chapter 2. The income tax computation is dealt with in Chapter 1. Overseas aspects of income tax are the subject of Chapter 10.

Top tips. Although there are no specific marks for presentation in this question, it would be advisable to set out the computations in part (a) neatly to make sure that relevant marks were awarded.

Easy marks. There were some easy marks in part (a) for basic income tax computations. In part (b), the remittance basis charge should have been well known.

Examining team's comments. Part (a) was in two closely related parts. It required candidates to calculate the benefit in respect of accommodation provided by an employer and to appreciate the effect on an individual's income tax liability of making pension contributions in excess of the annual allowance, where contributions of less than the annual allowance had been made in earlier years. Candidates also had to recognise that the pension contributions would affect the personal allowance available and the tax bands. This was a tricky question to get absolutely correct, and very few candidates did so, but there were plenty of marks available to candidates who knew how to put an income tax computation together and were aware of the rules relating to the determination of the annual allowance for a particular year. On the whole candidates scored reasonably well. In particular, most candidates handled the accommodation benefit well and knew that the tax bands needed to be extended. Many candidates were also aware that there was a three-year rule in respect of the annual allowance, although many were not absolutely clear as to how the rule worked. Many candidates missed the fact that the personal allowance would be available in full possibly because they did not pause and think at that stage of the calculation. Tax calculations should be done as a series of small steps with thought at each step in order to ensure that important matters are not missed.

Part (b) concerned the remittance basis and was not done particularly well. The problem here was that candidates did not have a clear set of rules. Instead, they had an awareness of a series of technical terms and time periods that were all confused. This made it very difficult to score well. The first thing candidates had to do was to explain whether or not the remittance basis was available to each of three individuals. This required a statement of the availability of the remittance basis together with a reason. For those who did not know the rules there was a 50:50 chance as regards the availability of the remittance basis. However, the reason for its availability or non-availability caused a lot more problems. Candidates must learn the rules and be able to apply them and state them clearly. In addition, the marks available for giving a reason are only awarded where the whole of the reason given is correct.

For example, the remittance basis was available to Lin because he was UK resident but not UK domiciled. Candidates who stated this together with various time periods of residency could not score the mark for the reason as it was not clear from their answer whether it was his residence and domicile status that was relevant or the time periods. The second thing candidates had to do was to state, with reasons, the remittance basis charge applicable to each of the individuals on the assumption that the remittance basis was available to all of them. Again, this was not done particularly well due to many candidates having a very confused knowledge of the rules. One particular area of confusion related to the automatic applicability of the remittance basis where **unremitted** income and gains are less than £2,000; many candidates thought the rule related to the level of **remitted** income and gains.

Marking scheme

				Marks
(a)	(i)	Benefit in respect of accommodation	2	
		Personal allowance	1	
		Tax bands	1½	
		Relevance of employer's pension contribution	1	
		Annual allowance	2½	
		Tax on excess pension contributions	1½	
		Max		8

					Marks
(ii)		Comparison with original liability		2½	
		Tax relief at source on pension contributions		1	
			Max		3
(b) (i)	(1)	Availability of remittance basis			
		General rule		1½	
		Application of the rule to the individuals		1½	
	(2)	The remittance basis charge			
		Lin		1	
		Nan		1½	
		Yu		1½	
					7
(ii)		Example of remittances – one mark each			2
					20

(a) Shuttelle

(i) Income tax liability for the tax year 2017/18

	£
Salary	204,000
Accommodation (W1)	6,000
Net income	210,000
Less personal allowance (W2)	(11,500)
Taxable income	198,500

Income tax liability

£(33,500 + £120,000) = £153,500 × 20%	30,700
£(198,500 – 153,500) = £45,000 × 40%	18,000
Excess pension contributions £59,000 (W3) × 40%	23,600
Income tax liability	72,300

Tutorial notes

1   The higher rate limit has been increased to £270,000 (£150,000 + £120,000), due to the pension contributions. Accordingly, the excess pension contributions will be taxed at 40%.

2   In the exam, equal credit was given to candidates who included the excess pension contributions within taxable income.

Workings

1   *Benefit in respect of accommodation*

	£
Basic benefit: annual value	10,000
Additional benefit £(635,000 – 75,000) = £560,000 × 2.5%	14,000
Total benefits for full tax year	24,000
Benefits in 2017/18: £24,000 × 3/12 (available 6.4 to 30.6)	6,000

2   *Personal allowance*

The adjusted net income is as follows:

	£
Net income	210,000
Less gross personal pension contributions	(120,000)
Adjusted net income	90,000

Since the adjusted net income does not exceed the limit of £100,000, the personal allowance is available in full.

3   *Excess pension contributions*

	£
Gross contributions by Shuttelle	120,000
Gross contributions by Din Ltd	4,000
Annual allowance available in 2017/18 (W4)	(65,000)
Excess pension contributions	59,000

4   *Annual allowance available in 2017/18*

	£	£
Annual allowance for 2017/18		40,000
Brought forward from 2015/16		
£(40,000 – 9,000 – 4,000)	27,000	
Less: Used in 2016/17		
£(40,000 – 38,000 – 4,000)	(2,000)	
		25,000
Annual allowance available in 2017/18		65,000

In 2017/18 Shuttelle's adjusted income is £(210,000 + 4,000) = £214,000 which exceeds £150,000 but her threshold income is £(210,000 – 120,000) = £90,000 which does not exceed £110,000. Therefore the annual allowance for 2017/18 is not reduced.

(ii)   **Total tax relief in respect of the gross personal pension contributions of £120,000**

	£
Income tax on taxable income of £210,000	
(ie ignoring the pension contributions)	
£33,500 × 20%	6,700
£(150,000 – 33,500) = £116,500 × 40%	46,600
£(210,000 – 150,000) = £60,000 × 45%	27,000
Income tax liability, ignoring the pension contributions	80,300
Less income tax liability, after pension contributions (part (i))	(72,300)
Add tax relief on pension contributions at source £120,000 × 20%	24,000
Total tax relief in respect of pension contributions	32,000

Tutorial notes

1   When calculating the liability ignoring the pension contributions, there would be no personal allowance (PA) due to the level of the net income.

2   By charging tax on the excess pension contributions, relief is effectively only given for the balance of the contributions, £61,000 (£120,000 – £59,000), as set out below:

	£
Tax saved in respect of pension contribution of £61,000	
£60,000 × 45%	27,000
£1,000 × 40%	400
Tax saved in respect of PA becoming available	
£11,500 × 40%	4,600
	32,000

(b)   **The three non-UK domiciled individuals**

(i)   *The availability of the remittance basis and the remittance basis charge*

(1)   The availability of the remittance basis

The remittance basis is available to UK resident individuals who are not domiciled in the UK. Accordingly:

o   The remittance basis is available to Lin and Yu.

o   The remittance basis is not available to Nan as he is not UK resident (and so his overseas income is not liable to UK income tax and so remittance is irrelevant).

(2)   The remittance basis charge

Lin has unremitted overseas income and gains of less than £2,000. Accordingly, the remittance basis will apply automatically, such that there will not be a remittance basis charge.

Nan has unremitted overseas income and gains of more than £2,000. If Nan were able to make a claim for the remittance basis, he would be liable for the remittance basis charge of £60,000 because Nan has been resident in the UK for 12 of the 14 tax years prior to 2017/18.

Yu has unremitted overseas income and gains of more than £2,000. If Yu made a claim for the remittance basis, he would be liable for the remittance basis charge of £30,000 because Yu has been resident in the UK for seven of the nine tax years prior to 2017/18.

(ii)   *Actions that would be regarded as remittances*

Bringing property into the UK which was purchased out of overseas income/gains.

Paying for services received in the UK out of overseas income/gains.

The use of overseas income/gains to pay the interest/capital on a debt where the funds borrowed have been brought into the UK or used to acquire property or services in the UK.

Tutorial note. Only **two** examples were required.

10 Ash (12/12)

Text references. Entrepreneurs' relief is covered in Chapter 13. Leases are dealt with in Chapter 14 and part disposals in Chapter 11. Value added tax (VAT) registration is covered in Chapter 28. Payments on account are covered in Chapter 15.

Top tips. Although Advanced Taxation (ATX – UK) is not primarily a computational exam, it is important to set out the computations you do produce in a way that is easy for marking. Look at the layout of the division of gains between those on which entrepreneurs' relief can be claimed and those on which it could not be claimed.

Easy marks. There were some easy marks in part (a) for basic capital gains computations. Even if you did not know the detail of the rules about leases, you could have guessed how to deal with the cost from the lease percentages given in the question. There were also some easy marks for explaining VAT registration – remember that the limits are in the Tax Tables.

Examining team's comments. Part (a)(i) required a statement of the conditions necessary for the disposal of an asset to be an associated disposal for the purposes of entrepreneurs' relief and was not done well. This is not an area of the syllabus that one would expect to see examined regularly and many candidates will have known immediately on reading the requirement that they did not know the answer. However, the sensible approach would then have been to write a very brief answer with some sensible comments on entrepreneurs' relief. It was pretty likely that this would then score one of the three marks available.

Part (a)(ii) was more straightforward and required candidates to calculate a capital gains tax liability. In order to do so, candidates had to know how to calculate a gain on the assignment of a lease and on the disposal of a remaining piece of land following an earlier part disposal. Entrepreneurs' relief was available in respect of some of the gains and there was also a capital loss and the annual exempt amount that needed to be offset correctly.

In general this question was done well by many candidates. There was no problem in deciding what needed to be done, so those candidates who did poorly simply did not have sufficient knowledge of the rules.

Part (b) concerned registration for the purposes of VAT. The majority of the question was done very well including, in particular, the advantages and disadvantages of registering for VAT. However, some candidates' answers lacked precision when it came to the circumstances where compulsory registration is required in that taxable supplies were not clearly defined and/or the 12-month period was not clearly stated. Other candidates wasted time by writing far too much on the recovery of input tax. The one area where performance was not good was the exceptions to the need to register, which were only referred to by a very small number of candidates.

The final part of the question concerned the matters to consider when making a claim to reduce a payment on account of income tax. This was an area that candidates would have been familiar with but the question approached it from a slightly unusual angle: it was not done well. Candidates needed to use their common sense as much as anything else here and to recognise that the claim would need to be made before the end of the tax year. This in turn meant that the tax liability would need to be estimated and that interest would be payable if the final liability turned out to be more than the estimated liability. Making these two points would have scored two of the three marks available for this part of the question.

Marking scheme

					Marks
(a)	(i)	Conditions – 1 mark each			3
	(ii)	*Taxable gains*			
		Assignment of lease		2½	
		Sale of land		2	
		Other matters		1½	
		Capital gains tax		1½	
			Max		7
(b)		Requirement to register		1½	
		Exceptions		2	
		Advantages		2	
		Disadvantages		2	
			Max		7
(c)		Context		1½	
		Circumstances in which a claim can be made		2	
		Interest and penalties		1½	
			Max		3
					20

(a) (i) **The availability of entrepreneurs' relief in respect of the assignment of the lease**

The following conditions must be satisfied in order for the assignment of the lease to qualify as an associated disposal so entrepreneurs' relief will be available.

(1) Ash's disposal of the shares in Lava Ltd (the main disposal) must qualify for entrepreneurs' relief.

(2) The lease of the building must have been owned by Ash and the building used for the purposes of the business of Lava Ltd for at least one year.

(3) Ash must have sold the shares in Lava Ltd and the lease as part of a withdrawal from participating in the business of Lava Ltd.

(ii) **Ash – capital gains tax (CGT) liability for the tax year 2017/18**

	Entrepreneurs' relief available £	Entrepreneurs' relief not available £
Gain on sale of shares	235,000	
Gain on assignment of lease £79,812 (W1) × 60:40	47,887	31,925
Gain on sale of land (W2)		21,780
Loss on sale of quoted shares (best use)		(17,300)
		36,405
Less: Annual exempt amount		(11,300)
	282,887	25,105
CGT @ 10%/20%	28,289	5,021

	Entrepreneurs' relief available £	Entrepreneurs' relief not available £
Total CGT liability £(28,289 + 5,021)		33,310

Workings

1   *Gain on the assignment of the lease*

	£
Proceeds	110,000
Less cost £31,800 × $\dfrac{93.497}{98.490}$	(30,188)
Gain	79,812

2   *Gain on the sale of the land*

	£
Proceeds	30,000
Less cost £27,400 − £(27,400 × $\dfrac{42,000}{42,000 + 18,000}$)	(8,220)
Gain	21,780

Tutorial notes

1   Entrepreneurs' relief in respect of the lease will be restricted to 60% (100% − 40%) of the gain, due to the rent charged by Ash to Lava Ltd.

2   Ash's taxable income is less than his basic rate limit. However, the gains qualifying for entrepreneurs' relief use up the remainder of the basic rate band so all of the non-qualifying gains are taxed at 20%.

(b)   **Vulcan Partnership (Vulcan) – value added tax (VAT) registration**

Whether or not Vulcan may be required to register

Subject to the exceptions noted below, Vulcan will be required to register for VAT once its cumulative taxable supplies (those that are standard rated or zero rated) in a 12-month period exceed £85,000.

However, Vulcan will not be required to register if HM Revenue & Customs is satisfied that its total supplies for the following 12 months will be less than £83,000.

Vulcan could request to be exempt from registration because only a small proportion of its supplies are standard rated. This exemption will be available provided it would normally be in a repayment position if registered.

Advantages of registration

Vulcan will be able to recover all of its input tax if the amount relating to exempt supplies is *de minimis* under the partial exemption rules. Where Vulcan does not satisfy one of the *de minimis* tests, it will still be able to recover the majority of its input tax.

Registration may give the impression of Vulcan being a substantial business.

Disadvantages of registration

Registration will add to the amount of work required to administer the business. In addition, Vulcan may be subject to financial penalties if it fails to comply with the obligations imposed by the VAT regime.

The partnership's customers would be unable to recover any output tax charged by the partnership as they are not registered for VAT. Accordingly, the prices charged to the small proportion of customers purchasing standard rated items would increase unless Vulcan decides to reduce its profit in respect of these sales.

Payment on account on 31 January 2019

The payment on account due on 31 January 2019 is the first payment in respect of Ash's income tax payable (income tax liability as reduced by tax deducted at source) for 2018/19. The payment due is half of the income tax payable for 2017/18 unless Ash makes a claim to reduce the payment.

Ash can make a claim to reduce the payment if he expects the amount payable for 2018/19 to be less than that for 2017/18. The income tax payable for 2018/19 is likely to be less than that for 2017/18 due, principally, to Ash receiving less profit from Vulcan.

Ash will need to estimate his income tax payable for 2018/19 in order to decide whether or not to reduce the payment on account. Ash will be charged interest if the payment on account is reduced to an amount that is less than half of the final agreed amount payable for 2018/19. In addition, a penalty may be charged if Ash is fraudulent or negligent when he makes the claim to reduce the payment.

11 Brad (06/13)

Text references. Overseas aspects of capital gains tax are covered in Chapter 14. The basics of inheritance tax are dealt with in Chapter 16. Related property valuation and business property relief are covered in Chapter 17. The basics of chargeable gains are in Chapter 11 and stamp taxes in Chapter 19.

Top tips. It is important to read the question very carefully and produce an answer which covers all of the requirements. For example, in part (a), you were given a very specific brief about what to include in your answer.

Easy marks. There were some easy marks in part (b)(i) for a basic description of inheritance tax advantages of making lifetime gifts to individuals.

Examining team's comments. This question was done well by many candidates. Part (a) required candidates to explain Brad's UK capital gains tax liability and the reasons for him being only temporarily non-UK resident and to state the payment date for the tax due. The majority of candidates had some knowledge of the temporary non-UK resident rules and quite a reasonable knowledge of capital gains tax generally, such that they scored reasonably well. Most candidates knew the five-year rule although a much smaller number stated the four years out of seven rule. A minority of candidates stated a rule correctly in general terms but failed to apply it to the facts of the question. For example, some candidates stated that assets bought and sold during the period of non-residence were not subject to UK capital gains tax but then went on to calculate a gain in respect of the antique bed. Other candidates failed to apply the basics. For example, a minority of candidates omitted the annual exempt amount whilst others either provided an incorrect payment date or failed to provide one at all. When providing a payment date it is important to make it clear which tax year is being addressed. There were three possible relevant tax years in this question so stating a date without a year could not score unless the candidate explained in general terms how the date is determined, ie 31 January after the end of the tax year.

Part (b)(i) was an invitation to candidates to be general rather than specific as it required an explanation of the advantages of lifetime giving. Many candidates did very well but the performance of the majority was unsatisfactory. The advantages of lifetime giving are scattered throughout the inheritance tax system with certain exemptions only being available in respect of lifetime gifts, potentially exempt transfers being exempt once the donor has lived for seven years, taper relief once the donor has lived for at least three years, and the value of a gift being frozen at the time of the gift together with the availability of relief for any fall in value of the assets gifted. Most candidates would have known all of these rules but many did not include them all in their answers. Instead they wrote at length about some of them whilst omitting others. In particular, many candidates did not address the exemptions available in respect of lifetime giving. This is likely to be because candidates simply started writing and kept writing until they felt they had written enough. These candidates would have benefited from thinking their way through the inheritance tax system and noting each of the advantages of lifetime giving before they started writing. Part (b)(ii) concerned a particular gift of shares and required knowledge of the valuation rules and business property relief. The valuation, which involved fall in value together with related property, was done well with many candidates scoring full marks. A minority of candidates were not aware that it is only the spouse's property that is related whilst others failed to appreciate that it is only the donor's property that is valued (the related property is only relevant when determining the valuation). The business property relief was done well, with the majority of candidates identifying the two year rule and the relevance of the investments. Fewer candidates stated the need for the donee to continue owning the shares until the death of the donor.

Candidates did not do so well when it came to identifying other tax issues. Most candidates simply repeated the basics of the inheritance tax rules in relation to potentially exempt transfers when what was required here was consideration of capital gains tax and stamp duty.

				Marks
(a)	Conditions		2	
	Antique bed and motor car		1½	
	Quoted shares		3	
	Tax liabilities		3½	
		Max		8
(b)	(i)	Seven year rule	1	
		Valuation	2	
		Exemptions	3	
		Taper relief	2	
			Max	7
	(ii)	Fall in value	3½	
		Availability of business property relief		
		Business of Omnium Ltd	1½	
		Brad's ownership of the shares	1	
		Circumstances on Brad's death	1	
		Calculation of business property relief		
		Rate of relief	1	
		Excepted assets	2	
		Other tax matters	2½	
			Max	10
				25

(a) **Capital gains tax**

Brad will be regarded as only temporarily non-UK resident whilst living in Keirinia because:

(i) He was non-UK resident for less than five years

(ii) Having always lived in the UK prior to moving to Keirinia, he was UK resident for at least four of the seven tax years immediately prior to the tax year of departure

As a temporary non-UK resident, Brad will be subject to UK capital gains tax on the assets sold whilst he was non-UK resident, which he owned at the date of his departure from the UK. Accordingly, the antique bed is excluded from these rules as it was both bought and sold during the period of temporary non-UK residence. The profit on the sale of the motor car is ignored as motor cars are exempt assets for the purposes of capital gains tax.

The shares were sold in 2014/15, the tax year of departure, so the gain on these shares was subject to tax in that year under general principles, as Brad was UK resident in that year. However, there will have been no tax to pay as the capital gain of £4,900 (£18,900 – £14,000) was covered by the annual exempt amount for 2014/15.

The capital gains tax due on the sale of the painting is calculated as follows:

	£
Capital gain £(36,600 – 15,000)	21,600
Less annual exempt amount	(11,300)
	10,300
Capital gains tax @ 20%	2,060

The gain on the sale of the painting is subject to tax in 2018/19, the tax year in which Brad became UK resident again, and not in the year of sale. Accordingly, the tax is due on 31 January 2020.

(b)   **Inheritance tax**

(i)   **The inheritance tax advantages of making lifetime gifts to individuals**

A lifetime gift to an individual is a potentially exempt transfer. It will be exempt from inheritance tax if the donor survives the gift by seven years.

If the donor dies within seven years of making the gift, such that the gift is chargeable to inheritance tax, the value used will be the value at the time of the gift and not the value at the time of death. Any increase in the value of the asset will be ignored, although relief will be available if the asset falls in value following the gift.

Certain exemptions are available only in respect of lifetime gifts. These exemptions are:

(1)   Annual exemption of £3,000 each year
(2)   Gifts in consideration of marriage/civil partnership up to certain limits
(3)   Regular gifts out of income that do not affect the donor's standard of living
(4)   Small gifts exemption of £250 per donee per tax year

Any inheritance tax due on the donor's death will be reduced by taper relief if the donor survives the gift by more than three years. The tax due will be reduced by 20% if the donor survives the gift by more than three but less than four years. The percentage reduction will increase by 20% for each additional year that the donor survives the gift.

(ii)   **In respect of the possible gift of 1,500 shares in Omnium Ltd to Dani**

Fall in value of Brad's estate

The fall in value of Brad's estate on a gift of 1,500 shares in Omnium Ltd will be calculated as follows:

	Related property	
	Included	*Ignored*
	£	£
Value of shares held prior to the gift:		
3,000 × £290 (30% + 45% = 75%)	870,000	
3,000 × £205 (30%)		615,000
Value of shares held after the gift:		
1,500 × £240 (15% + 45% = 60%)	(360,000)	
1,500 × £190 (15%)		(285,000)
Transfer of value	510,000	330,000

The higher fall in value of £510,000, produced by reference to related property, will be used.

Tutorial note. The value of Brad's shares is determined by reference to the shares held by him and his wife under the related property rules.

Business property relief

Business property relief will not be available if the business of Omnium Ltd consists wholly or mainly of dealing in securities, stocks or shares or land and buildings or the making or holding of investments. Accordingly, it will be necessary to determine the significance of the investment properties to the activities of Omnium Ltd as a whole.

Brad must have owned the shares for at least two years at the time of the gift. This condition is satisfied.

Business property relief will not be available unless Dani still owns the shares at the time of Brad's death (or had died whilst owning the shares) and the shares continue to qualify for the relief.

If all of the conditions set out above are satisfied, business property relief will be available at the rate of 100%, because Omnium Ltd is an unquoted company.

However, where there are excepted assets, business property relief will be restricted to:

$$100\% \times \text{the fall in value} \times \frac{\text{Omnium Ltd's non-excepted assets}}{\text{Omnium Ltd's total assets}}$$

Excepted assets are assets that have not been used for the purposes of the company's business in the two years prior to the transfer and are not required for such use in the future. Some or all of Omnium Ltd's investment properties may be classified as excepted assets.

Tutorial note. Business property relief will only be relevant if Brad were to die within seven years of making the gift, such that the potentially exempt transfer became a chargeable transfer. Business property relief would also be available if Dani has disposed of the shares prior to Brad's death and acquired qualifying replacement property within three years of the disposal.

Other tax issues

The gift of shares will be a disposal at market value for the purposes of capital gains tax. Gift relief will be available but will be restricted because of the investment properties owned by Omnium Ltd.

Gifts of shares are not subject to stamp duty.

Tutorial note. The question asked for a brief statement only of the other tax issues.

12 Sushi (12/10) (amended)

Text references. Basic principles of computing inheritance tax, including the residence nil rate band, are dealt with in Chapter 16. Inheritance tax overseas aspects and variations are covered in Chapter 18. Overseas aspects of income tax are dealt with in Chapter 10.

Top tips. Remember to use a letter format in your answer – there is a specific mark for this aspect.

Easy marks. The remittance basis is a favourite topic of the examining team and there were some easy marks for basic points.

Examining team's comments. Part (a) concerned inheritance tax and, in particular, the relevance of domicile to an individual's tax position. The level of knowledge here was good with some very strong, thorough answers. However, many candidates who scored well for this part of the question often did so in an inefficient manner which may have left them short of time for the remainder of the exam. As always, there was a need to pause; this time in order to determine the best way to say what needed to be said. Weaker candidates simply kept writing, often repeating themselves, until they finally got to where they wanted to be. Stronger candidates wrote short, precise phrases which earned all of the marks despite using very few words. Candidates should practise explaining areas of taxation making sure that their explanations are concise and clear.

There was a need to address the position of both the mother and the daughter but many candidates simply addressed 'inheritance tax' rather than the situation of the individuals. Candidates will be more successful in the exam if they think in terms of providing advice to individuals and companies rather than addressing technical issues as this will help them to stick to the point and to satisfy the questions' requirements.

A somewhat surprising error made by a significant minority of candidates was to state that the inheritance tax position on the death of Sushi's mother depended on the domicile status of Sushi as opposed to that of her mother. It is, of course, the status of the person whose estate has fallen in value that is relevant.

A final thought on this part of the question is that many candidates wasted time calculating inheritance tax, despite not having sufficient information, whilst others provided a considerable amount of detail regarding the taxation implications of making a potentially exempt transfer, despite being specifically told not to in the question.

Part (b) concerned overseas income and the remittance basis. The performance of candidates for this part was mixed. To begin with there was much confusion regarding the conditions that must be satisfied in order for the remittance basis to be available, with candidates mixing up domicile and residence with the remittance basis charge rules (and the rule for inheritance tax deemed domicile). The application of the £2,000 rule was also misunderstood by many.

Candidates were asked to explain the meaning of 'remittance' and the 'remittance basis'. Most candidates attempted to do this, which was very encouraging, but few had much knowledge beyond the absolute basics. Similarly, most candidates were aware of the remittance basis charge but a significant number were confused as to the situation in which the charge would be levied. On the plus side, the vast majority of candidates provided a conclusion (as requested) and many produced neat and reasonably accurate calculations.

Marks were available for professional skills in this question. In order to earn these marks candidates first had to satisfy the requirement in relation to the format of the document requested. Further marks were then available for providing clear explanations and coherent calculations.

On the whole, the performance of candidates in this area was good, with the majority of candidates producing correctly formatted documents in a style that was easy to follow. However, many candidates failed to maintain the correct style of a document throughout their answer such that, for example, the letters written in response to this question often referred to the client correctly as 'you' to begin with but then reverted to using the client's name later in the answer.

Marking scheme

			Marks
(a)	Assets subject to inheritance tax	1½	
	Mother's death	1	
	Sushi's death		
	UK assets	½	
	Foreign assets	½	
	Domicile and deemed domicile	1½	
	UK IHT on land and buildings in Zakuskia		
	Valuation	1½	
	UK IHT and double tax relief	3	
	The statue	3	
	Max		10
(b)	Meaning and availability of remittance basis	1½	
	Meaning of remittance	3	
	Calculations		
	Remittance basis not available	2	
	Remittance basis available		
	Remittance basis charge	1	
	Loss of personal allowance and annual exempt amount	2	
	Tax on remitted income	1	
	Explanatory notes (1 mark per sensible point) – maximum	3	
	Conclusion	1	
	Max		12
	Appropriate style and presentation	1	
	Effectiveness of communication	1	
	Approach to problem solving	1	
	Max		3
			25

Sushi's address
6 December 2018

Dear Sushi

Personal taxation

I set out below my advice in connection with the assets you have inherited from your mother.

(a)   **UK inheritance tax and the statue**

UK inheritance tax is charged on assets situated in the UK. It is also charged on assets situated overseas where the owner is domiciled or deemed domiciled in the UK. A person's domicile is, broadly speaking, the country in which they have their permanent home.

On the death of your mother

Your mother was domiciled in Zakuskia and did not own any UK assets. Accordingly, there will be no UK inheritance tax liability on her estate.

On your death

You now own both UK and Zakuskian assets. On your death, UK inheritance tax will, inevitably, be charged in respect of the UK assets but the treatment of the assets in Zakuskia will depend on your domicile position.

You have a domicile of origin in Zakuskia. However, you will be deemed domiciled in the UK (for the purposes of inheritance tax only) once you have been resident here for 17 of the 20 tax years ending with the year in which any assets are transferred. At the end of the tax year 2018/19 you will have been resident here for 15 years. Accordingly, 2020/21 will be your 17th year of UK residence and you will be deemed domiciled in the UK from that year onwards such that your Zakuskian assets, in addition to your UK assets, will then be subject to inheritance tax. Until 2020/21 your Zakuskian assets will not be subject to inheritance tax.

UK inheritance tax on land and buildings situated in Zakuskia

Land and buildings situated in Zakuskia but subject to UK inheritance tax will be included in your death estate at the market value in Zakuskia converted into sterling at the UK buying rate as this gives the lowest sterling equivalent. Expenses incurred in Zakuskia in connection with administering and realising the property will be deductible up to a maximum of 5% of the value of the property, so far as those expenses are attributable to the property's location overseas.

The residence nil rate band would usually be relevant in respect of your main residence in Zakuskia since you will be leaving it to your son on your death. However, your estate will exceed £2,200,000 which is the limit for the residence nil rate band to apply. Any available nil rate band will be deducted from your death estate and the balance will be subject to UK inheritance tax at 40%. The amount payable in respect of the land and buildings in Zakuskia is calculated by determining the percentage, by reference to market values, of your assets held at death represented by the land and buildings and applying that percentage to the total UK inheritance tax due. The inheritance tax due in Zakuskia will be deductible from the UK liability on these assets but cannot result in a repayment.

The statue

Once you bring the statue into the UK it will become a UK asset and the gift will be a potentially exempt transfer regardless of your country of domicile. However, the gift of the statue will not be a potentially exempt transfer whilst you retain your Zakuskian domicile and give the statue to your son whilst it is in Zakuskia. Such a gift would be outside UK inheritance tax as the asset would be overseas and you, the donor, would not be UK domiciled.

Alternatively, you could make a variation of your inheritance from your mother as if the statue had been left by your mother to your son. The variation must be made by you within two years of your mother's death, in writing and state that it is to have effect for inheritance tax purposes. The result would be that the transfer would be treated as made to your son by your mother on her death of an asset not situated in the UK. Accordingly, there will be no UK inheritance tax liability on this transfer.

(b) **The Zakuskian income**

If you are domiciled in Zakuskia you can choose to be taxed on the remittance basis such that you will only be taxed on remittances to the UK. If you have acquired a domicile of choice in the UK you will be taxed on all of the Zakuskian income regardless of whether or not it is remitted to the UK.

The most obvious example of a remittance occurs where the overseas income is brought into the UK. However, the definition of remittance is much wider than this. For example, it includes the situation where the overseas income is used to repay an overseas debt where the funds borrowed have been brought into the UK. A remittance would also occur where the overseas income is used to purchase items which are themselves brought into the UK. There are exceptions to this latter rule in respect of: items costing less than £1,000, items for personal use (clothes, watches etc), and items brought into the UK for repair or for no more than 275 days. There are also exceptions where money or property is brought into the UK to acquire shares in or make a loan to a trading company or a member of a trading group or to pay the remittance basis charge.

My calculations are included in the appendix to this letter.

You can see that if you remit £30,000 per annum, it will not be beneficial for you to claim the remittance basis due to the remittance basis charge (at £60,000 since you have been resident in the UK for at least 12 of the 14 tax years preceding 2018/19) and the loss of tax reliefs. The additional UK tax payable in respect of the Zakuskian income will therefore be £16,300 per year on the arising basis.

Please do not hesitate to contact me if I can be of any further assistance.

Yours sincerely

Tax manager

Appendix

Sushi – increase in UK tax liability due to the Zakuskian income

A   *Remittance basis not available*

	£
Zakuskian income gross of Zakuskian tax	55,000
Less savings income nil rate band (higher rate taxpayer)	(500)
Zakuskian income taxable at 40%	54,500
(as non-savings (property) and savings income) (N1)	
UK income tax at 40%	21,800
Less relief for Zakuskian tax at 10% (lower than UK tax)	(5,500)
Annual increase in UK tax payable	16,300

B   *Remittance basis available and claimed – Remit £30,000 (gross) per annum*

	£
Remittance basis charge (N2)	60,000
Loss of income tax personal allowance (£11,500 × 40%) (N3)	4,600
Loss of capital gains tax annual exempt amount (£11,300 × 20%) (N3)	2,260
Cost of claiming remittance basis	66,860

	£
Zakuskian income remitted to the UK, gross of Zakuskian tax	30,000
UK income tax at 40% (N4)	12,000
Less relief for Zakuskian tax at 10% (lower than UK tax)	(3,000)
UK income tax on remitted income	9,000
Annual increase in UK tax payable £(66,860 + 9,000)	75,860

Notes

1 Your taxable income, before taking into account the Zakuskian income, is £33,500. This amount is after deducting your personal allowance and means that your net income is £(33,500 + 11,500) = £45,000. When the Zakuskian income of £55,000 is added to this, your net income will rise to £100,000 which is the limit after which the personal allowance is gradually reduced. Therefore the Zakuskian income of £54,500 (after deduction of the savings income nil rate band of £500 since you are a higher rate taxpayer) is taxable at 40% (with no additional tax due to abatement of the personal allowance).

2 The remittance basis will not be available to you automatically because you will have unremitted income of more than £2,000. The remittance basis charge of £60,000 will be payable because you are claiming the remittance basis and you have been resident in the UK for at least 12 of the 14 preceding tax years.

3 On claiming the remittance basis you will no longer be entitled to the income tax personal allowance and the capital gains tax annual exempt amount.

4 Income taxed under the remittance basis is taxed as non-savings income regardless of its true nature. The savings income nil rate band will therefore not be applicable. Accordingly, the amount remitted will all be taxed at 40%.

Tutorial note. Where deceased's net estate, before the deduction of agricultural property relief, business property relief and any exemptions, exceeds £2,000,000, the residence nil rate band of £100,000 (2017/18) is tapered away. Tapering is £1 for every £2 that the net estate exceeds £2,000,000. Therefore, the residence nil rate band will be tapered to nil if the net estate exceeds £2,200,000, as in the case of Sushi.

13 Capstan (06/11)

Text references. Lifetime transfers for inheritance tax (IHT) are covered in Chapter 16. The enterprise investment scheme (EIS) is dealt with in Chapter 2. The capital gains tax (CGT) aspects of shares and securities are covered in Chapter 12.

Top tips. The Advanced Taxation (ATX – UK) exam is not just about technical tax knowledge. When thinking about advantages and disadvantages which might arise on delaying the sale of the shares in Agraffe Ltd, don't forget about practical and commercial aspects that might be important to the client.

Easy marks. The inheritance tax calculation was very straightforward. The sale of the loan stock after a takeover should also have given easy marks.

Examining team's comments. Part (a) required candidates to consider both the capital gains tax and inheritance tax implications of the transfer of a property to a discretionary trust. The inheritance tax implications were addressed very well by all but a tiny minority of candidates. The only common error was a failure to set out any assumptions made as required by the note to the question.

The capital gains tax element of this part was not answered well. The problem here was that most candidates did not think; instead they simply deducted the cost from the proceeds and addressed rates of tax. Some candidates then realised that gift relief was available and that, per the question, all available claims would be made. As a result, although they had wasted some time, they were still able to score full marks. Other candidates, however, did not address the gift relief point and consequently did not score any marks for the capital gains tax element of the question.

Part (b) concerned the sale of shares in respect of which EIS relief had been claimed. Almost all candidates identified the claw back of the relief if the shares were sold within three years of the acquisition. However, many stated that the whole of the relief obtained would be withdrawn as opposed to a proportion of it.

The implications of delaying the sale were not identified particularly well. Many candidates simply stated the opposite of what they had already written, ie that the relief obtained would not be withdrawn if the shares were held for three years. More thoughtful candidates considered other matters and recognised that delaying the sale delayed the receipt of the sales proceeds and that the value of the shares might change (for the better or the worse).

The final part of the question concerned the sale of shares and qualifying corporate bonds that had been acquired following a paper for paper exchange. This part was done well by those candidates who knew how to handle this type of transaction.

The first task was to recognise that the cost of the original shares needed to be apportioned between the new shares and the corporate bonds. Many candidates knew what they were doing here and were on the way to doing well in this part of the question.

However, there was often confusion as to the treatment of the sale of the corporate bonds. Many candidates who knew that corporate bonds are exempt from capital gains tax went on to calculate a gain on the sale and include it in the taxable capital gains for the year. Also, many candidates were not able to identify the gain on the original shares that was frozen at the time of the paper for paper exchange and then charged when the corporate bonds were sold.

Marking scheme

				Marks
(a)	**Inheritance tax**			
	Explanations and assumptions		3½	
	Calculations		2	
	Capital gains tax		1½	
				7
(b)	Withdrawal of EIS relief		2	
	Loss on sale		1½	
	Offset of loss		1	
	Advantages of delay		2	
	Disadvantages of delay		2	
		Max		8
(c)	Sale of loan stock		3½	
	Gain on sale of shares		1	
	Annual exempt amount		½	
				5
				20

(a)   **Transfer of a UK property to a discretionary trust**

Inheritance tax

A lifetime transfer to any form of trust is immediately chargeable to inheritance tax.

	£
Market value of property	425,000
Less: AE 2018/19	(3,000)
AE 2017/18 b/f	(3,000)
Net transfer of value (Capstan pays IHT)	419,000

			£
IHT	£325,000	× 0% =	Nil
	£94,000	× 20/80 =	23,500
	£419,000		23,500

The gross transfer of value for accumulation is £(419,000 + 23,500) = £442,500.

Check

			£
IHT	£325,000	× 0% =	Nil
	£117,500	× 20% =	23,500
	£442,500		23,500

It has been assumed that:

(i)   Capstan has made no other transfers of value in 2017/18 or in 2018/19 prior to 1 May 2018 such that there are two annual exemptions available.

(ii)   Capstan has made no chargeable lifetime transfers in the seven years prior to 1 May 2018 such that the whole of the nil rate band is available.

Since the transfer took place between 6 April and 30 September 2018, the tax will be due on 30 April 2019. Inheritance tax on land and buildings can be paid by instalments but not where the tax is being paid by the donor.

Capital gains tax

Gift relief will be available on the transfer because the gift is immediately chargeable to inheritance tax. Accordingly, there will be no capital gains tax liability in respect of the transfer.

(b) **Agraffe Ltd**

A sale on 1 July 2018 will result in a withdrawal of the EIS income tax relief as the shares will have been held for less than three years. On the assumption that the sale is a bargain at arm's length the withdrawal of relief will be £(20,000/32,000) × £9,600 = £6,000.

There will also be a loss on the sale of the shares. However, when calculating the loss, the allowable cost of the shares will be reduced by the EIS relief obtained.

	£
Proceeds	20,000
Less cost £(32,000 – (9,600 – 6,000))	(28,400)
Allowable loss	(8,400)

Capstan can offset the loss against his general income of 2018/19 and/or 2017/18 because the shares qualified for EIS relief.

This is advantageous as Capstan will save income tax at 40% (he is a higher rate taxpayer) rather than capital gains tax at 20%.

There would be no withdrawal of EIS relief if Capstan were to sell the shares after 1 February 2019 as he would then have held them for three years. However, this would reduce the allowable loss on the sale by £6,000 (because the allowable cost would be £6,000 less) such that the tax saved via the offset of the loss would be reduced by £2,400 (40% × £6,000). The overall saving to Capstan would be £3,600 (£6,000 – £2,400).

The disadvantages of delaying the sale are that the receipt of the sales proceeds will be delayed and the value of the shares could continue to fall such that Capstan's financial loss would increase.

(c) **Capstan's taxable capital gains for the tax year 2018/19**

	£
Gain arising on sale of Pinblock plc loan stock (W1)	4,224
Gain arising on sale of the shares in Pinblock plc (W2)	56,265
	60,489
Less annual exempt amount	(11,300)
Taxable gains	49,189

Tutorial note. Candidates who assumed in their answer to part (b) above that the loss arising on the sale of the shares in Agraffe Ltd would be set off against Capstan's capital gains were given full credit in this part of the question.

Workings

1   *Capital gain arising on sale of loan stock*

The profit on the sale of the 7% Pinblock plc non-convertible loan stock will not be subject to capital gains tax because qualifying corporate bonds are exempt assets.

However, a gain will have arisen when the shares in Wippen plc were exchanged for the loan stock. This gain will become chargeable on the sale of the loan stock.

	£
Market value of loan stock on 1 October 2013	9,000
Less cost £(26,000 × (9,000/(9,000 + 40,000)))	(4,776)
Chargeable gain	4,224

2 Capital gain arising on the sale of shares in Pinblock plc

	£
Proceeds	69,000
Less cost 12,000/20,000 × £(26,000 × (40,000/(9,000 + 40,000)))	(12,735)
Chargeable gain	56,265

14 Surfe (12/11) (amended)

Text references. Trusts are covered in Chapter 18. Inheritance tax, including the residence nil rate band, is dealt with in Chapters 16 to 18.

Top tips. Where there is a gift of unquoted shares, watch out for the loss to donor rules when computing the transfer of value. Also, think about the effect of related property.

Easy marks. There were some easy marks relating to inheritance tax exemptions.

Examiner's comments. Part (a) required an outline of the capital gains tax implications of various transactions relating to the trust and the inheritance tax charges that may be payable in the future by the trustees. It was important for candidates to be methodical in their approach to this question. There were three transactions to be addressed in relation to capital gains tax whereas the inheritance aspects of the question were more open ended.

The majority of candidates knew some of the capital gains tax implications of the transactions but very few knew all of them. In particular, there was a lack of understanding that capital gains would arise when the trustees transfer trust assets to the beneficiaries of the trust. As always, when dealing with capital gains tax, it is vital to consider the availability of reliefs; gift relief is available when assets are transferred to a discretionary trust and again when they are transferred to the beneficiaries.

The inheritance aspects of part (a) were not handled as well as the capital gains tax aspects. The majority of candidates failed to mention the ten-yearly charges and exit charges payable out of the trust's assets.

Part (b) required a calculation of the inheritance tax liability arising on the death of an individual who had made a number of lifetime gifts. This was a fairly straightforward question, albeit with a couple of tricky points within it, but it was not handled particularly well.

There was a lack of appropriate structure to candidates' answers that indicated that, perhaps, there had been insufficient practice of this area. Inheritance tax computations should all look the same, starting with the tax on any chargeable lifetime transfers, followed by the consideration of gifts within seven years of death and ending with the death estate. However, many candidates began with the death estate and worked their way backwards towards the lifetime gifts; a method that was never going to be successful.

There was confusion as to which gift benefited from the annual exemptions and in respect of the utilisation of the nil rate band. There was also a general lack of knowledge of the impact of related property on the valuation of a gift. Other technical errors, made by a minority of candidates, included the treatment of cash as an exempt asset and business property relief being given in respect of the shares owned by the taxpayer.

On the positive side, the majority of candidates identified the availability of the husband's nil rate band and the death estate was handled well. (**BPP note.** The residence nil rate band was not relevant when this question was originally set.)

Marking scheme

				Marks
(a)	(i)	Gift of shares	1½	
		Future sale of quoted shares	½	
		Transfer of trust assets to beneficiaries	1½	
		Election details	1	
	(ii)	Inheritance tax	2½	
		Max		6

			Marks
(b)	Inheritance tax in respect of lifetime gifts		
	Gift to charity	½	
	Gift to nephews	1½	
	Gift to trust		
	Shares – fall in value	2	
	Cash	½	
	Lifetime tax	1½	
	Gross chargeable transfer	½	
	Nil rate band available on death	2½	
	Inheritance tax payable on death	1½	
	Inheritance tax in respect of death estate		
	Death estate	1½	
	Residence nil rate band available	2½	
	Nil rate band not available	½	
	Death tax	1	
	Max		14
			20

(a)   (i)   **Capital gains tax**

A capital gain will arise on the gift of the shares to the trustees by reference to the market value of the shares. Gift relief will be available because the gift is a chargeable lifetime transfer for the purposes of inheritance tax. The gift relief election should be signed by Surfe and submitted by 5 April 2023 (within four years of the end of the tax year of the gift).

Capital gains made by the trustees whilst they are managing the assets of the trust will be subject to capital gains tax. The tax will be paid out of the trust assets.

A capital gain will arise on the transfer of trust assets from the trustees to Surfe's children by reference to the market value of the trust assets. Gift relief will be available because the transfer is immediately chargeable to inheritance tax. The gift relief election should be signed by the trustees and the recipient child and submitted within four years of the end of the tax year in which the transfer occurs.

Tutorial note. The detailed rules in connection with the calculation of capital gains tax payable by the trustees of a trust are not in the Advanced Taxation (ATX – UK) syllabus.

(ii)   **Inheritance tax**

It is assumed in the question that Surfe will die on 1 July 2021, ie within seven years of the gift of the shares and cash to the trust. Accordingly, the trustees will have to pay inheritance tax on the gift at 40% less the lifetime tax paid.

The trust will be subject to an inheritance tax charge every ten years (the 'principal' charge). The maximum charge will be 6% (30% of the lifetime tax rate of 20%) of the value of the trust assets at the time of the charge.

The transfer of trust assets from the trustees to the beneficiaries will also result in an exit charge to inheritance tax. The maximum charge will be 6% (30% of the lifetime tax rate of 20%) of the value of the assets transferred, times 39 quarters out of 40 quarters.

The principal charges are payable by the trustees, out of the trust assets. The trustees may also pay exit charges out of the trust assets.

(b) **Inheritance tax payable on Surfe's death on 1 July 2021**

Gifts in the seven years prior to death

The gift on 1 February 2007 to the charity was an exempt transfer.

The gifts on 1 October 2018 to Surfe's children were reduced by the annual exemptions for 2018/19 and 2017/18. The potentially exempt transfer of £164,000 ((£85,000 × 2) − (£3,000 × 2)) will be covered by the nil rate band.

The gift of the shares to the trust on 1 January 2019

	£
Gross chargeable transfer (W1)	543,750
Inheritance tax:	
£325,667 (W2) × 0%	0
£218,083 × 40%	87,233
£543,750	87,233
Less lifetime tax paid (W1)	(43,750)
	43,483

There will be no taper relief as the gift is less than three years prior to death.

Workings

1 *Gift to trust 1 January 2019*

	£
Value of Surfe's holding prior to gift 650 × £2,000 (Note)	1,300,000
Less value of Surfe's holding after gift 450 × £2,000 (Note)	(900,000)
	400,000
Cash	100,000
Net transfer of value	500,000
Inheritance tax:	
£325,000 × 0%	0
£175,000 × 20/80 (Surfe is paying tax – grossing up required)	43,750
£500,000	43,750
Gross transfer of value £(500,000 + 43,750)	£543,750

Note. The value per share of Surfe's holding is determined by reference to the number of shares she owns personally and any related property. Related property includes shares given by Surfe to a charity that the charity still owns. Accordingly, Surfe's holding prior to the gift, including related property, will be 100% (65% + 35%). Her holding after the gift, including related property, will be 80% (45% + 35%).

2 *Nil rate band on death to use against lifetime transfer*

	£
Nil rate band as at the date of death	325,000
Add: Unused nil rate band of Flud adjusted for increase in nil rate band	
£(300,000 − 148,000) = £152,000 × £325,000/£300,000	164,667
	489,667
Less amount utilised by gifts on 1 October 2018	(164,000)
Available nil rate band	325,667

Surfe's personal representatives will make a claim by 31 July 2023 to transfer Flud's unused nil rate band to Surfe.

The death estate on 1 July 2021

	£
Main residence	800,000
Quoted shares	200,000
Shares in Leat Ltd (450 × £2,400) (N1)	1,080,000
Net estate	2,080,000
Inheritance tax:	
£160,000 (N3) (60,000 (W) + 100,000 (N2)) × 0%	0
£1,920,000 × 40% (N4)	768,000
£2,080,000	768,000

Working: Surfe's own residence nil rate band

	£
Net estate	2,080,000
Less: Taper threshold	(2,000,000)
Excess	80,000
Surfe's maximum residence nil rate band	100,000
Less: Tapering £80,000/2	(40,000)
Surfe's reduced maximum residence nil rate band	60,000

Notes

1   Surfe's holding, including the related property held by the charity, will be 80% (45% + 35%).

2   Surfe's personal representatives will make a claim by 31 July 2023 to transfer Flud's unused residence nil rate band to Surfe. This is £100,000 since Flud died before 6 April 2017. It is not relevant whether Flud had a main residence at the date of his death.

3   The available residence nil rate band is the lower of the maximum residence nil rate band of £160,000 and the value of the main residence of £800,000 ie £160,000.

4   Surfe's nil rate band, including the amount transferred from Flud, is used by her lifetime gifts.

15 Una (06/12)

Text references. Inheritance tax is covered in Chapters 16 to 18. Stamp taxes are covered in Chapter 19. Capital gains tax computations are dealt with in Chapter 11 and reliefs in Chapter 13. Income tax administration is in Chapter 15 and ethics in Chapter 30.

Top tips. When you are asked to include 'other tax implications' in your answer as in part (a) of this question, it is a good idea to jot down the main taxes that might be relevant to an individual and then consider whether any points arise from the scenario you have been given. Don't forget stamp duties!

Easy marks. There were some easy marks for the inheritance tax calculations in part (a). The four professional marks should also have been easy to obtain.

Examining team's comments. Part (a) was answered reasonably well. In particular, only a minority of candidates confused the rules of inheritance tax and capital gains tax. Also, many candidates demonstrated strong technical knowledge of the mechanics of inheritance tax and agricultural property relief.

The one common error in relation to inheritance tax was a failure to realise that the earlier cash gift had no effect on the nil band in respect of the later gift as it was made more than seven years prior to death. Other, less common, errors included deducting taper relief from the value transferred rather than from the inheritance tax liability and deducting the annual exemptions from the death estate.

The capital gains tax elements of the question were not handled as well as inheritance tax. Many candidates did not know the conditions relating to the availability of capital gains tax reliefs and simply assumed, incorrectly, that gift relief would be available. A substantial minority also forgot the fundamental point that there is no capital gains tax on death and calculated liabilities in respect of both lifetime gifts and gifts via Una's will.

However, the main problems experienced by candidates related to exam technique. There were three particular problems; failing to read the question sufficiently carefully, failing to address all of the requirements and running over time.

When reading the question, many candidates failed to identify the relevance of the exemption clause in the Double Taxation Agreement. The effect of the clause was to exempt the overseas villa from UK inheritance tax. This meant that, when dealing with the villa, candidates needed only to consider the tax suffered overseas. Those candidates who failed to appreciate this did not lose many marks but wasted time calculating UK inheritance tax on the villa.

The question required calculations of the 'possible reduction in the inheritance tax payable as a result of Una's death' in respect of each of the possible lifetime gifts. This required candidates to compare the tax arising on a lifetime gift with that arising if the asset passed via Una's will for both of the assets. There was then the need to consider the capital gains tax on the lifetime gift whilst remembering that there would be no capital gains tax if the assets were retained until death. Finally, candidates were asked to provide a concise summary of their calculations 'in order to assist Una in making her decision'. The problem was that many candidates were not sufficiently methodical such that they did not carry out all of the necessary tasks and missed out on easy marks. In particular, many candidates did not provide the final summary.

The final problem in relation to exam technique related to time management: it was evident that some candidates did not have a sufficient sense of urgency when answering this question. This resulted in lengthy explanations of how inheritance tax and, to a lesser extent, capital gains tax is calculated together with details of Una's plans.

The question asked for 'explanations where the calculations are not self-explanatory, particularly in relation to the availability of reliefs'. Candidates need to think carefully before providing narrative as writing is very time consuming. They should identify, in advance, the points they are planning to make and should then make each point in as concise a manner as possible. There is likely to be a mark for each relevant point so each one should take no more than two short sentences.

Part (b) was done reasonably well. There were two elements to a good answer: the penalties that could be levied on the taxpayer and the professional issues relating to the firm of accountants. The two elements were indicated clearly in the question which stated that 'the letter should explain the implications for Una and our firm'. Those candidates who failed to address both elements struggled to do well.

Marking scheme

			Marks
(a)	Calculations		
	Farmland – inheritance tax		
	Owned at death	2	
	Lifetime gift	4	
	Farmland – capital gains tax	1	
	Villa – inheritance tax (Soloria)	1	
	Villa – capital gains tax (UK)	1½	
	Notes on availability of relevant reliefs – one mark each	3	
	Other relevant tax and financial requirements – one mark each	5	
	Relevant assumption	1	
	Summary of position re capital taxes	2	
	Payment of rent	3	
	Max		23
	Professional marks for the overall presentation of the memorandum and the effectiveness with which the information is communicated		3
(b)	Determination of taxable profit	1	
	The need to disclose	4	
	Interest and penalties	3	
			8
	Professional mark for overall presentation of the letter		1
			35

(a) To   The files
     From   Tax senior
     Date   15 June 2018
     Subject   Una – Gifts to son and granddaughter

The purpose of this memorandum is to provide advice to Una on the tax implications of a gift to be made to her son, Won, and the payment of rent on behalf of her granddaughter, Alona. For the purposes of this memorandum, it has been assumed that the gift to Won will be made on 18 November 2018 and that Una's death will occur on 31 December 2023.

(i)   **Gift to Won**

       Inheritance tax

       Farmland situated in England

       If Una owns the farmland at her death it will be included in her death estate. The inheritance tax on the farmland in the death estate will be as follows.

	£
Market value in death estate	1,100,000
Less APR £1,100,000 × 35% (100% of agricultural value)	(385,000)
Value included in death estate	715,000
Inheritance tax @ 40% (nil rate band used by other assets)	286,000

       If Una gifts the farmland to Won – it will be a potentially exempt transfer (N1). The death tax in relation to this gift will be as follows:

	£
Market value (N2)	900,000
Less annual exemptions 2018/19 and 2017/18 b/f	(6,000)
Potentially exempt transfer (PET)	894,000

Inheritance tax on death on 31 December 2023	
£325,000 (N3) @ 0%	0
£569,000 @ 40%	227,600
£894,000	227,600
Less taper relief (death within 5 to 6 years of gift) @ 60%	(136,560)
	91,040
Add additional tax on death estate due to use of nil rate band	
£325,000 @ 40%	130,000
Total death tax arising as a result of lifetime gift of farmland	221,040
Potential saving £(286,000 – 221,040)	64,960

       Notes

       1   There will be no UK inheritance tax when the gift is made as it will be a potentially exempt transfer.

       2   Agricultural property relief will not be available in respect of a gift on 18 November 2018 as Una will not have owned the farm for the requisite seven years. This is on the assumption that the farmland did not replace other agricultural property which, together with this farmland, had been owned for seven out of the previous ten years.

       3   The gift to Won in 2014 was initially partially exempt (two annual exemptions) and the remaining value was a PET. The PET element became an exempt transfer when Una survived until May 2021. Therefore the full nil rate band is available against the PET of the farmland.

       Villa situated in Soloria

       There will be no UK inheritance tax due to the exemption clause in the UK–Soloria Double Taxation Agreement. There will be no inheritance tax in Soloria until Una's death.

The gift will save inheritance tax in Soloria as set out below.

	£
Liability if Una owns the villa at her death on 31 December 2023	170,000
Liability if Una gifts the villa to Won on 18 November 2018	(34,000)
Inheritance tax saved	136,000

Capital gains tax

Farmland situated in England

A gift of the farmland would result in a liability to capital gains tax as set out below. No gift relief would be available as the farmland is an investment (as opposed to a business asset), does not qualify for agricultural property relief, and the gift does not give rise to an immediate charge to inheritance tax. The farmland is not a qualifying asset for entrepreneurs' relief as it is not a business asset and it is also not residential property.

	£
Proceeds (market value)	900,000
Less cost	(720,000)
Gain	180,000
Capital gains tax @ 20% (Una is a higher rate taxpayer)	36,000

Villa situated in Soloria

A gift of the villa would result in a liability to UK capital gains tax as set out below. The villa is an investment and not a business asset, so no capital gains tax business reliefs would be available. There is no capital gains tax in Soloria.

	£
Proceeds (market value)	745,000
Less cost (probate value)	(600,000)
Gain	145,000
Capital gains tax @ 28%	
(Una is a higher rate taxpayer and the villa is residential property)	40,600

Summary of capital taxes position

	Farmland £	Villa £
Inheritance tax – potential saving	64,960	136,000
Capital gains tax – liability	(36,000)	(40,600)
Net tax saving	28,960	95,400

Other tax implications in respect of the gift to Won

Inheritance tax

If Una were to die after 18 November 2024, there would be an additional 20% taper relief in the UK. If she were to survive the gift by seven years, there would be no UK inheritance tax in respect of the asset gifted and the inheritance tax nil rate band would be available against the death estate.

Stamp duty land tax

There is no charge to stamp duty land tax on a gift of land in England. The situation in Soloria would need to be investigated if a gift of the villa is proposed.

Financial implications in respect of the gift to Won

The potential gifts are income generating assets. Accordingly, Una should be aware that the gift will reduce her available income. The income in respect of the villa is subject to income tax in Soloria at the rate of 50%, so no UK income tax is payable due to double tax relief. The income in respect of the farmland is subject to UK income tax at a maximum rate of 40%.

The capital gains tax would be payable on 31 January 2020 (31 January following the end of the tax year in which the gift is made). This is at least four years prior to the eventual inheritance tax saving. Because there is a gift of land but gift relief is not available, it would be possible to pay the capital gains tax in ten equal annual instalments (provided Won continues to own the asset gifted), but interest would be charged on the balance outstanding.

(ii) **Payment of Alona's rent**

The payments will be exempt if they represent normal expenditure out of income. For this exemption to be available, Una would have to show that:

(1) Each gift is part of her normal expenditure
(2) The gifts are made out of income rather than capital
(3) Having made the gifts, she still has sufficient income to maintain her usual standard of living

Una must be able to demonstrate that her annual income exceeds her normal expenditure by the annual rental cost of £450 × 12 = £5,400 (maximum – less if Alona's rent is only payable during university term-time).

(b)

Firm's address

Una's address

15 June 2018

Dear Una

Income received in respect of the luxury motor car

I set out below our advice in relation to the income received in respect of the luxury motor car.

I have considered the circumstances surrounding the rental income in respect of the car and concluded that the profits from the hiring of the car are liable to income tax. In determining the taxable profit, the income you have received can be reduced by the expenses relating to the running and maintenance of the car. We can assist you in determining the taxable profit.

The taxable profit must be reported to HM Revenue & Customs; failure to disclose the profit would amount to tax evasion, which is a criminal offence. In addition, you will appreciate that we would not wish to be associated with a client who has engaged in deliberate tax evasion, as this poses a threat to the fundamental principles of integrity and professional behaviour. Accordingly, we cannot continue to act for you unless you are willing to disclose the hiring activity to HM Revenue & Customs and to pay any ensuing tax liabilities. We are required to notify the tax authorities if we cease to act for you, although we would not provide them with any reason for our action.

HM Revenue & Customs will charge interest on any tax liabilities that are overdue. A penalty may also be charged in respect of the non-declaration of the income. The maximum penalty is 70% of the tax liability for a deliberate non-disclosure of income where there is no attempt to conceal it (for example, by submitting false evidence in support). This penalty may be reduced if the income is disclosed to the authorities at a time when there is no reason to believe that the non-disclosure is about to be discovered and full assistance is provided to the authorities to enable them to quantify the error. The minimum penalty in these circumstances is 20% of the tax liability.

Yours sincerely

Tax manager

16 Kantar (12/14)

Text references. Inheritance tax exemptions and lifetime transfers are covered in Chapter 16. The basics of capital gains tax are dealt with in Chapter 11. Trading losses are the subject of Chapter 8. Self-assessment for individuals is covered in Chapter 15. Ethics will be found in Chapter 30. Value added tax (VAT) registration is dealt with in Chapter 28.

Top tips. In part (b)(i) there are a lot of figures involved so it was important to lay out your computations in an orderly manner so that the tax savings could be picked out easily when making the evaluation of which loss relief would be more beneficial.

Easy marks. There were some easy marks in part (a)(i) for describing the small gifts exemption. The ethical points in part (c) should have been well known. The registration requirements in part (d) were basic knowledge from Taxation (UK).

Examining team's comments. Part (a) was in two parts. Both parts were answered reasonably well but it felt as though many candidates spent too much time on them. This may have been because it was the first question and thus time may not have appeared to be such a pressing issue. However, of course, any overruns on this part would still have caused candidates to run out of time later on in the exam. Part (a) was only worth 8 marks in total and so should have been completed in less than 15 minutes, but some candidates found the time to explain the meaning of potentially exempt transfers, the manner in which they are taxed and the other exemptions that may be available rather than simply addressing the requirements of this particular question part. Candidates will always benefit from answering the specific requirements of the question and from not digressing into other, irrelevant, areas. Part (a)(i) related to inheritance tax and concerned the small gifts exemption and potentially exempt transfers. Candidates' knowledge in this area was satisfactory. The only common error was the failure to identify the fall in value of the donor's estate as a result of the gift. Part (a)(ii) related to capital gains tax and concerned the disposal of a piece of land in two stages. The key issue here was the A/A + B calculation of the cost in respect of the first disposal. The majority of candidates knew that such a calculation was necessary but many did not know exactly how to perform it. In addition, a minority of candidates failed to recognise that the base cost of the whole of the land was its value at the time of the uncle's death.

Part (b)(i) related to a trading loss and required candidates to calculate the tax which would be saved in respect of the offset of the trading loss depending on how the loss was relieved. This part of the question was not tackled particularly well. Many candidates did not know the rules for the offset of trading losses well enough and were unable to determine an approach to answer the question efficiently. As always, it was necessary to think first and decide how to approach the question in order to prepare the required answer. With trading losses there are two main things that candidates need to know; 1) what the losses can be offset against and 2) when. Many candidates did not possess this precise knowledge and others treated the individual taxpayer as a company or made other fundamental errors. Many candidates also failed to make use of the information in the question. In particular, the tax liability for the tax year [2017/18] was given in the question but many candidates calculated it themselves, thus wasting time. A final problem was that some candidates were unwilling to commit themselves to an answer, such that they described some of the issues but did not prepare calculations. This made it difficult for them to score particularly well. Part (b)(ii) concerned payments on account under self-assessment and was not done well. The question required candidates to have a precise knowledge of the manner in which payments of tax under self-assessment are determined and to be able to apply those rules in a chronological manner to the facts of the question and the three tax years concerned. Many candidates had an awareness of the rules but their knowledge was somewhat vague and confused, such that they were unable to apply it to the facts. Some candidates tried to describe the system but this did not satisfy the requirement. Other candidates presented their answers in confusing ways without explaining which tax year and/or which payments they were referring to. For a candidate who knew the rules, this part of the question was not particularly challenging, although it did require thought and care. Unfortunately, very few candidates had sufficient precise knowledge to produce an acceptable answer.

Part (c) was answered well by the majority of candidates. However, the problem here was that many candidates wrote far too much. There were only four marks available, so four decent sentences were sufficient, yet many candidates wrote the best part of a page. Candidates should think before they write and decide on the points they intend to make. They should then make each point concisely, and they should make it only once.

Part (d) concerned VAT registration and the recovery of pre-registration input tax. Answers to this part of the question were generally satisfactory. Candidates' knowledge of the rules regarding VAT registration was generally sound, although some candidates displayed a tendency to write generally rather than to address the specifics of the question. In addition, candidates need to take care to be precise in their use of language and terminology. The historic test relates to supplies in the 'previous 12 months', not the sales of 'the trading period', and HMRC must be notified 'within 30 days' as opposed to 'within a month'. Candidates' knowledge of the rules regarding the recovery of pre-registration input tax was not as strong as that relating to registration but was still generally of an acceptable standard.

Marking scheme

				Marks
(a)	(i)	Small gifts exemption	1½	
		Potentially exempt transfer	2½	
				4
	(ii)	Chargeable gain: Gift 1 February 2018	2	
		Chargeable gain: Sale 2 February 2018	1	
		Capital gains tax liability	1	
				4
(b)	(i)	Loss relieved as soon as possible		
		Income tax	1	
		Capital gains tax	3	
		Loss carried forward		
		Taxable incomes	2½	
		Tax liabilities and saving	2	
		£50,000 restriction	1	
		Evaluation	1	
		Explanatory notes	1½	
		Max		10
	(ii)	Payments required if loss carried forward		
		2017/18	2½	
		2018/19	1½	
		2019/20	2	
		Max		5
(c)		Implications for Kantar	2	
		Fundamental principles	1	
		Cease to act	2½	
		Max		4
(d)		When registration required	2	
		VAT incurred prior to registrar	2	
				4
		Format and presentation	1	
		Analysis	1	
		Quality of explanations	1	
		Quality of calculations	1	
				4
				35

Notes for meeting

(a)   (i)   **Inheritance tax**

Small gifts exemption

Outright gifts to individuals totalling £250 or less per donee in any one tax year are exempt. If gifts total more than £250 the whole amount is chargeable. Therefore, the small gifts exemption does not apply to the gifts of £400 each to Kantar's nephews.

Potentially exempt transfer on 1 February 2018

	£
Value of the land prior to gift	290,000
Less value of land after gift	(170,000)
Diminution in value (transfer of value)	120,000
Less: Annual exemption 2017/18	(3,000)
Unused annual exemption 2016/17 b/f £[3,000 − (3 × £400)]	(1,800)
Potentially exempt transfer	115,200

    (ii)   **Capital gains tax liability for tax year 2017/18**

	£	£
1 February 2018 gift		
Proceeds (market value)	100,000	
Less: Cost		
$£200,000 \times \dfrac{100,000}{100,000 + 170,000}$	(74,074)	
Gain		25,926
2 February 2018 sale		
Proceeds	170,000	
Less cost £(200,000 − 74,074)	(125,926)	
Gain		44,074
Chargeable gains		70,000
Less annual exempt amount		(11,300)
Taxable gains		58,700
Capital gains tax £58,700 × 20% (higher rate taxpayer)		11,740

Tutorial note. Rollover relief will not be available in respect of the chargeable gain on the sale of the land, as it is not a business asset.

(b)   (i)   **Budgeted trading loss for the year ended 31 March 2019**

    (1)   *Loss relieved as soon as possible*

The trading loss can be relieved against general income in the tax year of the loss (2018/19) and the previous tax year (2017/18).

Kantar should not make a claim to relieve the loss in 2018/19 as his only income for this tax year is £5,000 property business income which will be covered by the personal allowance.

If Kantar makes a claim to relieve the loss in 2017/18, he cannot choose the amount of loss to relieve so the loss must be set against income which would be covered by the personal allowance. He would therefore set off £(59,000 + 5,000) = £64,000 of the loss against general income and the tax saving would be the whole tax liability for the tax year 2017/18 of £14,300.

The £50,000 relief cap does not apply to trading income of the same trade and is therefore not relevant to the claim for the tax year 2017/18.

Kantar may include a further claim to set the remaining loss of £(68,000 – 64,000) = £4,000 against his chargeable gains for the tax year 2017/18. Also, since Kantar has no taxable income following loss relief against general income, his basic rate band is now available to be set against the taxable gains. The capital gains tax saved is £4,150 as shown below.

	£
Chargeable gains (part (a)(ii))	70,000
Less loss relief	(4,000)
	66,000
Less annual exempt amount	(11,300)
Taxable gains	54,700

Capital gains tax	
£33,500 × 10%	3,350
£(54,700 – 33,500) = £21,200 × 20%	4,240
	7,590

Capital gains tax saving £(11,740 (part (a)(ii)) – 7,590)	4,150

The total tax saving would therefore be £(14,300 + 4,150) = £18,450

(2) *Loss carried forward for future relief*

The loss would be set against Kantar's trading income for the tax year 2019/20. The tax saving would be £23,400 as shown below.

	Without loss relief £	With loss relief £
Trading income 2019/20		
£(85,000 + 4,000)	89,000	89,000
Less trading loss brought forward		(68,000)
		21,000
Property business income	5,000	5,000
Net income	94,000	26,000
Less personal allowance	(11,500)	(11,500)
Taxable income	82,500	14,500
Income tax		
£33,500/£14,500 × 20%	6,700	2,900
£(82,500 – 33,500) = £49,000 × 40%	19,600	
	26,300	2,900
Income tax saving £(26,300 – 2,900)		23,400

Carrying forward the loss would therefore increase the tax saving. However, Kantar cannot be certain that he will make the budgeted profit in the year to 31 March 2020. The tax saving will also be delayed.

(ii) **Future tax payments if loss carried forward**

	Notes	£
2017/18		
Balancing payment 31 January 2019		
Income tax £(14,300 – 8,400)	1	5,900
Capital gains tax (part (a)(ii))		11,740
		17,640

	Notes	£
2018/19		
Payments on account	2	0
Balancing payment		0
2019/20		
Payments on account	3	0
Balancing payment 31 January 2021 (part (b)(i)(2))		2,900

Notes

1. Kantar will have made payments on account equal to his tax liability for the previous tax year (2016/17).

2. Kantar should make a claim to reduce his payments on account to nil as he does not expect to have any tax liability for 2018/19.

3. Kantar will not have to make any payments on account for the tax year 2019/20 as he will not have a tax liability for the tax year 2018/19.

(c) **Reporting of chargeable gains**

Kantar may be liable to interest and penalties (based on potential lost revenue) if he does not report his chargeable gains to HM Revenue & Customs (HMRC).

The evasion or attempted evasion of tax by Kantar may also be the subject of criminal charges under both tax law and money laundering legislation. We may need to submit a report under the money laundering rules.

Our firm must not be associated with a client who has deliberately evaded tax as this is against the ACCA fundamental principles of integrity and professional behaviour.

We should not continue to act for Kantar if he does not agree to disclose the chargeable gains to HMRC. If he does not agree to disclosure, we are still under a professional duty to ensure that he understands the seriousness of offences against HMRC.

If we do cease to act for Kantar, we must inform HMRC of this cessation but not the reasons for it. We should advise Kantar that the notification that we are no longer acting for him may alert HMRC that tax irregularities have taken place and urge on Kantar the desirability of making a full disclosure.

(d) **Value added tax (VAT)**

Kantar will be liable to register for VAT if the value of his cumulative taxable supplies (excluding VAT) exceeds £85,000 in any 12-month period. At the end of every month he must therefore calculate his cumulative turnover of taxable supplies to date. Kantar is required to notify HMRC within 30 days of the end of the month in which the £85,000 limit is exceeded.

VAT incurred before registration can be treated as input tax and recovered from HMRC subject to certain conditions. For input tax on goods purchased prior to registration the following conditions apply:

(1) Acquired for the purposes of business carried on by Kantar at the time of supply
(2) Not supplied onwards or consumed before the date of registration
(3) Input tax incurred in the four years prior to the date of registration

For input tax on the supply of services prior to registration the following conditions apply:

(1) Supplied for the purposes of business carried on by Kantar at the time of supply
(2) Input tax incurred in the six months prior to the date of registration

Tutorial note. The recovery of input tax will reduce the expenses incurred by the business. It will also reduce the cost of the equipment purchased in the year ending 31 March 2019 for the purposes of capital allowances.

17 Pescara (12/13)

Text references. Valuation of quoted shares for inheritance tax (IHT) purposes is covered in Chapter 17. Lifetime transfers of value and the transfer of the nil rate band are dealt with in Chapter 16. The basic chargeable gains computation, the annual exempt amount, rates of capital gains tax (CGT) and the valuation of quoted shares for CGT purposes will be found in Chapter 11. Capital gains tax on disposals of shares, including takeovers, are covered in Chapter 12. Enterprise investment scheme (EIS) relief is covered in Chapter 2 and Chapter 13. Gifts with reservation of benefit are dealt with in Chapter 18.

Top tips. Where the nil rate band from a deceased spouse is transferred, account must be taken of the increase in the amount of the nil rate band between the date of death of the first spouse and the date of death of the second spouse.

Easy marks. There were some easy marks in part (a) for a basic inheritance tax computation on a potentially exempt transfer. The rules about gifts with reservation of benefit in part (c) should have been well known.

Examining team's comments. In part (a) the majority of candidates performed well and scored high marks. Less well-prepared candidates were unable to value the shares in Sepang plc and/or the amount of the nil rate band to be transferred from the donor's deceased husband. This was because they either did not know the rules or were unable to apply them to the facts in the question. Some candidates failed to identify that the husband's nil rate band was available for transfer.

Part (b) concerned capital gains tax and was in two parts; neither part was done particularly well.

Part (b)(i) required a calculation of the tax due on the sale of shares. The shares had been acquired via gift and had then been the subject of a share for share takeover and a bonus issue. Accordingly, the calculation of the base cost required a certain amount of work. It was first necessary to realise that, due to the fact that gift relief was not claimed on the original gift (the question stated that gift relief was not available), the base cost of the original shares was their market value [calculated for CGT purposes] at the time of the gift. Following the takeover, this original cost had to be split between the new shares and cash received by reference to the market value of the consideration. Finally, the bonus issue increased the number of shares but had no effect on the total base cost. A significant number of candidates lost marks here because they side-stepped the first two stages of this calculation by attributing a cost to the new shares equal to their market value at the time of the takeover. The majority of candidates had no problem with the bonus issue. When calculating the amount subject to capital gains tax it was necessary to deduct EIS deferral relief equal to the whole of the £50,000 invested in EIS shares. Many candidates confused this relief with the relief available in respect of income tax when EIS shares are acquired.

Part (b)(ii) required a statement of the capital gains tax implications of the future sale of the EIS shares. The first problem that some candidates had here was that they answered the question by reference to income tax rather than capital gains tax. Many of those who did address capital gains tax did not score as many marks as they might have done because they were not methodical in their approach. It was important to (briefly) consider four possible situations, ie sale of the shares at a profit or a loss both within and after the three-year period.

Part (c) was not done particularly well as those candidates who clearly had some knowledge did not pay sufficient attention to the requirement. The question asked how the gift would be treated for the purposes of calculating the inheritance tax due on death. This required consideration of the value to be used, whether or not the reservation was lifted prior to death and the relief available in order to avoid double taxation. Many candidates wrote more broadly about gifts with reservation, explaining the rationale behind the rules and the actions necessary in order for the reservation to be lifted. These generalisations did not score any marks.

Marking scheme

		Marks
(a)	Value of shares	2
	Annual exemptions	1
	Nil rate band	2½
	Inheritance tax liability	1½
		7

					Marks
(b)	(i)	Proceeds less cost		4		
		EIS deferral relief, annual exempt amount and liability		2		
						6
	(ii)	Zolder plc		1		
		EIS shares		3½		
			Max			3
(c)		Initial gift		1		
		Reservation lifted within seven years		1½		
		Reservation in place at death		1		
		Double taxation avoidance		2		
			Max			4
						20

(a) Marina – inheritance tax payable in respect of the gift of the shares in Sepang plc

	£
Value of shares: 375,000 × £1.86 (W1)	697,500
Less: Annual exemption 2013/14	(3,000)
Annual exemption 2012/13 b/f	(3,000)
Potentially exempt transfer now chargeable	691,500

	£
£476,667 (W2) @ 0%	0
£214,833 @ 40%	85,933
£691,500	85,933
Less taper relief (4 to 5 years) @ 40%	(34,373)
Death tax payable	51,560

Workings

1 *Value of shares in Sepang plc for IHT purposes as at 1 February 2014*

	£
Quarter up £1.84 + ([1.96 – 1.84]/4)	1.87
Average highest and lowest marked bargains £[1.80 + 1.92]/2)	1.86
Lower of quarter up and average bargains	1.86

2 *Nil rate band available*

	£	£
Nil rate band Marina		325,000
Nil rate band Galvez 2007/08	300,000	
Less legacies to Pescara/brother 2 × £80,000	(160,000)	
	140,000	
Increase pro-rata		
$\dfrac{£325,000}{£300,000} \times £140,000$		151,667
Total nil rate band available to Marina		476,667

(b) (i) Pescara – capital gains tax liability for the tax year 2018/19

	£
Proceeds sale of 1,000,000 shares in Zolder plc	445,000
Less cost (W)	(275,362)
Chargeable gain c/f	169,638

	£
Chargeable gain b/f	169,638
Less: EIS deferral relief	(50,000)
Annual exempt amount	(11,300)
Taxable gain	108,338
Capital gains tax @ 20%	21,668

Workings

1   *Base cost of 1,000,000 shares in Zolder plc*

	Number	Cost £
Sepang plc shares – MV of gift 375,000 × £1.90 (W2)	375,000	712,500
Zolder plc shares		
Cost of new shares $\dfrac{£2}{£2+£0.30} \times £712,500$	750,000	619,565
Bonus issue 2 for 1	1,500,000	0
	2,250,000	619,565
Disposal $\dfrac{1,000,000}{2,250,000} \times £619,565$	(1,000,000)	(275,362)
C/f	1,250,000	344,203

2   *Value of shares in Sepang plc for CGT purposes as at 1 February 2014*

£1.84 + ([1.96 – 1.84]/2)	£1.90

(ii)   **Pescara – capital gains tax implications of selling the EIS shares**

The gain deferred in respect of the sale of the shares in Zolder plc will be chargeable in the year the EIS shares are sold.

If the EIS shares are disposed of within the minimum holding period (usually three years from the date of issue), any gain on the EIS shares is computed in the normal way. If the shares are disposed of after the end of the minimum holding period, any gain is exempt from CGT.

If EIS shares are disposed of at a loss at any time, the loss is allowable but the acquisition cost of the shares is reduced by the amount of EIS income tax relief attributable to the shares which has not been withdrawn on sale.

(c)   **Pescara – gift of UK main residence**

The gift of Pescara's main residence will be a potentially exempt transfer (PET). The value of this PET will be the market value of the property at the time of the gift less any available annual exemptions.

The amount which will be subject to inheritance tax in respect of this gift with reservation depends on whether or not the reservation of benefit ceases before Pescara dies, for example if she stops using the property rent-free.

(i)   If the reservation ceases within the seven years before Pescara's death, then the gift is treated as a PET made at the time the reservation ceased. The charge is based on its value at that time. Annual exemptions cannot be used against such a PET.

(ii)   If the reservation still exists at the date of Pescara's death, the property is included in her death estate at its value at that time (not its value at the date the gift was made).

Where Pescara dies within seven years of the original PET such that the gift is taxable as a PET when made, as well as taxed under (i) or (ii) above, it will be taxed either as a PET when made, or under (i) or (ii) (but not both), whichever gives the higher total tax. The residence nil rate band will be available for computation (ii). The available residence nil rate band will be the lower of the maximum residence nil rate band at the date of Pescara's death and the value of the property at the date of Pescara's death.

Tutorial note. Pescara would be advised to stop using the property (or to start paying a market rent) if she wishes the gift to be advantageous from the point of view of inheritance tax.

18 Mirtoon (12/11)

Text references. Chargeable gains in outline are covered in Chapter 11. Principal private residence relief, entrepreneurs' relief and gift relief are covered in Chapter 13. Trading losses are dealt with in Chapter 8, the basis period in Chapter 6, and the basic income tax computation in Chapter 1. Value added tax (VAT) deregistration is covered in Chapter 28. Overseas aspects of income tax and capital gains are dealt with in Chapters 10 and 14 respectively. Associated operations and gifts with reservation of benefit will be found in Chapter 18.

Top tips. In scenario questions such as this, it is important to identify all the relevant information for each requirement which may appear in different parts of the question. For example, in this question, the overlap profits could have been overlooked as they were contained in the background information, whereas the remainder of the information about trading losses was in the extract from the email from Mirtoon.

Easy marks. The computations in this question were relatively uncomplicated. In part (b), the basic rules concerning gifts with reservation with benefit should have produced easy marks provided that your explanation was clear and succinct.

Examining team's comments. Part (a) concerned Mirtoon's financial position in view of his plans to sell his house, cease his business and leave the UK. It required a calculation of the total proceeds generated by the proposed transactions.

The sale of the house was handled well with almost all candidates identifying the availability of principal private residence relief and the need to restrict the relief to 80% of the gain arising. The crystallisation of the heldover gain in respect of the agricultural land (due to Mirtoon becoming non-resident), on the other hand, was spotted by only a small minority of candidates. However, this was an easy point to miss and it was possible to obtain a perfectly good mark without any reference to it.

The treatment of the losses arising on the cessation of the business was not handled well due to a lack of knowledge of the closing year rules. This meant that many candidates struggled to determine the assessment for the final years of trading. There were also a considerable number of candidates who erroneously treated the overlap profits brought forward as taxable profits in the final tax year as opposed to being part of the allowable loss. The unincorporated trader is examined with great regularity and candidates are likely to benefit from knowing, in particular, the opening and closing years rules.

A minority of candidates demonstrated a lack of precision when considering the tax due in respect of the sale of the house and the tax saving in respect of the offset of the trading losses. This lack of precision included a failure to take account of the capital losses brought forward and/or the annual exempt amount and the omission of the personal allowance from the income tax computations. It was important to consider the personal allowance as Mirtoon's income exceeded £100,000 such that the personal allowance was restricted.

Part (b) was in three parts and produced a wide variety of answers.

Part (i) concerned the VAT implications of Mirtoon ceasing to trade. This part was done reasonably well, although perhaps not as well as expected. Some candidates made it hard for themselves by writing generally rather than addressing the facts of the question. In particular, many candidates wrote at length about the sale of a business as a going concern. However, the question made it clear that the business was to cease with the assets then being sold. The vast majority of candidates identified the need to deregister. However, a considerably smaller number pointed out the possible need to account for output tax on business assets owned as at cessation.

Part (ii) concerned Mirtoon's liability to income tax and capital gains tax whilst living overseas. There were some good answers to this part but also two particular areas of confusion.

The first area of confusion related to the taxation of income where an individual is not resident in the UK. It needs to be recognised that where an individual is not resident in the UK, any foreign income will not be subject to UK income tax. Where many candidates went wrong was to imagine that the remittance basis was relevant here. This led candidates to write at length about the remittance basis thus wasting time.

The second area of confusion concerned the temporary non-resident rules. These rules relate to capital gains tax and cause gains that would otherwise not be taxable in the UK to be so taxable if the individual is non-UK resident for less than five years. However, a minority of candidates incorrectly treated these rules as an extension of the residency rules as they relate to income tax.

Part (iii) concerned two areas of inheritance tax; associated operations and gifts with reservation. The good news was that the vast majority of candidates knew all about gifts with reservation and answered this part of the question well. Knowledge of associated operations was less common but this was to be expected. The bad news, however, was that many candidates did not restrict their answers to the above two areas but wrote at length about inheritance tax generally. Candidates must take care in identifying what has been asked and try to avoid addressing other areas.

Marking scheme

				Marks
(a)	Sale of house			
		Capital gain	½	
		Principal private residence relief	1	
		Capital gains tax	1½	
	Agricultural land		2½	
	Trading losses			
		Loss available for relief	2	
		Tax relief	4	
	Total proceeds net of tax adjustments		2	
	Explanatory notes (1 mark each – maximum 4 marks)		4	
			Max	17
(b)	(i)	Requirement to deregister	1½	
		Output tax	2	
			Max	3
	(ii)	Status	2½	
		Income tax	1	
		Capital gains tax	5	
			Max	6
	(iii)	Associated operations	2½	
		Gift with reservation	5	
			Max	6
Approach to problem solving			1	
Appropriate style and presentation			1	
Effectiveness of communication			1	
				3
				35

(a) Mirtoon's financial position

	£
Proceeds from sale of home	850,000
Capital gains tax in respect of sale of home (W1)	(6,200)
Capital gains tax in respect of agricultural land (W2)	(11,520)
Proceeds from sale of business assets	14,000
Income tax relief in respect of trading losses £(43,010 – 20,570)(W3)	22,440
Total after-tax proceeds	868,720

Workings

1   *Capital gains tax in respect of the sale of the house*

	£
Sale proceeds	850,000
Less cost	(540,000)
Gain	310,000

		£
Capital gain in respect of business use £310,000 × 20% (N1)		62,000
Capital gains tax £62,000 × 10% (N2)		6,200

Notes

1 The capital gain on the disposal of an individual's principal private residence is exempt from tax. However, where part of the house has been used exclusively for business purposes an equal proportion of the gain is subject to tax.

2 The gain in respect of the business use of the house will qualify for entrepreneurs' relief. The relief is available because the house will be in use for the purposes of the business at the time at which the business ceases, the business has been owned for at least one year and the disposal will be within three years of the date of cessation. Accordingly, the rate of tax is 10%.

2 *Capital gains tax in respect of agricultural land*

	£
Chargeable gain held over subject to tax in 2018/19 (N1)	72,900
Less: Capital losses brought forward (N2)	(4,000)
Annual exempt amount (N2)	(11,300)
Gain	57,600
Capital gains tax £57,600 × 20% (N3)	11,520

Notes

1 Where an individual becomes non-resident within six years of receiving a gift in respect of which gift relief was claimed, the capital gain held over will become subject to capital gains tax immediately prior to their departure from the UK. Accordingly, the heldover gain on the agricultural land will become chargeable in January 2019 and will be taxed in the year 2018/19.

2 The capital losses and the annual exempt amount can be deducted from Mirtoon's capital gains in the most tax-efficient manner. Accordingly, they will be deducted from gains that would otherwise be taxed at 20%.

3 The taxable interest income in 2018/19 together with the capital gains qualifying for entrepreneurs' relief will clearly exceed the basic rate band such that all other capital gains will be taxed at 20%.

3 *Income tax relief in respect of trading losses*

	£
Loss in the year ended 30 June 2018	20,000
Loss in the six months ending 31 December 2018	17,000
Overlap relief	7,600
Loss for the tax year 2018/19 (N1)	44,600

Income tax liability for 2017/18

	Original £	Loss relief £
Trading income	90,000	90,000
Interest income	34,775	34,775
Total income	124,775	124,775
Less loss relief against general income	–	(44,600)
Net income	124,775	80,175
Less personal allowance (N2)	–	(11,500)
Taxable income	124,775	68,675

Tax	Original £	Loss relief £
Taxable income – no loss relief		
£33,500 × 20%	6,700	
£56,500 (90,000 – 33,500) × 40%	22,600	
£500 × 0% (higher rate taxpayer)	0	
£34,275 (34,775 – 500) × 40%	13,710	
Taxable income – after loss relief		
£33,500 × 20%		6,700
£400 (90,000 – 44,600 – 11,500 – 33,500) × 40%		160
£500 × 0% (higher rate taxpayer)		0
£34,275 (34,775 – 500) × 40%		13,710
Income tax liability	43,010	20,570

Notes

1. The basis period for 2018/19 runs from the end of the basis period for the previous tax year until the date of cessation, ie from 1 July 2017 until 31 December 2018. The loss will be increased by the unrelieved overlap profits.

2. An individual's personal allowance is reduced by £1 for every £2 by which adjusted net income exceeds £100,000. Accordingly, with adjusted net income of over £123,000, Mirtoon will have no personal allowance.

(b)

Firm's address

Mirtoon's address

9 December 2017

Dear Mirtoon

Departure from the UK

I set out below our advice in respect of the value added tax (VAT) consequences of your cessation of business and the tax implications of your departure from the UK.

(i) **VAT on the cessation of your business**

You must notify HM Revenue & Customs of the cessation of your business within 30 days of your ceasing to make taxable supplies, ie by 30 January 2019. You may be charged a penalty if you fail to do so.

You should charge VAT on any machinery and inventory that you sell whilst still registered for VAT. When you deregister you will need to account for output tax on all business assets that you still own in respect of which you have previously recovered input tax. There is no need to account for this output tax if it is less than £1,000.

(ii) **Liability to UK income tax and capital gains tax whilst living in Koro**

In 2018/19 18 you will be UK resident. This is because you do not meet any of the automatic overseas tests to be non-resident and you do meet one of the automatic UK tests of residence (being in the UK that year for 183 days or more). However, because you are leaving the UK to work full-time overseas, you are able to treat the year of departure as split into two parts, a UK part and an overseas part. You are treated as though you are non-UK resident during the overseas part (ie from 15 January to 5 April 2019). You will then be non-UK resident in the following tax years while you remain overseas.

Income tax

Generally, UK source income is subject to income tax regardless of the residence status of the individual. However, from 2019/20 since the only UK income you will have is savings income and this type of income is disregarded in computing your total income as a non-UK resident, you will not have any liability to UK income tax.

Whilst you are non-UK resident you will not be subject to UK income tax on any of your overseas income.

Capital gains tax

Generally, individuals who are not resident in the UK are not subject to UK capital gains tax. However, temporary non-residents who realise capital gains whilst non-UK resident, in respect of assets acquired when they were still UK resident, are subject to capital gains tax in the tax year when they become UK resident again.

You will be regarded as a temporary non-resident if you are not UK resident for less than five years. This is because you have been resident in the UK for at least four of the seven tax years prior to the tax year of departure from the UK.

Accordingly, if you become UK resident again before 15 January 2024, any gains you make whilst you were non-UK resident in respect of assets you owned when you ceased to be UK resident, for example your agricultural land, will be subject to UK tax on your return to the UK. If you did become UK resident in 2023/24, it may be possible to split that tax year into an overseas part and a UK part, as in the year of departure.

(iii) **Inheritance tax planning**

I summarise below the inheritance tax anti-avoidance rules you will need to be aware of when we discuss your inheritance tax planning ideas.

Associated operations

A scheme involving a series of transactions that seeks to reduce the value of a gift may be caught by the rules relating to associated operations. The definition of associated operations is quite broad but may be summarised as:

(1) Two or more operations which affect the same property

(2) Where one operation is carried out by reference to a second operation or in order to enable the second operation to be carried out

Where the rules apply, the series of transactions will be regarded as a single gift at the time of the final transaction in the series such that the total value transferred will be subject to tax.

Gifts with reservation

A donor of a gift who retains some interest in the asset transferred may be caught by the rules concerning gifts with reservation. A gift with reservation occurs where:

(1) Possession and enjoyment of the property is not genuinely obtained by the donee
(2) The property given is not enjoyed virtually to the entire exclusion of the donor

A gift will not be treated as a gift with reservation where:

(1) The donor gives full consideration for the benefit retained

(2) In respect of a gift of land, the donor is an elderly or infirm relative of the donee and, due to an unforeseeable change in circumstances, there is a need for a benefit to be provided to the donor in the form of reasonable care and maintenance

Where the rules apply:

(1) If the reservation is removed in the seven years prior to the death of the donor, the asset will be treated as having been gifted at the time the reservation is removed.

(2) If the reservation is not removed prior to the donor's death, the asset will be included in the donor's death estate at its value as at the time of death.

Provisions exist to ensure that the gift of the asset is not taxed twice, for example, at the time of the original gift and again at the time of death.

Please do not hesitate to contact me if you require any further information.

Yours sincerely

Tax manager

19 Cada (12/14)

Text references. The implications of lifetime transfers for inheritance tax and the death estate are dealt with in Chapter 16. The inheritance tax implications of altering dispositions made on death are dealt with in Chapter 18 and the capital gains aspects in Chapter 13. Capital losses are covered in Chapter 11 and negligible value claims in Chapter 14.

Top tips. In part (b) you can save some time by working out the original inheritance tax liability (based on the original gift to charity) and the reduced inheritance tax liability (based on the increased gift to charity) side by side.

Easy marks. There were some easy marks in part (a) for explaining taper relief. In part (d) the explanation of losses should have been straightforward.

Examining team's comments. Part (a) required candidates to explain the inheritance tax advantages that would have arisen if the deceased had made additional lifetime gifts. The first thing to note here was that this part of the question concerned inheritance tax and not capital gains tax. The question also stated that candidates should not consider lifetime exemptions, for example the annual exemption. Many candidates did not identify these important points and thus wrote about both of these areas rather than focusing on the question requirements. In addition, many candidates wrote at length about business property relief. This was not relevant because business property relief is available in respect of both lifetime gifts and the death estate and thus additional lifetime gifts by the deceased would not have resulted in additional relief. Other candidates were of the opinion that lifetime gifts will reduce the value of the death estate (true) and therefore reduce the inheritance tax due on death (not necessarily true). These candidates had failed to recognise the inheritance tax due in respect of potentially exempt transfers in the seven years prior to death (which these transfers inevitably would be due to the facts of the question). Most candidates would have benefited from reading the question more carefully (and, for example, ignoring the annual exemption) and thinking more (thus recognising that business property relief was not relevant) and then writing a shorter answer that may very well have scored more marks. Having said that, the majority of candidates correctly identified taper relief as an advantage of lifetime gifts and many explained the concept of value freezing. However, very few candidates were able to explain fall in value relief correctly.

Part (b) required candidates to calculate the increase in the legacy to charity that would be necessary for the reduced rate of inheritance tax to apply. Candidates appeared to be well prepared for a question on this area of the syllabus and this part was answered particularly well with the exception of a very small minority who were simply not aware of the rules regarding the 36% rate of tax.

Part (c) concerned the inheritance and capital gains tax advantages of varying the terms of the taxpayer's will and the procedures necessary to achieve a valid variation. The tax advantages are not obscure, but they do require some thought and they are not particularly easy to explain. Candidates would have benefited from slowing down and thinking about how best to express what they wanted to say rather than writing in the hope that the necessary words would eventually appear on the page. As always, candidates had to apply their knowledge to the facts in the question. As far as capital gains tax was concerned, many candidates knew that there was no capital gains tax on death but failed to think about the potentially undesirable implication of the proposed gift of the house and how that implication could be avoided. In respect of inheritance tax, many candidates saw that this was linked to generation skipping but mentioning the term 'generation skipping' was not in itself sufficient. Candidates had to explain that the variation would avoid the need for Raymer to make a potentially exempt transfer and therefore removed the possibility of such a transfer being chargeable to inheritance tax in the event that Raymer died within seven years of making the gift. The majority of candidates were able to explain the procedures necessary in order to achieve a valid variation of the terms of the will.

Part (d) was slightly more challenging and was, again, based on the specific facts of the question. It concerned capital gains tax and the beneficial actions that could have been taken in respect of the individual's shareholdings. Many candidates were unsure of the answer to this question despite having sufficient knowledge to deal with it. Unfortunately, instead of calmly thinking about it, they wrote about various aspects of capital gains tax, and inheritance tax, until they ran out of time. In particular, many candidates wrote about using any unused annual exempt amount despite being told in the question that the individual paid capital gains tax every year. The key issue here was that, because there is no capital gains tax on death, any unrealised losses in respect of shares worth less than cost are lost. Candidates simply had to point out, for example, that the quoted shares that were valued at less than cost at the time of death should have been sold prior to death in order to realise a loss that could then have been offset against chargeable gains.

Marking scheme

				Marks
(a)	Value of lifetime transfer	1		
	Relief for fall in value	1		
	Taper relief availability	1		
	Taper relief: effect	1½		
			Max	4
(b)	Original liability	3		
	Revised gift to charity	3		
	Net saving	1		
			Max	5
(c)	Additional gift to charity	1		
	House	3½		
	Procedure for variation	2		
			Max	6
(d)	No relief for losses accrued at death	1		
	Realisation of losses on FR plc shares	1		
	Negligible value claim on KZ Ltd shares	2		
	Use of losses	2		
			Max	5
				20

(a) Inheritance tax advantages of additional lifetime gifts

If Cada had made additional lifetime gifts of quoted shares between 1 December 2014 and her death, the transfers of value would have been based on the value of the quoted shares at the date of the gifts, rather than their value at the date of Cada's death. Therefore, although the transfers of value would be chargeable to inheritance tax because Cada died within seven years of making them, if the shares had increased in value between the lifetime transfers and her death that increase would not be subject to inheritance tax.

In addition, if the shares had fallen in value between the date the lifetime transfers and her death, fall in value relief could be claimed in computing the lifetime transfers of value chargeable at death.

Taper relief of 20% would also apply to the death tax on the additional gifts if they were made between 1 December 2014 and 20 November 2015 (three to four years before Cada's death) and to the extent that they exceeded the nil rate band available, taking into account transfers in the seven years before the additional gift.

(b)   **Additional gift to charity**

	Original gift to charity £	Increased gift to charity £
Assets owned at death	1,000,000	1,000,000
Less: Original gift to charity	(60,000)	
Increased gift to charity		
£(1,000,000 − 220,000) × 10%		(78,000)
Chargeable estate	940,000	922,000
Inheritance tax		
Residence nil rate band		
Lower of £100,000 and £500,000 ie £100,000 × 0%	0	0
Nil rate band		
£220,000 × 0%	0	0
£(940,000 − 100,000 − 220,000) = £620,000 × 40%	248,000	
£(922,000 − 100,000 − 220,000) = £602,000 × 36%		216,720
	248,000	216,720
Additional gift to charity £(78,000 − 60,000)		18,000
Reduction in inheritance tax £(248,000 − 216,720)		31,280

Tutorial note. There is a reduced rate of inheritance tax (36%, rather than 40%) available on the chargeable death estate if Cada gifts at least 10% of her net estate to charity. For the purpose of determining whether the 10% condition is met, the net estate is calculated as the assets owned at death as reduced by liabilities, exemptions, reliefs and the available nil rate band (not the residence nil rate band), but before the charitable legacy itself is deducted.

(c)   **Variation of Cada's will**

Gift to charity: Potential tax advantages

If Cada's will were varied to gift £78,000 to charity instead of £60,000, the inheritance tax liability on the estate would be reduced by £31,280 as shown above.

Gift of house by Raymer: Potential tax advantages

Cada's will could be varied to give the house directly to Raymer's son who would take the house at the probate value of £500,000 for capital gains tax purposes. Raymer would not be treated as making a disposal for capital gains tax purposes by making the variation.

If the will is not varied in this way, Raymer would make a disposal of house on 1 July 2019 at its market value at that time and there will be a chargeable gain if this value exceeds the probate value of £500,000. Raymer would not be able to claim principal private residence relief, as she does not intend to live in the house, and gift relief would not be available as the house is not a business asset nor is the gift a chargeable lifetime transfer for inheritance tax.

For inheritance tax, the variation would mean that the house is treated as being given to Raymer's son in Cada's will so would be chargeable to inheritance tax as part of the chargeable estate in the same way as if gifted to Raymer. Raymer would not be treated as making a transfer of value for inheritance tax purposes by making the variation.

If the will is not varied in this way, Raymer would make a potentially exempt transfer of the market value of the house on 1 July 2019 and this would become a chargeable transfer if she dies within seven years (ie on or before 30 June 2026).

Procedures

A written variation must be made by 19 November 2020 (two years after Cada's death) by Raymer and Yang as they are the persons who benefit under Cada's will and whose entitlements to property under the will are reduced by the variation.

As Raymer and Yang wish the relevant terms of the will to be treated as replaced by the terms of the variation for both inheritance tax and capital gains tax purposes, this must be stated in the variation.

Tutorial note. Yang's entitlement under Cada's will is reduced by the variation because the increased gift to charity must come from the remaining assets of Cada's estate which have been given to Yang. However, the value of Yang's entitlement will actually increase due to the reduction in inheritance tax.

(d)   **Capital gains tax – beneficial actions in respect of shareholdings**

The shares in Cada's estate will pass at probate value to Yang and the accrued losses up to the date of Cada's death will therefore not be available for relief.

The FR plc shares which are valued at less than cost could have been sold in the tax year of Cada's death, thus realising the loss on those shares. This loss could have been offset against chargeable gains in that tax year and then carried back against chargeable gains of the three tax years before death on a last in, first out (LIFO) basis.

A negligible value claim could have been made in respect of the KZ Ltd shares to treat them as sold, and immediately reacquired, for no value so realising the loss on those shares. The sale and reacquisition would have been treated as taking place when the claim was made, or at a specified earlier time. The earlier time could have been any time up to two years before the start of the tax year in which the claim was made. The loss would be relieved in a similar way to the loss on the FR plc shares.

20 Meredith and Adrian

Text references. Chapter 14 deals with overseas aspects of CGT including residential property owned by a non-UK resident. Chapter 15 covers penalties for non-compliance. Chapter 13 includes entrepreneurs' relief.

Top tips. You must make sure that your tax knowledge is up to date for the examination you will be sitting. The rules on serial tax avoiders are new in 2017/18 and are covered in the Finance Act 2017 edition of the BPP Study Text. Changes in tax rules are often examined shortly after they come into force.

			Marks	
(a)	(i)	Normal penalty for error	2	
		Offshore matter	1	
		Further penalty	2	
				5
	(ii)	Serial tax avoidance notice	1	
		Sanctions (one mark for each)	3	
				4
(b)		Entrepreneurs' relief conditions	1	
		Shop	½	
		Goodwill	1	
		CGT liability	2½	
				5
				14

(a) (i) **Meredith – offshore matter penalties**

As a UK resident, Meredith is taxable on her worldwide income including the income from the overseas assets. A penalty for error might be imposed on her if she submits an inaccurate return by making a deliberate error which results in an understatement of her tax liability. The amount of the penalty for error is based on the Potential Lost Revenue (PLR) to HMRC as a result of the error. For a deliberate, but not concealed, error the maximum penalty is 70% of PLR.

Since the error relates to an offshore matter, the penalty may be increased. The rate of this increased penalty is linked to how much information the territory, in which the assets are situated, shares with HMRC. The harder it is for HMRC to obtain information from the territory, the higher the penalty.

There is a further penalty which may be imposed where there is a relevant offshore asset move intended to prevent or delay HMRC from discovering a potential loss of revenue once a non-compliance penalty for deliberate failure has been imposed. A relevant offshore asset move includes one where an asset ceases to be situated in a territory which automatically shares information with HMRC and becomes situated in a territory which does not.

(ii) **Meredith – serial tax offender**

Meredith may be issued with a serial tax avoidance warning notice which has effect for five years. This will require her to submit additional information to HMRC about her tax affairs annually, for example her use of tax avoidance schemes.

Meredith could also be liable to penalties if she enters into further tax avoidance schemes during the notice period, the level of which increase with the number of such schemes entered into. She may be publicly named by HMRC as a serial tax avoider. Meredith may also have restrictions on direct tax reliefs imposed on her for up to three years.

(b) **Adrian**

Entrepreneurs' relief is available where there is a material disposal of business assets which includes a disposal of the whole of a business which has been owned by the individual throughout the period of one year ending with the date of the disposal.

Therefore, the disposal of Adrian's business is a material disposal of business assets and qualifies for entrepreneurs' relief on the gain on the freehold shop (a relevant business asset). However, since the disposal of the goodwill is to a close company of which Adrian is a participator, the goodwill is not a relevant business asset.

Adrian's capital gains tax (CGT) liability on the sale of his business to Better Ltd is therefore as follows:

	Gains £	CGT £
Gains qualifying for entrepreneurs' relief		
Gain on shop	50,000	
CGT @ 10%		5,000
Gains not qualifying for entrepreneurs' relief		
Gain on goodwill	42,000	
Less annual exempt amount (best use)	(11,300)	
Taxable gain	30,700	
CGT @ 20%		6,140
CGT liability		11,140

Tutorial note. The question states that Adrian has no intention of selling his shares in Better Ltd in the near future. Since he holds 5% or more of the ordinary share capital of Better Ltd, if he sold the whole of the shareholding to another company (Company A) within 28 days and he held less than 5% of the ordinary share capital or voting rights of Company A, the goodwill would be a relevant business asset on the incorporation. This relaxation is designed to cover the situation where an individual incorporates his business to facilitate the sale of the newly incorporated company.

21 Klubb plc (12/14)

Text references. Corporation tax administration is covered in Chapter 22. Share schemes are dealt with in Chapter 5. Controlled foreign companies are covered in Chapter 27.

Top tips. In part (c)(i), state the conditions for a controlled foreign company to exist and then apply them to the question. The key point is the residence of the individual shareholder.

Easy marks. There were easy marks in part (a) for basic corporation tax administration. The computation of the CFC charge in part (c)(ii) was also straightforward.

Examining team's comments. Part (a) concerned a company with a long period of account. Candidates were required to state when any corporation tax returns needed to be filed and explain any penalties for late filing. The first thing candidates had to point out was the need to split the long period of account into two accounting periods. Unfortunately, many candidates failed to identify this point. Candidates then had to know the filing dates and the penalty rules. However, many candidates wrote about the dates on which corporation tax has to be paid as opposed to the filing dates of the returns, such that they did not answer the requirement set.

Part (b) of the question was more substantial. It required a comparison of two tax-advantaged share schemes: a share incentive plan and a share option scheme, by reference to certain specified areas. It was very important to identify clearly the particular areas that needed to be addressed, and to stick to them. Failure to do this could result in irrelevant parts of an answer that would score no marks, despite being technically accurate. Unfortunately many candidates were insufficiently disciplined in their approach and regarded the question as being about the two share schemes generally as opposed to being about certain aspects of the two schemes. Generally, candidates' knowledge of this area was good with many candidates providing satisfactory answers. The candidates who did best were those who structured their answer in a very clear manner so that it was always clear which aspect of which scheme was being addressed. This clear structure enabled candidates to keep their answers relatively brief whilst addressing all of the precise requirements of the question. However, a minority of candidates appeared to be making up their answer as they went along, such that they were setting out each thought as it occurred to them. The problem with this approach was that some points were repeated, other points were made which were not relevant and some aspects of the requirement were omitted altogether. Most candidates knew that under a share incentive plan, shares need to be offered to, broadly, all employees whereas, under a company share option plan, the employer can choose certain employees to join the scheme. Candidates' knowledge of the number or value of shares that could be offered under each scheme was also satisfactory notwithstanding that some candidates confused the two schemes or confused the different categories of shares that can be offered under a share incentive plan.

When it came to the tax implications of acquiring and selling the shares it was important for candidates to stick to the facts of the question. It was clear from the question how long the shares would be held for and when they would be sold. Accordingly, there was no need to address all of the different tax implications that could occur if the shares were sold at other times. Candidates who failed to realise this wasted time writing lengthy answers that were not addressing the requirements of the question. When explaining the tax implications, stronger candidates were clear as to which scheme they were writing about and which tax (income tax or capital gains tax) they were addressing. The answers of other candidates were more confused and used the general term 'tax' as opposed to the specific tax concerned.

Part (c)(i) was done reasonably well by many candidates. Candidates had two main problems when answering this first part of the question. First, they confused the definition of a controlled foreign company with the exemptions that are available. Secondly, there was a tendency to write about all of the available exemptions as opposed to the particular one in the question requirement; this resulted in irrelevant parts of answers.

Part (c)(ii) required a calculation of a controlled foreign company charge. Candidates had to remember to exclude the gains from the calculation, bring in only 30% of the trading profits, and deduct an appropriate amount of creditable tax. Answers here were generally not as accurate as might have been hoped.

Marking scheme

				Marks
(a)	Two accounting periods		1	
	Filing date		1	
	Penalty		2	
				4
(b)	Employees included		2	
	Number or value of shares acquired			
		SIP	4	
		CSOP	2	
	Tax implications of acquiring and selling shares			
		SIP	2	
		CSOP	2	
		Max		9
(c)	(i)	Status of Hartz Co	2½	
		Low profits exemption	2	
		Max		4
	(ii)	Profits apportioned	1½	
		Calculation of charge	1½	
				3
				20

(a)   **Late submission of corporation tax returns**

There are two accounting periods within the long period of account. These are for the 12-month period ended 30 November 2016 and the 4-month period ended 31 March 2017.

As the relevant period of account is not more than 18 months long, the filing date for both periods is 12 months from the end of the period of account which is 31 March 2018.

There is a £100 penalty for a failure to submit each return on time, as each return is made within 3 months of the filing date.

The £100 penalty is increased to £500 when a return was late (or never submitted) for each of the preceding 2 accounting periods.

Tutorial note. It has been assumed that HM Revenue & Customs issued notices requiring the returns to be made before 1 January 2017 so that the later three-month filing date rule does not apply.

(b) Comparison of share incentive plan (SIP) with company share option plan (CSOP)

(i) *Employees*

Klubb plc would need to offer all full- and part-time employees the opportunity to participate in a SIP, although a minimum qualifying period of employment of up to 18 months may be specified.

All the employees and full-time directors of Klubb plc can participate in a CSOP, but the scheme need not be open to all of them. Klubb plc can therefore select the employees it wishes to include.

A CSOP is therefore more likely to achieve the flexibility that Klubb plc wants, rather than a SIP.

Number or value of shares which can be acquired by each plan member

In a SIP, employees would be given free shares in Klubb plc, which are held in the plan, up to the value of £3,600 each tax year. Employees must be awarded free shares on similar terms to all of the plan members. This means that any variation in the number of free shares must be made by reference to objective criteria, such as level of remuneration, length of service or hours worked. However, Klubb plc can also specify that the award can be conditional on the meeting of performance targets (within rules prescribed in the legislation) but there can be no deliberate weighting of rewards in favour of directors and the more highly paid employees. Employees can also purchase partnership shares through deduction from pre-tax salary up to the lower of £1,800 and 10% of salary in any tax year. Klubb plc can also award matching shares free to employees who purchase partnership shares at a maximum ratio of 2:1.

In a CSOP employees can be granted options to buy shares in Klubb plc up to the value of £30,000 (at the date of grant). Subject to that maximum amount, Klubb plc can decide how many options to grant to each employee.

Again, a CSOP is therefore more likely to achieve the flexibility that Klubb plc wants, rather than a SIP.

(ii) *Tax implications of acquiring and selling the shares*

There are no income tax implications when shares are given to employees in a SIP. Since the shares will be held within the SIP for five years, there will be no income tax charge when the shares are taken out of the SIP. There will also be no charge to capital gains tax on shares taken out of the SIP and sold immediately because their base cost will be equal to their market value at the time they are withdrawn from the SIP.

There is no income tax on the grant of options in a CSOP, nor on the exercise of an option under a CSOP since it will be exercised between three and ten years after the grant, which is a condition for a CSOP. When the shares acquired under a CSOP are sold, any gain is subject to capital gains tax. The cost in the gain calculation is the option price paid by the employee to acquire the shares. It is a condition for a CSOP that the option price must not be less than their market value at the time of the grant of the option.

Therefore, there will be no charge to income tax on either the SIP or the CSOP, but capital gains tax may be payable on the disposal of shares acquired under a CSOP, but not on those acquired under a SIP.

Tutorial note. It was not necessary to make all of the above points in order to score full marks for this question.

(c) (i) Status of Hartz Co and availability of low profits exemption

A controlled foreign company is a company which is not resident in the UK but is controlled by persons resident in the UK.

Hartz Co is owned 30% by Klubb plc (UK resident), 45% by Kort Co (non-UK resident) and 25% by Mr Deck. Therefore, Hartz Co will be a controlled foreign company (CFC) only if Mr Deck is UK resident.

The chargeable profits of Hartz Co will not be exempt from apportionment under either of the conditions for the low profits exemption. This is because its profits are more than £50,000 and, although they are under £500,000, its non-trading profits (chargeable gains) exceed £50,000.

	£
Chargeable profits of Hartz Co	330,000
Apportioned to Klubb plc £330,000 × 30%	99,000
Tax on apportioned profits £99,000 × 19%	18,810
Less creditable tax £99,000 × 10%	(9,900)
CFC charge	8,910

Tutorial note. Chargeable gains are not part of chargeable profits for the purposes of the CFC charge so only the trading profits are included.

22 Sank Ltd and Kurt Ltd (06/12)

Text references. Payment of corporation tax and administration are covered in Chapter 22. Capital allowances in general are dealt with in Chapter 7. The division of the annual investment allowance is covered in Chapter 26 and research and development expenditure in Chapter 20.

Top tips. In a two-part question such as this, you must produce a reasonable answer to both parts.

Easy marks. In part (a), the computation of corporation tax should have been easy marks. In part (b), the availability of the annual investment allowance and the writing down allowance were straightforward, even if you did not know the detail about the restriction for related companies.

Examining team's comments. In part (a)(i), the payment of corporation tax appeared to be fairly straightforward but care was needed if sufficient marks were to be earned. It was not enough to state that the company would pay corporation tax quarterly because it was large. Candidates needed to explain how they knew this (ie by reference to its profits and the number of related 51% group companies). There was also a need to point out that the company was large in the previous accounting period. **[BPP Note.** These comments have been amended to reflect terminology and rule changes since the question was originally set.] Weaker candidates confused quarterly accounting with the payments of income tax by individuals and thought that the payments were paid on account by reference to the liability for the previous year.

Part (a)(ii) required candidates to explain the validity of the compliance check enquiry 'in relation to the date on which (it)...... was raised'. Many candidates simply wrote about compliance check enquiries generally such that this part of the question was not answered well.

Most candidates produced reasonable answers to part (b), but many would have done better if they had simply read the question more carefully and identified the relevance of all of the information and slowed down. In particular, many candidates wrote about the basic rules at some length rather than thinking about the particular situation of the question.

The owner of the company concerned owned three other companies. This information was intended to elicit a discussion of the need to split the annual investment allowance between the companies. However, many candidates wrote instead about the unavailability of group relief. The question also pointed out that the relevant accounting period was only eight months. This meant that the annual investment allowance and the writing down allowance needed to be multiplied by 8/12. However, this point was missed by many candidates.

A significant number of candidates were of the opinion that, because the company was loss-making, it should not claim all of its capital allowances. It should be remembered that, where the annual investment allowance is concerned, failing to claim allowances in full will considerably slow down the time it takes for a tax deduction to be obtained for the cost incurred as, in the future, there will only be an 18% writing down allowance on a reducing balance basis. Accordingly, there needs to be a strong reason not to claim allowances in full. Such a reason might include the situation where there are insufficient profits in the group to relieve a company's losses in the current year and any losses carried forward are likely to be locked inside the company for a considerable period of time.

In such a situation it may be worthwhile claiming reduced capital allowances in the current year in order to have increased capital allowances in future years that can then be group relieved.

The tax treatment of the expenditure on scientific research was explained well by the majority of candidates, many of whom were aware that there was a possibility of claiming a 14.5% repayment. However, very few candidates attempted to evaluate whether or not the repayment should be claimed.

Marking scheme

				Marks
(a)	(i)	Corporation tax	½	
		Why required to pay by instalments	3	
		Payments required	3	
		Payment already made	1½	
		Interest	1	
		Future payments	½	
		Max		9
	(ii)	Deadlines	2½	
		Conclusion	1	
		Max		3
(b)		Equipment		
		Annual investment allowance	3	
		Writing down allowance	1	
		Scientific research		
		Tax deduction	1	
		Repayment	1	
		Evaluation	2	
				8
				20

(a) (i) **Sank Ltd – increase in the budgeted corporation tax liability for the 11 months ended 30 September 2018**

Sank Ltd's corporation tax liability for the period is expected to be £750,000 × 19% = £142,500.

It is required to pay its corporation tax liability for the period in instalments because its profits exceed the profit threshold of £(1,500,000/3 × 11/12) = £458,333 for the period and it was a large company in previous years.

The payments required are as follows.

14 May 2018	3/11 of the final liability for the period
14 August 2018	3/11 of the final liability for the period
14 November 2018	3/11 of the final liability for the period
14 January 2019	2/11 of the final liability for the period (balance)

A payment should have been made on 14 May 2018 of £640,000 × 19% × 3/11 = £33,164, based on the budget prepared on 31 March 2018. However, if the new figure of taxable total profits is correct, the payment required on that day was £750,000 × 19% × 3/11 = £38,864.

Interest will be charged from 14 May 2018 until the additional £(38,864 – 33,164) = £5,700 is paid. The total interest due will be calculated by HM Revenue & Customs, once the corporation tax return has been submitted.

Future payments, ie from 14 August 2018 onwards, should be based on the latest budgeted figures in order to minimise interest charges.

(ii)   **Sank Ltd – circumstances necessary for the notice of the compliance check to be regarded as valid**

The deadline for raising a notice of the compliance check depends on when the corporation tax return was filed.

Where the return was filed on time (ie by 31 October 2016), the compliance check must be notified, at the latest, by 31 October 2017. Where the return was submitted late, the compliance check must be notified by the 31 January, 30 April, 31 July or 31 October next following the first anniversary of the actual date of delivery of the return. Accordingly, a notice of a compliance check dated 31 May 2018 will only be valid if the corporation tax return was submitted after 30 April 2017.

(b)   **Kurt Ltd**

Machinery

A 100% annual investment allowance is available for expenditure on machinery up to a maximum of £200,000 for a 12-month period. The maximum amount available to Kurt Ltd for the period ended 31 March 2018 is therefore £200,000 × 8/12 = £133,333.

However, only one annual investment allowance is available to companies that are related to each other. The other companies controlled by Mr Quinn will be regarded as related to Kurt Ltd if they share premises or carry on similar activities. Mr Quinn can choose to allocate the allowance available to related companies in the most tax-efficient manner.

The excess of the expenditure over the available annual investment allowance will be eligible for a writing down allowance of 18% × 8/12 = 12% in the period to 31 March 2018.

Scientific research

Kurt Ltd is a small enterprise for the purposes of research and development. Accordingly, the expenditure of £28,000 will result in tax deductions of £28,000 × 230% = £64,400.

Kurt Ltd can choose to claim a tax credit of 14.5% of the lower of its trading loss and £64,400. This relief is an alternative to carrying the loss forward against future profits of the same trade.

Kurt Ltd should consider claiming the 14.5% tax credit if cash flow is its main priority. Alternatively, if the company wishes to maximise the tax saved in respect of the expenditure, it should carry the loss forward; it will then save tax at 20% (provided it succeeds in becoming profitable).

23 Opus Ltd group (06/14)

Text references. Groups and consortia are the subject of Chapter 26. Chargeable gains for companies are covered in Chapter 21. Ethics are dealt with in Chapter 30.

Top tips. It is a good idea to ascertain the membership of the 75% group relief group and the 75% capital gains group before you start to work out how profits can be moved around each group.

Easy marks. There were easy marks in part (b) if you applied the test for the substantial shareholding exemption. The ethics in part (c) should have been well known.

Examining team's comments. Part (a) concerned relief for trading losses within the group. The question was all about identifying various individual points in respect of each of the companies. That's why the email from the manager suggested 'you should think carefully about the tax position of each company'. Akia Ltd, the loss-making company, had realised a chargeable gain against which the loss could be offset. There was also the possibility of carrying the loss back 12 months, although very few candidates identified this point. Once the position of Akia Ltd, the loss-making company, had been considered it was then necessary to consider the group and consortium position. The group position was handled well but many candidates failed to spot that because Venere Ltd was a 75% subsidiary of Jarrah Ltd, it could not be a consortium company. Ribe Ltd had trading losses brought forward. These could not be group relieved (because only current period losses can be group relieved) and therefore could only be used against that company's trading profits. However, a minority of candidates simply added the losses of Ribe Ltd to those of Akia Ltd and then addressed the total losses together.

Finally, Binni Ltd was not a member of the group for the whole of the period so it was necessary to determine the maximum loss that could be surrendered to it by Akia Ltd. This is a straightforward point but it was missed by many candidates.

The second part of the question concerned the sale of shares by one of the group companies and the availability of the substantial shareholding exemption (SSE). This was not done well for two main reasons. First, many candidates failed to consider the SSE despite it being an important exemption in Advanced Taxation (ATX – UK). There were follow through marks available for those who found themselves in this predicament but only if they answered the question set. Unfortunately, many candidates failed to do so. Two lessons may be learned from what happened here.

Firstly, it is always worth thinking about how to do a calculation in an efficient manner rather than to just immediately start it. Those candidates who thought it was necessary to calculate a chargeable gain on each of the possible disposal dates should have realised that the only difference was an increase in sales proceeds of £20,000. This would, of course, increase the gain by £20,000; there was no need to repeat the whole calculation to determine this. The second lesson is that you must answer the question set. Candidates were asked to consider on which of the two dates it would be more financially advantageous to sell the shares. This required candidates to consider the post-tax proceeds on each of the potential disposal dates, but the majority of candidates simply focused on the amount of the chargeable gain.

The final part of the question concerned an error in a corporation tax return and the matters that needed to be considered in relation to the disclosure of the error to HM Revenue & Customs. This was a standard question and an opportunity for all candidates to earn some straightforward marks. Unfortunately, a minority of candidates decided to address the penalties aspect of the question in great detail without thinking about the other relevant issues. Stronger candidates recognised the need to consider the importance of disclosing the error from the point of view of tax evasion, money laundering and the acceptability of continuing to act for the company. These stronger candidates were able to score well on this part of the question.

Marking scheme

			Marks
(a)	**Loss of Akia Ltd**		
	Offset against total profits of Akia Ltd		
	Against own total profits	2	
	Against gain from Lido Ltd	2	
	Group relief		
	Members of group and consortium	2	
	Opus Ltd	2½	
	Binni Ltd	1½	
	Ribe Ltd	1	
	Loss carried forward	2	
	Loss of Ribe Ltd	1	
	Capital allowances	2	
	Max		14
(b)	Sale on 30 June 2018	1½	
	Sale on 30 April 2019	3	
	Comparison	1	
	Max		5
(c)	Interest on underpaid tax	2	
	Action required		
	Necessary to disclose	2	
	Implications of failure to disclose	3½	
	Max		6
			25

(a) **Trading losses of Akia Ltd and Ribe Ltd**

	Notes	£	£
Akia Ltd			
Trading loss for the year ended 31 March 2018			93,000
Offset of losses in Akia Ltd:			
Year ended 31 March 2018	1		(27,000)
Year ended 31 March 2017	2		Unknown
Group relief:	3		
Opus Ltd			
Trading profit		10,000	
Property business income		8,000	
Gain on shares in Venere Ltd	4	0	
			(18,000)
Binni Ltd	5		(31,000)
Ribe Ltd	6		0
Amount unrelieved	7		17,000
Ribe Ltd			
Trading loss b/f at 1.4.17			68,000
Offset against trading profit y/e 31.3.18	6		(41,000)
Trading loss c/f at 31.3.18			27,000

Notes

1   Lido Ltd is in a chargeable gains group with Akia Ltd. This is because Opus Ltd has a direct interest of at least 75% in Akia Ltd and has direct interest of at least 75% in Ribe Ltd which, in turn, has a direct interest of at least 75% in Lido Ltd and Opus Ltd has an effective interest in Lido Ltd of more than 50% (80% × 85% = 68%). The chargeable gain of £21,000 can therefore be transferred to Akia Ltd and added to its own gain of £6,000 to give total chargeable gains of £27,000.

2   Akia Ltd can offset its trading losses against its total profits (income and chargeable gains) of the loss-making period and those of the previous 12 months. We therefore need to know the company's total profits for the year ended 31 March 2017.

3   Akia Ltd is in a 75% group relief group with Opus Ltd, Ribe Ltd and Binni Ltd. Lido Ltd is not in the group as the effective interest of Opus Ltd is less than 75%.

    Venere Ltd is not a consortium company because it is a 75% subsidiary of Jarrah Ltd.

4   The chargeable gain on the sale of shares in Venere Ltd is exempt under the substantial shareholding exemption. This is because Opus Ltd and Venere Ltd are trading companies and Opus Ltd owned at least 10% of the shares in Venere Ltd for a continuous period of at least 12 months in the 2 years prior to the disposal.

5   Binni Ltd joined the Opus Ltd group on 1 December 2017, such that it is in a group relief group with Akia Ltd for the four months from 1 December 2017 to 31 March 2018.

    The maximum loss which can be surrendered by Akia Ltd to Binni Ltd is the lower of:

    Loss of Akia Ltd for the overlapping period £93,000 × 4/12   £31,000

    Total profits of Binni Ltd for the overlapping period £78,000 × 4/10   £31,200

6   The trading losses brought forward in Ribe Ltd must be offset against the first available trading profits of the same trade. Therefore, the company has no profits which can be relieved through group relief.

    Ribe Ltd and Lido Ltd form a 75% group relief group. However, the remaining losses cannot be surrendered as group relief to Lido Ltd as only current period losses can be group relieved.

7   The use of losses carried forward in Akia Ltd will be delayed because the company is not expected to be profitable for some time. Akia Ltd can turn what would otherwise be trading losses **carried forward** into future **current period** trading losses (available for immediate relief via group relief) by not claiming capital allowances equal to its unrelieved current period trading loss.

Reducing the capital allowances would increase the tax written down value of the main pool and consequently the capital allowances and trading loss in future periods. The increased trading loss could then be group relieved.

Reducing the capital allowances would reduce the trading loss of Akia Ltd for the year ended 31 March 2018. This in turn would reduce the maximum loss which could be surrendered to Binni Ltd.

Tutorial note. The chargeable gain of Lido Ltd could alternatively be transferred to Opus Ltd or Ribe Ltd, rather than Akia Ltd, and be relieved with Akia Ltd's loss via group relief. It would not be beneficial to transfer the gain to Binni Ltd because of the restriction on the surrender of losses to that company.

(b)   **Sale of shares in Venere Ltd**

If the shares are sold on 30 June 2018, the chargeable gain arising will be exempt under the substantial shareholding exemption. This is because Opus Ltd would have owned at least 10% of the shares in Venere Ltd for a continuous period of at least 12 months (from 1 July 2016 to 30 September 2017) during the 2 years prior to the sale. Accordingly, the post-tax proceeds will be equal to the gross proceeds of £80,000.

If the shares are sold on 30 April 2019, there will not be a continuous 12-month period in the previous 2 years where Opus Ltd has owned at least 10% of the shares in Venere Ltd. Therefore, on the assumption that the shares are sold for £100,000, there will be a chargeable gain of £73,235 (W). This gain will be subject to corporation tax of £(73,235 × 19%) = 13,915. The post-tax proceeds will be £(100,000 – 13,915) = £86,085.

Therefore, while there may be a marginal increase in the post-tax proceeds from delaying the sale until after the results for the year ending 31 March 2019 are known, there is no guarantee that a higher level of sales proceeds will be achieved and there will be a significant delay in obtaining the sales proceeds. Also, these figures assume that any costs of sale will be the same at both dates, which may not be the case.

Working

	£
Proceeds	100,000
Less: cost £65,000 × 50,000/170,000	(19,118)
indexation allowance £19,118 × 0.400 (assumed)	(7,647)
Chargeable gain	73,235

(c)   **Error in the corporation tax return of Binni Ltd**

Interest on underpaid tax

Binni Ltd will be regarded as having underpaid corporation tax on each of the four payment dates for the year ended 31 May 2016. Accordingly, interest may be charged from 14 December 2015, 14 March 2016, 14 June 2016 and 14 September 2016 on any amounts of underpaid corporation tax.

Disclosure of the error

The directors of Binni Ltd must be advised to make full disclosure of the error or authorise our firm to make such disclosure, without delay. If they refuse, we can no longer act for the company. The directors should be advised of this, and also that we must inform HMRC that we have ceased to act for the client. We should not, however, advise HMRC of the error unless the directors consented to such disclosure.

Even if we cease to act for Binni Ltd, we are still under a professional duty to ensure that the directors understand the seriousness of offences against HMRC, including the possibility of criminal prosecution.

Tax evasion may also constitute money laundering and we are also bound by legislation to report suspicions to the appropriate authority. Again, this may lead to criminal prosecution.

24 Helm Ltd group (06/15)

Text references. Groups, including pre-entry losses, are the subject of Chapter 26. Chargeable gains for companies, including the substantial shareholding exemption and rollover relief, are covered in Chapter 21. Stamp duty land tax is covered in Chapter 19. The loan relationship rules are explained in Chapter 20 and deficits on non-trading loan relationships in Chapter 24. Ethics are dealt with in Chapter 30.

Top tips. It is very important to answer the question set and not give a lot of irrelevant detail which will waste time and not score marks.

Easy marks. There were some easy marks in part (a) for working out the degrouping charge gain and the gain on the sale of shares in Bar Ltd. The identification of the non-availability of rollover relief in part (c) was very easy.

Examining team's comments. Part (a) consisted of various aspects of corporation tax with some easy and some more challenging marks. Candidates who did well had a good knowledge of the subject and addressed all of the issues briefly rather than writing about a small number of issues in great detail. When calculating the gain on the sale of the shares in Bar Ltd, the majority of candidates recognised that there would be a degrouping charge and most candidates explained the reasons for the charge arising. However, a minority of candidates were unable to calculate the indexation allowance correctly and so failed to gain some of the available marks. Candidates who performed less well often confused the sale of shares with the sale of assets and calculated gains on the individual assets owned by the company. Candidates must take the time to ensure that they understand the transactions that have taken place in a scenario. It was then necessary to consider the availability of the substantial shareholding exemption. Most candidates knew that at least 10% of the company's shares needed to be owned for 12 months in the 2 years prior to the sale. However, fewer candidates pointed out that the companies needed to be trading companies. The final element, which was only picked up by a small number of candidates, was the fact that the ownership period was satisfied in this particular situation due to the trade of Bar Ltd having been owned by another group company, Aero Ltd, previously. The stamp duty land tax aspects of the question were not handled well, with very few candidates recognising that the inter-group exemption that was available when the trade and assets of Aero Ltd were transferred to Bar Ltd would be withdrawn due to the sale of Bar Ltd within three years.

Part (b) concerned the loan relationships rules and produced a great variety of answers. Those candidates with a good knowledge of the rules were able to present a brief, methodical answer that scored very well. Candidates who were less confident in this area did not pursue the question to its conclusion and therefore did not address the detail of the offset of non-trading loan relationship deficits. This made it difficult to pick up many marks.

Part (c) concerned rollover relief and the offset of capital losses within a capital gains group. Most candidates identified the fact that rollover relief was not available because the building had never been used in the company's trade. The problem was that many candidates described all of the rules relating to rollover relief in addition to making the one relevant point that was worth a mark. Performance in respect of capital losses was mixed. The majority of candidates knew that, in certain circumstances, capital losses can effectively be transferred between companies in capital gains groups. The problem was that this could not occur in this question because the capital losses concerned were pre-entry capital losses, such that their use was restricted. Many candidates did not identify this point but I suspect that they would have done if they had simply paused and thought before they started writing.

The final part of the question concerned the information required and the actions to be taken before becoming tax advisers to a new client. Many candidates did well here. Those who did not either did not have the necessary knowledge or did not make a sufficient number of points briefly, but instead wrote at length about a small number of matters.

			Marks
(a)	Chargeable gain on the sale of Bar Ltd		
	Calculations		
	Degrouping charge	2	
	Chargeable gain on sale of Bar Ltd	2½	
	Explanations	2	
	Substantial shareholding exemption	3	
	Stamp duty land tax	3	
	Max		11
(b)	Loan arrangement fee	1	
	Split of loan	1½	
	Tax treatment of costs	4	
	Max		5
(c)	Rollover relief	1	
	Capital losses	3	
			4
(d)	Information needed	3	
	Action to take	3	
	Max		5
			25

(a) **Sale of Bar Ltd**

Degrouping charge

The transfer of the building on 1 December 2016 by Aero Ltd to Bar Ltd was deemed to have been made for consideration such that Aero Ltd had neither a gain nor a loss (a 'no gain, no loss' disposal). This was because Aero Ltd and Bar Ltd were members of a chargeable gains group at that date since Helm Ltd owned at least 75% of the shares of both companies.

A degrouping charge arises because Bar Ltd left the chargeable gains group while it owned the building transferred to it by Aero Ltd on a no gain, no loss basis within the previous six years. Bar Ltd is treated as though it had, at the time of its acquisition of the building, sold and immediately reacquired it at its then market value.

The gain arising is therefore:

	£
Deemed proceeds (MV on 1 December 2016)	830,000
Less cost	(425,000)
	405,000
Less indexation allowance	
$\dfrac{267.1 - 157.5}{157.5}(0.696) \times £425,000$	(295,800)
Indexed gain	109,200

This gain is added to the sale proceeds received by Helm Ltd when computing the gain on sale of the shares in Bar Ltd.

Chargeable gain on sale of shares in Bar Ltd

	£
Proceeds	1,200,000
Degrouping charge gain (above)	109,200
	1,309,200
Less cost	(1,000,000)
	309,200
Less indexation allowance	
$\dfrac{269.6 - 264.8}{264.8} \times £1,000,000$	(18,127)
Indexed gain	291,073

Tutorial note. The indexation factor should not be rounded to three decimal places because the disposal is from a share pool.

Substantial shareholding exemption

There is an exemption from corporation tax on a gain arising when a trading company (Helm Ltd) disposes of a shareholding in another trading company (Bar Ltd) where the first company has held a substantial shareholding in the second company for a certain period.

Helm Ltd has held a substantial shareholding in Bar Ltd because it held at least 10% of ordinary share capital of Bar Ltd. The 10% test must have been met for a continuous 12-month period during the 2 years preceding the disposal. Since Bar Ltd was only incorporated on 1 October 2016, this test initially appears not to be met.

However, the 12-month period condition can also be satisfied by including a period during which assets, which are being used in its trade by Bar Ltd, were being used in the trade of another chargeable gains group company (Aero Ltd) and then transferred to Bar Ltd before the sale of its shares. Therefore the substantial shareholding exemption will apply to the sale of shares in Bar Ltd by Helm Ltd.

Stamp duty land tax (SDLT)

Relief from SDLT was given for the transfer of the building between Aero Ltd and Bar Ltd because at the date of the transfer they were members of an SDLT group since Helm Ltd had beneficial ownership of at least 75% of the ordinary share capital of both companies. However, the relief will be withdrawn because Bar Ltd leaves the group within three years of the transfer whilst still owning the building. Bar Ltd will therefore have to pay SDLT as follows:

	£
£150,000 × 0%	0
£100,000 (£250,000 – 150,000) × 2%	2,000
£580,000 (£830,000 – 250,000) × 5%	29,000
£830,000	31,000

(b) **Drill Ltd**

If the company is a borrower in a loan relationship, it will have loan relationship debits which include loan interest payable and incidental costs including those incurred in bringing a loan relationship into existence such as the loan arrangement fee.

If the loan relationship is for a trade purpose (trading loan relationship), any debits charged through its accounts are allowed as a trading expense and are therefore deductible in computing trading profits. If the loan relationship is for a non-trade purpose (non-trading loan relationship) non-trade debits must be netted off against non-trade credits such as the £50 bank interest received by Drill Ltd each year.

In this case, one-quarter of the building will be rented out as an investment so that one-quarter of the cost of the building (£1,200,000 × ¼ = £300,000) will be for non-trading purposes. Therefore £(300,000/1,350,000 × 100) = 22.2% of the loan will be a non-trading loan relationship and the remaining 77.8% will be a trading loan relationship which will be dealt with as described above.

There will be a deficit on the non-trading loan relationship which can be relieved as follows:

(i) Deducted from any profit of the same accounting period
(ii) Surrendered for group relief
(iii) Deducted from non-trading loan relationship credits in the previous 12 months
(iv) Deducted from non-trading profits of the company for succeeding accounting periods

(c) **Cog Ltd**

Replacement of business assets (rollover) relief

Rollover relief will not be available to relieve the chargeable gain arising on the sale of Cog Ltd's warehouse. This is because the warehouse was not a qualifying asset when it was sold since it was not used in the trade of Cog Ltd.

Drill Ltd's capital losses

In general, two members of a chargeable gains group, such as Drill Ltd and Cog Ltd, can elect to transfer all or part of a capital gain between them in order to utilise a brought forward capital loss.

However, Drill Ltd's capital losses are pre-entry capital losses since they were made before Drill Ltd joined the Helm Ltd group. These losses can therefore only be relieved against gains on assets which:

(i) Drill Ltd disposed of before joining the Helm Ltd group
(ii) Drill Ltd already owned when it joined the Helm Ltd group
(iii) Drill Ltd acquired after joining the Helm Ltd group from someone outside that group

Therefore, Drill Ltd's capital losses cannot be transferred to Cog Ltd and used to relieve the chargeable gain on the sale of the warehouse.

(d) **Becoming tax advisers to Gomez and the Helm Ltd group**

Information required

(i) Gomez: independent evidence of identity (such as a passport, driving licence, HM Revenue & Customs document such as a notice of coding) and proof of address.

(ii) Helm Ltd group: proof of incorporation of each company; primary business addresses and registered office; identifying members and directors of the companies; establishing the identities of those persons giving instructions on behalf of the companies and verifying that those persons are authorised to do so.

Actions to take

(i) Consider any threats to compliance with the fundamental principles of professional ethics (such as integrity and professional competence) which may arise by becoming tax advisers to Gomez and the Helm Ltd group.

(ii) If any such threats are identified, determine whether safeguards can be implemented to reduce those threats to an acceptable level. If appropriate safeguards cannot be implemented, we should decline to act.

(iii) Ascertain whether there are any professional or other reasons for not accepting the engagement, for example by direct communication with the existing accountant to establish the facts and circumstances behind the proposed change.

25 Flame plc group (12/12)

Text references. Chargeable gains for companies are covered in Chapter 21 and the degrouping charge in Chapter 26. Capital allowances are dealt with in Chapter 7 and the calculation of taxable total profits in Chapter 20. Corporation tax liability is in Chapter 20. Company share option plans are covered in Chapter 5. Value added tax (VAT) on land and buildings will be found in Chapter 29. Ethics is covered in Chapter 30, which also has a section on approaching questions on the impact of taxes.

Top tips. There was a key piece of information in the email from the manager concerning the substantial shareholding exemption. This emphasises the need to read the whole question before starting your answer – don't expect all the information you need to be in one place in the question.

Easy marks. The capital allowances and gains calculations in section (a) were straightforward. The ethical matters in section (b) should have been well known.

Examining team's comments. Answers to part (a)(i) varied in quality quite considerably. There were many candidates who clearly understood the two alternatives and the related tax implications whilst weaker candidates were unsure of the precise nature of the transactions and the related tax implications, such that they produced confused answers. A small minority of candidates treated the companies as individuals.

The sale of Inferno Ltd had two main implications; a chargeable gain on the sale of the shares and a degrouping charge. The chargeable gain was worth one mark. However, it took some candidates half a page or more to calculate and write about this gain in order to score that mark. This was most likely because it was the first thing they did in the exam and there were still almost three hours to go, such that the pressure was not yet on. Candidates must approach every mark in the exam in the same way and get on with it. There is no time to dither when there is so much to do.

Frustratingly, it was not uncommon for some candidates to only score half a mark for this gain because they based the indexation allowance on the unindexed gain rather than the cost. This may have been a lack of concentration rather than a lack of knowledge but the half mark was still lost.

It was stated in the question that the substantial shareholding exemption was not available. Many candidates simply included a statement to that effect in their report and earned a mark. However, a small minority of candidates wasted time writing at length about the exemption rather than getting on with the question.

The degrouping charge was done well on the whole. Those candidates who did not do so well were divided into two groups. The first group missed the degrouping charge altogether. This was perhaps due to a lack of knowledge but, in view of the fact that degrouping charges are examined regularly, was more likely due to a lack of thought. Candidates must give themselves time in the exam to think about issues before they start writing; it is difficult to successfully think of one issue whilst writing about a different one.

The second group of candidates knew that there would be a degrouping charge somewhere in the answer and earned most of the marks available for saying why and for calculating it. However, they did not know which of the two possible transactions would give rise to the charge and either put it into the wrong section of the report or put it into both sections. This was not particularly costly, but would have been in a different question which was only concerned with one of these two transactions. Candidates must know their stuff; degrouping charges only occur on the sale of a company, ie on the sale of shares, and not on the sale of assets.

The sale by Inferno Ltd of its trade and assets was not done particularly well. A small minority of candidates treated the disposal as the disposal of a single asset by adding up all of the proceeds and then deducting the total cost. Even those candidates who knew that each asset had to be handled separately failed to apply basic rules concerning capital allowances and chargeable gains.

Capital allowances were handled particularly poorly with very few candidates identifying that where the tax written down value is zero, any sale of machinery must result in a balancing charge. In addition, most candidates calculated capital losses on the sale of the machinery, thus failing to recognise that, due to the claiming of capital allowances, no capital losses would be available. Finally, only a minority of candidates identified that the deferred gain of £8,500 would crystallise on the sale of the milling machine; most candidates thought, incorrectly, that the gain would be deducted from the asset's base cost. A final thought on part (a)(i) relates to the narrative provided by candidates in their reports. The question required candidates to include concise explanations of matters where the calculations were not self-explanatory. On the whole this was done well. Most candidates kept their answers brief and very few fell into the trap of writing down everything they knew about the broad technical areas relating to the question.

Part (a)(ii) concerned a Schedule 4 company share option plan. This was a straightforward question that tested candidates' knowledge of a particular share scheme. In order to do well, candidates needed to slow down for a moment and make sure that they were about to write about the correct scheme. They then needed to ensure that they addressed all of the issues set out in the question. The majority of candidates did both of these things and therefore scored well.

In part (b), candidates needed to realise that this refund had been received some time ago and that, if it had been paid in error, it had to be returned to HM Revenue & Customs. Most candidates recognised this situation and were able to list the actions that the firm needed to take and the matters that needed to be drawn to the attention of Bon Ltd.

Marking scheme

				Marks
(a)	(i)	*Sale of share capital*		
		Calculations		
		Gain (including degrouping charge)	2	
		Corporation tax	½	
		Narrative – one mark for each relevant point	5	
		Sale of trade and assets		
		Calculations		
		Equipment and milling machine	2	
		Goodwill	½	
		Premises	1½	
		Liability	½	
		Narrative – one mark for each relevant point	3	
				15
	(ii)	*Advantages*		
		Timing	2½	
		Taxes	3½	
		Suitability of CSOP	1	
		Restrictions	2	
		Max		8
	(iii)	Nature of supply	1	
		Recoverable input tax	2	
				3
		Format and presentation	1	
		Analysis	2	
		Quality of calculations and explanations	1	
				4
(b)		The need to repay the tax	3	
		Ceasing to act	3	
		Max		5
				35

(a) (i) Flame plc – sale of Inferno Ltd

Sale by Flame plc of the whole of the ordinary share capital of Inferno Ltd for £1 million

A sale of the share capital will result in a liability to corporation tax calculated as follows:

	£	£
Proceeds on sale of shares		1,000,000
Degrouping charge – deemed sale proceeds		
Market value of the premises at 15 March 2014	300,000	
Less: Cost of premises 1 January 2010	(240,000)	
Indexation allowance £240,000 × 0.169	(40,560)	
		19,440
Total sale proceeds		1,019,440
Less: Cost of shares in Inferno Ltd 1 March 2014		(600,000)
Indexation allowance £600,000 × 0.100		(60,000)
Chargeable gain		359,440
Corporation tax £359,440 @ 19%		68,294

Due to the unavailability of the substantial shareholding exemption, the sale of Inferno Ltd will result in a gain chargeable to corporation tax.

A degrouping charge will arise in respect of the building because it was transferred at no gain, no loss (Flame plc and Inferno Ltd are members of a capital gains group) within the six years prior to the sale of Inferno Ltd. Inferno Ltd will be regarded as having sold the building at the time of the no gain, no loss transfer for its market value at that time. In the computation of the degrouping charge, Inferno Ltd's base cost in the building, resulting from the no gain, no loss transfer, is the original cost to Flame plc plus indexation allowance up to 15 March 2014, the date Inferno Ltd purchased the building. The degrouping charge will increase the sales proceeds on the disposal of Inferno Ltd.

Sale by Inferno Ltd of its trade and assets for their market value

A sale of the trade and assets will result in a liability to corporation tax calculated as follows:

	£	£
Balancing charge on sale of equipment and milling machine £([60,000 + 80,000] – 0)		140,000
Profit on sale of goodwill £(530,000 – 0)		530,000
Additional trading profits		670,000
Crystallisation of gain deferred on milling machine		8,500

Chargeable gain on sale of premises

	£	£	£
Proceeds		490,000	
Cost	240,000		
Indexation allowance to March 2014			
£240,000 × 0.169	40,560		
Indexed cost: No gain, No loss transfer		(280,560)	
Indexation allowance to January 2019			
£280,560 × 0.100		(28,056)	
			181,384
Taxable profits			859,884
Corporation tax £859,884 @ 19%			163,378

The excess of the sales proceeds (market value) of the equipment and the milling machine over the balance on the main pool will result in a taxable balancing charge.

The goodwill is a trading asset so the profit on its sale will be additional trading income.

When a rollover relief claim has been made in respect of the purchase of a depreciating asset, as in the case of the milling machine, the deferred gain crystallises on the sale of that replacement asset.

The equipment and the milling machine are to be sold for less than cost. However, no capital loss will arise because capital allowances have been claimed.

As noted above, Inferno Ltd's base cost in the building is the original price paid by Flame plc plus indexation allowance up to March 2014.

(ii) **Flame plc – employee share scheme**

The tax advantages of a Schedule 4 company share option plan (CSOP) over a non-tax advantaged scheme

(1) With a CSOP, there would be no income tax or national insurance contributions liability on the grant or exercise of the option, provided it is exercised between three and ten years after it is granted. Under a non-tax advantaged scheme, there would be a liability when the option is exercised.

(2) With a CSOP, the whole of the employee's profit on the shares will be subject to capital gains tax when the shares are sold. Under a non-tax advantaged scheme, the excess of the market value of the shares at the time the option is exercised over the amount paid by the employee for the shares will be taxable as specific employment income and so subject to income tax and national insurance contributions in the year the option is exercised; any subsequent increase in the value of the shares will be subject to capital gains tax when the shares are sold.

The advantages of a charge to capital gains tax over charges to income tax and national insurance contributions are the availability of the annual exempt amount and the lower tax rates.

Suitability of a CSOP

Gordon wants to use the scheme to reward the company's senior managers as opposed to all of the company's staff. Accordingly, he needs to use a scheme that allows him to choose which employees are able to join. The two tax-advantaged schemes that allow this are the CSOP and the enterprise management incentive scheme.

Restrictions

(i) The value of shares in respect of which an employee holds options cannot exceed £30,000.

(ii) The exercise price of the shares must not be less than the value of the shares at the time of the grant of the option.

(iii) **Bon Ltd – the grant of a lease**

If Bon Ltd were to opt to tax the building, the proposed granting of the lease would be a standard rated supply rather than an exempt supply, so Bon Ltd would have to charge value added tax (VAT) on the rent. A lessee that was registered for VAT and making wholly taxable supplies would be able to recover all of the VAT charged. However, some or all of the VAT would be a cost for a lessee that was not registered or one that was partially exempt and not within the *de minimis* limits.

(b) **Refund of corporation tax**

We should review the tax affairs of Bon Ltd in order to identify the reason for the tax refund.

If, as would appear likely, it is an error on the part of HM Revenue & Customs (HMRC), we should inform Bon Ltd that it should be repaid immediately. Failure to return the money in these circumstances may be a civil and/or criminal offence.

We should advise Bon Ltd to disclose the matter to HMRC immediately in order to minimise any interest and penalties that might otherwise become payable.

In addition, unless the money is returned, we would have to consider ceasing to act as advisers to Bon Ltd. In these circumstances, we are required to notify the tax authorities that we no longer act for the company, although we would not provide them with any reason for our action. We should also consider whether or not we are required to make a report under the money laundering rules.

26 Bond Ltd group (12/14)

Text references. Computation of taxable total profits and the patent box election are dealt with in Chapter 20. Losses are covered in Chapter 24. Capital allowances are the subject of Chapter 7 and the allocation of the annual investment allowance (AIA) is dealt with in Chapter 26. Rollover relief for companies is covered in Chapter 21. Partial exemption and the capital goods scheme are dealt with in Chapter 29.

Top tips. In part (a), 11 marks were available for the written notes on the calculation of the corporation tax liability of Bond Ltd so it was important that you dealt with the matters raised in detail.

Easy marks. There were some easy marks in part (a) for explaining basic principles such as capital allowances in a short period of account, losses brought forward and rollover relief.

Examining team's comments. Part (a) required candidates to calculate the corporation tax liability of a company for a six-month accounting period and to include notes on various aspects of the computation. Almost all candidates identified that they were dealing with a six-month accounting period, but many of them did not recognise the areas where this point was relevant, ie the annual investment allowance and the rate of writing down allowance. It was stated in the question that the required notes represented approximately two-thirds of the marks available and it was pleasing that most candidates picked up on this guidance and addressed all three areas on which notes were required in various levels of detail. The capital allowances were handled reasonably well with most candidates recognising the mistake the client had made. However, many candidates did not recognise that the expenditure that did not qualify for the additional investment allowance would qualify for writing down allowances. Of those that did, many forgot to reduce the rate of the writing down allowance by 6/12 to reflect the length of the accounting period. The use of the company's brought forward trading losses required candidates to consider two matters. First, had the company changed its trade? If it had, the losses brought forward could not be used in the future. Secondly, because there had been a change in ownership of the company, it was necessary to consider if there had been a major change in the nature or conduct of the trade. The company's trade continued to be the baking and selling of bread and baked products. However, the changes made to its products and customers were likely to represent a major change in the nature or conduct of the trade, such that the losses could not be carried forward beyond the date of the change of ownership of the company. The third area of explanatory notes concerned rollover relief. In order to score well here, candidates had to first be aware of the meaning of a qualifying business asset for the purposes of rollover relief and the qualifying period for reinvestment. Qualifying business assets include land and buildings and fixed plant and machinery used in the business. Most candidates were not sufficiently clear on these rules. The qualifying time period was identified by the majority of candidates. Candidates then had to consider the chargeable gains group aspects of rollover relief. A sizeable minority of candidates did not consider this aspect and, of those who did, a minority thought that Madison Ltd, a 65% subsidiary, was a member of the gains group because the holding was more than 50%. However, the direct holding between each company in the group has to be at least 75%; it is any indirect holding between the principal company and a non-directly held subsidiary that has to be more than 50%. Finally, candidates had to point out that only part of the gain can be rolled over if only part of the sales proceeds are reinvested in qualifying replacement assets. Although many candidates were aware of this point, not all of them were able to calculate the amount of gain that could be rolled over given a specific level of reinvestment in the question.

Part (b) required candidates to write briefly about the patent box regime. This aspect of the question was mainly knowledge-based. A minority of candidates were not aware of the regime and consequently did not score well. Those who knew about the regime scored well provided they took care to address the requirement and made separately identifiable points rather than repeating themselves. As always, time spent identifying relevant points before putting pen to paper was time well spent.

Part (c) concerned the value added tax (VAT) capital goods scheme. Despite this being examined regularly, it was not tackled particularly well. Many candidates thought, incorrectly, that the scheme applies to plant and machinery generally. The way in which the scheme operates was also misunderstood by many candidates who were unable to explain the adjustments that would be made in future years. This aspect of VAT is not part of the Taxation (TX – UK) syllabus and thus is new knowledge in Advanced Taxation (ATX – UK). It should be regarded as an area that is likely to continue to be examined regularly in future Advanced Taxation (ATX – UK) exams.

		Marks	
(a)	Corporation tax computation		
	Taxable total profits	2	
	Corporation tax liability	½	
	Capital allowances		
	Maximum AIA for short accounting period	1	
	Group aspect	1	
	Calculation of adjustment to capital allowances	1½	
	Losses brought forward		
	Set against future profits of same trade	2	
	Major change in the nature or conduct of trade	3	
	Replacement of business assets relief	5	
			16
(b)	Identification of each relevant point – one mark		
	Possible points include:		
	Availability of scheme		
	Election for treatment		
	Meaning of patent profits		
	10% rate		
			4
(c)	Building		
	Original recovery	1	
	Capital goods scheme	1	
	Example	2	
	Machinery	1	
			5
			25

(a) **Bond Ltd – corporation tax computation for the six months ended 30 September 2018**

	Notes	£
Tax-adjusted trading income as previously calculated		470,000
Add: Reduction in capital allowances		
£(180,000 – 107,200)	1	72,800
Less trading losses brought forward	2	(0)
Revised tax-adjusted trading income		542,800
Chargeable gain	3	40,000
Taxable total profits		582,800
Corporation tax @ 19%		110,732

Notes

1   *Capital allowances*

The maximum annual investment allowance (AIA) for the 6-month period to 30 September 2018 is £200,000 × 6/12 = £100,000. Bond Ltd and Ungar Ltd are in a group and therefore are entitled to a single AIA between the group companies. Bond Ltd and Ungar Ltd can decide how to allocate the AIA between them and they should do so in the most beneficial way, taking into account the nature of the expenditure by each company (eg main pool, special rate pool).

Assuming that the AIA is wholly allocated to Bond Ltd, the capital allowances for the period are:

	AIA £	Main pool £	Allowances £
Additions qualifying for AIA	180,000		
AIA	(100,000)		100,000
Transfer to pool	80,000	80,000	
WDA @ 18% × 6/12		(7,200)	7,200
TWDV c/f		72,800	
Maximum capital allowances			107,200

2 *Trading losses brought forward*

Trading losses can be carried forward and deducted from income of the same trade in future accounting periods. Bond Ltd is carrying on the same trade before and after 1 April 2016 (baking and selling bread and other baked profits).

However, trading losses may be restricted where there is a change in ownership of a company and, for example, there has been a major change in the nature or conduct of the trade within three years after the change of ownership. This restriction will probably apply in the case of Bond Ltd as it previously only sold low-cost products to schools, hospitals and prisons but now 65% of its turnover and 90% of its profits relate to high-quality products sold to supermarkets and independent retailers.

If the restriction applies, losses incurred before the change in ownership on 1 April 2016 cannot be carried forward against post-acquisition profits. Therefore, the trading losses which arose up to 31 March 2016 cannot be set against the profits for the period ended 30 September 2018.

Tutorial note. If the restriction is relevant, it also applies to the two previous accounting periods ended 31 March 2017 and 31 March 2018. This means that it will be necessary to recalculate Bond Ltd's corporation tax liability for those periods.

3 *Rollover relief*

A gain on a qualifying business asset may be relieved where the proceeds on the disposal of that asset are matched with expenditure on another qualifying business asset under replacement of business assets (rollover) relief. The members of a chargeable gains group are treated as a single unit for the purpose of claiming such relief. Bond Ltd and Ungar Ltd are in a chargeable gains group because Bond Ltd owns at least 75% of Ungar Ltd. Madison Ltd is not in the chargeable gains group because Bond Ltd only owns 65% of that company.

Bond Ltd can therefore match its gain with acquisitions made by itself or by Ungar Ltd within the period starting 1 May 2017 and ending 30 April 2021. Full relief will be available if the expenditure is at least £350,000. Otherwise, there will be a chargeable gain equal to the amount of proceeds not reinvested, up to a maximum equal to the gain of £180,000.

The only qualifying acquisition about which there is information is the building acquired by Ungar Ltd on 1 July 2017 for £310,000. Rollover relief of £140,000 (£180,000 – £40,000) would be available on this acquisition as £(350,000 – 310,000) = £40,000 of the gain is left in charge.

Further relief may be available if there are more acquisitions of qualifying assets, for example if there are items of fixed plant within the purchases of plant and machinery made by Bond Ltd.

(b) **Ungar Ltd – patent box election**

The patent box scheme could apply to Ungar Ltd as it has patent profits attributable to qualifying patents because it has carried on qualifying development in relation to the patents for new baking processes and techniques.

Ungar Ltd would need to make an election to HM Revenue & Customs for the patent box scheme to apply.

Patent profits within the patent box would include royalty income received directly from qualifying patents and a proportion of Ungar Ltd's profits in respect of the sale of products incorporating the use of those patents.

A reduced rate of corporation tax applies to profits within the patent box by deducting an amount from the company's taxable profits so that, when the corporation tax rate is applied to the reduced figure, the effective rate is 10% on the patent box profits.

(c) **Recovery of value added tax (VAT) on assets acquired by Madison Ltd**

Building

The capital goods scheme will apply to the building because it cost £250,000 or more.

Madison Ltd will be able to recover (£400,000 × 20% = £80,000) × 80% = £64,000 on the building in the year ended 30 September 2019.

For each subsequent VAT year, during the recovery period of ten years, an adjustment will be made to the VAT recovery. The adjustment is equal to the difference in percentage use between the first VAT year and the VAT year under review × 1/10 × the original input tax. For example, if the percentage in the year to 30 September 2020 is 75%, Madison Ltd would need to repay to HM Revenue & Customs:

((80% − 75%) = 5%) × 1/10 × £80,000 = £400.

Machinery

The capital goods scheme does not apply to machinery. Madison Ltd will be able to recover £300,000 × 20% × 80% = £48,000 on the machinery in the year ended 30 September 2019 and there will be no adjustment in later years.

27 Maria and Granada Ltd (Mar/Jun 16) (amended)

Text references. Purchase of own shares will be found in Chapter 23 and losses in Chapter 24. Intangible assets are covered in Chapter 20. Value added tax (VAT) on a transfer of a going concern is dealt with in Chapter 28 and on land and buildings in Chapter 29.

Top tips. Make sure you follow each requirement carefully in this question to ensure you are answering each sub-requirement fully. It's actually lots of smaller questions about separate topics which will make the question less intimidating. If you don't remember the rules for a purchase of own shares to be treated as capital then look them up quickly in your notes and then have a go at the calculations.

Easy marks. The tax treatment for companies for intangibles and the transfer of a going concern rules are commonly examined and thus should have allowed you easy marks in this question.

Examining team's comments. Part (a)(i) of this question focused on the requirement for the sale of shares by an individual shareholder to the company to result in a 'substantial reduction' in their shareholding in order to receive capital treatment on the disposal. Unfortunately, it would appear that this is an aspect of a company purchasing its own shares which many candidates are not comfortable with. A small number of candidates just reproduced the conditions to be satisfied in order to obtain capital treatment, which was not required and so scored no marks.

Of those candidates who did try to answer this part of the question, the most common mistake was to forget that when a company repurchases shares from a shareholder, the shares are cancelled so that the total issued share capital of the company is reduced as a consequence.

Part (a)(ii) of this question required the calculation of after-tax proceeds on the disposal of two alternative numbers of shares from a shareholding, one of which did qualify for capital treatment and one of which didn't. This information was given in the requirements. In spite of this, a lack of technical knowledge or inadequate reading of the question meant that a significant number of candidates did not apply this and treated both disposals as giving rise to chargeable gains, rather than correctly treating one of them as a distribution. Additionally, many candidates failed to recognise that the disposal which attracted capital treatment would also qualify for entrepreneurs' relief. In any question regarding the disposal of shares by an individual, candidates should automatically consider the application of entrepreneurs' relief. This is an area where it is very important to know the precise conditions and to be able to state definitively whether or not the relief applies, and the reasons why or why not. Candidates who went on to calculate the after-tax proceeds generally identified the correct starting point on this occasion, which was pleasing.

Part (b)(i) concerned the tax deductions available to a company on the acquisition of an intangible asset. There were very few good answers to this part of the question. Intangible assets are examined frequently in Advanced Taxation (ATX – UK), so candidates need to be aware of their tax treatment as trading assets, rather than capital assets, for companies, and the consequential tax treatment of these for corporation tax purposes.

Part (b)(ii) required candidates to explain how the company could get tax relief for a loss incurred by a recently acquired trade. Several candidates incorrectly discussed group relief here. This was not the acquisition of shares in a company, which would have created a group, but the acquisition of trade and assets from a partnership. The two situations are completely different, and candidates must take care to ensure that they read and interpret the facts in this type of question correctly.

It appeared that many candidates would have benefited from pausing and thinking more before they started to write. It is important in any question dealing with relief for losses that a well-considered and logical approach is taken. Well-prepared candidates were able to identify that at least part of the trading loss would have to be carried forward, relief for which would be restricted to profits from the same trade, and discussed the relevance of proposed changes to the trade in this context.

Part (c) required an explanation of the VAT implications of the acquisition of the business and additional information needed to fully clarify the VAT position in relation to a building. The majority of candidates were able to identify that the transaction would not be liable to VAT as it concerned the transfer of a going concern. Candidates who performed less well on this part, however, then went on to explain why the going concern rules applied, stating all the conditions, but reasons **why** a particular treatment applies aren't required in a discussion of the VAT implications of that treatment. The VAT rules relating to property are very frequently tested in Advanced Taxation (ATX – UK) and it was good to see that the majority of candidates were aware of the main facts here in relation to the age of the building and the existence, or otherwise of an option to tax.

Marking scheme

					Marks
(a)	(i)	Sale of 2,700 shares		3½	
		Sale of 3,200 shares		1	
			Max		4
	(ii)	Sale of 2,700 shares		2½	
		Sale of 3,200 shares		2	
			Max		4
(b)	(i)	Entitled to deduction		1	
		Writing down allowance		1	
		Impairment/consistent treatment		1	
					3
	(ii)	Current year relief		2	
		Carry forward		1½	
		Relevance of change in nature of trade		2	
			Max		5
(c)		General implications of going concern transfer		1	
		Additional information		4	
			Max		4
					20

(a)   (i)   **Sale of 2,700 shares back to Granada Ltd**

For capital gains tax treatment to apply, Maria's shareholding in Granada Ltd must be reduced to no more than 75% of her pre-sale holding.

Maria has a 25% shareholding before the sale. Therefore, after the sale her shareholding must be reduced to no more than 75% × 25% = 18.75%.

The total number of shares in issue after the sale will be reduced as the shares repurchased by the company are cancelled.

Maria will hold 10,000 – 2,700 = 7,300 shares out of (10,000 × 4) – 2,700 = 37,300 total shares in issue. This is a (7,300/37,300) × 100% = 19.6% holding, ie greater than 18.75%, so that the condition relating to the reduction in the level of shareholding will not be met.

Sale of 3,200 shares back to Granada Ltd

Maria will now hold 10,000 – 3,200 = 6,800 shares out of 40,000 – 3,200 = 36,800 total shares in issue. This is an (6,800/36,800) × 100% = 18.5% holding, ie less than 18.75%, so that the condition relating to the reduction in the level of shareholding will be met.

(ii) **Sale of 2,700 shares back to Granada Ltd**

The income tax payable in respect of each share is £(12.80 – 1.00) × 32.5% = £3.83.

The post-tax proceeds per share are therefore £(12.80 – 3.83) = £8.97.

Tutorial notes

1   As Maria does not satisfy all of the conditions for this sale to be dealt with under the capital gains tax rules, the disposal will be treated as an income distribution and Maria will have an income tax liability.

2   The dividend is the difference between the sale proceeds and the amount originally subscribed.

3   The dividend nil rate band of £5,000 has already been used.

Sale of 3,200 shares back to Granada Ltd

The capital gains tax payable in respect of each share is £(12.80 – 1.00) × 10% = £1.18.

The post-tax proceeds per share are therefore £(12.80 – 1.18) = £11.62.

Tutorial note. The disposal will qualify for entrepreneurs' relief as Maria holds more than 5% of the ordinary shares of Granada Ltd and is a director of the company. The capital gain arising will therefore be taxed at 10%.

(b)   (i)   **Acquisition of the patent**

As the patent is an intangible asset which has been acquired as part of the Starling Partners' trade, it will be treated as a trading asset by Granada Ltd and an allowable deduction will be available in calculating the taxable trading income for each accounting period.

Although Granada Ltd has not made any charge for amortisation in its statement of profit or loss, it may take an annual writing down allowance for tax purposes equal to 4% of the cost of the patent, on a straight line basis. This would be £40,000 × 4% = £1,600 per year.

If an election is made to claim the 4% writing down allowance, any accounting debits for impairment would be disallowable for tax purposes. Such an election would be irrevocable.

(ii)   **Relief for the expected loss from the former Starling Partners' trade**

As Starling Partners is an unincorporated business, Granada Ltd took over ownership of the assets and responsibility for the trade following its acquisition on 1 January 2019.

The forecast trading loss of £130,000 from Starling Partners' handbag trade could be offset against Granada Ltd's total income for the year ending 31 December 2019, comprising the trading profit from the knitwear business of £100,000 and the chargeable gain of £10,000.

So a loss of £20,000 (£130,000 – £110,000) will be left unrelieved.

As Granada Ltd does not want to carry any of the loss back, the unrelieved loss of £20,000 must be carried forward for relief against the first available future profits from the same trade. This will exclude any future profits from Granada Ltd's knitwear manufacturing business.

Granada Ltd wishes to change the nature of the Starling Partners' trade, by starting to sell to the export market from 1 January 2020. Although this may be seen as a major change in the nature of the trade, it should not serve to prevent the loss incurred in the year ended 31 December 2019 from being carried forward providing HM Revenue & Customs (HMRC) agree that, essentially, the same trade is being carried on. The impact of a major change in the nature or conduct of a trade in restricting loss relief is only relevant where it precedes or follows a change in ownership of a company, not the acquisition of the trade and assets from an unincorporated business.

Accordingly, based on the expected profit, £15,000 of the carried forward loss may be relieved in the year ending 31 December 2020, and the remaining £5,000 will be carried forward for relief in future years.

(c)   **Value added tax (VAT) implications following the acquisition of the trade and assets of Starling Partners**

For VAT purposes, the transfer of Starling Partners' trade and assets qualified as a transfer of a going concern (TOGC). Therefore no VAT will have been charged on the transfer of the assets generally, and so there will have been no input VAT for Granada Ltd to reclaim.

However, additional information is needed in respect of the building, as its treatment will depend on its age and whether or not the option to tax has been exercised.

Age of the building: If the building was less than three years old at 1 January 2019, its sale would have been a taxable supply, chargeable to VAT at the standard rate.

Option to tax: If the building was more than three years old, its sale would have been exempt from VAT, unless Starling Partners exercised the option to tax.

If the building was less than three years old or Starling Partners had opted to tax the building, then the transfer would have been a taxable supply, chargeable to VAT at the standard rate. In either case, to bring the transfer of the building within the TOGC regime, so that no VAT is charged, Granada Ltd must also have opted to tax the building, prior to the date of transfer. Alternatively, if Granada Ltd did not opt to tax the building, but uses the building in its business, it may obtain an input credit for the VAT charged.

28 Bamburg Ltd (06/14)

Text references. The flat rate scheme for value added tax (VAT) is covered in Chapter 28. Capital allowances are covered in Chapter 7 and replacement of business assets relief in Chapter 13. The computation of income tax is dealt with in Chapter 1 and national insurance contributions on employment income in Chapter 4. Close companies are covered in Chapter 25.

Top tips. In part (c), don't forget to consider the national insurance implications of a loan benefit.

Easy marks. There were some easy marks for describing the flat rate scheme in part (a). The rules on close companies in part (c) are frequently examined.

Examining team's comments. Part (a) concerned the VAT flat rate scheme. Candidates were required to explain whether or not a particular company could join the scheme and the matters that needed to be considered in order to determine whether or not it would be financially beneficial to do so. Almost all candidates realised that the ability of the company to join the scheme depended on its taxable supplies being below the limit of £150,000. However, a small minority did not apply their knowledge to the facts of the question where there was sufficient information to reach a conclusion in respect of the company concerned. The matters that needed to be considered in relation to the financial implications of joining the scheme were not handled particularly well, with many candidates appearing to be somewhat confused as to the implications of joining the scheme. This was partly due to mixing up the flat rate scheme with other VAT special schemes and also due to a lack of methodical thought. In particular, candidates should have slowed down and tried to explain the payments made to HM Revenue & Customs (HMRC) under the existing arrangements and the payments that would be made under the flat rate scheme so that a comparison could be made.

In part (b), candidates were required to explain 'the tax and financial implications' of proposals to sell a machine and rent a replacement. When candidates read the model answer to this question they will realise that this was not a challenging requirement. However, very few candidates scored well. The problem here was that candidates started writing before they had identified the issues. As a consequence of this, most candidates addressed the chargeable gain point and very little else. This was unfortunate as the chargeable gain point was not as easy as it appeared, such that many candidates got it wrong. Other points that most candidates should have been well equipped to tackle if they had thought to do so included: a balancing charge would arise, the inability to offset capital losses against trading profits and the rent representing a cost to the company that would reduce its taxable profits.

The final part of the question concerned the extraction of funds from the company by its owner, Charlotte, and was split into two sub-requirements. The first part required calculations of the cost to the company of providing Charlotte with post-tax income of £14,000. This was relatively challenging and was not done particularly well. Candidates needed to identify that Charlotte was a higher rate taxpayer and paying national insurance contributions at the margin at the rate of 2% in order to gross up the amount required at the appropriate rate. They then had to identify that the company would have to pay employer's national insurance contributions and that this would be a tax-deductible expense for the purposes of corporation tax. A minority of candidates did not read the question carefully enough, such that they calculated the cost to Charlotte of being paid a bonus or a dividend of £14,000.

Marking scheme

				Marks
(a)	Eligibility		1½	
	VAT due normally		1	
	VAT due under flat rate scheme		3	
	Conclusion		1	
		Max		5
(b)	One mark for each relevant point			5
(c)	(i) Payment of bonus		3½	
	Payment of dividend		2	
		Max		5
	(ii) Charlotte		1½	
	Bamburg Ltd			
	Close company loan to participator		2½	
	Class 1A national insurance contribution		1	
	Exemption not applicable		1	
		Max		5
				20

(a) VAT flat rate scheme

Bamburg Ltd will be permitted to join the flat rate scheme provided its taxable supplies for the next year are not expected to exceed £150,000. On the basis that its budgeted taxable supplies for the year ending 31 March 2019 are expected to be £114,000 (£120,000 – £6,000), it is likely that this condition will be satisfied.

Bamburg Ltd currently pays VAT to HMRC equal to the output tax on its standard rated sales less its recoverable input tax.

Under the flat rate scheme, the company would pay HMRC a fixed percentage of the total of its VAT inclusive sales. Exempt supplies are included in sales for this purpose. The percentage usually depends on the particular business sector in which Bamburg Ltd operates. There is a rate of 16.5% for traders who purchase no, or a limited amount, of goods.

Whether or not it is financially beneficial for Bamburg Ltd to join the flat rate scheme will depend on the percentage which it is required to use. However, the scheme is primarily intended to reduce administration and any financial benefit is unlikely to be significant.

(b) Implications of selling the 'Cara' machine

The balance on the main pool of Bamburg Ltd is nil. This means that the sale of the machine will result in a balancing charge equal to the sales proceeds received of £80,000 which will increase the taxable trade profit of Bamburg Ltd.

The 'Cara' machine is a depreciating asset for the purposes of replacement of business assets. Therefore the chargeable gain of £13,000 which was deferred in respect of the purchase of the 'Cara' machine will become chargeable when the machine is sold. This will increase the taxable total profit of Bamburg Ltd in the year of sale.

No allowable capital loss will arise on the sale of the machine because it qualified for capital allowances.

In summary, Bamburg Ltd will receive proceeds of £80,000 but will have to pay additional corporation tax of £(80,000 + 13,000) × 19% = £17,670.

Once the machine has been sold, Bamburg Ltd will have to pay rent in respect of the replacement machine. This represents an outflow of cash for the company, although it will be an allowable deduction when computing the company's taxable trading profit.

(c) (i) Bamburg Ltd to make an additional payment to Charlotte of £14,000

Payment of bonus

	£
Bonus required £(14,000/(100 − 42)%)	24,138
Employer's national insurance £24,138 × 13.8%	3,331
	27,469
Less reduction in corporation tax £27,469 × 19%	(5,219)
Total cost to Bamburg Ltd	22,250

Payment of dividend

	£
Dividend covered by dividend nil rate band	5,000
Dividend taxed at basic rate	
£([14,000 − 5,000]/(100 − 32.5)%)	13,333
Cash dividend	18,333

Tutorial note. Charlotte's salary of £46,000 will mean that the bonus will be subject to income tax at 40% and national insurance contributions at 2%.

(ii) Tax implications of Bamburg Ltd making a loan of £14,000 to Charlotte

Charlotte

The interest-free loan will result in an annual employment income benefit for Charlotte because she is an employee of Bamburg Ltd. The benefit will be £350 (£14,000 × 2.5%) on which Charlotte will have to pay income tax at 40%.

Bamburg Ltd

Bamburg Ltd is a close company as it is wholly owned and controlled by Charlotte. When a close company makes a loan to a participator (eg a shareholder), it must pay HMRC an amount equal to 32.5% of the loan, in this case £4,550. This will be payable at the same time as Bamburg Ltd's corporation tax liability by 1 January 2020.

Bamburg Ltd will also have to pay Class 1A national insurance contributions of £(350 × 13.8%) = £48 in respect of the loan benefit. These contributions will be allowable when computing the company's taxable trading profits.

The payment to HMRC will be required even though the loan will be for less than £15,000. This is because Charlotte owns more than 5% of the company.

29 Liza (06/13)

Text references. Chargeable gains for companies are covered in Chapter 21 with chargeable gains groups dealt with in Chapter 26. Capital allowances are the subject of Chapter 7. Value added tax (VAT) groups are covered in Chapter 28.

Top tips. If you choose to answer this type of multiple topic question in the exam, it is important that you are confident that you can achieve reasonable marks on all parts.

Easy marks. The computation of the chargeable gain in part (a) should have yielded easy marks. Group registration for VAT (part (c)) is a standard exam topic.

Examining team's comments. Part (a)(i) required a calculation of the chargeable gain on the sale of a building and the correct treatment of the various expenses incurred in acquiring, enhancing and maintaining the property. This was a gentle introduction to the question and was done well. Part (a)(ii) concerned rollover relief and groups for the purposes of chargeable gains. It was done well by those candidates who knew the rules and who expressed themselves carefully.

This part required candidates to know three things: that rollover relief can be claimed where one company in a gains group sells a qualifying business asset and another company in the group buys one, the definition of a gains group, and the time period in which a replacement asset needs to be purchased in order for rollover relief to be available. The majority of candidates knew the first and third points although a small minority failed to address the third point despite, probably, knowing the rule.

The difficulty came in dealing with the second point and the definition of a gains group where a minority of candidates revealed a level of confusion. This stemmed from a problem in distinguishing the 75% aspect of the rule from the 51% aspect and led to some candidates concluding erroneously that Vault Ltd and Bar Ltd were in a gains group. For there to be a chargeable gains group, the direct holding between each company in the chain must be at least 75%; if it isn't, the two companies cannot be in a group regardless of the level of the indirect holding. Part (a)(iii) concerned the amount that needed to be invested in order for the maximum amount of gain to be rolled over. This was the hardest part of the question and was not done particularly well. It required candidates to know the basic rule whereby the whole of the relevant proceeds has to be spent on replacement assets in order for the maximum gain to be rolled over, whilst recognising the relevance of the non-business use of both the asset sold and the asset acquired. Almost all candidates knew the basic rule but the majority struggled to apply it in these particular circumstances.

Part (b) concerned the availability of capital allowances in respect of electrical, water and heating systems acquired as part of a building and was done well.

Part (c) concerned VAT groups. The idea here was to test another aspect of groups in order to ensure that candidates appreciated the difference between a group for the purposes of VAT and one for the purposes of chargeable gains as tested in part (a). Candidates were also required to identify the advantages and disadvantages of registering as a group for the purposes of VAT. The majority of candidates made a reasonable job of discussing the advantages and disadvantages of registering as a VAT group and made a series of concise points. However, the definition of a group for the purposes of VAT was not handled particularly well. In particular, a sizeable minority of candidates thought that the required holding was 75% as opposed to control. In addition, many candidates did not appreciate that control could be exercised by an individual, ie Liza, as well as by a company, such that all of the companies in the question were able to register as a single group. As always, a minority of candidates wrote in general terms, for example, about partial exemption, rather than addressing the specifics of the question, such that they wasted time.

				Marks
(a)	(i)	Chargeable gain	Max	3
	(ii)	Chargeable gains group	2	
		Identification of relevant companies	1½	
		Qualifying period	1	
			Max	4
	(iii)	Amount relievable via rollover relief	2	
		Total acquisitions necessary	1	
		Further acquisitions necessary	1½	
			Max	4
(b)		Plant and machinery as integral feature	1	
		Special rate pool	½	
		Use of AIA	1	
			Max	2
(c)		Ability to register as a group	2	
		Discussion	6	
			Max	7
				20

(a) (i) **The chargeable gain on the sale of Building I**

	£	£
Net sale proceeds		860,000
Less: Purchase price	315,000	
Legal fees	9,000	
Work on roof to make fit for use	38,000	
		(362,000)
		498,000
Less indexation allowance		
$\frac{277.2 - 241.8}{241.8} = 0.146 \times £362,000$		(52,852)
Chargeable gain		445,148

Tutorial note. A deduction is available for the legal fees incurred in acquiring the building and the costs incurred shortly afterwards in order to make the building fit for use (see *Law Shipping Co Ltd v CIR 1923*). The cost of repainting the building would have been an allowable deduction in calculating the company's trading profits and would not be allowable when computing the chargeable gain.

(ii) **Acquisition of qualifying assets for the purposes of rollover relief**

The assets can be purchased by companies within the Bar Ltd chargeable gains group. A chargeable gains group consists of a principal company, Bar Ltd, its 75% subsidiaries, the 75% subsidiaries of those subsidiaries and so on. Bar Ltd must have an effective interest of more than 50% in all of the companies in the group. Accordingly, the only companies able to purchase qualifying replacement assets are Bar Ltd and Pommel Ltd. Ring Ltd is not a 75% subsidiary of Bar Ltd, such that it and Vault Ltd cannot be members of the Bar Ltd chargeable gains group. The Hoop Ltd group is a separate group.

The qualifying replacement assets must be purchased in the period from 1 June 2017 to 31 May 2021.

(iii) **The additional amount that would need to be spent on qualifying assets**

Bar Ltd owned the building from 1 June 2012 to 31 May 2018, a period of 72 months. The building was not used for trading purposes from 1 January 2014 to 30 June 2015, a period of 18 months.

Accordingly, the building was used for the purposes of the trade for a period of 54 (72–18) months, such that only 54/72 of the gain can be relieved via rollover relief.

Therefore, qualifying business assets costing £645,000 (£860,000 × 54/72) will need to be acquired in order to relieve the whole of the gain qualifying for rollover relief.

Only two-thirds of the new building is to be used for trading purposes, such that only £480,000 (£720,000 × 2/3) of its cost will be a qualifying acquisition for the purposes of rollover relief. Accordingly, the additional amount that would need to be spent on qualifying acquisitions in order to relieve the whole of the gain that qualifies for rollover relief would be £165,000 (£645,000 – £480,000).

(b) **Capital allowances available in respect of the new building**

Electrical, water and heating systems qualify for plant and machinery capital allowances.

They are classified as integral features, such that they are included in the special rate pool where the writing down allowance is only 8%.

The annual investment allowance available to the Bar Ltd group should be set against these additions in priority to those assets which qualify for the 18% writing down allowance.

(c) **Group registration for the purposes of value added tax (VAT)**

The companies able to register as a group

Two or more companies may register as a group provided they are established in the UK, or have a fixed establishment in the UK, and they are controlled by the same person. The person can be an individual, a company, or a partnership. Accordingly, all of the companies in the Bar Ltd and Hoop Ltd groups can register as a single group for the purposes of VAT.

The potential advantages and disadvantages of registering as a group

The advantage of a group registration would be that there would be no need to charge VAT on the transactions between the group companies. This would reduce administration and improve the group's cash flow.

The group would have to appoint a representative member which would account for the group's VAT liability as if the group were a single entity. Consequently, there would be a need to collate information from all of the members of the group and to present it in a single VAT return. This may not be straightforward, depending on the accounting systems and procedures used by the various companies within the two separate groups.

Vault Ltd makes zero rated supplies and will therefore be in a repayment position, such that it can improve its cash flow by accounting for VAT on a monthly basis. However, if it were registered as part of a VAT group, it would not be able to do this as the group, as a single entity, is very unlikely to be in a regular repayment position. Accordingly, if a group registration is to be entered into, consideration should be given to excluding Vault Ltd from that registration.

Finally, it should be recognised that all of the companies within the group registration would have joint and several liability for the VAT due from the representative member. Liza, and the minority shareholders, should give careful consideration to the possible dangers of linking the two groups in such a manner.

30 Banger Ltd and Candle Ltd (12/12)

> **Text references.** Close companies and investment holding companies are covered in Chapter 25. Liquidations are dealt with in Chapter 23. Chargeable gains for companies is the topic of Chapter 21 and overseas aspects are covered in Chapter 27.
>
> **Top tips.** In part (a)(ii), it was important that you dealt with the tax implications for the company and then for the shareholders (which include Katherine who will receive both cash and the building).
>
> **Easy marks.** The treatment of close companies is often examined and there should have been easy marks on the use of the motor car in part (a)(i). The double taxation relief in part (b) was straightforward.

Examining team's comments. Part (a)(i) required candidates to explain the taxable income arising out of the use by a minority shareholder of a car owned by the company. Almost all candidates were able to calculate the benefit in respect of the use of the car but not all of them realised that this would be taxed as a distribution rather than employment income. Many of those who knew this point still failed to earn full marks because they did not state the reasons for this treatment; those reasons being that the company is a close company and that the individual is not an employee.

Part (a)(ii) concerned the treatment of company distributions before and after the appointment of a liquidator. Performance in this part of the question was mixed. Those candidates who did not do well either did not know the rules or were not careful enough in addressing the requirements. A lack of knowledge of the rules was unfortunate and not something that could easily be rectified in the exam room. Failure to address the requirements carefully was a greater shame as potentially easy marks were lost. The requirement asked for the tax implications for 'Banger Ltd, the minority shareholders and Katherine'. Most candidates dealt with the minority shareholders and Katherine but many omitted the implications for Banger Ltd. Candidates should always read the requirement carefully and identify all of the tasks. It would have been helpful then to use sub-headings for each of the three aspects of the requirement to ensure that all of the aspects of the requirement were addressed.

Part (b) required candidates to calculate the corporation tax liability of Candle Ltd. On the whole, this part was done quite well by many candidates.

The two more difficult areas of this part of the question concerned loan relationships and a share for share disposal. The loan relationships issue was not done well. The vast majority of candidates failed to apply the basic rules such that they did not offset the amounts in order to arrive at a deficit on non-trading loan relationships. This was not a difficult or obscure matter; it simply felt as though candidates were not giving themselves the time to think before answering the question.

The share for share disposal was identified by the vast majority of candidates who went on to point out that no chargeable gain would arise in respect of the shares. There was then a further mark for recognising that there would also be no gain in respect of the cash received as it amounted to less than 5% of the total consideration received. This point was picked up by only a small number of candidates.

Marking scheme

					Marks
(a)	(i)	Explanation		2	
		Calculations		1½	
			Max		3
	(ii)	Banger Ltd		2½	
		Shareholders		1½	
		Katherine			
		Capital gain		1½	
		Taxation		2½	
			Max		7
(b)		*Taxable total profits*			
		Loan relationships		3½	
		Chargeable gains		1½	
		Sale of shares in Rockette plc		½	
		Management expenses		½	
		Corporation tax liability			
		Corporation tax		½	
		Double taxation relief		1	
		Explanations		3	
			Max		10
					20

(a) **Banger Ltd**

(i) **Minority shareholder's taxable income in respect of the use of the motor car**

The minority shareholder is not employed by Banger Ltd. Accordingly, because Banger Ltd is a close company (it is controlled by Katherine), the use of the motor car will be treated as a distribution. The distribution will equal the amount that would have been taxable as employment income in respect of the motor car:

Amount by which CO_2 emissions exceed base level: (105 (rounded down) − 95) = 10/5 = 2

Add to 18% = 20%.

The car benefit is therefore £22,900 (list price) × 20% = £4,580.

The taxable income will be equal to the car benefit.

(ii) **The tax implications of the distributions being considered**

Banger Ltd

The distribution of cash will be a normal dividend with no tax implications for Banger Ltd.

The distribution of the building is a dividend *in specie* and therefore a deemed disposal of the building by Banger Ltd at market value. This will result in a chargeable gain or allowable loss equal to the market value of the building less its cost. Indexation allowance will be deducted from any chargeable gain arising.

The shareholders

(1) The distribution of cash to all the shareholders

The distribution of cash is to be made prior to the appointment of the liquidator and will therefore be taxed as a normal dividend. It will be subject to income tax at 0% (within the dividend nil rate band of £5,000), 7.5%, 32.5% and 38.1%, depending on the income tax position of the individual shareholders.

(2) The distribution of the building to Katherine

The distribution is to be made after the appointment of the liquidator and will therefore be taxed as a capital receipt in relation to Katherine's shares. The market value of the building will be treated as the sales proceeds of Katherine's shares in Banger Ltd from which the base cost (or part of the base cost if there are to be further distributions to Katherine) will be deducted in order to calculate the capital gain.

The gain will be taxable at 10% and/or 20% depending on Katherine's income tax position or, alternatively, at 10% where entrepreneurs' relief is available regardless of her income tax position. Banger Ltd is a trading company. Accordingly, entrepreneurs' relief will be available, provided that Katherine has owned at least 5% of the ordinary share capital and can exercise at least 5% of the voting rights in the company by virtue of that holding of shares, and has been an officer or employee of Banger Ltd. Both these conditions must have been satisfied throughout the period of one year ending with the date of disposal (ie the date of the distribution).

(b) **Candle Ltd – corporation tax liability for the year ended 31 March 2018**

	Total £	UK £	Non-UK £
Chargeable gain realised in Sisaria			
£15,770 × 100/83	19,000		19,000
Chargeable gains realised in the UK	83,700	83,700	
Sale of shares in Rockette plc (Note)	0	0	
	102,700	83,700	19,000
Less: Deficit on non-trading loan relationship (W1)	(25,800)	(25,800)	
General expenses of management	(38,300)	(38,300)	
Taxable total profits	38,600	19,600	19,000

	Total	UK	Non-UK
	£	£	£
Corporation tax @ 19%	7,334	3,724	3,610
Less double taxation relief (W2)	(3,230)		(3,230)
	4,104	3,724	380

Note. The acquisition of the shares in Rockette plc by Piro plc was a qualifying 'paper for paper' takeover because Piro plc acquired more than 25% of Rockette plc and the acquisition was a commercial transaction that did not have the avoidance of tax as one of its main purposes. Accordingly, no gain arose in respect of the shares in Piro plc received by Candle Ltd.

In addition, no gain arose in respect of the cash received because the cash represented less than 5% of the value of the total consideration received:

	£
Value of shares received in Piro plc	147,100
Cash received	7,200
Total value received	154,300

The cash received is $\dfrac{7,200}{154,300} \times 100 = 4.67\%$ of the total consideration.

Workings

1   *Deficit on non-trading loan relationship*

	£
Interest receivable	41,100
Less: Interest payable	(52,900)
Fees charged by financial institution	(14,000)
Net deficit	(25,800)

It has been assumed that the company has chosen to offset the deficit against its current period profits.

2   *Double taxation relief*

Lower of:

UK tax	£3,610
Overseas tax £(19,000 – 15,770)	£3,230
ie £3,230	

31 Christina (Sep/Dec 15)

Text references. Chapter 20 covers the computation of taxable total profits and Chapter 22 deals with the computation of corporation tax. Chargeable gains for companies is the subject of Chapter 21. Groups are dealt with in Chapter 26. Registration issues for value added tax are dealt with in Chapter 28. Reliefs for chargeable gains are covered in Chapter 13. Computation of income tax is covered in Chapter 1.

Top tips. It is really important to comply with the requirements of the question. For example, you were told to keep your points to be made to Christina brief. This should have alerted you to the fact that there were a relatively small number of marks for each point and that you should make your points clearly and concisely.

Easy marks. Stating the dates for payment of corporation tax in part (a) should have been easy marks if you realised that there were two accounting periods in the long period of account. There were also some easy marks for basic chargeable gains computations in the same part.

Examining team's comments. Part (a) required a calculation of the corporation tax payable for a company in respect of a 16-month set of accounts, including consideration of two asset disposals where rollover relief had been claimed previously. It was surprising, and indeed disappointing, to see that the majority of candidates calculated the corporation tax payable for the 16-month period as a whole, rather than recognising the need to split this into 2 separate accounting periods, the first covering the first 12 months and the second covering the remaining 4 months. Candidates are reminded that a good level of familiarity with the Taxation (TX – UK) syllabus is required for Advanced Taxation (ATX – UK). It is not enough to just focus on the new areas; candidates must ensure that they are also confident in dealing with more basic issues. The majority of candidates recognised that the sale of the two business assets would cause the gain rolled over on the acquisition of these assets to become chargeable. However, the different treatments in respect of the depreciating asset (fixed machinery) and non-depreciating asset (building) was identified by only a small number of candidates.

Part (b) was the largest part of the question. It required a comparison of the tax implications of a company being acquired by an individual as opposed to by another company. Candidates who did well had a good knowledge of the subject, adopted a sensible, logical approach and addressed all of the issues briefly, as instructed in the question. Weaker candidates fell down in at least one of these areas. The adoption of a logical approach in this sort of question requiring a comparison of two alternatives can save considerable confusion and avoid wasting time due to needless repetition. Candidates should pause and think before they start writing. Dealing fully with the implications of one of the alternatives first, and then the other, tended to provide a much clearer answer than those who adopted a less logical approach, apparently writing points as they occurred to them, without making it clear which alternative they were dealing with, constantly swapping between the two, and leading to a confusing answer. Candidates should avoid repetition, including making the same point from different angles. An example in this case would be where a candidate has stated that if the company is acquired by another company, they would form a group for group relief purposes. Stating separately at a later point that if acquired by an individual there will not be a group for group relief purposes scored no additional marks.

Part (c) concerned the often-tested area of registration for value added tax (VAT), an area which the vast majority of candidates are very technically comfortable with. However, all but a handful failed to read the question in sufficient detail, and provided a very detailed account of the tests applied to determine whether compulsory registration is required, but this did not address the question and wasted a good deal of time. Where the subject coverage is very familiar it is particularly important to understand the context in which it is being tested. In this case, the key issue was recognition that monitoring the level of cash receipts is not relevant; it is the level of taxable supplies, ie the invoiced value of taxable sales, which is relevant.

Marking scheme

		Marks
(a)	Trading income	1
	Chargeable gains	
	Industrial building	2
	Machinery	1½
	Crystallisation of deferred gain	1
	Chargeable gains in correct period	½
	Corporation tax payable	1½
	Due dates	1½
		9

(b) Ongoing

Group relief	2
Relief for capital losses	2
Rollover relief	1
No gain, no loss transfers	1
Annual investment allowance	1
Related 51% group companies	1
VAT group registration	2

Sale of Iron Ltd

Sprint Ltd owns Iron Ltd	3½
Christina owns Iron Ltd	2

	Max	13

(c)

Taxable supplies as monitoring basis	1	
Implications of late registration	2½	
	Max	3
		25

(a) **Iron Ltd – corporation tax payable for the period ending 30 June 2019**

	Year ending 28 February 2019 £	4 months ending 30 June 2019 £
Trading income		
£30,000 × 12/16	22,500	
£30,000 × 4/16		7,500
Chargeable gains (below)		
Industrial building	86,276	
Fixed machinery	0	
Crystallisation of deferred gain re sale of fixed machinery	3,200	
Taxable total profits	111,976	7,500
Corporation tax payable		
£111,976/£7,500 × 19%	21,275	1,425
Due date	1 December 2019	1 April 2020

Tutorial note. If Christina owns Iron Ltd it will not be a related 51% group company with Sprint Ltd or Olympic Ltd. The profit threshold, for determining whether Iron Ltd is a large company for payment of corporation tax by instalments, will therefore be £1,500,000 for the year ending 28 February 2019 and 4/12 × £1,500,000 = £500,000 for the 4 months to 30 June 2019. Therefore, Iron Ltd does not have to pay its corporation tax by instalments.

Chargeable gains

	Industrial building £	Fixed machinery £
Proceeds	160,000	14,000
Less: Cost (£100,000 – £31,800)	(68,200)	(13,700)
Indexation allowance (June 2015 to December 2018)		
(0.081 (280.0 – 258.9/258.9) × £68,200)	(5,524)	
(0.081 × £13,700 – but restricted because indexation allowance cannot create a loss)		(1,110)
Chargeable gain	86,276	0

(b)   **Ownership of Iron Ltd**

Ongoing ownership of Iron Ltd

Corporation tax

It would be advantageous for Sprint Ltd, rather than Christina, to purchase Iron Ltd for the following reasons.

(i)   It is possible that Iron Ltd will make a trade loss for the period ending 30 June 2019. If this were to occur, a proportion of the loss could be surrendered by way of group relief to Sprint Ltd and/or Olympic Ltd and be deducted in arriving at the taxable total profits of the recipient company. Whilst all three companies remain in the group, group relief would also be available between them in respect of any losses in future periods.

(ii)   Iron Ltd will join Sprint Ltd's capital gains group on 1 November 2018. The capital loss to be made by Sprint Ltd on the sale of the warehouse could therefore be relieved against the chargeable gains to be realised by Iron Ltd on the sale of the industrial building and the fixed machinery. This would reduce the corporation tax liability of Iron Ltd by £7,220 (£38,000 × 19%).

(iii)   A gain made by one of the companies in the group on the disposal of a qualifying business asset (land, buildings or fixed machinery used in the business) could be deferred if a qualifying business asset is purchased by any other company in the group during the qualifying period.

(iv)   Any future transfers of assets from one group company to another would take place on a no gain, no loss basis.

There is a possible disadvantage in Iron Ltd joining the Sprint Ltd group of companies in relation to capital allowances. The annual investment allowance will be split between the three companies if they are members of a group, whereas an additional full annual investment allowance would be available to Iron Ltd if Christina were to own Iron Ltd personally (unless Iron Ltd were to share premises or carry on activities similar to those of Sprint Ltd or Olympic Ltd).

There is another possible disadvantage as Iron Ltd would become a related 51% group company with Sprint Ltd and Olympic Ltd. The profit threshold for determining whether any of the companies are large for payment of corporation tax by instalments would then be reduced in future accounting periods.

Value added tax (VAT)

It may be beneficial for Sprint Ltd and Iron Ltd (and possibly Olympic Ltd) to register as a group for the purposes of VAT. This is because it would remove the need for Iron Ltd to charge VAT on the sales it makes to Sprint Ltd. This will, however, be possible regardless of who owns Iron Ltd because Christina will have effective control of all three companies in both situations.

Sale of Iron Ltd

Sprint Ltd owns Iron Ltd

Any chargeable gain (or loss) on the sale of the shares will be exempt due to the substantial shareholding exemption (SSE). This exemption will be available because Sprint Ltd will have owned at least 10% of the ordinary share capital of Iron Ltd for more than a year and both companies are trading companies.

Although the existence of the SSE would appear to be a significant advantage, it should be recognised that the proceeds of sale will then need to be transferred to Christina. This could be carried out via, for example, the payment of a dividend to Christina. As Christina is a higher rate taxpayer, she would have an income tax liability of 32.5%, or even 38.1%, of the dividend in excess of the dividend nil rate band of £5,000.

Tutorial notes

1   The dividend could cause Christina to become an additional rate taxpayer.

2   Credit was also available for reference to other ways in which the proceeds of sale could be transferred to Christina, for example, via the payment of a bonus.

Christina owns Iron Ltd personally

On a sale by Christina of the shares in Iron Ltd, there will be a chargeable gain equal to the excess of the sales proceeds over the price paid for the shares. This gain, after the deduction of any annual exempt amount not used against any other gains, will be subject to capital gains tax at 10% regardless of Christina's taxable income due to the availability of entrepreneurs' relief.

Entrepreneurs' relief will be available because Iron Ltd is a trading company and Christina will have owned at least 5% of its shares for more than a year, and Christina will be a director of Iron Ltd.

Tutorial note. It can be seen from the marking guide that it was not necessary to make all of the above points in order to score full marks.

(c) **VAT registration**

Iron Ltd should be monitoring the level of its taxable supplies (excluding sales of capital assets), as opposed to its cash receipts, in order to determine when it needs to register for VAT.

The implications of registering late are:

(i) Iron Ltd will be required to account for output tax on the sales it has made after the date on which it should have been registered. This will be a cost to Iron Ltd unless it is able to recover the VAT from its customers.

(ii) A penalty may be charged for failing to register by the appropriate date. This penalty would be a percentage of the potential lost revenue where the percentage depends on the reason for the late registration.

(iii) Interest may be charged in respect of the VAT paid late.

32 Drake Ltd, Gosling plc and Mallard Ltd

Text references. Intangible assets and research and development relief are covered in Chapter 20. Disincorporation relief is dealt with in Chapter 21.

Top tips. The treatment of goodwill in part (a) is highly topical. Note the difference between the tax treatment of a credit on the disposal of goodwill (trading) and a debit on the sale of goodwill (non-trading). In part (b), don't forget to deduct the research and development (R&D) expenditure as well as dealing with the additional elements which give extra relief.

Easy marks. In part (c), you should learn the conditions for disincorporation relief for easy marks.

Marking scheme

		Marks	
(a)	No deduction for amortisation	1	
	Disposal of goodwill calculation	1	
	Tax treatment of credit	½	
	Tax treatment of debit	1½	
			4
(b)	Add tax credit	1	
	Deduct R&D expenditure	½	
	Corporation tax	½	
	Deduct tax credit	1	
			3

			Marks
(c)	(i)	Going concern transfer to shareholder	1
		All assets except cash	½
		MV does not exceed £100,000 – information needed	1
		Individuals and shares held at least 12 months	1
		Dates	½
			4
	(ii)	Election by company and shareholder	1
		Date for election	1
			2
	(iii)	Shop	1½
		Goodwill	2
		Max	3
	(iv)	Motor car	1
		Inventory	1
			2
			18

(a) Drake Ltd

Whilst Drake Ltd owns the goodwill no tax deduction will be available for the amortisation of the goodwill so this must be added back in calculating the company's tax adjusted trading profit.

On a disposal of the goodwill, a credit (profit) or debit (loss) must be calculated. This is the difference between the proceeds received and the original cost of the goodwill.

If there is a credit on the sale of the goodwill, this is taxable as trading income.

If there is a debit on the sale of the goodwill this is a non-trading debit. The non-trading debit can be set off against total profits in the same accounting period or a claim can be made for group relief. Any remaining debit is carried forward to the next accounting period as a non-trading debit of that period.

(b) Gosling plc – Corporation tax payable year ended 31 March 2018

	£
Taxable total profit before R&D expenditure	4,500,000
Add ATL credit £500,000 × 11%	55,000
Less R&D expenditure	(500,000)
Taxable total profit	4,055,000
Corporation tax £4,055,000 × 19%	770,450
Less ATL credit £500,000 × 11%	(55,000)
Corporation tax payable	715,450

(c) Mallard Ltd – Disincorporation relief

(i) An election for disincorporation relief may be made where:

(1) The company is transferring its business as a going concern to an individual who is a shareholder

(2) All of the assets of the business (except cash) are being transferred

(3) Market value of the goodwill and land and buildings does not exceed £100,000 – further information is required to confirm whether this condition is met

(4) The transfer is to individuals who have held shares in the company for at least 12 months prior to the transfer

(5) The transfer will occur after 1 April 2013 but before 31 March 2018

(ii) Mallard Ltd and Nathan must make a joint election for disincorporation relief.

The election must be made within two years of the transfer to Nathan.

(iii)   The freehold shop is deemed to have been disposed of by Mallard Ltd at the lower of market value and cost. Therefore no chargeable gain will arise. Nathan will acquire the shop at the deemed disposal value.

The goodwill is deemed to have been disposed of at the lower of market value and cost. Since the goodwill has been built up since incorporation (rather than being purchased), the cost is nil and so the deemed proceeds are therefore nil. Therefore no profit will arise on disposal. Nathan will acquire the goodwill at nil value.

(iv)   Motor car – since Mallard Ltd and Nathan are connected persons, an election can be made to transfer the motor car at its tax written down value.

Inventory – since Mallard Ltd and Nathan are connected persons, an election can be made to transfer the inventory at the greater of original cost and transfer price.

33 Jerome (06/12)

Text references. Value added tax (VAT) on the sale of a business is covered in Chapter 28. Taxable benefits and expenses for employees are dealt with in Chapter 4. Allowable expenses for business are covered in Chapter 6. Corporation tax payable is covered in Chapter 20.

Top tips. It is important to state that the transfer of assets on incorporation will be a supply for VAT unless the conditions for transfer of the business as a going concern are satisfied.

Easy marks. The conditions for VAT transfer of a going concern (TOGC) in part (a) should have been well known. In part (b), the calculation of car and fuel benefits and the mileage allowance were straightforward.

Examining team's comments. In part (a), candidates first needed to recognise that the sale was a transfer of a business as a going concern such that VAT should not be charged. This was done well with the majority of candidates listing the conditions that needed to be satisfied. Candidates were then expected to realise that the building being sold was a commercial building that was less than three years old. Accordingly, VAT would need to be charged in respect of the building unless the purchaser made an election to tax the building at the time of purchase. Very few candidates identified this point.

Part (b) required calculations of the total tax cost for Tricycle Ltd and Jerome in relation to the lease of car. The car would be leased by Jerome, an employee of the company, or by Tricycle Ltd. This was a practical problem that was not particularly technically difficult but required care and thought in order to score well. It was not done as well as it should have been.

The point here was that Jerome owned Tricycle Ltd such that he was interested in the total tax cost to himself and the company in respect of each of the two options. Candidates needed to recognise that there were tax implications for both the employer, Tricycle Ltd, and the employee, Jerome, in each situation. For example, if Jerome leased the car, the payment of 50 pence per business mile was tax deductible for the company but resulted in taxable income for Jerome. There was also the need to consider national insurance contributions as well as income tax and corporation tax.

The main problem for candidates was a lack of exam technique. In particular, weaker candidates did not spend sufficient time thinking about the different tax implications for both parties in each situation but focused on Jerome when he leased the car and on Tricycle Ltd when it leased the car.

					Marks
(a)	Administration – one mark for relevant point			1	
	Charge VAT unless transfer of a going concern			1	
	Conditions (one mark each, maximum three marks)			3	
	Land and buildings			2½	
			Max		7
(b)	(i)	Motor car leased by Tricycle Ltd			
		Income tax payable by Jerome		2½	
		Net taxes saved by Tricycle Ltd		3	
		Net tax cost		½	
	(ii)	Motor car leased by Jerome			
		Total tax payable by Jerome		3	
		Net taxes saved by Tricycle Ltd		1½	
		Net tax saved		½	
					11
(c)	Conditions – one mark each				2
					20

(a) **Value added tax (VAT) on the sale of the business**

HM Revenue & Customs should be notified of the sale of the business within 30 days.

Jerome's VAT registration will need to be cancelled unless it is to be taken over by Tricycle Ltd.

VAT must be charged on the sale of the business assets unless it qualifies as a transfer of a going concern. For the sale of the business to be regarded as a transfer of a going concern, the following conditions must be satisfied:

(i) The business must be a going concern.

(ii) Tricycle Ltd must use the assets to carry on the same kind of business as that carried on by Jerome.

(iii) Tricycle Ltd must be VAT registered or be required to be VAT registered as a result of the purchase (based on the turnover of the purchased business in the previous 12 months).

(iv) There should be no significant break in trading before or after the purchase of the business.

Even if the transfer satisfies the above conditions, Jerome will need to charge VAT on the sale of the building as it is a commercial building that is less than three years old. The only exception to this is if Tricycle Ltd makes an election to tax the building at the time of purchase.

(b) **Tax costs incurred in respect of the motor car**

(i) **Motor car is leased by Tricycle Ltd**

Jerome

	£
Taxable benefit in respect of the private use of the motor car	
135 (rounded down) – 95 = 40/5 =	
8% + 18% + 3% (diesel) = 29%	
29% × £31,000	8,990
Taxable benefit in respect of the private fuel	
29% × £22,600	6,554
	15,544
Income tax at 40% payable by Jerome	6,218

Tricycle Ltd

	Allowable expenses £	Tax £
Lease payments		
£4,400 × 85% (100% − 15%)	3,740	
Running costs	5,000	
Class 1A NICs £15,544 × 13.8%	2,145	2,145
	10,885	
Reduction in corporation tax £10,885 × 19%		(2,068)
Net taxes increased for Tricycle Ltd		77
Total tax cost £(6,218 + 77)		6,295

Tutorial notes

1. Jerome's salary of £48,000 per year exceeds the personal allowance plus the basic rate band, such that he will be a higher rate taxpayer.

2. 15% of the lease payments will be disallowed because the CO_2 emissions of the car are above 130 g/km.

(ii) **Motor car is leased by Jerome**

Jerome

	£
Taxable mileage allowance	
10,000 × (50 − 45)p	500
(14,000 − 10,000) × (50 − 25)p	1,000
	1,500
Income tax at 40% payable by Jerome	600
Class 1 NICs payable by Jerome	
14,000 × (50 − 45)p × 2%	14
Total tax payable by Jerome	614

Tricycle Ltd

	Allowable expenses £	Tax £
Mileage allowance paid 14,000 × 50p	7,000	
Class 1 NICs payable by Tricycle Ltd		
14,000 × (50 − 45)p × 13.8%	97	97
	7,097	
Reduction in corporation tax £7,097 × 19%		(1,348)
Net taxes saved by Tricycle Ltd		(1,251)
Net taxes saved £(1,251 − 614)		637

Tutorial notes

1. The calculations reflect the tax implications of the two alternatives. Jerome controls the company such that the non-tax costs incurred (lease payments, running costs and mileage allowances) are going to be incurred regardless of who leases the car and are therefore only relevant to the extent that they increase or reduce a tax liability. However, Jerome may need to extract funds from the company in order to pay the costs relating to the motor car. This would give rise to further tax liabilities that would need to be considered.

2 Class 1 national insurance contributions are payable in respect of mileage allowances on the excess of the rate paid over the HMRC rate for up to 10,000 miles. Jerome's salary of £48,000 exceeds the upper earnings limit of £45,000 so the rate of Jerome's national insurance contributions will be 2%.

(c) **Conditions for deduction of travel costs**

(i) The employee must be absent from the UK for a continuous period of at least 60 days for the purposes of performing the duties of his employment.

(ii) The journey must be from the UK to the place where the employee is carrying out the duties of his employment.

Tutorial note. A deduction is only available for two outward and two return journeys by the same person(s) in the same tax year.

34 Spetz Ltd group (12/13)

Text references. Value added tax partial exemption is dealt with in Chapter 29. Company residence is covered in Chapter 20 and double taxation relief and the exemption for overseas branches in Chapter 27.

Top tips. Remember to round up the percentage recovery for partial exemption to the nearest whole number.

Easy marks. The computation of corporation tax and double tax relief in part (b)(ii) was not particularly complicated. You might have guessed that travel for a private holiday in part (c) was not relevant for tax purposes.

Examining team's comments. Part (a) was done reasonably well by those candidates who had a working knowledge of the *de minimis* rules. A minority of candidates had very little awareness of the rules, such that their performance was poor. Candidates who did not have a precise knowledge of the rules were able to score reasonably well provided they satisfied the requirement and attempted to address all three *de minimis* tests.

Part (b)(i) required an explanation of how to determine whether or not the company was resident in the UK. This simply required a statement of the rules regarding country of incorporation and place of management and control but the majority of candidates were unable to state these fundamental rules.

Part (b)(ii) required an explanation of the company's corporation tax liability together with the advantages and disadvantages of making an election to exempt the profits of an overseas permanent establishment from UK tax. This was done well. The majority of candidates prepared a short accurate calculation and were able to state the particular disadvantages of making such an election.

Part (c) concerned the travel and subsistence costs of an employee seconded to work overseas. This was relatively tricky but was done reasonably well by those candidates who were methodical in their approach. In particular, candidates who did not necessarily know all of the detailed rules were still able to score an acceptable mark if they applied basic principles to all three elements of the question. Very few candidates identified that the overseas workplace would be a temporary workplace. In addition, a minority of candidates discussed the tax implications for the company rather than for the employee. Candidates must read the requirement for each question carefully and ensure that their answer is always focused on satisfying that requirement.

Marking scheme

		Marks
(a)	Test 1	1
	Test 2	1½
	Input tax attributed to taxable supplies and unattributed input tax	1½
	Test 3	1½
	Adjustment and date	1½
		7

				Marks
(b)	(i)	Not incorporated in UK	1	
		Central management and control	2	
				3
	(ii)	Calculation of liability	1½	
		Taxation of worldwide profits	1	
		Discussion of election		
		Advantage	1½	
		Disadvantage	2	
		Max		5
(c)		Flights at start and end of contract	3	
		Return flight in February	1½	
		Laundry and telephone calls	2	
		Max		5
				20

(a) **Novak Ltd – value added tax (VAT) partial exemption annual adjustment**

Test 1 is not satisfied, as the total input tax exceeds an average of £625 per month (£625 × 12 = £7,500).

Test 2 is not satisfied, as the total input tax less that directly attributed to taxable supplies exceeds an average of £625 per month (£12,200 + £4,900 + £16,100 – £12,200 = £21,000, £21,000/12 = £1,750).

	£
Input tax attributable to taxable supplies	12,200
Unattributed input tax £16,100 × 74% (W1)	11,914
Recoverable input tax (W2)	24,114
Less input tax recovered on quarterly returns	(23,200)
Annual adjustment – additional input tax recoverable	914

The annual adjustment must be made on the final VAT return of the year, which is the return for the period ended 30 September 2018, or the first VAT return after the end of the year at the option of the company.

Workings

1 *Recoverable unattributed input tax*

$$\frac{£1,190,000}{£1,190,000 + £430,000} \times 100 = 73.4\%, \text{ rounded up to } 74\%.$$

2 *Recoverable input tax*

Exempt input tax of (£4,900 + £[16,100 – 11,914]) = £9,086 exceeds the Test 3 limit of £625 per month and is therefore irrecoverable.

(b) (i) **Residence status of Kraus Co**

A company is regarded as resident in the UK if it is incorporated in the UK or if its central management and control is exercised in the UK. Kraus Co was incorporated in the country of Mersano.

Accordingly, Kraus Co will only be resident in the UK if its central management and control is exercised in the UK. The central management and control of a company is usually regarded as being exercised in the place where the meetings of the board of directors are held.

(ii) **Kraus Co**

UK resident companies are subject to corporation tax on their worldwide income.

	£
Corporation tax: £520,000 × 19%	98,800
Less unilateral double taxation relief £520,000 × 16%	(83,200)
UK corporation tax liability	15,600

Tutorial note. The profits will be subject to tax because no election has been made to exempt the profits and losses of the overseas permanent establishment from UK corporation tax.

Election to exempt the overseas profits from UK tax

The advantage of making such an election would be that the profits made in Mersano would not be subject to UK corporation tax. Based on the current rates of corporation tax in the two countries, this would save corporation tax at the rate of (19% – 16%) = 3%.

When considering this election, it should be recognised that it is irrevocable and would apply to all future overseas permanent establishments of Kraus Co. Accordingly, there would be no relief in the UK for any losses incurred in the trade in Mersano in the future or for any other losses incurred in any additional overseas trades operated by Kraus Co.

(c) **Meyer's secondment to Kraus Co**

The reimbursement of expenses by an employer represents taxable income for an employee under general principles. However, the reimbursement of the travel expenses to Meyer at the start of the contract should be automatically exempt because they would be fully allowed as deductions for him since:

(i) It is necessary for Meyer to travel to Mersano in order to perform the duties of his employment

(ii) The workplace in Mersano is a temporary workplace (the secondment is for less than 24 months), so the travelling does not constitute ordinary commuting

The cost of the return journey to the UK in February 2019 has no UK tax implications. Meyer will not be able to claim a tax deduction for the costs incurred because the journey is for a private purpose and he, rather than Spetz Ltd, will bear the cost.

The reimbursement of the cost of laundry and telephone calls home will be exempt from tax in any event if less than £10 per night. If this limit is exceeded, the whole of the amount reimbursed will be subject to UK income tax.

Tutorial note. Credit was also available to candidates who focused their answers on the special rules relating to travel cost where duties are performed abroad.

35 Nocturne Ltd (06/15)

Text references. Close companies are covered in Chapter 25 and capital allowances in Chapter 7. Chattels are dealt with in Chapter 14. The income tax computation is covered in Chapter 1. Value added tax (VAT) partial exemption is dealt with in Chapter 29.

Top tips. Make sure you read the question carefully and do not jump to conclusions about what it is asking you!

Easy marks. There were some easy marks for applying the partial exemption tests in part (c).

Examining team's comments. Part (a) concerned two alternative ways in which a computer was to be provided to a shareholder who was not employed by the company. Despite knowing the relevant rules, candidates did not perform as well as they could have done in this part for two reasons. Firstly, they failed to consider all of the aspects of the situation and secondly, they did not answer the question set. Most candidates appreciated that the provision of the computer would give rise to a distribution but many failed to address the capital allowances position of the company. This was important because it differed in the two alternative situations. Similarly, many candidates failed to address the tax treatment of the loss on the transfer of the existing computer in the second alternative. Candidates will benefit if they think before they write and identify all the different aspects of the transaction. They should then address each of the aspects in a concise manner. The failure to answer the question set related to the need to determine the after-tax cost for the company. Most candidates focused on the tax treatment for the individual, which meant that they missed out on some of the available marks.

Part (b) concerned Siglio, the company's managing director, who was going to borrow money from a bank and then lend it to the company. Many candidates provided unsatisfactory answers to this question part because they wanted the question to deal with a loan from a close company to a participator in that company – but it wasn't. It was also important to deal with the two loans separately. The loan to the company was a normal commercial loan. The company would obtain a tax deduction for the interest paid and Siglio would pay income tax on the interest income in the normal way. It was no more complicated than that. The loan from the bank to Siglio was more interesting in that it would be a qualifying loan, such that the interest paid by Siglio would be tax deductible. Some candidates were aware of this point but very few stated the detailed reasons for the tax deduction being available.

The final part of the question concerned VAT and was in two parts. Part (i) concerned the partial exemption *de minimis* tests. It was a straightforward test of the rules and was done well by those candidates who knew them. As always, it was important to read the question carefully and to address the requirement and nothing more; some candidates wasted time by addressing other aspects of VAT that were not required. Candidates should recognise that VAT is tested at every sitting and that the partial exemption rules are tested regularly. Part (ii) concerned the annual test for computing recoverable input tax and was not done well. The problem here was that the majority of candidates addressed the annual accounting scheme rather than the subject of the question. This was unfortunate and meant that very few candidates did well on this part of the question. Candidates should always try to be sure as to what the question is about; both parts of part (c) related to partial exemption.

Marking scheme

					Marks
(a)	Close company		1		
	Purchase of new computer for Jed		2½		
	Transfer of existing computer to Jed		3½		
	Conclusion		½		
		Max			7
(b)	Treatment of interest received		1½		
	Conditions for income tax deduction		2½		
	Conclusion		½		
		Max			4
(c)	(i)	Test 1	2		
		Test 2	2		
		Conclusion	½		
		Max			4
	(ii)	Annual test			
		Conditions	2		
		Application to Nocturne Ltd	1		
		Implications	3		
		Max			5
					20

(a) **Provision of laptop computer for Jed**

Option 1: Purchase of new laptop computer

Nocturne Ltd is a close company because it is under the control of five or fewer shareholders (in this particular case it is controlled by any three out of its four shareholders) who are called 'participators'. Jed is a participator in Nocturne Ltd.

As Jed does not work for Nocturne Ltd, the provision of the laptop is not taxable under the benefits code, but since he is a participator of Nocturne Ltd he will be treated as receiving a deemed distribution of the amount that would otherwise be taxed as a benefit (the use of asset benefit). No national insurance contributions are payable. Nocturne Ltd cannot deduct capital allowances on the new laptop.

Nocturne Ltd cannot deduct any further capital allowances on the old laptop because it already has a tax written value of nil.

Option 1 therefore has an after-tax cost to Nocturne Ltd of the cost of the laptop which is £1,800.

Option 2: Transfer of existing laptop computer

As Jed is a participator of Nocturne Ltd he will be treated as receiving a deemed distribution of the amount that would otherwise be taxed as a benefit (the gift of asset benefit). No national insurance contributions are payable.

The transfer of the old laptop computer to Jed will result in a balancing charge of £150 (market value less tax written down value of pool) for Nocturne Ltd. This will result in additional corporation tax of £150 × 19% = £28.

The transfer of the old laptop will also be a disposal of a chattel by Nocturne Ltd but this is an exempt disposal as both cost and deemed proceeds are less than £6,000.

The new laptop will be eligible for capital allowances as it is to be used in Nocturne Ltd's business. The annual investment allowance will be available to cover the full amount of £1,800 and so there will be a corporation tax saving of £1,800 × 19% = £342 so the net cost of the new laptop will be £(1,800 − 342) = £1,458.

Option 2 therefore has an after-tax cost to Nocturne Ltd of £(28 + 1,458) = £1,486.

Conclusion

Option 2 is therefore the preferable option for Nocturne Ltd as it would result in a lower after-tax cost.

(b) **Provision of loan finance by Siglio**

Siglio will receive interest on the loan from Nocturne Ltd net of basic rate tax. The gross amount of interest will be taxable on Siglio as savings income. Interest in excess of the available savings income nil rate band will be taxed at his marginal rate of tax. Credit will be given for tax deducted at source.

The money lent by the bank to Siglio is then lent by him to a close company (Nocturne Ltd) to be used wholly and exclusively for the purpose of its business. Interest paid on a loan taken out to make a loan to a close company can be deductible against income. To be deductible, when the interest is paid, Siglio either must hold some shares in Nocturne Ltd and work the greater part of his time in the actual management or conduct of the company (almost certainly the case since he is the managing director) or must have a material interest in Nocturne Ltd (ie hold more than 5% of the shares). So in fact Siglio probably meets both of these alternative conditions.

The interest payable by Siglio on the loan from his bank is therefore deductible from Siglio's total income to compute his net income and he is thus given tax relief.

(c) (i) **Recoverable input VAT for the year ended 31 March 2018**

Test 1

All the input VAT is recoverable if the amount of input VAT relating to exempt supplies is small (*de minimis*). Under Test 1, the *de minimis* condition is satisfied if the total input VAT incurred is no more than £625 per month on average (£7,500 a year) and the value of exempt supplies is no more than 50% of all supplies.

As the total input VAT incurred by Nocturne Ltd for the year to 31 March 2018 is £(7,920 + 1,062 + 4,150) = £13,132, Test 1 is not satisfied even though the value of exempt supplies is only 14% of all supplies.

Test 2

Under Test 2, the *de minimis* condition is satisfied if the total input VAT incurred less input VAT directly attributed to taxable supplies is no more than £625 per month on average (£7,500 a year) and the value of exempt supplies is no more than 50% of the value of all supplies.

Test 2 is satisfied because the total input VAT incurred by Nocturne Ltd less input VAT directly attributed to taxable supplies is £(13,132 − 7,920) = £5,212 and the value of exempt supplies is 14%.

(ii) **Annual test**

The annual test gives Nocturne Ltd the option of applying the *de minimis* test once a year rather than for every VAT return period.

To use the annual test, Nocturne Ltd must satisfy the following conditions:

(1) Have been *de minimis* in the previous partial exemption year

(2) Will consistently apply the annual test throughout any given partial exemption year

(3) Have reasonable grounds for not expecting to incur more than £1 million input tax in its current partial exemption year

As Nocturne Ltd was *de minimis* in the partial exemption year to 31 March 2018 and should satisfy the other conditions for the partial exemption year ended 31 March 2019, Nocturne Ltd can opt to treat itself as *de minimis* in that year.

This means that there will be provisional recovery of all input tax in the year which will give a cash flow benefit and an administrative time saving. The administrative time saving is particularly useful as the company's turnover and associated costs are expected to increase in the year ended 31 March 2019 so that Tests 1 and 2 may no longer be satisfied and the more complex Test 3 might otherwise have to be applied for each return period.

At the end of the year to 31 March 2019, Nocturne Ltd must review its status using the *de minimis* tests applied to the year as a whole. If one of the tests is failed, it must carry out an annual adjustment which will result in a repayment of part of the input VAT previously recovered in full.

36 Loriod plc group (06/11)

Text references. Overseas aspects of corporation tax are covered in Chapter 27. Transfer pricing is dealt with in Chapter 20.

Top tips. Read the question carefully. For example, in part (c), you are told to consider the position for transfer pricing if Strategy B is adopted. (You might like to think why the question directs you to do this.)

Easy marks. There were some easy marks in this question for basic comparisons between permanent establishments and subsidiaries, and transfer pricing.

Examining team's comments. Part (a) required candidates to explain the relief available in respect of the expected loss to be made by the business depending on whether it was established as a branch or a subsidiary of the UK company. This was an area where candidates had a certain amount of knowledge but, on the whole, did not score as well as they could have done because they wrote generally about branch versus subsidiary as opposed to addressing the particular facts and requirements of this question.

In particular, despite being asked to address loss relief, many candidates wrote about the taxation of profits. Many of those who did address losses did not address them as precisely as they could have done in the context of the question such that they did not consider the relevance of the tax rates provided.

Part (b) concerned group relief and the preservation of double tax relief. It required technical knowledge that almost all candidates had regarding double tax relief being the lower of the UK tax and the overseas tax on the overseas income. However, it also required candidates to be able to work out how to ensure that sufficient overseas profits remained within the charge to tax such that relief in respect of the overseas tax was not wasted. This task was carried out elegantly by a minority of candidates but the majority struggled with the problem. Credit was available for approaching the question by reference to double tax relief but many candidates simply stated that group relief was restricted to the lower of the losses available and the profits subject to tax.

The final part of the question concerned transfer pricing and was done reasonably well by many candidates who had a good knowledge of the transfer pricing rules. However, only a small minority made reference to the relevance of the size of the companies in determining whether or not the rules would apply or to the possibility of reaching an agreement with HM Revenue & Customs (HMRC).

The question also required candidates to explain how the prices charged between the group companies would affect the total tax paid by the group. In order to do this, candidates had to focus on the difference between the tax rate in the UK and that in Kuwata and the possibility of group profits being taxed at the lower rate. It was important here to address the situation from a group perspective rather than that of a particular company. However, the majority of candidates did not address this element of the question.

			Marks
(a)	Use of permanent establishment	4	
	Use of subsidiary	3	
	Comparison	1	
			8
(b)	Explanations		
	Double taxation relief	2	
	UK tax on overseas profits	2	
	Calculations	2	
			6
(c)	Impact of prices on total tax paid by the group	2	
	Transfer pricing		
	Why the rules apply	2	
	Application of the rules	1½	
	HMRC confirmation of pricing arrangements	1	
	Max		6
			20

(a) **The relief available in respect of the expected loss**

Strategy A – Elivar Ltd purchases the trade and all of the assets of Syme Inc

The business in Kuwata would be an overseas permanent establishment of Elivar Ltd. The permanent establishment would be an extension of Elivar Ltd. Accordingly, because the overseas operations are to be controlled from the UK, the loss made in the year following the acquisition will be offset in calculating Elivar Ltd's trading income. If Elivar Ltd makes a trading loss, the overseas losses can be included in a group relief surrender to other group companies. Any unrelieved losses will be carried forward for relief against future profits of the same trade. The relief of the overseas losses will save UK corporation tax at 19%.

Strategy B – Elivar Ltd purchases the share capital of Syme Inc

Syme Inc would be a subsidiary of Elivar Ltd resident in Kuwata. It would be a separate legal entity and its losses would be subject to the tax regime of Kuwata. This will save tax in Kuwata at only 16% as opposed to the 19% relief available under Strategy A. However, it may be possible for the loss generated by the 'Frager' business to be carried back for relief in earlier years in Kuwata if Strategy B is adopted.

(b) **Strategy A – 'Frager' business operated via a permanent establishment**

Maximum loss to be surrendered to Elivar Ltd

The tax suffered in Kuwata of £19,200 (£120,000 × 16%) can be offset against the corporation tax liability of Elivar Ltd up to a maximum of the UK tax on the overseas income. Accordingly, in order not to waste double tax relief, the UK tax on the overseas profits must be at least £19,200.

In determining the UK tax on the profits of Elivar Ltd, the company can choose to offset the qualifying charitable donations and the group relief in the most tax-efficient manner. Accordingly, the qualifying charitable donations and the group relief will be deducted first from the UK profits, reducing them to zero. It should then be used to reduce the overseas profits to the amount that results in the UK corporation tax being equal to the tax suffered in Kuwata.

The overseas profits in respect of the permanent establishment should not be reduced below £101,053 (£19,200/19%).

The maximum loss that should be surrendered to Elivar Ltd is set out below.

	£
In respect of:	
UK profits less qualifying charitable donations £(90,000 – 2,000)	88,000
Overseas profits £(120,000 – 102,000)	18,000
Maximum loss to be surrendered to Elivar Ltd	106,000

(c)   **Strategy B – 'Frager' business operated via a subsidiary**

Transfer pricing

The rate of corporation tax in Kuwata is lower than that in the UK. Accordingly, the total tax paid by the group will be reduced if more of the group's profits are generated in Kuwata. This could be achieved by increasing the prices charged by the subsidiary in Kuwata.

The transfer pricing rules will apply to transactions between Elivar Ltd and its subsidiary in Kuwata because Elivar Ltd controls the subsidiary. The exemption for small and medium-sized enterprises is unlikely to be available, regardless of the size of the Loriod plc group, as there is no double tax treaty between the UK and Kuwata.

Any reduction in Elivar Ltd's profits caused by paying inflated prices to the subsidiary in Kuwata would be regarded as a potential tax advantage. The transfer pricing rules would counteract such an advantage by requiring Elivar Ltd to calculate its taxable profits as if it had been charged arm's length prices by its overseas subsidiary.

Elivar Ltd could approach HMRC for confirmation that its pricing arrangements with its overseas subsidiary are acceptable in order to remove uncertainty in this area.

37 Ziti (06/14)

Text references. Trade profits are covered in Chapter 6 and capital allowances in Chapter 7. The income tax computation is dealt with in Chapter 1. Capital gains tax computations are covered in Chapter 11 and reliefs in Chapter 13. Value added tax on land and buildings is dealt with in Chapter 29 and the conditions for transfer of a going concern in Chapter 28. Inheritance tax on lifetime transfers is covered in Chapter 16 and business property relief in Chapter 17.

Top tips. It is important to adopt a methodical approach to questions where there are alternative dates for actions. First, work out the income tax position for a cessation on 31 January 2019 and, second, the position for a cessation on 30 April 2019. Then repeat for the capital gains tax disposals. As required in the question, finally bring the computations together in a summary.

Easy marks. There were some easy marks for basic income tax computations in part (a)(i) and inheritance tax computations in part (b).

Examining team's comments. Part (a)(i) was quite substantial and was worth 17 marks. Stronger candidates structured their answers in such a way that it was very clear which of the possible methods of disposal they were addressing and then dealt with the two methods one at a time. Weaker candidates did not spend sufficient time thinking about the facts of the question and simply dealt with a disposal without making it clear which of the possibilities they were considering. The income tax aspects of the disposal revolved around the closing year rules for the unincorporated trader. It was important to be able to identify the tax years of the proposed disposal and the basis of assessment for each of the relevant years. Many candidates did not have a clear understanding of these basic rules, such that they were not able to identify the relevant tax years or to accurately calculate the taxable profits for each of the relevant tax years. The trader had purchased equipment, which was then to be sold on the cessation of the business. Most candidates identified the annual investment allowance (AIA) but many then omitted to follow the story through to the disposal, such that the balancing charge was left out. In addition, weaker candidates prepared comprehensive (and time-consuming) calculations of capital allowances in order to arrive at an AIA of £6,000. The treatment of overlap profits, the personal allowance and the calculation of income tax was done well by the vast majority of candidates.

The capital gains tax implications of the sale of the business were straightforward and were handled reasonably well. However, one common error was to treat the sale of the business as if it were a sale of a single asset as opposed to a sale of the individual assets of the business. Many candidates concluded that the capital gains tax implications were the same regardless of which of the methods of disposal took place. However, this was not the case because there was a disposal of goodwill only where the business was sold as a going concern. Finally, candidates were required to prepare a summary. In order to score the maximum three marks available, candidates had to include the trading income and the proceeds from the sale of the assets together with both the income tax and the capital gains tax. It was also important to exclude any non-cash items. Very few candidates managed to score all three marks and many candidates failed to produce any sort of summary.

Part (a)(ii) concerned the value added tax (VAT) implications of the disposal. This was handled well by the majority of candidates with many candidates demonstrating a good knowledge of the various conditions necessary for a sale to be regarded as a transfer of a going concern.

Part (b) concerned the basic mechanics of inheritance tax; it was done well by many candidates. Almost all candidates identified the gift of the business as a potentially exempt transfer that would become chargeable following the death of the donor within seven years. They were also competent at dealing with the annual exemptions, the nil rate band (with one exception – see below), the tax rate and taper relief.

The one area where a lot of candidates did not perform as well was when it came to business property relief (BPR). To begin with, many candidates omitted BPR altogether. Those candidates who did include BPR in their answers often failed to realise that if the business was sold by Ziti (the donee) before the death of his father (the donor), BPR would not be available because the rules require the donee to own the assets gifted at the date of the donor's death.

The point referred to above regarding the nil rate band relates to the relevance of the chargeable lifetime transfer (CLT) made by the donor of the business on 1 May 2010. It was thought by some candidates that this gift would have no effect on the nil rate band available as it was more than seven years prior to the death of the donor. However, because the CLT was made within seven years of the gift of the business on 1 July 2014, the nil rate band available when calculating the tax due in respect of the gift of the business has to be reduced by the amount of the CLT.

Marking scheme

			Marks
(a)	(i)	Income tax position	
		Cessation on 31 January 2019	
		Trading income	1
		Capital allowances	1½
		Overlap profits	½
		Basis period	1
		Income tax payable	1
		Cessation on 30 April 2019	
		Basis period	1
		Trading income	½
		Capital allowances	1½
		Overlap profits	½
		Income tax payable	1

Capital gains tax position		
Cessation on 31 January 2019		
Capital gains	2	
Capital gains tax	1	
Availability of entrepreneurs' relief	1	
Cessation on 30 April 2019		
Capital gains	½	
Capital gains tax	½	
Availability of entrepreneurs' relief	1	
Summary	3	
Assumption	1	
Max		17
(ii) Sale on 31 January 2019	1½	
Sale on 30 April 2019		
Charge VAT unless TOGC	1	
TOGC conditions	3	
Max		5
(b) Death prior to disposal of business	2	
Death post disposal of business		
Value of transfer	1½	
Annual exemptions	1	
Business property relief not available	1½	
Taper relief	1	
Nil rate band available	1½	
Inheritance tax liabilities	2	
Max		9
Approach to problem solving	1	
Clarity of calculations	1	
Effectiveness of communication	1	
Overall presentation	1	
		4
		35

Notes for meeting

Prepared by: Tax senior
Date: 6 June 2018
Subject: Ziti – sale of business and inheritance tax

(a) **Sale of business**

(i) **Post-tax income and sales proceeds**

Income tax position

Business cessation on 31 January 2019

Taxable trading profits

Y/e 30.4.18

	£
Profits 12 × £5,000	60,000
Less annual investment allowance on equipment 1.8.17	(6,000)
Taxable trading profits	54,000

P/e 31.1.19

	£
Profits 9 × £5,000	45,000
Add balancing charge on equipment £(0 – 10,000)	10,000
Less overlap profit on commencement	(9,000)
Taxable trading profits	46,000

Income tax 2018/19

Final year of trading: basis period 1 May 2017 to 31 January 2019

	£
Trading income £(54,000 + 46,000)/Net income	100,000
Less personal allowance	(11,500)
Taxable income	88,500

	£
Income tax:	
£33,500 @ 20%	6,700
£55,000 @ 40%	22,000
Income tax liability	28,700

Business cessation on 30 April 2019

Taxable trading profits

Y/e 30.4.18

	£
As above	54,000

Y/e 30.4.19

	£
Profits 12 × £5,000	60,000
Add balancing charge on equipment £(0 – 10,000)	10,000
Less overlap profit on commencement	(9,000)
Taxable trading profits	61,000

Income tax 2018/19

Current year basis: basis period 1 May 2017 to 30 April 2018

	£
Trading income/Net income	54,000
Less personal allowance	(11,500)
Taxable income	42,500

	£
Income tax:	
£33,500 @ 20%	6,700
£9,000 @ 40%	3,600
Income tax liability	10,300

Income tax 2019/20

Final year of trading: Basis period 1 May 2018 to 30 April 2019

	£
Trading income/Net income	61,000
Less personal allowance	(11,500)
Taxable income	49,500
Income tax:	
£33,500 @ 20%	6,700
£16,000 @ 40%	6,400
Income tax liability	13,100

Capital gains tax position

Sale of assets on 31 January 2019

Capital gains tax 2018/19

	£
Building £(330,000 – 60,000(Note 1))	270,000
Equipment (Note 2)	0
Chargeable gains	270,000
Less annual exempt amount	(11,300)
Taxable gains	258,700
Capital gains tax:	
£258,700 @ 10% (Note 3)	25,870

Notes

1   The base cost of the building for Ziti is the original cost for Ravi as gift relief was claimed on the disposal of the business assets from Ravi to Ziti.

2   All of the equipment has a market value and cost of £6,000 or less and so is exempt from capital gains tax.

3   Entrepreneurs' relief is available on the disposal of the assets because the business has been owned by Ziti throughout the period of one year ending with the date on which the business ceased to be carried on and the date of cessation is within three years before the date of the disposal.

Sale of business on 30 April 2019

Capital gains tax 2019/20

	£
Capital gains tax:	
On gains as above (Note)	25,870
Goodwill £40,000 @ 10% (Note)	4,000
Capital gains tax	29,870

Note. Entrepreneurs' relief is available as this is the disposal of whole or part of a business by Ziti who has owned the business throughout the period of one year ending with the date of the disposal. As with the building, the base cost of the goodwill for Ziti is the original cost to Ravi ie nil, because of gift relief on the disposal from Ravi to Ziti.

Summary of post-tax cash position

	Sale on 31.1.19 £	Sale on 30.4.19 £
Trading income £(60,000 + 45,000)	105,000	
Trading income £(60,000 + 60,000)		120,000
Equipment purchase 1 August 2017	(6,000)	(6,000)
Proceeds of sale:		
Goodwill	0	40,000
Building	330,000	330,000
Equipment	10,000	10,000
Less: Income tax 2018/19	(28,700)	(10,300)
Income tax 2019/20	0	(13,100)
Capital gains tax 2018/19	(25,870)	0
Capital gains tax 2019/20	0	(29,870)
	384,430	440,730

Conclusion

Delaying the sale until 30 April 2019 would be financially beneficial.

It would also delay the payment of some of the income tax and all of the capital gains tax by one year.

Assumptions

Ziti has not used his annual exempt amount for 2018/19 (for a sale on 31 January 2019) or 2019/20 (for a sale on 30 April 2019).

(ii) **Value added tax (VAT)**

Sale of assets on 31 January 2019

VAT @ 20% will need to be charged on the sale of the equipment.

The sale of the building will be exempt since it is more than three years old and the option to tax has not been exercised.

Sale of assets on 30 April 2019

VAT @ 20% will need to be charged on the sale of the equipment and the goodwill unless the sale qualifies as the transfer of a going concern.

The conditions for the transfer of assets not to be treated as a supply for VAT purposes and to be treated as a transfer of a going concern are as follows:

(1) The assets are to be used by the purchaser in the same kind of business (whether or not as part of an existing business) as that carried on by Ziti, the business being transferred as a going concern.

(2) The purchaser is a taxable person when the transfer takes place or immediately becomes one as a result of the transfer.

(3) There is no significant break in the normal trading pattern before or immediately after the transfer.

As above, the sale of the building is exempt.

(b) Inheritance tax

Date of death	Notes	IHT liability £
7 June 2018 to 30 April 2019	1	0
1 May 2019 to 30 June 2019	2	48,480
1 July 2019 to 30 June 2020	3(i)	32,320
1 July 2020 to 30 June 2021	3(ii)	16,160

Notes

1   If Ravi dies whilst Ziti still owns the business, business property relief at 100% will apply on the value of the transfer. This is because the transfer was of an unincorporated trading business owned by Ravi for at least two years.

2   Business property relief will not apply as Ziti does not own the business when Ravi dies and he has not reinvested the whole of the proceeds in replacement business assets.

   Taper relief applies as there are at least three years between the transfer and the death of Ravi.

   The inheritance on the transfer is computed as follows:

	£	£	£
Transfer of value			
£(40,000 + 300,000 + 9,000)			349,000
Less: Annual exemptions			
2014/15 and 2013/14 b/f			(6,000)
Chargeable transfer			343,000
Nil rate band at death of Ravi		325,000	
Transfer of value 1 May 2010	190,000		
Less: Annual exemptions			
2010/11 and 2009/10 b/f	(6,000)		
		(184,000)	
Available nil rate band		141,000	
Inheritance tax:			
£141,000 @ 0%			0
£202,000 @ 40%			80,800
			80,800
Less: Taper relief (4 to 5 years)			
£80,800 @ 40%			(32,320)
Inheritance tax liability			48,480

3   IHT liability after additional taper relief

		£
(i)	Taper relief of 60% (5 to 6 years) £(80,800 − 48,480)	32,320
(ii)	Taper relief of 80% (6 to 7 years) £(80,800 − 64,640)	16,160

38 King (06/15)

Text references. The calculation of chargeable gains and liability to capital gains tax is covered in Chapter 11. Gift relief is dealt with in Chapter 13. Inheritance tax on lifetime transfers is covered in Chapter 16. Income tax on trusts is dealt with in Chapter 3. Associated operations are covered in Chapter 18 and related property valuation in Chapter 17.

Top tips. In part (a) it is important to think through what is meant by post-tax proceeds. You need to separate out the calculation of the capital gains tax for each share and then deduct this tax from the proceeds of each share to work out the net proceeds of sale. Then it is a simple matter to work out how many shares need to be sold to produce total net proceeds of £30,000.

Easy marks. There were some easy marks in part (b)(i) for explaining basic inheritance tax concepts.

Marking scheme

					Marks
(a)	Calculation of number of shares				3
(b)	(i)	Capital gains tax		4	
		Inheritance tax		3	
			Max		6
	(ii)	Life tenant entitled to income		1	
		Receipt as dividend income with 7.5% tax credit		1	
		Recovery of tax credit, with reasons		1	
					3
(c)	Explanation of associated operations			1	
	Application to gift of flat			1½	
	Implication (value with vacant possession)			1	
	Increase in inheritance tax liability			4½	
					8
					20

(a) **Minimum number of Wye Ltd shares to be sold to generate £30,000 after tax**

Each share will be sold for £45 and so will result in a gain of £(45 – 5) = £40.

King has already used his annual exempt amount for 2018/19 so the full gain will be taxable.

King will pay tax at 20% on the gain since his income exceeds the basic rate threshold. The tax per share sold is therefore £40 × 20% = £8.

The after-tax proceeds for each share is therefore £(45 – 8) = £37.

King will therefore have to sell £(30,000/37) = <u>811</u> shares to generate total after-tax proceeds of £30,000.

Tutorial note: alternative algebraic calculation

Let x be the number of shares to be sold.

$45x - ([45 - 5]x \times 20\%) = 30,000$

$45x - 8x = 30,000$

$37x = 30,000$

$x = 811$ (rounded up)

(b)   (i)   **Gifts into interest in possession trust**

Capital gains tax (CGT)

Cash is an exempt asset for CGT and so there are no CGT implications of the gift of £30,000 to the trust.

There will be disposal at market value of the cottage in Newtown on its transfer to the trust, probably resulting in a chargeable gain. Gift relief will be available to defer this gain because the transfer is subject to an immediate inheritance tax (IHT) charge as it is a chargeable lifetime transfer as a gift to a trust. King alone (without the trustees) can elect within four years after the end of the tax year of the transfer (by 5 April 2023 as the disposal is in 2018/19) for gift relief to apply. The full gain can be deferred since there is no consideration for the transfer.

Inheritance tax (IHT)

The transfer of the cash and the cottage to the trust will be a transfer of value for IHT of £(30,000 + 315,000) = <u>£345,000</u>.

The annual exemption for 2018/19 of £3,000 is available. The annual exemption for 2017/18 has already been used against the transfer of value to Florentyna on 1 June 2017. The net chargeable lifetime transfer is therefore £(345,000 – 3,000) = <u>£342,000</u>.

The available nil rate band is £325,000 since there are no chargeable lifetime transfers in the 7 years prior to this transfer. The lifetime IHT payable by King is therefore £(342,000 – 325,000) = £17,000 × 20/80 = <u>£4,250</u>.

Tutorial note. The potentially exempt transfer to Florentyna is treated as exempt during King's lifetime and so has no effect on the nil rate band while King is alive.

(ii)   **Income tax payable by Florentyna on trust income**

Since Florentyna is the life tenant of the trust, she is entitled to receive all the income of the trust during her lifetime.

The only income is dividend income from the quoted shares and it will be received by Florentyna as dividend income with a 7.5% tax credit.

Florentyna will be able to recover this tax credit as the dividend income will fall within her dividend nil rate band.

(c)   **Gift of flat in Unicity**

Associated operations for IHT are broadly defined as:

(i)   Two or more operations which affect the same property

(ii)   Any two or more operations, where one is effected with reference to the other(s)

Where the rules apply, the series of transactions will be regarded as a single gift at the time of the final transaction in the series so that the total value transferred will be subject to tax.

The flat gifted to Axel is subject to a pre-existing rental agreement between King and Joy, as original owners of the property, and Axel's daughter as tenant. Because of this agreement, there is no right to vacant possession of the flat and so its value is reduced. The creation of the rental agreement and subsequent gift of the property may therefore be associated operations. If this is the case, the rental agreement with Axel's daughter and the transfer of the property to Axel will be a single transaction for IHT so that the transfer of the flat will be valued on a vacant possession basis, even though the rental agreement was made on a commercial basis.

If the associated operations rules do not apply, the transfer of value will be the greater of the stand alone value of a 75% share of the flat without vacant possession (£160,000) and the related property valuation since King and his wife jointly own the flat. The related property valuation is:

$$\frac{160,000}{160,000 + 40,000} \times £250,000 \qquad\qquad £200,000$$

The related property valuation therefore applies.

If the associated operations rules do apply, the transfer of value will be the greater of the standalone value of a 75% share of the flat with vacant possession (£220,000) and the related property valuation of:

$$\frac{220,000}{220,000 + 60,000} \times £340,000 \qquad\qquad £267,143$$

Again, the related property valuation therefore applies.

The increase in the value of the transfer if the associated operation rules apply is therefore £(267,143 − 200,000) = £67,143.

If King dies on 1 May 2020, the potentially exempt transfer will become chargeable. The annual exemptions for 2017/18 and 2018/19 have already been used and King's nil rate band will have been used up by his previous lifetime transfers. The additional IHT payable if the associated operations rules apply is therefore £67,143 × 40% = £26,857.

39 Cinnabar Ltd (Sep/Dec 15)

Text references. Research and development expenditure is dealt with in Chapter 20. Intra-group transfers of intangible assets are covered in Chapter 26. Chargeable gains for companies are the subject of Chapter 21. Groups and consortia are covered in Chapter 26.

Top tips. Whenever you see the disposal of shares in a company by another company, consider whether the substantial shareholding exemption applies (unless you are specifically told otherwise).

Easy marks. There were some easy marks for computing the gain in part (b). The fact that the date of disposal was important should have led you to consider the conditions for substantial shareholding exemption.

Examining team's comments. The first part required an explanation of the tax relief available for a small company in respect of expenditure on research and development. The majority of students were aware that directly related revenue expenditure qualifies for an additional [130]% deduction, but were rather vague in their explanations as to why items were or were not included. A small minority wasted time by discussing the tax credit which could be obtained in respect of a loss created by the enhanced deduction, despite there being no mention of a loss in the question, nor sufficient information to be able to calculate one. The first of the two assets sold was an intangible asset, which was sold to a wholly owned subsidiary. Intangible assets are examined fairly frequently in Advanced Taxation (ATX − UK), so candidates need to be aware of their tax treatment as trading assets, rather than capital assets, for companies, which will give rise to a balancing charge or allowance on sale, rather than a capital gain or loss. In the case of a transfer between two companies in a 75% group, the asset will be transferred at its written down value, thereby giving rise to neither profit nor loss. Interestingly, the majority of candidates identified one or other of these points, but very few identified both.

The second asset disposal related to shares in an unquoted trading company. This was the sale of an 8% shareholding in a company following a sale of 4% the previous year. In any question regarding the sale of shares in one company by another, candidates should automatically consider the application of the substantial shareholding exemption (SSE). This is an area where it is very important to know the precise conditions and to be able to state definitively whether or not the exemption applies, and the reasons why or why not. In this case the timing of the disposal was critical; bringing the date of disposal forward would mean that the requirement to hold at least 10% of the shares for a continuous 12-month period in the 2 years prior to sale would be satisfied, whereas this would not be the case if the disposal was delayed. An ability to advise on the timing of transactions in respect of all taxes is an important skill in Advanced Taxation (ATX – UK).

The final part of this question concerned a proposed joint venture between two companies, where two alternative group structures were being considered. The new company to be set up would be loss-making initially. The key issue here was to be able to differentiate between a group for group relief purposes (which requires one company to have a minimum 75% holding in another) and a consortium (which is formed where two or more companies hold a minimum of 75% between them in a third company, each with at least 5%, but none holding 75% or more on their own). It was disappointing to see that a good number of candidates were unclear on these definitions, thereby producing incorrect answers and scoring few marks. However, well-prepared candidates who were able to make this distinction tended to go on and score well in respect of the way in which the new company's trading losses could be relieved.

Marking scheme

					Marks
(a)	(i)	Computer hardware – 100% capital allowance	1		
		Revenue expenditure qualifying for additional deduction	3½		
		Calculation of total deduction	1		
			Max	5	
	(ii)	Intra-group disposal of intangible asset		2	
(b)		After-tax proceeds	2		
		Advantage of disposal in October	3		
				5	
(c)		Structure 1	2		
		Structure 2 – Consortium	2		
		Relief available	5½		
			Max	8	
				20	

(a) (i) **Research and development expenditure**

The computer hardware qualifies for a 100% capital allowance as capital expenditure on an asset related to research and development.

As Cinnabar Ltd is a small enterprise for research and development purposes, the revenue expenditure which is directly related to undertaking research and development activities qualifies for an additional 130% deduction in calculating its taxable trading income. This additional deduction applies to the software and consumables and the staff costs. However, as the external contractor is provided by an unconnected company, only £6,500 (65% of the £10,000 fee) will qualify for this additional deduction.

The rent payable is not a qualifying category of expense, so is not eligible for the additional deduction.

The total deduction from taxable trading profit for the year ended 31 March 2018 is therefore £423,650 (£228,000 + 130% × £(18,000 + 126,000 + 6,500)).

(ii) **Intra-group transfer of an intangible asset**

As Cinnabar Ltd owns more than 75% of Lapis Ltd, the intangible asset will be treated for corporation tax purposes as having been transferred intra-group at its tax written down value, thereby giving rise to neither profit nor loss in Cinnabar Ltd's corporation tax computation.

(b) **Disposal of Garnet Ltd shares**

A chargeable gain will arise on the proposed disposal in November 2018, calculated as follows:

	£
Sale proceeds	148,000
Less: Cost £120,000 × 2/3	(80,000)
Indexation allowance 0.1549 × £80,000	(12,392)
Chargeable gain	55,608
Corporation tax payable (£55,608 × 19%)	10,566
After-tax proceeds (£148,000 – £10,566)	137,434

The substantial shareholding exemption would not be available in respect of a disposal in November 2018. This is because Cinnabar Ltd's shareholding was reduced to 8% following the disposal on 20 October 2017 and consequently it has not held at least 10% of the shares in Garnet Ltd for a continuous 12-month period in the 2 years prior to disposal.

As Cinnabar Ltd held 12% of the shares prior to the first disposal on 20 October 2017, the sale should be brought forward to a date prior to 20 October 2018 in order for the substantial shareholding exemption to apply to the sale. In this case, Cinnabar Ltd's corporation tax liability in relation to the disposal of these shares will be reduced to nil.

Tutorial note. The shares in Garnet Ltd are in the FA 1985 share pool. Accordingly, the indexation factor is not rounded to three decimal places.

(c) **Loss relief implications of the alternative structures**

Structure 1:

Under this structure, Amber Ltd will own more than 75% of the shares in Beryl Ltd, so Beryl Ltd will be in a group with Amber Ltd for the purposes of group relief for trading losses. Accordingly, none of Beryl Ltd's trading loss will be available for surrender to Cinnabar Ltd.

Structure 2:

Under this structure, Beryl Ltd will be a consortium-owned company, with Amber Ltd and Cinnabar Ltd as the consortium members. This is because each of the companies owns at least 5% of the shares in Beryl Ltd, and together they hold at least 75% of the shares.

Beryl Ltd's trading loss for the year ending 31 December 2019 may be surrendered to the consortium members according to their respective shareholdings. Cinnabar Ltd may therefore claim a maximum of £19,200 (24% of Beryl Ltd's loss of £80,000) in respect of this year. Relief will be taken against Cinnabar Ltd's taxable total profits for the corresponding accounting period(s).

As Cinnabar Ltd prepares accounts to 31 March annually, the maximum loss which can be claimed for relief in the year ending 31 March 2019 will be the lower of £4,800 (3/12ths of the available loss of £19,200) and 3/12ths of Cinnabar Ltd's taxable total profit for the year ending 31 March 2019. Similarly, the maximum loss which can be claimed for relief in the year ending 31 March 2020 is the lower of £14,400 (9/12ths of £19,200) and 9/12ths of Cinnabar Ltd's taxable total profit for the year ending 31 March 2020.

Cinnabar Ltd expects to pay corporation tax by instalments so, as it has one related 51% group (Lapis Ltd), its taxable total profit must exceed the profit threshold of £750,000 (£1,500,000/2). Therefore, the loss relief must be the lower figure for each 12-month period, which will be £4,800 in the year ending 31 March 2019 and £14,400 in the year ending 31 March 2020.

40 Hyssop Ltd (Sep/Dec 15)

Text references. Employment income is covered in Chapter 4. Property income is dealt with in Chapter 3. Chargeable gains for companies is covered in Chapter 21. Value added tax (VAT) on land and buildings and the capital goods scheme are dealt with in Chapter 29.

Top tips. In part (a), make sure you follow the requirements and deal first with Corin's position for both alternatives and then with Hyssop Ltd's position for both alternatives, rather than all the tax implications for each alternative. Don't forget that both employers and employees are liable for Class 1 national insurance contributions, but only employers pay Class 1A contributions.

Easy marks. There were some easy marks for dealing with the premium on the acquisition of the short lease in part (b).

Examining team's comments. The first part required candidates to consider two possible ways in which an employer could provide financial assistance to an employee in respect of home to work travel and to advise on the most cost-efficient method. Although this was, arguably, very straightforward, it was not easy to get right. As always, those candidates who thought before writing did considerably better than those who simply wrote. In particular, they recognised the importance of national insurance contributions. Most candidates identified the income tax and corporation tax implications of the two alternatives. The one point that many missed out on was the fact that the provision of a parking space is an exempt benefit. The problems related to the national insurance position. Some candidates missed this out completely. Others were simply not orderly enough, such that they did not earn as many marks as they could have done. Candidates needed to recognise that the provision of a motorcycle to an employee would result in a liability to Class 1A national insurance contributions for the employer but no liability to national insurance contributions for the employee, whereas making a payment towards an employee's driving costs would result in a liability to Class 1 national insurance contributions for both the employer and the employee. Many candidates wrote about the statutory mileage rates, but these are only relevant where payments are in respect of journeys made when carrying out employment duties, which was not the case here.

The second part of the question concerned a premium paid in respect of a lease and the availability of rollover relief. This part was not done particularly well. There were two distinct aspects to this part of the question. The first concerned the tax deduction available in respect of the premium paid. Most candidates were able to make a start on this but very few made it to the end. The first task was to determine the amount of the premium that would be taxed on the landlord as income. This amount was then divided by the number of years of the lease in order to determine the annual deduction. The deduction in the current period was then 11/12 of the annual deduction because the lease was entered into when there were 11 months of the accounting period remaining. The second part of the question concerned the availability of rollover relief. Most candidates knew the basics of rollover relief. However, they did not score as well as they could have done for two reasons:

(a) The asset sold had not been used for the purposes of the trade for the whole of the period of ownership. As a result, although rollover relief was available, only the business-use proportion of the gain could be relieved and only that proportion of the proceeds needed to be reinvested in qualifying business assets.

(b) They failed to realise that the lease was a depreciating asset for the purposes of rollover relief, such that the gain would be deferred until the earliest of the date of disposal of the lease, the date the leased building ceased to be used in the business and ten years after the acquisition of the lease.

The final part of the question concerned the capital goods scheme for VAT and was not done particularly well. The capital goods scheme is not easy to explain and many candidates were unable to organise their thoughts and provide a coherent explanation of the implications of the disposal of a building. Candidates would help themselves if they told the story from the beginning.

(a) The first point to make was that the input tax on the purchase of the building would have been recovered in full.

(b) It was then necessary to recognise that the sale of the building would be an exempt supply.

(c) As a result of the exempt supply, there will be deemed to be 0% taxable use of the building for the remainder of the 10-year adjustment period resulting in a repayment of VAT to HM Revenue & Customs (HMRC).

				Marks
(a)	(i)	Cost of motorcycle	1½	
		Cost of driving costs reimbursement	3	
		Conclusion	½	
				5
	(ii)	Cost of provision of motorcycle	1½	
		Cost of driving costs reimbursement	1	
		All costs deductible for corporation tax	½	
		Conclusion	½	
		Max		3
(b)		Deduction:		
		Available against taxable trading income	1	
		Amount	3	
		Deferral relief available	3	
		Date gain crystallises	2	
		Max		8
(c)		Disposal exempt	1½	
		Initial reclaim	1	
		Repayment of VAT reclaimed previously y/e 31 December 2018	2	
		Max		4
				20

(a) **Assistance with home to work travel costs for Corin**

(i) **Cost to Corin**

Alternative 1 – provision of a motorcycle

Corin is a higher rate taxpayer, so will pay income tax at 40% on the annual taxable benefit. This will be £1,264 (£3,160 × 40%).

Corin will have no national insurance liability in respect of this benefit, so the total cost to him is £1,264.

Alternative 2 – payment towards the cost of driving and provision of parking place

Provision of a parking place at or near an employee's normal place of work is an exempt benefit for income tax.

Corin will pay income tax at 40% on the cash received as reimbursement of his driving costs, together with Class 1 national insurance contributions at 2%. This will give rise to a total tax cost of £941 (£2,240 × 42%).

The additional driving costs not reimbursed are £580 (£2,820 – £2,240). The total cost to Corin of this option is therefore £1,521 (£941 + £580).

The most cost-efficient option for Corin is therefore provision of the motorcycle.

Tutorial note. The statutory mileage rates are not relevant in this case as the driving costs are not related to journeys made in the course of Corin carrying out his duties of employment.

(ii)   **Cost to Hyssop Ltd**

Alternative 1 – provision of a motorcycle

Hyssop Ltd will have to pay Class 1A national insurance contributions of £436 (£3,160 × 13.8%) in respect of the provision of the motorcycle. The total cost to Hyssop Ltd is therefore £3,596 (£3,160 + £436).

Alternative 2 – payment towards the cost of driving and provision of parking place

As the provision of the parking place is an exempt benefit for income tax, there will be no Class 1A liability for Hyssop Ltd.

Hyssop Ltd will have a Class 1 national insurance liability in respect of the reimbursement of driving costs. This will be £309 (£2,240 × 13.8%).

The total cost to Hyssop Ltd is therefore £3,469 (£2,240 + £309 + £920).

The most cost-efficient option for Hyssop Ltd is therefore the payment towards the cost of driving and provision of the parking place.

Hyssop Ltd will be able to deduct all the costs for corporation tax purposes under both options.

Tutorial note. As the amounts are deductible for corporation tax purposes under both options, there is no need to calculate the after-tax cost to Hyssop Ltd.

(b)   **Corporation tax implications of the acquisition of the 40-year lease**

As Hyssop Ltd has paid a premium on the grant of a short lease on a property which is going to be used in its trade, a deduction is available for each year of the lease in calculating Hyssop Ltd's taxable trading income.

The annual deduction is calculated as $\dfrac{\text{Amount of premium taxed as income on the landlord}}{\text{Number of years of the lease}}$

The amount of the premium which is taxed as income on the landlord is £57,200 (£260,000 – (£260,000 × (40 – 1) × 2%)).

The annual deduction available to Hyssop Ltd is £1,430 (£57,200/40).

As the lease was only acquired on 1 February 2018, the deduction available in the year ended 31 December 2018 is restricted to £1,311 (£1,430 × 11/12).

The factory is used in Hyssop Ltd's trade, so the lease is a qualifying business asset, and it was acquired within the 12 months before the disposal of the warehouse. Therefore the full business use element of the gain arising may be deferred to the extent that the proceeds relating to the business use of the warehouse have been reinvested in the lease.

The warehouse will have been owned by Hyssop Ltd for four years (1 January 2015 to 31 December 2018).

The warehouse has been used by Hyssop Ltd in its trade for three years (1 January 2015 to 31 December 2017).

The proceeds relating to the business use element of the gain are £236,250 (75% × £315,000). This is less than the £260,000 premium reinvested in the acquisition of the lease, therefore the full 75% of the chargeable gain relating to the business use of the warehouse can be deferred against the acquisition of the lease. Accordingly, £12,390 (£16,520 × 75%) may be deferred.

The lease is for less than 60 years and so is a wasting asset for capital gains purposes. Accordingly, the gain will be deferred until the earliest of:

(i)   The date of disposal of the lease
(ii)   The date the leased factory ceases to be used in Hyssop Ltd's business
(iii)   1 February 2028 (ten years after the acquisition of the lease)

The remaining gain of £4,130 (£16,520 × 25%), relating to the non-business use, will be included in Hyssop Ltd's corporation tax computation for the year ending 31 December 2018.

(c)   **Value added tax (VAT) implications of the disposal of the warehouse**

At the date of sale, the warehouse is more than three years old. Accordingly, because Hyssop Ltd has not opted to tax it, the disposal will be exempt from VAT.

As the warehouse was newly constructed when it was purchased, VAT of £54,000 (£270,000 × 20%) would have been charged and, as the warehouse was used in its standard rated business, this would have been wholly reclaimed by Hyssop Ltd in the year ended 31 December 2015.

As the disposal is exempt from VAT, VAT will have to be repaid to HM Revenue & Customs (HMRC) as the warehouse is deemed to have 0% taxable use for the remainder of the 10-year adjustment period under the capital goods scheme. The amount of £32,400 (£54,000 × 6/10 × (100% – 0%)) will be repayable to HMRC as a result of the disposal.

Tutorial note. A further £5,400 (£54,000 × 1/10 × (100% – 0%)) will also be repayable to HMRC in respect of the year ending 31 December 2018 as the warehouse has been rented out throughout this year, with no option to tax.

41 Jonny (Sep/Dec 15)

Text references. The basics of income tax computation are dealt with in Chapter 1. Trade profits (including basis periods on commencement) are covered in Chapter 6 and trading losses in Chapter 8. Tests of employment versus self-employment are dealt with in Chapter 4. Ethics are covered in Chapter 30. The death estate is covered in Chapter 16 and the reduced rate of inheritance tax is dealt with in Chapter 17.

Top tips. In part (a)(i) you were required to work out Jonny's post-tax income. You need to adopt a logical approach to this requirement. First, you need to work out what is the profit or loss for each tax year if demand is weak. Then you need to consider how this will be taxed (if a profit) or relieved (if a loss). You should have been able to spot that early years trading loss relief was available. Next work out how much income tax is payable or repayable. This will then enable you to work out the post-tax income position using the proforma given in the question.

Easy marks. There were some easy marks for identifying the factors which would indicate self-employment in part (a)(ii). The ethical issues in part (a)(iii) should have been well known.

Examining team's comments. A small number of candidates achieved full, or nearly full marks for part (a)(i) but a significant minority made no or very little attempt to address this part of the question, suggesting a lack of preparation for this type of question. Unincorporated businesses are tested in every paper, and questions frequently demand consideration of basis periods and/or relief for trading losses, so question practice on these areas should always form an important part of all candidates' preparation for this exam. Relief for trading losses is a technically demanding area, which requires accurate knowledge of what reliefs are available in which situations, and the precise rules or conditions in each case. Many candidates confined themselves to discussing just one method of loss relief, whereas careful reading of the question indicated that there were different options available and a decision was to be made regarding the optimum method of relief, thereby suggesting that more than one method of relief was available. It appeared that many candidates would have benefited from pausing and thinking more before they started to write. It is important in a question dealing with relief for losses that a well-considered and logical approach is taken. Weaker candidates prepared detailed income tax computations for several tax years in the apparent hope that this would eventually lead to being able to determine the rate of tax paid in each year, and an ability to calculate the tax refund suggested by the question. The problem with this approach was that it was very time consuming and tended to produce redundant information as tax years were included for which it was not possible to offset the loss. Candidates should be advised to consider first of all the tax years in which they believe loss relief is available, before launching into a series of detailed computations for which there are no marks available.

Part (a)(ii) concerned the employment status of two part-time salesmen and was done extremely well. The majority of candidates were able to identify which of the specific contractual arrangements given in the question concerning the work to be done by the salesmen indicated self-employment and any changes required to the other arrangements in order to maximise the likelihood of the salesmen being treated as self-employed. Many candidates gave the impression of being very confident with this topic, and happy to write at length about the different arrangements, giving the impression that they may well have exceeded the four marks' worth of time which should have been allocated to this part. Candidates should always take note of the number of marks available for each question part and resist the temptation to elaborate unnecessarily on areas with which they are very comfortable.

Part (a)(iii) covered the ethical issue of confidentiality in relation to using knowledge and experience gained from dealing with both current and ex-clients to assist a new client. This part was done very well by the vast majority of candidates, with many scoring full marks. It was pleasing to see that most candidates related well to the specific client and the facts given in the scenario.

Part (b) of this question required candidates to identify errors in an inheritance tax computation on a death estate, and to calculate the amount to be received by the sole beneficiary of the estate, after the correct inheritance tax had been paid. Performance on this part of the question was mixed, with a disappointing number of candidates believing that the capital gains tax exemption for chattels with a value below £6,000 also applies to inheritance tax, and that inheritance tax annual exemptions are available against assets in the death estate. These are fundamental errors which candidates in Advanced Taxation (ATX – UK) should not be making. Candidates should ensure that they are able to identify and apply correctly the different exemptions available for capital gains tax and inheritance tax as these are tested on a very regular basis. In order to calculate the correct amount of inheritance tax to be paid after correcting the errors found, the majority of candidates rewrote the entire death estate. This succeeded in gaining the relevant marks, but was probably fairly time consuming, and candidates are encouraged to try to adopt a more efficient approach, focusing on the effect of correcting the error on the value of the chargeable estate as this would save time. (**BPP note**: The residence nil rate band was not relevant when this question was originally set so the examining team made no comments on this aspect but it is likely that some candidates would have missed this error in a similar way to the other errors.) Questions in Advanced Taxation (ATX – UK) frequently ask for a calculation of after-tax proceeds – here, the amount receivable by the sole beneficiary of the estate. Candidates need to think more carefully about the starting point for this type of calculation. Here, it wasn't the value of the chargeable estate, as this includes a deduction for the nil rate band. Candidates needed to identify the actual value which would be received prior to making this deduction. Failure to identify the correct starting point is a common error.

Marking scheme

				Marks
(a)	(i)	Taxable trading profit/(loss) for weak demand	3	
		Income tax payable or refundable		
		Strong demand	2	
		Weak demand	2	
		Advice on use of loss		
		Options available	3	
		Recommendation	3	
		Summary	1	
		Calculation only an approximation	2	
		Max		15
	(ii)	One mark for each relevant point	Max	4
	(iii)	One mark for each relevant point	Max	4
(b)		Identification of errors	5½	
		Calculations		
		Inheritance tax liability	2½	
		Inheritance received by Jonny	1½	
		Max		8

Memorandum

To:	The files
Prepared by:	Tax senior
Date:	10 September 2018
Subject:	Jonny – New business
	Inheritance tax
	Other matters

(a) **Unincorporated business**

(i) **Jonny's post-tax income**

Weak demand – taxable trading profit/(loss) for the first two tax years

	£	£
2018/19 (1 November 2018 to 5 April 2019)		
Loss (£15,200 × 5/8)		(9,500)
2019/20 (1 November 2018 to 31 October 2019)		
1 November 2018 to 30 June 2019		
Loss	(15,200)	
Less recognised in 2018/19	9,500	
		(5,700)
1 July 2019 to 31 October 2019		
Profit (£18,000 × 4/12)		6,000
Profit		300

Total income tax payable/refundable

	Notes	2018/19 £	2019/20 £	Total £
Strong demand				
Taxable trading profit		5,750	19,200	
Income tax (payable)/refundable	1, 2	Nil	(1,640)	(1,640)
Weak demand				
Taxable trading profit/(loss)		(9,500)	300	
Income tax (payable)/refundable	3, 4	3,800	Nil	3,800

Notes

1. Strong demand – 2018/19

   The taxable trading income will be covered by the personal allowance.

2. Strong demand – 2019/20

   The tax liability will be £1,540 ((£19,200 − £11,500) × 20%).

3. Weak demand – 2018/19

   The taxable trading income will be nil, such that the tax liability will be nil.

   The loss of £9,500 can be offset against:

   (i) Total income of 2018/19 and/or 2017/18

       In 2018/19, Jonny will have no taxable income.

In 2017/18, Jonny had employment income of £24,000 (12 × £2,000), such that he was a basic rate taxpayer.

Or:

(ii)   Total income of 2015/16, 2016/17 and 2017/18 in that order

In 2015/16, Jonny had employment income of £72,000 (12 × £6,000), such that he had more than £9,500 of income taxable at the higher rate.

The loss should therefore be offset in 2015/16, resulting in a tax refund of £3,800 (£9,500 × 40%).

4   Weak demand – 2019/20

The taxable trading income will be covered by the personal allowance.

Post-tax income position

	Strong £	Weak £
Aggregate budgeted net profit of the first two trading periods (per email)	39,200	2,800
Aggregate income tax (payable)/refundable for the first two tax years	(1,640)	3,800
Budgeted post-tax income	37,560	6,600

These post-tax income figures are an approximation because the total income arises in a period of 20 months (1 November 2018 to 30 June 2020), whereas the total income tax payable is in respect of only 17 months (5 months in 2018/19 and the whole of 2019/20).

(ii)   **Salesmen**

Proposed contractual arrangements indicating self-employed status

(1)   The salesmen will be paid a fee by reference to the work they do. This will enable them to earn more by working more efficiently and effectively.

(2)   The salesmen will not be paid sick pay or holiday pay; such payments would be indicative of employed status.

(3)   The salesmen will be required to use their own cars.

Suggested changes in order to maximise the likelihood of the salesmen being treated as self-employed

(1)   It would be helpful if the salesmen were able to work on the days they choose rather than being required to work on specific days.

(2)   The salesmen should be required to provide their own laptop computer rather than borrowing one from Jonny.

Tutorial note. The period for which the salesmen will work is not a relevant factor in determining their status. However, the longer they are appointed for, the more likely it is that the factors indicating employment (for example, the degree of control over the worker) will be present.

(iii)   **New contracts for the business**

(1)   ACCA's Code of Ethics and Conduct includes confidentiality as one of the fundamental principles of ethics on which we should base our professional behaviour.

(2)   Where we have acquired confidential information as a result of our professional and business relationships, we are obliged to refrain from using it to our own advantage or to the advantage of third parties.

(3)   This principle of confidentiality applies to both ex-clients and continuing clients.

(4)   As a result of this, we should not use any confidential information relating to our existing clients or ex-clients to assist Jonny.

(5)   We are permitted to use the experience and expertise we have gained from advising our clients.

(b) **Jonny's inheritance from his mother**

Errors identified

(i) Chattels (for example, furniture, paintings and jewellery) with a value of less than £6,000 are not exempt for the purposes of inheritance tax (although they are exempt for the purposes of capital gains tax).

(ii) The annual exemption is not available in respect of transfers on death.

(iii) The residence nil rate band will apply because Jonny's mother left her main residence to Jonny. The residence nil rate band is the lower of £100,000 and the value of the house of £530,000 ie £100,000.

(iv) The reduced rate of inheritance tax of 36% will apply. This is because:

    (1) The chargeable estate, before deduction of the charitable donation but after deduction of the nil rate band (not the residence nil rate band), is £689,000 (£619,000 (£591,000 + £25,000 + £3,000) + £70,000)

    (2) The gift to the charity of £70,000 is more than 10% of this amount

Value of inheritance receivable by Jonny

	£
Chargeable estate per draft computation	892,000
No exemption for chattels valued at less than £6,000	25,000
No annual exemption	3,000
	920,000
Less: Residence nil rate band	(100,000)
Nil rate band	(301,000)
	519,000
Inheritance tax at 36%	186,840
Assets inherited by Jonny	
(£530,000 + £400,000 + £40,000 + £20,000 – £70,000)	920,000
Less inheritance tax payable	(186,840)
Inheritance receivable by Jonny	733,160

Mock exams

ACCA Strategic Professional – Options

Advanced Taxation (ATX – UK)

Mock Exam 1

(ACCA September/December 2016 Sample questions updated to FA 2017)

Question Paper	
Time allowed	**3 hours 15 minutes**
This paper is divided into two sections	
Section A	**BOTH questions are compulsory and MUST be attempted**
Section B	**BOTH questions are compulsory and MUST be attempted**

DO NOT OPEN THIS PAPER UNTIL YOU ARE READY TO START UNDER EXAMINATION CONDITIONS

SECTION A – BOTH questions are compulsory and MUST be attempted

1 Hahn Ltd group (Sep/Dec 16)

Your manager has had a meeting with the finance director of Hahn Ltd, which is a client of your firm. Extracts from the memorandum she prepared following the meeting, and an email from her in connection with the Hahn Ltd group are set out below:

Extracts from the memorandum – dated 8 September 2018

Hahn Ltd group

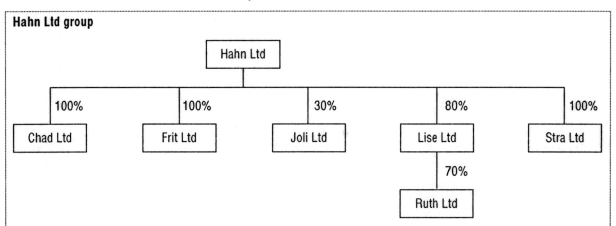

Notes

1   All of the companies are UK resident trading companies with a year end of 31 March.

2   All of the companies are registered for the purposes of value added tax (VAT).

3   With the exception of Chad Ltd, all of the companies have been members of the Hahn Ltd group for many years.

4   Hahn Ltd purchased Chad Ltd from Zeno Ltd on 1 September 2018. Prior to its disposal to Hahn Ltd, Zeno Ltd had owned Chad Ltd, and six other wholly-owned subsidiaries, for many years.

5   Joli Ltd is not a consortium company.

Budgeted results for the year ending 31 March 2019

	Hahn Ltd £'000	Chad Ltd £'000	Frit Ltd £'000	Joli Ltd £'000	Lise Ltd £'000	Ruth Ltd £'000	Stra Ltd £'000
Tax adjusted trading profit/(loss)	180	675	(540)	410	375	320	38
Chargeable gains	–	–	65	–	–	–	–
Trading loss brought forward	–	–	–	–	–	–	46
Capital loss brought forward	–	–	31	–	–	–	–
Assets purchased which qualify for rollover relief	–	–	14	–	–	6	10

Extracts from the memorandum – dated 8 September 2018 (continued)

Notes

Notes

1   The budgeted results include £94,000 of sales made by Hahn Ltd to Stra Ltd. The arm's length price of these sales would be £104,000. Both of these figures are exclusive of VAT. No tax adjustments have been made in respect of these sales. The Hahn Ltd group is a large group for the purposes of the transfer pricing rules.

2   Frit Ltd's chargeable gain will be in respect of the sale of a building to an unconnected third party for £125,000. The building is a qualifying business asset for the purposes of rollover relief.

3   None of the companies will receive any dividends in the year ending 31 March 2019.

4   Frit Ltd will not be able to carry its loss back to the year ended 31 March 2018.

5   All of the companies, with the exception of Frit Ltd and Stra Ltd, were required to pay their corporation tax liabilities for the year ended 31 March 2018 by instalments.

VAT

(a)   The Hahn Ltd group is considering registering as a VAT group. Frit Ltd makes some exempt supplies, such that it is a partially exempt company. The other six companies all make standard rated supplies only. Stra Ltd uses both the annual accounting scheme and the cash accounting scheme.

(b)   On 1 September 2018, Chad Ltd received a refund of VAT from HM Revenue and Customs (HMRC). The company has not been able to identify any reason for this refund.

Email from your manager – dated 8 September 2018

Please prepare a memorandum for the client files which addresses the following issues:

(a)   (i)   **Chargeable gain of Frit Ltd**

Calculate the additional amount which would need to be spent on assets qualifying for rollover relief, such that the unrelieved gain would be fully covered by Frit Ltd's brought forward capital loss.

(ii)   **Relieving the trading loss of Frit Ltd**

(1)   Prepare explanations, together with supporting calculations, to show how the trading loss of Frit Ltd should be allocated between the companies in the group. The group's priority is its cash flow position and the need to minimise the corporation tax payable by instalments.

When preparing these calculations, you should assume that the whole of the chargeable gain of Frit Ltd will be relieved by rollover relief.

(2)   Prepare a schedule setting out the amounts of corporation tax payable by Hahn Ltd, and the companies it controls (ie not Joli Ltd) in respect of the year ending 31 March 2019, together with the related payment dates.

(b)   **Group registration for the purposes of VAT**

By reference to the specific information in my memorandum only, set out the matters which will need to be considered when deciding which of the companies should be included in a group registration.

(c)   **Chad Ltd – refund of VAT**

Prepare a summary of the actions which we should take, and any matters of which Chad Ltd should be aware, in respect of the refund of VAT.

Tax manager

Required

Prepare the memorandum as requested in the email from your manager. The following marks are available:

(a) (i)   Chargeable gain of Frit Ltd   **(3 marks)**

     (ii) Relieving the trading loss of Frit Ltd   **(18 marks)**

(b) Group registration for the purposes of VAT   **(5 marks)**

(c) Chad Ltd – refund of VAT.   **(5 marks)**

Professional marks will be awarded for the approach taken to problem solving, the clarity of the explanations and calculations, the effectiveness with which the information is communicated, and the overall presentation. **(4 marks)**

(Total = 35 marks)

2 Waverley (Sep/Dec 16)

Your manager has been advising a client, Waverley, on his plans to sell his business. An email from your manager setting out the current situation and some notes on the tax system in the country of Surferia are set out below:

Email from your manager – dated 8 September 2018

Waverley

Waverley was born in 1978. He divorced his wife in 2016. His three children, all of whom are under 18, live with his ex-wife in the UK.

Waverley began trading as a sole trader on 1 March 2010. We are advising him on the sale of this unincorporated business with the objective of minimising his capital gains tax liability. It has been concluded that it will be very difficult to sell the business as an unincorporated entity, so Waverley is going to sell the business to a newly-formed company which he owns, Roller Ltd. Waverley will then sell his shares in Roller Ltd.

Waverley has decided to emigrate to the country of Surferia. He wants to make a fresh start and has heard from friends that moving abroad could be advantageous from the point of view of UK tax. He will move to Surferia on 5 April 2019.

Waverley wants to see his children regularly and is also an enthusiastic member of an amateur football team in the UK. As a result, he intends to spend as many days as possible in the UK in the tax year 2019/20. He will continue to work for Roller Ltd until the company is sold and it is also possible that the purchaser of Roller Ltd will ask Waverley to do further work for the company whilst he is in the UK.

Waverley will sell his home in the UK in March 2019. The house is Waverley's principal private residence, such that there will be no capital gains tax in respect of its disposal. Once the house has been sold, whenever Waverley is in the UK he will stay in a hotel, as he does not have any other UK property available for his use. When he is not in the UK, he will live in a new house which he plans to buy in Surferia.

Unincorporated business

Waverley will cease trading as a sole trader on 15 January 2019 when he sells his unincorporated business to Roller Ltd. Roller Ltd will be wholly-owned by Waverley.

The tax adjusted trading profits of the business (actual and budgeted) up to the date of cessation are:

Year ended 30 June 2018   £125,400
Period ended 15 January 2019   £72,150

The assets of the unincorporated business are expected to be worth £540,000 on 15 January 2019. They will be sold at market value to Roller Ltd in exchange for 270,000 £1 ordinary shares in the company. This will result in chargeable gains, before incorporation relief, of £160,000 on the business premises and £30,000 in respect of goodwill.

The shares in Roller Ltd will be sold for £600,000 at some point during the six months following Waverley's emigration to Surferia on 5 April 2019.

Residence status

Waverley has always been resident and domiciled in the UK, but it is likely to be beneficial for him to be non-UK resident for the tax year 2019/20.

Investment property

Waverley owns an investment property located in the UK. The property is a residential house, which is tenanted under a lease which expires on 31 October 2023. This house has never been Waverley's principal private residence and it is not available for him to use.

Waverley plans to sell this house as soon as possible following the end of the lease. He will then give the proceeds from the sale to his sister.

Please carry out the following work:

(a)   **Unincorporated business**

(i)   State the basis period for 2018/19, the final tax year of trading, and calculate the taxable trading profits for that year, noting any further information required in order to finalise this figure.

(ii)   State the conditions which must be satisfied in order for incorporation relief to be available on the sale of the unincorporated business to Roller Ltd.

(iii)   Prepare calculations in order to conclude whether or not it will be advantageous for Waverley to disclaim incorporation relief on the sale of the unincorporated business to Roller Ltd.

To do this you will need to calculate Waverley's total capital gains tax liability, in the UK and in the country of Surferia, in respect of both the sale of the unincorporated business to Roller Ltd in the tax year 2018/19 and the sale of the Roller Ltd shares in the tax year 2019/20. In respect of the sale of the Roller Ltd shares, you should consider two possible situations: first, where Waverley is resident **only** in the UK at the time of the sale; and, second, where he is resident **only** in Surferia at the time of the sale. You should not consider the rules concerning individuals who are temporarily non-UK resident.

You should assume that Waverley will be a higher rate taxpayer in the tax years 2018/19 and 2019/20 (if UK resident) and that he realises sufficient additional chargeable gains every year to use his annual exempt amount.

(b)   **Residence status**

Explain the maximum number of days which Waverley will be able to spend in the UK in the tax year 2019/20 without being UK resident. I have already concluded that for the tax year 2019/20, Waverley will be neither automatically resident overseas nor automatically resident in the UK.

(c)   **Investment property**

(i)   Explain the capital gains tax implications in the tax year 2023/24 of the sale of the investment property, assuming that it gives rise to a chargeable gain and that Waverley is resident only in the country of Surferia in that tax year.

(ii)   Discuss, by reference to Waverley's domicile status, whether or not Waverley's gift to his sister of the proceeds from the sale of the investment property will be within the scope of UK inheritance tax.

Tax manager

Notes on the tax system in the country of Surferia

(1)	Individuals who are resident in Surferia are subject to capital gains tax on disposals of worldwide assets at the rate of 11%. There is no annual exempt amount.
(2)	For the purposes of capital gains tax in Surferia, Waverley's chargeable gains will be the same as they would be in the UK.
(3)	The payment date for capital gains tax in Surferia is the same as the payment date for capital gains tax in the UK.
(4)	There is no inheritance tax in Surferia.
(5)	There is a double tax treaty between the UK and Surferia.

Required

Carry out the work requested in the email from your manager. The following marks are available:

(a)	Unincorporated business	**(12 marks)**
(b)	Residence status	**(6 marks)**
(c)	Investment property	**(7 marks)**
		(Total = 25 marks)

Section B – BOTH questions are compulsory and MUST be attempted

3 Juanita (Sep/Dec 2016)

Juanita has contacted you following the death of her husband, Don. As the executor of his estate, she is seeking advice regarding the inheritance tax liability arising as a result of his death on shares which he owned. She also requires advice on the timing of her ceasing to trade.

Don:

- Died on 1 July 2018
- Had always been UK resident and domiciled
- Was married to Juanita, and they have one daughter, Lexi

Lifetime gifts:

- Don made only two lifetime gifts.
- On 9 May 2013, Don gifted his overseas villa to Lexi.
- The villa was valued at £355,000 on 9 May 2013, and at £370,000 on 1 July 2018.
- On 1 March 2015, on the advice of a financial adviser, Don gifted 3,500 of his shares in Estar Ltd to Lexi.
- Prior to receiving this advice, Don had been planning to leave these shares to Lexi on his death.
- Under the terms of Don's will, Don's cousin will inherit the remaining 3,500 shares in Estar Ltd owned by Don at his death.

Estar Ltd:

- Estar Ltd is an investment company; no business property relief is available on the transfer of its shares.
- Before the gift on 1 March 2015, Don owned 7,000 ordinary shares in Estar Ltd.
- The remaining 3,000 ordinary shares issued by Estar Ltd are held by Juanita.
- The shares were valued as follows:

Percentage shareholding	Value per share	
	1 March 2015	1 July 2018
0%–50%	£9.00	£10.80
51%–75%	£15.00	£18.00
76%–100%	£20.00	£24.00

Juanita:

- Has carried on a business as a sole trader for many years, preparing accounts to 30 June annually
- Following Don's death, intends to cease trading and retire
- Would like to cease trading on 28 February 2019, in which case the business will be sold to an unconnected person
- Is willing to continue to trade until 30 April 2019, when Lexi will be able to take over the business
- Does not anticipate having any other source of taxable income in either of the tax years 2018/19 or 2019/20

Juanita's business:

- Has taxable trading profits of £51,000 for the year ended 30 June 2018

- Has budgeted tax-adjusted profits of £48,000 (before capital allowances) in the period ending 28 February 2019

- Has budgeted further taxable profits of £4,000 per month if Juanita continues to trade after 28 February 2019

- Has overlap profits from commencement of £17,000

- The tax written down value on the main pool was £Nil at 1 July 2018

- The market value of the assets in the main pool will be £6,000 at the date of cessation

Required

(a)   Advise Juanita of the reduction in the inheritance tax liability arising on Don's death in respect of the shares in Estar Ltd as a result of Lexi having received her shares as a lifetime gift, rather than on Don's death.

(8 marks)

(b)   Advise Juanita, by reference to the increase in her trading income after tax and national insurance contributions, whether it would be beneficial for her to continue to trade until 30 April 2019, rather than ceasing to trade on 28 February 2019. You should assume any elections which are beneficial to Juanita are made and should support your advice with a brief explanation of the available capital allowances in each case.

Note. Where necessary, you should assume that there are four weeks in each month of the years 2018 and 2019.

(12 marks)

(Total = 20 marks)

4 Acryl Ltd and Cresco Ltd (Sep/Dec 2016)

Acryl Ltd and Cresco Ltd are two unrelated companies. Acryl Ltd requires advice on the implications of being placed into liquidation, particularly the timing of distributions to its shareholders. Cresco Ltd requires advice on the relief for losses on the cessation of trade, and its obligations in relation to value added tax (VAT).

(a)   **Acryl Ltd:**

- Is a UK resident trading company
- Has always prepared accounts to 30 June annually
- Has substantial distributable profits
- 70% of the company's share capital is owned by Mambo Ltd
- The remaining 30% of the share capital is owned by Mambo Ltd's managing director, Alan
- Mambo Ltd and Alan both subscribed for their shares at par value on 1 March 2012

Mambo Ltd:

- Is a UK resident trading company

Alan:

- Will be an additional rate taxpayer in the tax year 2018/19
- Will be eligible for entrepreneurs' relief on the disposal of his shares in Acryl Ltd

Liquidation of Acryl Ltd:

- Winding up will commence on 1 January 2019 with the appointment of a liquidator.

- It is anticipated that the winding up will be completed on 31 March 2019, when the company will cease trading.

Alternative timing of distributions being considered by Acryl Ltd:

- Acryl Ltd is prepared to distribute the available profits to its shareholders on 31 December 2018.

- Alternatively, Acryl Ltd will delay the distribution until the completion of the winding up of the company on 31 March 2019.

Required

(i) State the corporation tax consequences arising from the commencement of Acryl Ltd's winding up on 1 January 2019. **(2 marks)**

(ii) Explain the tax implications for both Mambo Ltd and Alan if the distribution to be made by Acryl Ltd occurs either on 31 December 2018, or alternatively on 31 March 2019, and conclude as to which date would be preferable. **(7 marks)**

(b) **Cresco Ltd:**

- Is a UK resident trading company

- Commenced trading on 1 April 2014

- Is registered for the purposes of VAT

- Has made significant trading losses in recent months such that the company will need to cease trading on 31 October 2018

Cresco Ltd – trading losses:

- Recent and anticipated results are as follows:

	Year ended 31 March 2015 £	Year ended 31 March 2016 £	Year ended 31 March 2017 £	Year ended 31 March 2018 £	Period ending 31 October 2018 £
Trading (loss)/profit	(5,000)	21,000	8,000	(24,000)	(40,000)
Bank interest receivable	1,000	3,000	3,000	Nil	Nil

- Cresco Ltd always claims relief for trading losses as early as possible.

Required:

(i) Set out, together with supporting explanations, how Cresco Ltd will claim relief for the trading losses incurred and identify the amount of trading losses which will remain unrelieved after all available loss reliefs have been claimed. **(8 marks)**

(ii) Advise Cresco Ltd of the VAT implications of the cessation of its trade. **(3 marks)**

(Total = 20 marks)

Answers

DO NOT TURN THIS PAGE UNTIL YOU HAVE
COMPLETED THE MOCK EXAM

A plan of attack

We've already established that you've been told to do it 101 times, so it is of course superfluous to tell you for the 102nd time to **take a good look at the paper before diving into the answers.**

What's the worst thing you could be doing right now if this was the actual exam paper? Wondering how to celebrate the end of the exam in about three hours' time?

Turn back to the paper and let's sort out a **plan of attack!**

First things first

Look through the paper and work out the order in which to attack the questions. You've got **two options**. Option 1 is the option recommended by BPP.

Option 1 (if you're thinking 'Help!')

If you're a bit worried about the paper, do the questions in the order of how well you think you can answer them. If you find the questions in Section B less daunting than the questions in Section A, start with Section B.

There are **two questions** in Section B. **Question 3** has two parts. Part (a) is about the rules for valuing shares for inheritance tax purposes. You should be familiar with the concept of a transfer of value being the diminution in value of the donor's estate from Taxation (TX – UK) but this question also tests related property which is new in Advanced Taxation (ATX – UK). There are also some easy marks for a basic inheritance tax (IHT) computation.

Part (b) is about choosing a date for the cessation of trade. Again, the technical content is brought forward knowledge from Taxation (TX – UK). Don't forget to answer the requirement about giving a brief explanation of the capital allowances in each case.

Question 4 also has two parts. Part (a) has two sub-parts. Sub-part (i) simply requires a statement of the corporation tax consequences on the start of a winding-up for two marks. Be brief and to the point. Sub-part (ii) relates to the tax consequences of distributions being made **before** winding-up commenced and **during** winding-up. Hint – they are treated in different ways! Winding-up is a new topic in Advanced Taxation (ATX – UK).

Part (b) also has two sub-parts. Sub-part (i) concerns relief for trading losses for a company which you should remember from Taxation (TX – UK). Use the standard pro-forma layout for corporate losses and keep a loss memorandum. Sub-part (ii) tests another topic from Taxation (TX – UK), the value added tax treatment of cessation, for three marks.

Do not spend longer than about 75 minutes on Section B. When you've spent the allocated time on the questions in Section B turn to the **two case-study questions** in Section A.

Read the Section A questions through thoroughly before you launch into them. Once you start make sure you allocate your time to the parts within the questions according to the marks available and that, where possible, you attempt the easy marks first.

Question 1 has three parts. Part (a) is the largest part of the question and has two sub-parts. Sub-part (i) is about reinvestment of business assets (rollover) relief. Note that it only has three marks allocated to it so you should be spending not more than six minutes on it. Sub-part (ii) is about transfer pricing (new in Advanced Taxation (ATX – UK)) and group relief and payment of corporation tax (brought forward knowledge from Taxation (TX – UK)). You are told that the priority of the group is cash flow and the need to minimise corporation tax payable by instalments so you first need to work out which group companies might be liable to pay tax this way by considering their profit thresholds. Then work out how to use the loss of Frit Ltd to reduce their taxable total profits to their profit threshold.

Part (b) is about group registration for value added tax which should be familiar from your Taxation (TX – UK) studies. Make sure you deal with the facts of the situation given rather than just giving a summary of the rules.

BPP
LEARNING MEDIA

Part (c) is the five marks on ethics. It is straightforward and should give some easy marks.

Finally, don't forget that there are four professional marks in this question. In order to earn these marks you need to demonstrate a professionally acceptable style and presentation, provide calculations and explanations that are clear and logical and demonstrate effective communication and problem solving skills.

Question 2 has three parts. Part (a) is the largest part and you should spend just over 20 minutes answering it. The main focus is on the treatment of chargeable gains on the disposal of shares acquired with or without incorporation relief and also where the taxpayer is UK resident or not UK resident. You must deal with all the alternative circumstances to obtain good marks in this part. Most of part (a) is new at Advanced Taxation (ATX – UK).

Part (b) is about the residence status of an individual and tests brought forward knowledge from Taxation (TX – UK). Once again, remember to address the specific circumstances in the question.

Part (c) is about the capital gains tax treatment of the sale of a UK investment residential property and the inheritance tax implications of the gift of cash, both with overseas aspects and new in Advanced Taxation (ATX – UK). The rules concerning the first part of the question changed in 2015 and is a good example of how recent changes in tax law are examined in Advanced Taxation (ATX – UK).

Lastly, what you mustn't forget is that you have to **answer BOTH questions in Section A and BOTH questions in Section B**.

Option 2 (if you're thinking 'This paper's alright')

It never pays to be overconfident but if you're not quaking in your shoes about the exam then **turn straight to the case-study questions in Section A**.

Once you've done these questions, **move to Section B**. The question you attempt first really depends on what you are most confident at. If you are undecided look at the requirements. It may be easier to obtain more marks if these are broken down into several smaller parts. For example, Question 4 is about two unrelated companies and is broken down further into sub-parts.

No matter how many times we remind you...

Always, always **allocate your time** according to the marks for the question in total and then according to the parts of the question. And **always, always follow the requirements** exactly. For example in Question 1(a)(ii) you needed to produce a schedule of corporation tax payable and to state the payment dates. These would have gained you some easy marks.

You've got spare time at the end of the exam...?

If you have allocated your time properly then you **shouldn't have time on your hands** at the end of the exam. But if you find yourself with five or ten minutes to spare, check over your work to make sure that you have answered all the requirements of the questions and all parts of all requirements.

Forget about it!

And don't worry if you found the exam difficult. More than likely other candidates will too. If this were the real thing you would need to **forget** the exam the minute you leave the exam hall and **think about the next one**. Or, if it's the last one, **celebrate**!

1 Hahn Ltd group

Text references. Groups are dealt with in Chapter 26 and chargeable gains for companies in Chapter 21. Transfer pricing is dealt with in Chapter 20. Payment of corporation tax is covered in Chapter 22. Group registration for value added tax is covered in Chapter 28. Ethics are dealt with in Chapter 30.

Top tips. It is important to deal with the specific points asked in the question rather than provide a general explanation of topics examined. For example, in part (b) it was important to discuss the interaction between group registration, the annual accounting scheme and the partial exemption rules.

Easy marks. There were easy marks in part (a)(ii) for computation of corporation tax and the schedule of payments. In part (c), the ethical issues arising from an unexpected refund of tax should have been well known.

Examining team's comments. Part (a), which was in two parts, related to a group of UK resident companies. The first of these parts required candidates to calculate the amount to be reinvested in qualifying assets in order to leave no gain on the disposal of a building chargeable to corporation tax. Most candidates made a reasonable attempt at this, but a very significant proportion also included detailed explanations to accompany their calculations, despite these clearly not being required. The fact that this question part was worth only three marks should have led candidates to realise that a lengthy discussion was not required. Accordingly, these candidates wasted time, which could have beneficially been spent elsewhere. Candidates would be advised to double check what is required by each question before making a start. The main technical error was a failure to realise that the total investment needed must equal the sale proceeds of the building, not the chargeable gain. The second part of part (a) required candidates to relieve a trading loss within a group so as to minimise the amount of corporation tax payable by the group companies in instalments. Clearly, the majority of candidates were not aware of how this could be achieved, and therefore did not state a strategy for relieving the loss. The loss was therefore relieved in a somewhat random manner within the group. With the introduction of a unified rate of corporation tax, cash-flow issues such as this are going to be more important for groups of companies and are therefore likely to appear in future questions. There were a good number of easy marks in this part for calculating the amount of corporation tax payable by each company, which most candidates achieved, but a few didn't appear to have read this part of the requirements and so failed to produce the necessary schedule. The answers to the requirement to state the due dates for payment of the instalments, where necessary, elicited a significant number of incorrect answers in relation to the starting date as many candidates thought that this was after the end of the accounting period, rather than within it. Practical issues such as due dates for payment of tax by both companies and individuals are essential knowledge within many tax planning scenarios in Advanced Taxation (ATX – UK). Overall, group aspects of corporation tax remain a key topic in Advanced Taxation (ATX – UK) and candidates should endeavour to practise a wide range of questions on these to ensure that they are confident in dealing with different aspects of this area.

Part (b) of this question related to the consideration of specific matters relating to the group of companies when deciding which companies should be included in a group registration for value added tax (VAT) purposes. Despite the requirement stating that candidates were to refer only to the specific matters within the memorandum provided, a significant number wrote in detail about the general advantages and disadvantages of registering as a group, which was not relevant, and so wasted time. However, many candidates did identify the specific issues – one of the companies being partially exempt, and another using the annual accounting scheme and the cash accounting scheme – but then discussed what this meant for the relevant companies themselves, rather than the implications of including that company within a group registration. Unfortunately though, having identified the issues, they didn't go on to score as many marks as they could have done by answering the precise requirement.

Part (c) of this question concerned an unexpected refund of tax from HM Revenue & Customs (HMRC), and the actions to be undertaken by the firm in respect of this. This is a frequently tested area of ethics, and on the whole, candidates' performance was good, with clear explanations of the advice to be given to the client, and the consequences of the client not following this advice. Candidates generally appeared to have practised this type of question, and a good number scored full marks.

Marks were available for professional skills in this question. On the whole, the performance of candidates in this area was reasonably good with the majority of candidates producing a document in a style that was easy to follow and appropriately written, but, in many cases, failed to demonstrate problem-solving skills. The main problem in this question was the relief of a trading loss within a group of companies. A significant number of candidates went ahead with this without setting out a strategy for taking relief at the outset and so were unable to provide a structured solution which addressed the particular criteria stipulated in the requirement.

Marking scheme

					Marks
(a)	(i)	Calculation		3½	
			Max		3
	(ii)	Transfer pricing		3½	
		Rationale for loss planning		2	
		Threshold for payment by instalments		2½	
		Members of group relief group		1	
		Allocation of loss between group companies		4	
		Corporation tax liabilities		5	
		Payment schedule		4	
			Max		18
(b)		Companies to be included		2	
		Sales between members of the VAT group		1	
		VAT schemes		2	
		Frit Ltd		1	
			Max		5
(c)		The need to repay the tax		3	
		Ceasing to act		3	
			Max		5
		Problem solving		1	
		Clarity of explanation and calculations		1	
		Effectiveness of communication		1	
		Overall presentation		1	
					4
					35

(a) **Memorandum**

Client	Hahn Ltd group
Subject	Group loss planning and other matters
Prepared by	Tax senior
Date	8 September 2018

(i) **Chargeable gain of Frit Ltd**

The additional qualifying assets which would need to be purchased in order for the chargeable gain realised by Frit Ltd to be fully relieved by its capital losses brought forward is calculated as follows:

	£'000
Sales proceeds of asset sold	125
Proceeds retained to equal capital losses brought forward	(31)
Proceeds to be spent	94
Qualifying assets already purchased by group companies (14 + 10)	(24)
Additional amount to be spent	70

Tutorial notes

1   The amount of the chargeable gain which cannot be rolled over will be the amount of sales proceeds not reinvested. Accordingly, an amount of £31,000 should not be reinvested, such that only £34,000 of the gain will be rolled over and the remaining £31,000 of the gain will be relieved by the capital losses brought forward.

2   The additional assets can be purchased by any member of the capital gains group. The group consists of all of the companies apart from Joli Ltd (not a 75% subsidiary of Hahn Ltd) and Ruth Ltd (not a 75% subsidiary of Lise Ltd). Therefore, the £6,000 spent on purchases of assets by Ruth Ltd does not represent a qualifying reinvestment for the purposes of rollover relief.

(ii)   Relieving the trading loss of Frit Ltd

Intercompany trading

A transfer pricing adjustment will be required in respect of the sales at undervalue from Hahn Ltd to Stra Ltd. This is because Hahn Ltd controls Stra Ltd, and the group is large for the purposes of the transfer pricing rules. Accordingly, the trading profit of Hahn Ltd must be increased by £10,000 (£104,000 – £94,000), the excess of the arm's length price over the price charged for the intra-group sales. As Stra Ltd is also within the charge to UK corporation tax, its trading profits can be reduced by the same amount.

Rationale for the allocation of the trading loss

In order to maximise the benefit to the group's cash flow position, Frit Ltd's trading loss should be surrendered to those companies paying corporation tax by quarterly instalments.

*   First to any company whose profits can be reduced to the payment by instalments threshold, such that instalments will no longer be required;

*   Then to any other company with profits in excess of the payment by instalments threshold, such that their instalments will be reduced; and

*   Finally, to any other company.

The payment by instalments threshold for the Hahn Ltd group companies (excluding Chad Ltd) for the year ending 31 March 2019 is £300,000. This is the threshold of £1,500,000 divided by five (the number of related 51% group companies as at 31 March 2018 being Hahn Ltd, Frit Ltd, Lise Ltd, Ruth Ltd and Stra Ltd).

The threshold for Chad Ltd for the year ending 31 March 2019 is £187,500. This is the threshold of £1,500,000 divided by eight (the number of related 51% group companies in the Zeno Ltd group as at 31 March 2018, being Zeno Ltd and its effective 51% subsidiaries).

Tutorial note. The instalments threshold is divided by the number of related 51% group companies as at the end of the **previous** accounting period.

Allocation of the loss

	Notes	£'000
Frit Ltd – trading loss		540
Surrender to:		
Lise Ltd (375 – 300)	1	(75)
Chad Ltd	2	(315)
Hahn Ltd – the balance	3, 4	150

Notes

1   The taxable total profits of Lise Ltd should be reduced to no more than £300,000 so that the company will not have to pay corporation tax by instalments.

2   Chad Ltd will have been a member of the group relief group for only seven months of the accounting period. Accordingly, the maximum loss which can be surrendered by Frit Ltd to Chad Ltd is £315,000, ie the lower of:

    Frit Ltd – loss for the corresponding seven-month period of £315,000 (£540,000 × 7/12); and

    Chad Ltd – profit for the corresponding seven-month period of £393,750 (£675,000 × 7/12).

    This is not sufficient to reduce the taxable total profits of Chad Ltd to £187,500 but it will reduce the company's corporation tax liability and therefore the instalments due.

3   The trading profit of Stra Ltd of £28,000 (£38,000 – £10,000) will be reduced to zero by its trading loss brought forward.

4   Joli Ltd and Ruth Ltd are not effective 75% subsidiaries of Hahn Ltd and are therefore not in the group relief group.

Tutorial note. It would be equally acceptable to surrender the balance of the loss of £150,000 to Lise Ltd rather than Hahn Ltd because the corporation tax liability of both companies is due on 1 January 2020 rather than by quarterly instalments.

Corporation tax liabilities for the year ending 31 March 2019

	Hahn Ltd £'000	Chad Ltd £'000	Lise Ltd £'000	Ruth Ltd £'000
Taxable total profit	180	675	375	320
Transfer pricing adjustment	10			
Group relief	(150)	(315)	(75)	Nil
	40	360	300	320
Corporation tax at 19%:				
Due in instalments		68.4		60.8
Due on 1 January 2020	7.6		57.0	

Frit Ltd and Stra Ltd will have no taxable total profits and therefore will not have a corporation tax liability.

Payment schedule

Date	Payment £'000	Working £'000
14 October 2018	32.3	(¼ × (68.4 + 60.8))
14 January 2019	32.3	
14 April 2019	32.3	
14 July 2019	32.3	
1 January 2020	64.6	(7.6 + 57)

(b)   **Group registration for the purposes of value added tax (VAT)**

A group registration could be made in respect of all of the companies in the Hahn Ltd group with the exception of Joli Ltd (because this company is not controlled by Hahn Ltd). However, it is not necessary to include all of the qualifying companies within the group registration.

Sales from one company in the VAT group to another would be disregarded for the purposes of VAT. Therefore, there would be no requirement to charge VAT on the sales made by Hahn Ltd to Stra Ltd.

The annual accounting scheme is not available where companies are registered as a group. The cash accounting scheme would be available but only if the group's taxable turnover was less than £1,350,000. These matters should be considered before deciding whether or not Stra Ltd should be included in the group registration.

The inclusion of Frit Ltd in the group registration would result in the group being partially exempt. This could increase the total input tax recovered by the group, for example, if the results of the group as a whole satisfy the partial exemption *de minimis* limits. Alternatively, the calculation of the recoverable input tax for the group as a whole could result in a reduction in the total input tax recovered. Accordingly, further consideration is required before deciding whether or not Frit Ltd should be included in the group registration.

(c)   **Chad Ltd – refund of VAT**

We should investigate the VAT reporting of Chad Ltd in order to determine whether or not there is a valid reason for the refund.

If we are unable to identify a valid reason, we would have to conclude that the refund was made as a result of error on the part of HM Revenue and Customs (HMRC), in which case it should be repaid immediately. We should inform Chad Ltd that failing to return the money in these circumstances may well be a civil and/or a criminal offence.

We should also advise Chad Ltd to inform HMRC of their error as soon as possible in order to minimise any interest and penalties which may otherwise become payable.

If Chad Ltd is unwilling to return the money, we would have to consider ceasing to act as advisers to the company. We would then have to notify the tax authorities that we no longer act for Chad Ltd, although we would not provide them with any reason for our action. We should also consider whether or not it is necessary to make a report under the money laundering rules.

2 Waverley

Text references. Trade profits are the subject of Chapter 6. Incorporation relief is covered in Chapter 13, the computation of capital gains tax in Chapter 11 and overseas aspects of chargeable gains in Chapter 14. Residence status is dealt with in Chapter 10. The overseas aspects of inheritance tax will be found in Chapter 18.

Top tips. In part (a) it was important to deal with each of the scenarios in turn. There were two aspects to be considered – first whether to disclaim incorporation relief or not and secondly the residence status of Waverley. Advanced Taxation (ATX – UK) questions often involve considering alternative scenarios so it is vital to practice how to approach such requirements.

Easy marks. There were some easy marks in part (a) for basic capital gains tax computations. The residence tests ties in part (b) were brought forward knowledge from Taxation (TX – UK).

Examining team's comments. Part (a) of this question required candidates to deal with various aspects of incorporating a business, including the income tax implications of the cessation of trade for the sole trader, and the capital gains tax implications of a disposal of shares in the new company, on the assumption that incorporation relief was taken, or, alternatively, disclaimed.

An ability to identify the basis periods for taxation of a business in its opening and closing years, is a fundamental skill which candidates are expected to apply in Advanced Taxation (ATX – UK). Relatively few candidates were able to do this correctly in the case of the final tax year for this business. This is regarded as essential brought forward knowledge, and is tested on a regular basis.

The assets of the business were transferred to the company on incorporation in return for consideration comprising wholly of shares, such that the total gains on the chargeable assets were eligible for incorporation relief. Alternatively, if incorporation relief was disclaimed, the chargeable gains would be taxable.

The two most common errors in this part of the question were:

(i)   Failure to recognise that goodwill transferred to a company which is a close company and in which the transferor is a participator, will not qualify for entrepreneurs' relief.

(ii)   Failure to realise that the nominal value of the shares issued as consideration does not necessarily equal the market value of the shares. The nominal value of the shares issued is irrelevant; their market value must equal the total market value of the assets transferred where they represent the total consideration. This is a commonly tested examination point in this area, but was only picked up by a few candidates.

A logical approach was required for the final aspect of this part of the question, to calculate the capital gains tax liability arising on the subsequent disposal of shares, both with and without disclaiming incorporation relief, and on the alternative assumptions that the taxpayer was UK resident or overseas resident. Candidates needed to take a step back and ensure that they understood the full picture, before embarking on the calculations. This advice is also applicable more generally to Section A questions, where candidates need to stop and think about the scenario as a whole before starting to undertake the detailed work required.

Part (b) required candidates to identify the relevant 'ties' to determine the residence status, which applied to the taxpayer who has left the UK. The question clearly stated that the automatic tests for determining both UK and overseas residence were not satisfied, but a minority of candidates still discussed these rules, gaining no marks, and wasting time. However, overall this part of the question was done well, with candidates being aware of the relevant ties, and applying them to the taxpayer's situation.

Part (c) concerned the capital gains tax implications, both in the UK and overseas, of an overseas resident taxpayer disposing of a UK investment property acquired when previously resident in the UK. Most candidates realised that this was chargeable overseas, but very few appeared to be aware of recent legislation (FA 2015), which now includes disposals of UK residential property by a non-resident individual as being within the scope of UK capital gains tax. The taxpayer's domicile, rather than residence status, was relevant to the second part of this requirement, which related to the gift of the proceeds from the sale of the investment property. This was not particularly well done, with many candidates not recognising the relevance of the concept of deemed domicile, and of the location of the asset being gifted. The definition and relevance of an individual's residence and domicile for the purposes of both capital taxes is a frequently tested area in Advanced Taxation (ATX – UK), and candidates should ensure that they are confident with applying these in context.

			Marks
(a)	Taxable trading profits	2½	
	Sale of business to Roller Ltd		
	Incorporation relief conditions	2	
	Calculations without incorporation relief	2	
	Calculations with incorporation relief	1	
	Sale of Roller Ltd		
	Chargeable gain on disposal	2½	
	Capital gains tax	2	
	Conclusion	2	
		Max	12
(b)	Consideration of each tie	5	
	Conclusions	2	
		Max	6
(c)	Capital gains tax		
	Gain on UK property	2	
	Relief under the treaty	2	
	An additional discretionary mark may be given for the administrative requirements of capital gains tax		
	Inheritance tax		
	Liability to UK inheritance tax	1	
	Cessation of UK domicile	2	
	Deemed domicile	1	
	Conclusion	1	
		Max	7
			25

(a) **Unincorporated business**

Final tax year of trading

The basis period for 2018/19, the final tax year of trading, is from 1 July 2017 to 15 January 2019. Accordingly, the taxable trading profit will be £197,550 (£125,400 + £72,150).

Any overlap profits from when Waverley began trading are deductible from this figure; this information is required in order to finalise the taxable trading profit.

Incorporation relief – conditions

- Waverley's unincorporated business must be transferred to Roller Ltd as a going concern.

- All of the assets of the unincorporated business, other than cash, must be transferred.

- The whole or part of the consideration for the transfer must be the issue of shares by Roller Ltd to Waverley.

Sale of the unincorporated business to Roller Ltd and subsequent sale of Roller Ltd

Disclaim incorporation relief

Sale of the unincorporated business to Roller Ltd (2018/19)

Country of residence of Waverley:		UK
	£	£
Chargeable gains arising (per question)	190,000	
Capital gains tax (CGT): £160,000 × 10%		16,000
£30,000 × 20%		6,000
		22,000

Sale of shares in Roller Ltd (2019/20)

Country of residence of Waverley:		UK	Surferia
	£	£	£
Proceeds	600,000		
Less: Cost	(540,000)		
Chargeable gain	60,000		
CGT in the UK at 20%		12,000	
CGT in Surferia at 11%			6,600
Total CGT (£22,000 + £12,000/£6,600)		34,000	28,600

Tutorial note. Entrepreneurs' relief is not available in respect of goodwill transferred to a close company by a shareholder in that company unless the shares are sold within 28 days.

With incorporation relief

Sale of the unincorporated business to Roller Ltd (2018/19)

Country of residence of Waverley:		UK
	£	£
Chargeable gains arising (£160,000 + £30,000)	190,000	
Less: Incorporation relief	(190,000)	
	Nil	Nil

Sale of shares in Roller Ltd (2019/20)

Country of residence of Waverley:		UK	Surferia
	£	£	£
Proceeds	600,000		
Less: Cost (£540,000 – £190,000)	(350,000)		
Chargeable gain	250,000		
CGT in the UK at 20%		50,000	
CGT in Surferia at 11%			27,500
Total CGT		50,000	27,500

Conclusion

Whether or not Waverley should disclaim incorporation relief depends on whether he is resident in the UK or Surferia in the tax year 2019/20. If he is resident in the UK, he should disclaim incorporation relief as this will result in a lower overall CGT liability. However, if he is resident in Surferia, he should not disclaim incorporation relief as the relief will result in a lower overall CGT liability as well as a deferral of the date on which the tax is payable.

(b)   **Residence status**

The number of days which Waverley can spend in the UK in 2019/20 without being UK resident will depend on the number of ties he has with the UK.

Waverley will definitely satisfy two ties:

- He was in the UK for more than 90 days in 2018/19, the previous tax year.
- In 2019/20 Waverley will have children under the age of 18 who are resident in the UK.

Waverley will also satisfy a third tie if he works in the UK for 40 days or more in 2019/20.

Waverley will not satisfy the following two ties in respect of 2019/20:

- He will not have accommodation in the UK available for his use.
- He will not be in the UK for more days than in any other country.

Accordingly, Waverley will satisfy either two or three ties.

Waverley was UK resident in the previous three tax years. Accordingly, if he works in the UK for 40 days or more, such that he satisfies three ties, he will only be able to spend up to 45 days in the UK without becoming UK resident.

If Waverley does not work in the UK for 40 days or more, he will only satisfy two ties, and will therefore be able to spend up to 90 days in the UK without becoming UK resident.

Tutorial note. The question states that Waverley will not be automatically UK resident in the tax year 2019/20. Accordingly, he must be in the UK for less than 183 days. The question also states that he will live in Surferia when he is not in the UK. Accordingly, he will spend more days in Surferia than he will in the UK.

(c)   **Investment property**

CGT

The gain on the sale of the property will be subject to Surferian CGT because Waverley will be resident in Surferia when he sells the property.

That part of the gain which has accrued since 5 April 2015 will also be subject to CGT in the UK because residential property situated in the UK is subject to UK CGT regardless of the residence status of the person making the disposal.

It will therefore be necessary to consider the terms of the double tax treaty between the UK and Surferia. For example, the treaty might provide that the part of the gain on the property which would otherwise be taxed twice is only taxed in one of the two countries (double tax relief by exemption). Alternatively, it might allow the tax chargeable in one country to be deducted from the tax charged in the other (double tax relief by credit).

Inheritance tax (IHT)

Whether or not Waverley's gift to his sister will be within the scope of UK IHT will depend on Waverley's domicile status and the country in which the money is situated.

If the money is in a UK bank account it will be a UK asset, such that the gift will be within the scope of UK IHT regardless of Waverley's domicile status. If the money is in an overseas bank account it will be an overseas asset, such that it will only be subject to UK IHT if Waverley is domiciled or deemed domiciled in the UK.

In order to acquire a domicile of choice outside the UK, Waverley will need to leave the UK permanently and sever all of his links with the UK. Accordingly, whilst he has young children in the UK, and wishes to continue with his UK-based social activities, he will remain domiciled in the UK even though he will be living overseas.

In addition, even if Waverley were able to acquire a domicile of choice overseas, such that he loses his UK domicile status, for the purposes of IHT he will be deemed domiciled in the UK for a further three years and for any year where he has been UK resident for 17 out of the 20 tax years prior to the gift.

In conclusion, the gift of the proceeds from the sale of the investment property will be within the scope of UK IHT unless Waverley has acquired a domicile of choice overseas and is not deemed domiciled in the UK for the purposes of IHT.

3 Juanita

Text references. Inheritance tax transfers and diminution in value are covered in Chapter 16. Trade profits are the subject of Chapter 6 and capital allowances are covered in Chapter 7.

Top tips. Working out income tax and national insurance contributions at marginal rates is an important aspect of answering questions set in Advanced Taxation (ATX – UK).

Easy marks. There were some easy marks in part (a) for applying basic inheritance tax principles which should have been familiar from your Taxation (TX – UK) studies.

Examining team's comments. Part (a) examined two key principles in valuing unquoted shares which are gifted in lifetime, namely related property and diminution in value (comparing the value of the shareholding before and after the gift). Both of these were relevant in respect of the gift in this case, and it was pleasing to see that a significant number of candidates identified these, but unfortunately in many cases were not then able to apply them correctly to the figures given. An earlier lifetime gift was included, so that candidates had to recognise that there would be no annual exemption to bring forward, and no nil rate band available. This is a common examination technique which candidates should be familiar with if they have practised similar past examination questions. However, a common issue here was for candidates to provide a full calculation of the inheritance tax payable in respect of this earlier gift, despite this being totally irrelevant in order to address the requirement, which was to focus on the tax payable only in respect of the shares. In some cases, this wasted a considerable amount of time for no marks. This highlights the need to read the wording of the requirement very carefully to ensure that the right approach is taken and time is not wasted on unnecessary calculations.

Follow through marks were given in respect of the valuation of the shares where they were included, alternatively, in the deceased's estate on death, but a surprising number of candidates tried to apply the diminution in value principle again, with 'before' and 'after' figures, when, of course, on death, the whole of a person's holding must be transferred.

Part (b) required advice on which of two proposed dates for ceasing to trade would be beneficial for the taxpayer. The focus of the decision was the additional income after tax and national insurance contributions in each case. The requirement was deliberately worded, instructing candidates to do this by reference to the **increase** in net trading income, to encourage them to adopt a marginal approach to the question, considering only the **additional** income tax, and national insurance contributions in each case, but the majority of candidates ignored this, and produced full computations, resulting in unnecessary and repetitive computations, including figures which were common to both scenarios. It was still possible to score full marks on this basis, but would have been much more time-consuming, and care had to be taken to ensure that comparable calculations were prepared in each case in order to come to a meaningful conclusion.

In Advanced Taxation (ATX – UK) questions involving opening or closing years for an unincorporated business, it is extremely important always to identify the relevant tax years for which the assessments are being calculated. This is something which several candidates omitted to do, and as a consequence missed the significance of the fact that the second proposed cessation date fell into a later tax year such that a new personal allowance, and Class 4 national insurance contributions threshold would be available.

The majority of candidates did not address the final part of the requirements relating to an explanation of the capital allowances available. There were two aspects to this; the first is the need to calculate a balancing adjustment in the final period, and explain why, in this case it is a balancing charge. The second relates to the 'beneficial election' which was referred to in this context in the requirements. This concerns the succession election to transfer assets at written down value when the business is transferred to her daughter. This is an important election, and one which Advanced Taxation (ATX – UK) candidates should always consider when a business is being transferred to a connected person.

(a) **Inheritance tax (IHT) liability on the Estar Ltd shares**

Regardless of whether the shares in Estar Ltd were gifted to Lexi in Don's lifetime or on his death, IHT will be payable at the rate of 40% because the gift of the villa in 2013 has used the full nil rate band.

However, whether the shares were gifted or not will impact on their value in Don's death estate under the related property valuation rules.

The IHT due in respect of the Estar Ltd shares on Don's death as a result of his making the lifetime gift to Lexi is £52,240 (£27,040 + £25,200) (W).

If all the shares had been retained by Don until his death, the IHT payable in respect of the shares would have been £67,200 (7,000 × £24 × 40%).

Therefore there is a reduction in the IHT liability on the Estar Ltd shares of £14,960 (£67,200 – £52,240).

Working: Value of the lifetime gift of 3,500 shares

Related property rules apply as the shares in Estar Ltd were held by both Don and Juanita at the date of the gift.

	£
Value before the gift: 7,000 shares at £20 (70% + 30%)	140,000
Value after the gift: 3,500 shares at £15 (35% + 30%)	(52,500)
Diminution in value	87,500
Business property relief not available (as per question)	
Annual exemption 2014/15	(3,000)
2013/14 (used on gift of villa)	0
Gross chargeable transfer	84,500
IHT at 40%	33,800
Less: Taper relief at 20%	(6,760)
IHT payable by Lexi	27,040

The remaining 3,500 shares held by Don at the date of his death will give rise to an IHT liability on his death of £25,200 (40% × 3,500 × £18 (35% + 30%)).

(b) **Cessation of trade on 28 February 2019**

The profits of the year ended 30 June 2018 of £51,000 will be taxed in the tax year 2018/19.

If Juanita ceases to trade on 28 February 2019, the profits of her final accounting period will also be taxed in this tax year. The tax liability in respect of the profits of the final accounting period will therefore be as follows:

	£
Tax-adjusted profit for the eight months ending 28 February 2019	48,000
Add: Balancing charge (£Nil – £6,000)	6,000
Less: Overlap profits	(17,000)
Taxable trading profit	37,000
Income tax (£37,000 × 40%)	14,800
Class 4 NIC (£37,000 × 2%)	740
Class 2 NIC (£2.85 × 8 × 4)	91
Total deductions	15,631

Income after tax and national insurance contributions is £32,369 (£48,000 – £15,631).

Cessation of trade on 30 April 2019

If Juanita continues to trade until 30 April 2019, the profits of her final accounting period will be taxed in 2019/20. The liability for this final period will therefore be:

	£
Tax-adjusted profit for the ten months ending 30 April 2019	
(£48,000 + £4,000 + £4,000)	56,000
Add: Balancing charge	Nil
Less: Overlap profits	(17,000)
Taxable trading profit	39,000
Income tax ((£39,000 – £11,500) × 20%)	5,500
Class 4 NIC ((£39,000 – £8,164) × 9%)	2,775
Class 2 NIC (£2.85 × 10 × 4)	114
Total deductions	8,389

Income after tax and national insurance contributions is £47,611 (£56,000 – £8,389).

The increase in income after tax and national insurance contributions of £15,242 (£47,611 – £32,369) exceeds the amount of the additional two months profits of £8,000 (2 × £4,000). It is therefore beneficial for Juanita to continue to trade until 30 April 2019.

Availability of capital allowances

No writing down allowance is available in the final accounting period of a business. A balancing adjustment will, however, arise on the disposal of the assets. The sale proceeds will exceed the written down value of the assets at the start of the final period, so a balancing charge will arise.

If the sale is delayed until 30 April 2019, and the business is transferred to Lexi, then as Juanita and Lexi are connected persons, a succession election can be made to transfer the plant and machinery to Lexi at its written down value at 30 April 2019 thereby avoiding the balancing charge.

4 Acryl Ltd and Cresco Ltd

Text references. Liquidations are covered in Chapter 23. Chargeable gains for companies is the subject of Chapter 21. Losses for companies are dealt with in Chapter 24. Value added tax (VAT) implications of cessation are covered in Chapter 28.

Top tips. Don't forget your basic taxation knowledge when tackling Advanced Taxation (ATX – UK) questions! Most candidates would have known that companies do not pay corporation tax on dividends but did not stop to think carefully when approaching part (a)(ii).

Easy marks. There were some easy marks in part (b)(ii) for explaining the VAT implications of ceasing business.

Examining team's comments. Part (a)(i) required candidates to state the corporation tax implications arising for a company as a result of the appointment of a liquidator. The commencement of winding up/appointment of a liquidator is one of the factors which will bring a company's accounting period for corporation tax purposes to an end. This was worth only two marks, but most candidates appeared to not be aware of the impact on a company's accounting periods and so scored zero on this question part.

Part (a)(ii) was a 'textbook' question requiring an explanation of the tax implications for both an individual and a corporate shareholder of a distribution being made alternatively before the commencement of liquidation or on completion of the winding up. Answers were very mixed. A good number of candidates realised that the distribution would be taxed as a dividend prior to commencement of liquidation, but as a capital receipt once liquidation had commenced, although a surprising number were not aware of this distinction. For those candidates who realised this, the majority were able to go on and correctly identify the tax implications for the individual shareholder, but, disappointingly, not for the corporate shareholder. Many candidates referred to the corporate shareholder paying corporation tax on both of these, thereby failing to recognise that dividends are not taxable on corporate shareholders, and that the substantial shareholding exemption would apply in the case of the capital receipt. These are both fundamental points which candidates in Advanced Taxation (ATX – UK) need to be very familiar with, as they can be tested in a variety of different scenarios.

In part (b)(i) candidates were required to show how a company could relieve trading losses incurred in its last few periods of account. This involved consideration of loss relief in an ongoing company, in addition to the availability of terminal loss relief. It is important in any question dealing with relief for losses that a well-considered and chronological approach is taken. Precise explanations of the reliefs are required in these sorts of questions. Well-prepared candidates were able to deal correctly with the earlier losses in accounting periods prior to the final period, and were aware that, on cessation, an extended three year carry back is available, but almost all neglected to correctly calculate the loss which was available for this terminal loss relief. Nevertheless, those who adopted a sensible, logical approach scored well on this question part.

Part (b)(ii) required candidates to explain the VAT implications for the company of ceasing to trade. Many candidates were clearly confident with this situation and scored the full three marks available.

Marking scheme

					Marks
(a)	(i)	Effect on accounting periods		1	
		Two computations required		1	
					2
	(ii)	Distribution 31 December 2018		3	
		Distribution 31 March 2019		5	
		Recommendation with reason		1	
			Max		7
(b)	(i)	Loss year ended 31 March 2015		1½	
		Loss year ended 31 March 2018		1½	
		Terminal loss		5	
		Loss unrelieved		1	
			Max		8
	(ii)	Notify HMRC		1	
		Output tax on assets held on cessation		2	
					3
					20

(a) Acryl Ltd

(i) Implications of the commencement of winding up

The commencement of winding up will lead to the end of an accounting period on 31 December 2018 and the commencement of a new accounting period on 1 January 2019.

Acryl Ltd will remain liable to corporation tax until the winding up is completed. Accordingly, a corporation tax computation is required for each of the two accounting periods: the first from 1 July 2018 to 31 December 2018, and the second from 1 January 2019 to 31 March 2019.

(ii) Distribution on 31 December 2018

In this case the distribution will be made prior to the commencement of winding up and therefore will be treated as an income distribution (ie a normal dividend) for tax purposes for both shareholders.

Mambo Ltd will not be subject to corporation tax on this dividend as companies are not subject to corporation tax on dividends.

Alan will be subject to income tax on the dividend. It will be subject to income tax at 38.1% as Alan is an additional rate taxpayer to the extent that it exceeds his available dividend nil rate band.

Distribution on 31 March 2019

As the distribution will be made while the company is in liquidation, it will be treated as a capital receipt on disposal of the shares in Acryl Ltd for both shareholders.

Mambo Ltd should not be subject to corporation tax on the disposal as it should qualify as a disposal out of a substantial shareholding. Mambo Ltd will have held more than 10% of the shares in Acryl Ltd for more than 12 continuous months out of the 2 years preceding the disposal. Although Acryl Ltd is not trading because it is in liquidation, the second subsidiary exemption will apply since it is controlled by Mambo Ltd.

Alan will be subject to capital gains tax on any gain arising. As Alan is eligible for entrepreneurs' relief on the disposal of his Acryl Ltd shares, capital gains tax will be charged at 10% on the taxable gain.

Conclusion

Mambo Ltd will not be subject to corporation tax under either alternative but Alan would probably prefer 31 March 2019 as he is likely to suffer a lower rate of tax if the distribution is made on this date.

Tutorial note.

It is not necessary to consider the possibility of a capital loss on receipt of the distribution on 31 March 2019. Mambo Ltd and Alan subscribed for the shares at par, so they will have a very low base cost and Acryl Ltd has substantial distributable profits.

(b) (i) Cresco Ltd – relief for trading losses

	Year ended 31 March 2015 £	Year ended 31 March 2016 £	Year ended 31 March 2017 £	Year ended 31 March 2018 £	Year ended 31 March 2018 £
Trading income	Nil	21,000	8,000	Nil	Nil
Less: Loss brought forward (note 1)		(4,000)			
		17,000			
Bank interest receivable	1,000	3,000	3,000	—	—
c/f	1,000	20,000	11,000	Nil	Nil

	Year ended 31 March 2015 £	Year ended 31 March 2016 £	Year ended 31 March 2017 £	Year ended 31 March 2018 £	Year ended 31 March 2018 £
b/f					
Less:					
Loss for the year ended 31 March 2015 (note 1)	(1,000)				
Loss for the year ended 31 March 2018 (note 2)			(11,000)		
Loss for the year ended 31 October 2018 (note 3)		(20,000)			
	Nil	Nil	Nil	Nil	Nil

Losses unrelieved:

	£
Year ended 31 March 2018: (£24,000 – £11,000 – £10,000)	3,000
Terminal loss: (£50,000 – £20,000)	30,000
Total unrelieved:	33,000

Tutorial note. £10,000 of the trading loss in the year ended 31 March 2018 is included as part of the terminal loss and used against the profits of the year ended 31 March 2016 (see Note 3 below).

Notes

1   The trading loss for the year ended 31 March 2015 of £5,000 will have been relieved against the £1,000 of bank interest (total profits) in the year, and then carried forward against the £21,000 of trading profit in the following year. A trading profit of £17,000 (£21,000 – £4,000) remains in the year ended 31 March 2016.

2   As there is no other income or gains in the year ended 31 March 2018, the trading loss of £24,000 will have been carried back and offset against the total profits in the year ended 31 March 2017 of £11,000 (£8,000 + 3,000). £13,000 of the loss remains unrelieved. However, £10,000 of this forms part of the terminal loss (see note 3).

3   As Cresco Ltd has ceased to trade on 31 October 2018, the loss of the last 12 months of trading is a terminal loss which is eligible to be carried back up to 36 months. The loss available for such relief is £50,000 (£40,000 + (£24,000 × 5/12), including the five months of loss for the period from 1 November 2017 to 31 March 2018. As there are no profits remaining in the years ended 31 March 2018 or 2017, the loss can be offset against the total profits of £20,000 (£17,000 + £3,000) in the year ended 31 March 2016.

(ii)   **Value added tax (VAT) implications of the cessation of trade**

Cresco Ltd must notify HM Revenue & Customs of the cessation of its business within 30 days of ceasing to make taxable supplies.

Output tax must be accounted for on any business assets it still holds at the date of cessation of trade in respect of which input tax was previously recovered. However, there is no need to account for this output tax if it is less than £1,000.

ACCA Strategic Professional – Options

Advanced Taxation (ATX – UK)

Mock Exam 2

(ACCA Specimen exam updated to FA 2017)

Question Paper	
Time allowed	**3 hours 15 minutes**
This paper is divided into two sections	
Section A	**BOTH questions are compulsory and MUST be attempted**
Section B	**BOTH questions are compulsory and MUST be attempted**

DO NOT OPEN THIS PAPER UNTIL YOU ARE READY TO START UNDER EXAMINATION CONDITIONS

SECTION A: BOTH questions are compulsory and MUST be attempted

1 FL Partnership

Your manager has had a meeting with Farina and Lauda, potential new clients, who are partners in the FL Partnership. The memorandum recording the matters discussed, together with an email from your manager, is set out below.

Memorandum

To:	The Files
From:	Tax manager
Date:	5 December 2018
Subject:	FL Partnership

Background

Farina and Lauda began trading as the FL Partnership on 1 May 2013. Accounts have always been prepared to 31 March each year. They are each entitled to 50% of the revenue profits and capital profits of the business.

On 1 March 2019, the whole of the FL Partnership business will be sold as a going concern to JH plc, a quoted trading company. The consideration for the sale will be a mixture of cash and shares. Capital gains tax relief on the transfer of a business to a company (incorporation relief) will be available in respect of the sale.

Farina and Lauda will both pay income tax at the additional rate in the tax year 2018/19 and anticipate continuing to do so in future years. They are very wealthy individuals, who use their capital gains tax annual exempt amounts every year. Both of them are resident and domiciled in the UK.

The sale of the business on 1 March 2019

The assets of the FL Partnership business have been valued as set out below. All of the equipment qualified for capital allowances.

	Value £	Cost £
Goodwill	1,300,000	Nil
Inventory and receivables	30,000	30,000
Equipment (no item to be sold for more than cost)	150,000	200,000
Total	1,480,000	

The total value of the consideration will be equal to the value of the assets sold. Farina and Lauda will **each** receive consideration of £740,000; £140,000 in cash and 200,000 shares in JH plc. Following the purchase of the FL Partnership, JH plc will have an issued share capital of 8,400,000 shares.

Future transactions

Farina:

On 1 August 2019, Farina will make a gift of 15,000 of her shares in JH plc to the trustees of a discretionary (relevant property) trust for the benefit of her nieces and nephews. Farina will pay any inheritance tax liability in respect of this gift. The trustees will transfer the shares to the beneficiaries over the life of the trust.

Farina has already made the following gifts:

1 May 2017	Cash of £300,000 to a discretionary (relevant property) trust
1 July 2018	Cash of £40,000 to one of her nephews

Email from your manager

I want you to prepare a memorandum for the client file in respect of the following:

(i)   **Capital allowances**

A **detailed** explanation of the calculation of the capital allowances of the FL Partnership for its final trading period ending with the sale of its equipment to JH plc for £150,000 on 1 March 2019.

(ii)   **Farina**

(1)   A calculation of the inheritance tax payable by Farina in her lifetime in respect of the gift of the shares to the trustees of the discretionary (relevant property) trust on 1 August 2019 and the date on which the tax would be payable.

(2)   A **brief** explanation of the availability of capital gains tax gift relief in respect of the transfer of the shares to the trustees of the discretionary (relevant property) trust and the subsequent transfers of shares from the trustees to the beneficiaries.

(iii)   **Lauda**

A review of whether or not Lauda should disclaim incorporation relief.

The review should encompass the sale of the FL Partnership business, the gift of the shares to Lauda's son and the effect of incorporation relief on the base cost of the remaining shares owned by Lauda, as she intends to sell all of her shares in JH plc in the next few years.

It is important that you include a summary of your calculations and a statement of the key issues for me to discuss with Lauda. You should also include **brief** explanations of the amount of incorporation relief available, the availability of any additional or alternative reliefs, and the date(s) on which any capital gains tax will be payable.

Tax manager

(a)   It is anticipated that Farina and Lauda will require some highly sophisticated and specialised tax planning work in the future.

Required

Prepare a summary of the information which would be required, together with any action(s) which should be taken by the firm before it agrees to become the tax advisers to Farina and Lauda.   **(5 marks)**

(b)   Prepare the memorandum requested in the email from your manager. The following marks are available:

(i)   Capital allowances   **(5 marks)**
(ii)   Farina   **(7 marks)**
(iii)   Lauda   **(14 marks)**

Note. Ignore value added tax (VAT).

Professional marks will be awarded in part (b) for the overall presentation of the memorandum, the provision of relevant advice and the effectiveness with which the information is communicated.   **(4 marks)**

(Total = 35 marks)

2 Forti Ltd group

You have received an email from your manager with an attached schedule in connection with the Forti Ltd group of companies. The schedule and the email are set out below.

Email from your manager

Forti Ltd group

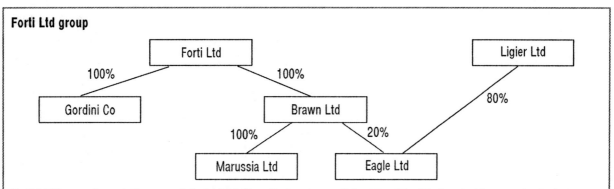

Forti Ltd has an issued share capital of 120,000 ordinary shares. It is owned by 12 shareholders, each of whom owns 10,000 ordinary shares.

All six of the companies are trading companies. Gordini Co is resident in and trades in the country of Arrowsia; it does not carry out any activities in the UK. The other five companies are all resident in the UK. There is no double tax treaty between Arrowsia and the UK.

The only changes to the group structure in recent years relate to the purchase and subsequent sale of Marussia Ltd as set out in note 3 to the attached schedule.

Ligier Ltd has no links to the Forti Ltd group other than its shareholding in Eagle Ltd.

The work I require you to do is set out below.

(a) **Brawn Ltd – Review of the corporation tax computation**

I attach a schedule detailing the corporation tax computation for Brawn Ltd for the year ended 31 March 2018. This schedule has been prepared by an inexperienced tax assistant.

Brawn Ltd is a medium-sized enterprise for the purposes of tax relief on research and development expenditure relief. I can confirm that the substantial shareholding exemption is not available and that the figures given for the indexed cost of Marussia Ltd in the schedule, the degrouping charge in note 3, and the tax adjusted trading losses referred to in notes 4 and 5 have all been calculated correctly.

Review the computation and related notes in order to identify any errors and prepare a revised schedule showing calculations of the correct taxable total profits and the corporation tax liability. You should include notes explaining the errors you have identified and the changes you have made.

(b) **Other corporate matters**

(i) Brawn Ltd will only be a close company if Forti Ltd is a close company.

Set out the matters which need to be considered in order to determine whether or not Forti Ltd is a close company.

(ii) Set out the matters which need to be considered in connection with the sale of components to Gordini Co referred to in note 6 to the schedule.

(c) **Value added tax (VAT) annual accounting scheme**

The management of the Forti Ltd group have asked for advice on the annual accounting scheme.

State the conditions which must be satisfied by any company wishing to operate the annual accounting scheme and explain the operation of the scheme.

Tax manager

Schedule prepared by a tax assistant

Brawn Ltd – Corporation tax computation for the year ended 31 March 2018

	Notes	£	£
Tax adjusted trading income	1, 2		240,500
Sale of Marussia Ltd – Proceeds	3	484,000	
Less: Indexed cost		(390,000)	
Annual exempt amount		(11,300)	
			82,700
			323,200
Less: Losses transferred from:			
Marussia Ltd (£60,000 × 5/12)	4		(25,000)
Eagle Ltd (£52,500 × 20%)	5		(10,500)
Taxable total profits			287,700
Corporation tax @ 19%			54,663

Notes

1   The treatment of the following items of expenditure needs to be checked.

	£	
The cost of establishing a company share option plan (CSOP)	6,000	Disallowed
The cost of entertaining overseas customers	4,000	Disallowed
Accrued management bonuses to be paid on 1 February 2019	7,000	Allowed

2   The tax adjusted trading income is after deducting a total of £120,000 (£48,000 × 250%) in respect of research and development expenditure. The expenditure consisted of salaries paid to Brawn Ltd staff of £21,000 and payments for subcontracted labour of £27,000.

3   Marussia Ltd was purchased on 1 August 2017. On 1 November 2017, Brawn Ltd signed a contract to sell Marussia Ltd for £484,000, and the sale took place on 31 December 2017. Accordingly, the substantial shareholding exemption was not available. The sale of Marussia Ltd resulted in a degrouping charge of £21,500. This has been included as a chargeable gain in the corporation tax computation of Marussia Ltd.

4   Marussia Ltd made a tax adjusted trading loss of £60,000 in the year ended 31 March 2018.

5   Eagle Ltd made a tax adjusted trading loss of £52,500 in the year ended 31 March 2018 and did not pay a dividend.

6   During the year ended 31 March 2018, Brawn Ltd began selling components to Gordini Co. Are there any issues which need to be considered in respect of these sales in relation to Brawn Ltd's corporation tax liability?

Required

Carry out the work required as set out in the email from your manager. The following marks are available.

(a)   Brawn Ltd – Review of the corporation tax computation

    Note. Ignore value added tax (VAT).   **(12 marks)**

(b)   Other corporate matters:

    (i)   Close companies   **(5 marks)**

    (ii)   Note 6 to the schedule   **(3 marks)**

(c)   VAT annual accounting scheme   **(5 marks)**

    (Total = 25 marks)

SECTION B: BOTH questions are compulsory and MUST be attempted

3 Kesme and Soba

Kesme and Soba, a married couple, require advice on Kesme's taxable income and rent a room relief, the letting exemption available on a future sale of the family home, the remittance basis, and the assets which will be received by Soba under Kesme's will.

Kesme:
- Has been UK resident since the tax year 2014/15 but is non-UK domiciled
- Is married to Soba
- Has not made any lifetime gifts for the purposes of inheritance tax

Soba:
- Has been UK resident since the tax year 2003/04 but is non-UK domiciled

Kesme's income for the tax year 2017/18 includes:

- Salary (gross) and benefits from Noodl plc, his current employer, of £48,500

- Pension from a former employer of £24,100 (gross)

- Rental income in respect of a furnished room in the main residence he owns jointly with Soba; the joint rental income receivable was £17,650

- Allowable expenses in respect of the joint rental income of £1,600, none of which are finance costs

Share-based remuneration provided to Kesme by Noodl plc in the tax year 2017/18:

- 400 shares in Noodl plc were issued to Kesme for £2,500.

- Kesme was granted share options which were not tax advantaged to purchase 300 shares for £4 per share.

- Kesme exercised not tax advantaged share options and purchased 250 shares for £3 per share. Kesme had paid 50 pence for each of these options.

- A share in Noodl plc can be assumed to be worth £12 throughout the tax year 2017/18.

- Noodle plc offers its staff share-based remuneration but does not operate any tax advantaged share schemes.

Income to be received in future years in respect of investments in the country of Penne:

- Kesme will receive £1,400 per year.
- Soba will receive £19,500 per year.
- Neither Kesme nor Soba plan to remit any of this income into the UK.
- There is no income tax in the country of Penne.

Kesme's estate and his will:

- Kesme's gross chargeable estate will have a value of £1,280,000.
- This value includes a plot of land situated in the UK worth £370,000.
- Kesme has left the plot of land to his daughter and the residue of his estate to his wife, Soba.

Required

(a) Explain the availability and operation of rent a room relief in relation to Kesme and calculate his taxable income for the tax year 2017/18 on the assumption that the relief is claimed. **(8 marks)**

(b)   State, with reasons, whether or not the remittance basis is available to Kesme and Soba and, on the assumption that it is available to both of them, explain whether or not it is likely to be beneficial for each of them.

(6 marks)

(c)   Explain why it would not be beneficial for Soba to elect to be treated as UK domiciled for the purposes of inheritance tax and calculate the value of the residue of the estate which Soba would receive under Kesme's will if Kesme were to die today.

(6 marks)

(Total = 20 marks)

4 Spike

Spike requires advice on the loss relief available and the value added tax (VAT) position following the cessation of his business and on the tax implications of a relocation payment provided by his new employer.

Spike:

*   Ceased to trade on 30 September 2017 and sold the assets used in his unincorporated business
*   Sold his house, 'Sea View', on 1 March 2018 for £125,000 more than he had paid for it
*   Began working for Set Ltd on 1 May 2018
*   Has no income or chargeable gains other than the amounts referred to in the information below

Spike's unincorporated business:

*   There are overlap profits from the commencement of the business of £8,300.
*   The sale of the business resulted in net capital gains of £78,000.
*   The tax adjusted profits/(loss) of the business have been:

		£
Year ended 31 December 2013	Profit	52,500
Year ended 31 December 2014	Profit	68,000
Year ended 31 December 2015	Profit	54,000
Year ended 31 December 2016	Profit	22,500
Nine months ending 30 September 2017	Loss	(13,500)

Sale of the business:

*   The majority of the business assets were sold to unrelated purchasers during September and October 2017.

*   Spike retained some of his business assets for his own use.

Remuneration from Set Ltd:

*   Spike is being paid a salary of £65,000 per year.
*   On 1 July 2018, Set Ltd will pay Spike a relocation payment of £33,500.

The relocation payment of £33,500:

*   Spike sold 'Sea View', and purchased a new house, in order to live near the premises of Set Ltd.
*   £22,000 of the payment is to compensate Spike for having to sell his house at short notice at a low price.
*   £11,500 of the payment is in respect of the costs incurred by Spike in relation to moving house.

Required

(a) (i) Calculate the trading loss for the tax year 2017/18, and the terminal loss, on the cessation of Spike's unincorporated business. **(4 marks)**

     (ii) Explain the reliefs available in respect of the losses calculated in part (a)(i) and quantify the potential tax savings for each of them. **(10 marks)**

(b) State the VAT implications of the cessation of the business and the sale of the business assets. **(4 marks)**

(c) Explain the income tax implications for Spike of the relocation payment. **(2 marks)**

Notes

1   You should assume that the tax rates and allowances for the tax year 2017/18 apply to all tax years.
2   Ignore national insurance contributions throughout this question.

(Total = 20 marks)

Answers

DO NOT TURN THIS PAGE UNTIL YOU HAVE
COMPLETED THE MOCK EXAM

A plan of attack

We've already established that you've been told to do it 101 times, so it is of course superfluous to tell you for the 102nd time to **take a good look at the paper before diving into the answers.**

What's the worst thing you could be doing right now if this was the actual exam paper? Wondering how to celebrate the end of the exam in about three hours' time?

Turn back to the paper and let's sort out a **plan of attack!**

First things first

Look through the paper and work out the order in which to attack the questions. You've got **two options**. Option 1 is the option recommended by BPP.

Option 1 (if you're thinking 'Help!')

If you're a bit worried about the paper, do the questions in the order of how well you think you can answer them. If you find the questions in Section B less daunting than the questions in Section A, start with Section B.

There are **two questions** in Section B. **Question 3** has three parts. Part (a) concerns rent a room relief, which should be familiar to you from your Taxation (TX – UK) studies, and computing taxable income including non-tax advantaged share options, which are new in Advanced Taxation (ATX – UK).

Part (b) requires an explanation of the remittance basis in relation to two taxpayers. It is important to **apply** the rules to the particular circumstances of each taxpayer, not just give a general overview.

Part (c) is about whether a non-UK domiciled individual should elect to be treated as UK domiciled for inheritance tax purposes. You need to think about the advantage and the disadvantage of making the election. This part also deals with a special rule on working out tax on death where there is a chargeable specific legacy and exempt residue. This is new in Advanced Taxation (ATX – UK).

Question 4 has three parts. Part (a) concerns trading loss relief and terminal loss relief for a sole trader. In sub-part (i) there are two losses you need to work out. Then you need to consider how each can be relieved in sub-part (ii). Don't forget that a trading loss relief claim against general income can be extended to chargeable gains. Terminal loss relief is only against trading income. Both these topics should be familiar from your Taxation (TX – UK) studies.

Part (b) is about value added tax on the cessation of a business and the sale of business assets. Again, this is basic knowledge from your Taxation (TX – UK) studies.

Part (c) is about relocation payments, another Taxation (TX – UK) topic. Notice that there are only two marks for this part so you only need to write a couple of sentences.

Do not spend longer than about 75 minutes on Section B. When you've spent the allocated time on the questions in Section B turn to the **two case-study questions** in Section A.

Read the Section A questions through thoroughly before you launch into them. Once you start make sure you allocate your time to the parts within the questions according to the marks available and that, where possible, you attempt the easy marks first.

Question 1 has two parts. Part (a) is the ethics question. There will always be five marks on ethics in Section A and they are relatively easy to obtain.

Part (b) has three sub-parts and involves preparing a memorandum about capital allowances for a partnership and the tax position of two partners which involves inheritance tax and capital gains tax. Use the headings in the email from the manager to plan your answer. There are four professional marks in this question for presentation, providing relevant advice (not just stating the rules) and the effectiveness of communication. You should be familiar with the format of presenting a memorandum to obtain these marks.

Question 2 has three parts. Part (a) is a review of a corporation tax computation. A good way to approach a question like this is to redraft the computation using the information provided and then compare your answer with the one in the question to identify the errors. Some of the points should be obvious and so easy marks.

Part (b) has two sub-parts, sub-part (i) is about close companies and sub-part (ii) is about transfer pricing, both of which are new in Advanced Taxation (ATX – UK).

Part (c) is about the value added tax annual accounting scheme which should be familiar from Taxation (TX – UK).

Lastly, what you mustn't forget is that you have to **answer BOTH questions in Section A and BOTH questions in Section B**.

Option 2 (if you're thinking 'This paper's alright')

It never pays to be overconfident but if you're not quaking in your shoes about the exam then **turn straight to the case-study questions in Section A**.

Once you've done these questions, **move to Section B**. The question you attempt first really depends on what you are most confident at. If you are undecided look at the requirements. It may be easier to obtain more marks if these are broken down into several smaller parts. For example, Question 4 (a) has two subparts so it is easier to see how to allocate your time.

No matter how many times we remind you...

Always, always **allocate your time** according to the marks for the question in total and then according to the parts of the question. And **always, always follow the requirements** exactly. For example in Question 1(b)(i) you needed give a **detailed** explanation of the capital allowances available to the partnership. It would not be sufficient to write a few general sentences.

You've got spare time at the end of the exam...?

If you have allocated your time properly then you **shouldn't have time on your hands** at the end of the exam. But if you find yourself with five or ten minutes to spare, check over your work to make sure that you have answered all the requirements of the questions and all parts of all requirements.

Forget about it!

And don't worry if you found the exam difficult. More than likely other candidates will too. If this were the real thing you would need to **forget** the exam the minute you leave the exam hall and **think about the next one**. Or, if it's the last one, **celebrate**!

1 FL Partnership

Text references. Ethics are covered in Chapter 30. Capital allowances are dealt with in Chapter 7. Inheritance tax basic principles are covered in Chapter 16, reliefs in Chapter 17 and trusts in Chapter 18. Capital gains tax principles will be found in Chapter 11 and reliefs in Chapter 13.

Top tips. Did you remember to include a summary of your calculations and a statement of the key issues in part (b)(iii)? These were awarded four valuable marks.

Easy marks. You should have been able to obtain some easy marks in part (a) for common-sense points. In part (b) there were some easy marks for basic computations. Make sure you get the easy mark for format and presentation!

Marking scheme

				Marks
(a)	Information required		1	
	Contact existing tax adviser		1	
	Fundamental principles		1	
	Competence		1	
	Conflict of interest		2	
		Max		5
(b)	(i) Allowances available		1½	
	Calculation of balancing adjustment		2	
	Consideration of transfer at tax written down value		1½	
				5
	(ii) Inheritance tax			
	Chargeable lifetime transfer		2	
	Inheritance tax liability		3	
	Due date		1	
	Capital gains tax: gift relief		1½	
		Max		7
	(iii) Capital gains tax on sale of business		1½	
	With incorporation relief			
	Incorporation relief		1½	
	Capital gains tax and due date		1	
	Capital gains tax on gift of shares		2	
	Capital gains tax and due date		1	
	Without incorporation relief			
	Capital gains tax on sale of business		1	
	Capital gains tax on gift of shares		1½	
	Explanations		4	
	Summary and key issues		4	
		Max		14
Format and presentation			1	
Analysis			1	
Quality of explanations and calculations			2	
				4
				35

(a) **Becoming tax advisers to Farina and Lauda**

Information required in respect of Farina and Lauda:

- Evidence of their identities; and
- Their addresses.

Action to be taken by the firm

(i) The firm should contact their existing tax advisers. This is to ensure that there has been no action by either Farina or Lauda which would, on ethical grounds, preclude the acceptance of the appointment.

(ii) The firm should consider whether becoming tax advisers to Farina and Lauda would create any threats to compliance with the fundamental principles of professional ethics. unless the threats can be reduced to an acceptable level via the implementation of safeguards.

With this in mind, the firm must ensure that it has sufficient competence to carry out the sophisticated tax planning required by Farina and Lauda.

In addition, it is possible that providing advice to Farina and Lauda on the sale of their business could give rise to a conflict of interest, as a course of action (for example, the timing of the sale) which is beneficial for one of them may not be beneficial for the other. The firm should obtain permission from both Farina and Lauda to act for both of them and should consider making a different member of the firm responsible for each of them.

(b)
To: The files
From: Tax senior
Date: 6 December 2018
Subject: The FL Partnership

The purpose of this memorandum is to advise Farina and Lauda, the partners in the FL Partnership, on the sale of the business to JH plc and on the proposed disposals of shares in JH plc in the future.

(i) **Capital allowances of the FL Partnership for its final trading period**

There will be no annual investment allowance, first year allowances or writing down allowances in the period in which the partnership business ceases. Instead, there will be a balancing adjustment which will be either a balancing allowance or a balancing charge.

The balancing adjustment will be calculated as follows:

	£
Tax written down value brought forward at the start of the period	X
Add additions in the period	X
Less disposals during the period at the lower of cost and sales proceeds	(X)
	X
Less proceeds on the sale of the equipment on 1 March 2019	(150,000)
Balancing allowance/(balancing charge)	X/(X)

It is not possible for an election to be made to transfer the equipment to JH plc at its tax written down value because Farina and Lauda will not be connected with JH plc. This is because they will not control the company.

(ii) **Farina**

(1) *Inheritance tax*

	£
Value of shares 15,000 × £4	60,000
Less annual exemption 2019/20	(3,000)
Net chargeable lifetime transfer	57,000
£31,000 (£325,000 – 294,000 (300,000 – 3,000 – 3,000)) × 0%	0
£26,000 (£57,000 – 31,000) × 20/80	6,500
Inheritance tax liability	6,500

The inheritance tax will be payable on 30 April 2020.

Tutorial notes

1   Farina's gift to her nephew on 1 July 2018 will used her annual exemption for 2018/19 but will otherwise be a potentially exempt transfer and so is ignored in the computation of lifetime tax on the chargeable lifetime transfer.

2   Business property relief will not be available as JH plc is a quoted company and Farina will not be a controlling shareholder.

(2) *Capital gains tax gift relief*

Gift relief will be available in respect of the transfer of the shares to the trustees because the transfer is immediately subject to inheritance tax. For the same reason, gift relief will also be available in respect of any subsequent transfers of shares from the trustees to the beneficiaries.

(iii) **Lauda**

The sale of the business will result in a chargeable gain in respect of the goodwill. The gain, equal to the market value of the goodwill of £1,300,000, will be split equally between Farina and Lauda. Lauda's chargeable gain will therefore be £650,000. As all of the equipment qualified for capital allowances, no capital losses will arise on its disposal.

With incorporation relief

Sale of business on 1 March 2019

	£
Chargeable gain on the sale of the goodwill	650,000
Less incorporation relief £650,000 × $\dfrac{£600,000}{£740,000}$ (note 1)	(527,027)
Chargeable gain after incorporation relief	122,973
Capital gains tax @ 10% (note 2)	12,297

The tax will be payable on 31 January 2020.

Shares in JH plc – Lauda's base cost

	£
Market value of shares received 200,000 × £3	600,000
Less incorporation relief	(527,027)
Base cost	72,973

Gift of 40,000 shares on 1 June 2020 (note 3)

	£
Deemed proceeds (market value) 40,000 × £5	200,000
Less cost £72,973 × $\frac{40,000}{200,000}$	(14,595)
Chargeable gain	185,405
Capital gains tax @ 20% (note 4)	37,081

The tax will be payable on 31 January 2022.

Notes

1   The relief is restricted by reference to the value of the shares divided by the value of the total consideration received. Lauda will receive a total of £740,000, consisting of cash of £140,000 and shares worth 200,000 × £3 = £600,000.

2   Capital gains tax will be charged at 10% because entrepreneurs' relief will be available. This relief is available because the business is to be sold as a going concern and has been owned for at least a year. It is assumed that Lauda has not exceeded the lifetime limit of £10,000,000 and will claim this relief. The restriction for goodwill does not apply because JH plc is not a close company.

3   Gift relief will not be available in respect of this gift because the shares are quoted and Lauda will hold 200,000/8,400,000 = 2.38% of the shares which is less than 5% of the company so it is not Lauda's personal company.

4   Capital gains tax will be charged at 20% because Lauda pays income tax at the additional rate and so has used up her basic rate band. Entrepreneurs' relief will not be available because Lauda will hold less than 5% of JH plc.

   Tutorial note. In order for entrepreneurs' relief to be available in respect of the gift of the shares, Lauda would also need to be an officer or employee of JH plc. Investors' relief cannot be available because JH plc is a quoted (listed) company.

Without incorporation relief

Sale of business on 1 March 2019

	£
Chargeable gain on the sale of the goodwill	650,000
Capital gains tax @ 10% (note 2 above)	65,000

The tax will be payable on 31 January 2020.

Shares in JH plc – Lauda's base cost

	£
Market value of shares received 200,000 × £3	600,000

Gift of 40,000 shares on 1 June 2020 (note 3 above)

	£
Deemed proceeds (market value) 40,000 × £5	200,000
Less cost £600,000 × $\frac{40,000}{200,000}$	(120,000)
Chargeable gain	80,000
Capital gains tax @ 20% (note 4 above)	16,000

The tax will be payable on 31 January 2022.

Summary

	With incorporation relief	Without incorporation relief
	£	£
Capital gains tax on sale of business	12,297	65,000
Capital gains tax on gift of shares 1 June 2020	37,081	16,000
	49,378	81,000

Effect of incorporation relief on base cost of shares

	With incorporation relief	Without incorporation relief
	£	£
Base cost	72,973	600,000
Less used on gift of shares 1 June 2020	(14,595)	(120,000)
	58,378	480,000
Increase in gain on eventual disposal of shares if incorporation relief applies £(480,000 − 58,378)		421,622
Increase in capital gains tax £421,622 @ 20%		84,324

Key issues

If Lauda were to disclaim incorporation relief, she would have higher initial capital gains tax liabilities.

However, disclaiming incorporation relief will result in a higher base cost in the shares such that, on a sale of the shares in the future, there will be tax savings which will exceed the increased initial liability.

Tutorial notes

1   Incorporation relief reduces the capital gains tax payable on the sale of the business and the gift of the shares by £31,622 (£81,000 − £49,378). When this amount is deducted from the additional tax due because of the reduced base cost, we arrive at an overall increase in the capital gains tax liability of £52,702 (£84,324 − £31,622).

This overall increase in the capital gains tax liability is simply the tax on the deferred gain of £527,027 at 20% in the future rather than at 10%, due to the availability of entrepreneurs' relief, now: £527,027 × 10% (20% − 10%) = £52,703 (and a rounding difference of £1).

2   Capital gains tax gift relief in respect of gifts of business assets will not be available on the sale of the business to JH plc, because Farina and Lauda are not gifting the business to the company. They are selling the business for market value, which is received in the form of cash and shares.

2 Forti Ltd group

Text references. Computing taxable total profits, including research and development and transfer pricing, is the subject of Chapter 20. Chargeable gains for companies are covered in Chapter 21. Computing corporation tax payable is dealt with in Chapter 20. Close companies are covered in Chapter 25. Groups and consortia are the subject of Chapter 26. The value added tax annual accounting scheme is covered in Chapter 28.

Top tips. If you are asked to correct a computation, don't assume that **all** the figures are incorrect. You were specifically told that some were correct, but there was an adjustment which was correct as well.

Easy marks. There were some easy marks in part (a) for computing taxable total profits and the corporation tax liability, even if you were not sure why some of the corrections to the original schedule needed to be made. The adjustment for transfer pricing should have been well known in part (b)(ii). The annual accounting scheme in part (c) was brought forward knowledge from Taxation (TX – UK).

Marking scheme

					Marks
(a)	Notes				
		Tax adjusted trading income – other matters	2		
		Research and development	2		
		Chargeable gains	2		
		Losses transferred from Marussia Ltd	1½		
		Losses transferred from Eagle Ltd	2		
	Calculation		5		
			Max		12
(b)	(i)	Definition of close company	2½		
		Associates	1½		
		Application	2		
			Max		5
	(ii)	Reasons why transfer pricing rules apply	2½		
		Adjustment required	1		
			Max		3
(c)	Conditions		3		
	Operation of the scheme		3		
			Max		5
					25

(a) **Brawn Ltd – Corporation tax computation for the year ended 31 March 2018**

		Notes	£
Tax adjusted trading income per original schedule			240,500
Less:	Costs relating to company share option plan	1	(6,000)
Add:	Accrued management bonuses	2	7,000
	Research and development expenditure		
	£(120,000 – 98,115)	3	21,885
Tax adjusted trading income			263,385
Add:	Sale of Marussia Ltd:		
	Chargeable gain £(82,700 + 21,500 + 11,300)	4, 5	115,500
Total taxable profits before loss relief			378,885
Less:	Losses transferred from:		
	Marussia Ltd £60,000 × 3/12	6	(15,000)
	Eagle Ltd	7	(0)
Taxable total profits			363,885
Corporation tax @ 19%			69,138

Notes

1   The cost of establishing a company share option plan is an allowable deduction when computing tax adjusted trading income.

2   The management bonuses are not an allowable cost as they have not been paid within nine months of the end of the accounting period.

3   The additional tax deduction in respect of research and development expenditure is 130%, not 150%. In relation to payments for subcontracted labour, this additional deduction is only available in respect of 65% of the amount paid. Accordingly, the total deduction is £98,115 (£21,000 + (£21,000 × 130%) + £27,000 + (£27,000 × 65% × 130%)).

4   The degrouping charge must be added to the sales proceeds on the sale of Marussia Ltd so it increases the chargeable gain arising.

5   The capital gains tax annual exempt amount of £11,300 is not available to companies.

6   For the purposes of group relief, Marussia Ltd is regarded as having left the group once there were arrangements in force for it to leave the group. The signing of the contract on 1 November 2017 amounts to such arrangements. This means that Marussia Ltd is only a member of the group relief group for the three months from 1 August 2017 until 31 October 2017 and the loss must therefore be apportioned on a time basis.

7   Eagle Ltd is not a consortium company because it is in a group relief group with Ligier Ltd. Accordingly, it is not possible for any of Eagle Ltd's trading losses to be transferred to Brawn Ltd.

Tutorial note. The costs of entertaining customers (whether UK or overseas) are disallowable in computing the trading profit. The distinction between UK and overseas customers is only relevant for value added tax purposes.

(b)   **Other corporate matters**

(i)   *Close companies*

Forti Ltd will be a close company if it is controlled by:

(1)   Any number of directors who are shareholders; or

(2)   Its five largest shareholders.

A company is controlled by those shareholders who own more than half of the company's share capital.

When determining whether or not a company is close within this definition, each shareholder is regarded as owning any shares owned by their associates as well as the shares owned personally. A person's associates include their direct relatives, business partners and the trustees of certain trusts set up by the shareholder or their direct relatives.

Control of Forti Ltd can be exercised by seven shareholders holding 58.3% (7/12) of the shares.

Accordingly, unless Forti Ltd is controlled by shareholder directors, it will only be close if some of its shareholders are associated with each other.

Tutorial note. There are further complexities when determining whether or not a company is close but the points set out above were sufficient to score full marks.

(ii)   *Transfer pricing (Note 6 to the schedule)*

The transfer pricing rules will apply to the sale of components by Brawn Ltd to Gordini Co because these two companies are both controlled by Forti Ltd. The exemption for small and medium-sized enterprises is unlikely to be available, regardless of the size of the Forti Ltd group, as there is no double tax treaty between the UK and the country of Arrowsia.

Under the transfer pricing rules, if Brawn Ltd has sold components to Gordini Co for less than an arm's length price, it is required to increase its taxable profits by the excess of the arm's length price over the price charged.

(c)   **Value added tax (VAT) annual accounting scheme**

Conditions

(i)   The company's VAT reporting and payments must be up to date, such that its VAT debt is not increasing.

(ii)   Taxable supplies (excluding VAT) must not be expected to exceed £1,350,000 in the following 12 months.

(iii)   The company must notify HM Revenue and Customs (HMRC) if it expects its taxable supplies for a year to exceed £1,600,000. The company must leave the scheme if its taxable supplies for a year exceed £1,600,000.

(iv)   The scheme is not available where registration is in the name of a group.

Tutorial note. Companies which are normally in a repayment situation can account for VAT annually if they wish, but this would not be advisable from a cash flow point of view as they would only receive one repayment for the whole year.

(i) The company will be required to make nine monthly payments starting at the end of the fourth month of the year.

(ii) Each payment is equal to 10% of the company's liability for the previous year as adjusted for any additional information provided to HMRC.

(iii) Alternatively, a company can choose to make three larger interim payments equal to 25% of its liability for the previous year.

(iv) The company must submit its VAT return within two months of the end of the year together with any final balancing payment.

3 Kesme and Soba

Text references. Property income is covered in Chapter 3 and taxable income in Chapter 1. Employment income is the subject of Chapter 4 and share based remuneration is dealt with in Chapter 5. Overseas aspects of income tax are the subject of Chapter 10. Further aspects of the death estate for inheritance tax are covered in Chapter 17. Overseas aspects of inheritance tax (IHT) are covered in Chapter 18.

Top tips. In part (b), make sure that you deal with the implications of the remittance basis for both Kesme and Soba.

Easy marks. There were easy marks in part (a) for a basic computation of taxable income.

Marking scheme

				Marks
(a)	Rent a room relief			
	Availability		1	
	Operation		1½	
	Claim		1½	
	Employment income		1	
	Property business income		½	
	Share options		3	
	Personal allowance		½	
		Max		8
(b)	Availability of remittance basis		1	
	Kesme		3	
	Soba		3	
		Max		6
(c)	Election to be treated as UK domiciled		2½	
	Value of residue of estate			
	Calculation of amount received by Soba		1½	
	Inheritance tax liability		2	
				6
				20

(a)   **Income tax**

Availability and operation of rent a room relief

Rent a room relief is relevant because Kesme and Soba are letting furnished rooms in their main residence. The limit for each of them is £7,500/2 = £3,750.

Since gross rents exceed the limit, Kesme and Soba would be taxed under the normal property business income rules unless they elect for the 'alternative basis'. If they so elect, they will each be taxable on gross receipts less £3,750, with no deductions for expenses.

An election for the alternative basis must be made by 31 January 2020 (22 months after the end of the tax year 2017/18). The election will then continue to apply until it is withdrawn.

Tutorial note. The election would also cease to apply in the unlikely event that the gross annual rent fell below £7,500.

Taxable income for the tax year 2017/18

	£
Salary and benefits	48,500
Pension from former employer	24,100
Property business income £((17,650/2) – 3,750)	5,075
Shares acquired ((400 × £12) – £2,500)	2,300
Grant of non-tax advantaged share options – no tax on grant	0
Exercise of non-tax advantaged options (250 × £(12 – 0.5 – 3))	2,125
Net income	82,100
Less personal allowance	(11,500)
Taxable income	70,600

(b)   **The remittance basis**

The remittance basis is available to UK resident individuals who are not domiciled in the UK. Accordingly, it is available to both Kesme and Soba.

Kesme will have unremitted overseas income of less than £2,000. Accordingly, the remittance basis will apply automatically, such that there will be no loss of his personal allowance, and the unremitted income will not be subject to income tax in the UK. There will also be no remittance basis charge. This is clearly beneficial for Kesme, as the income will also not be subject to tax in the country of Penne.

Soba will have unremitted overseas income of more than £2,000, such that the remittance basis will not apply automatically. In addition, because she has been resident in the UK for 12 of the 14 tax years prior to 2018/19, if Soba were able to claim the remittance basis there would be a remittance basis charge of £60,000 as well as the loss of her personal allowance. This is clearly not beneficial for Soba as it exceeds the amount of income which she would be sheltering from UK tax.

(c)   **Soba**

Election to be treated as UK domiciled

This election will remove the limit (equal to the nil band of £325,000) on the spouse exemption which would otherwise apply on transfers from Kesme to Soba.

However, it will also mean that any overseas assets owned by Soba will be subject to UK inheritance tax in the future as they will no longer be excluded property for inheritance tax purposes. This would not be beneficial.

Tutorial note. The limit of £325,000 on the spouse exemption applies where the transferor spouse is UK domiciled and the transferee spouse is non-UK domiciled.

Value of the residue of the estate

Soba will receive the residue of the estate, ie the estate less the gift to the daughter and the inheritance tax on that gift. The inheritance tax is calculated as follows:

	£
£325,000 @ 0%	0
£45,000 @ 40/60	30,000
£370,000	30,000

The gross transfer is £(370,000 + 30,000) = £400,000.

The residue available to Soba is £(1,280,000 − 400,000) = £880,000.

Tutorial notes

1   Although Kesme is non-UK domiciled, the specific legacy to his daughter will be chargeable to UK IHT because it is a UK asset.

2   The residence nil rate band does not apply because Kesme's share of the main residence passes to his spouse Soba.

3   The inheritance tax due on the specific gift to the daughter will be paid out of the residue of the estate, such that it will be borne by Soba. Because the residue of the estate is exempt, due to the spouse exemption, the gift must be grossed up.

4   *Proof of Kesme's IHT liability*

	£
Kesme's estate	1,280,000
Less: Legacy to Soba (spouse exemption)	(880,000)
Chargeable estate	400,000
£325,000 @ 0%	0
£75,000 @ 40%	30,000
£400,000	30,000

4 Spike

Marking scheme

				Marks
(a)	(i)	Loss for the tax year 2017/18	1	
		Terminal loss	3	
				4
	(ii)	Relief of the loss for the tax year 2017/18		
		The reliefs available	2	
		Tax savings 2017/18		
		Business assets	1½	
		House	2	
		Tax savings 2016/17	1	
		Relief of the terminal loss		
		The reliefs available	3	
		Tax savings – terminal loss	1	
		Tax savings – excess of trading loss over terminal loss	1½	
		Max	10
(b)		Requirement to deregister	2	
		Output tax	2	
				4
(c)		Relocation payment		2
				20

(a) (i) **Loss relief available on the cessation of the trade**

Trading loss for the tax year 2017/18

	£
Loss for the period from 1 January 2017 to 30 September 2017	13,500
Add overlap profits	8,300
Trading loss 2017/18	21,800

Tutorial note. The basis period for the tax year 2017/18 runs from 1 January 2017 (the end of the basis period for the previous year) until 30 September 2017 (the cessation of trade).

Terminal loss

	£	£
6 April 2017 to 30 September 2017		
Loss £13,500 × 6/9		9,000
Add overlap profits		8,300
		17,300
1 October 2016 to 5 April 2017		
1 October 2016 to 31 December 2016		
Profit £22,500 × 3/12	5,625	
1 January 2017 to 5 April 2017		
Loss £13,500 × 3/9	(4,500)	
Net profit ignored for the purposes of terminal loss	1,125	
		0
Terminal loss		17,300

(ii) **The reliefs available in respect of the trading loss and the terminal loss**

Relief of the loss for the tax year 2017/18

The loss for the tax year 2017/18 can be offset against Spike's general income of 2017/18 and/or 2016/17.

Once the loss has been offset against the general income of a particular tax year, it can also be offset against the capital gains of that same year.

Spike has no general income in the tax year 2017/18. However, a claim can be made for the whole of the loss to be relieved against his 2017/18 capital gains.

Relieving the loss against the gains on the sale of the business assets would save capital gains tax at the rate of 10% due to the availability of entrepreneurs' relief. The tax saved would be £21,800 × 10% = £2,180.

Spike's sale of his house will be an exempt disposal of his principal private residence if he has always occupied it, or is deemed to have always occupied it. If part of the gain on the house is taxable, capital gains tax will be payable at 28% because it is residential property and the gains on the business assets will have used the basic rate band. Accordingly, if this is the case, the loss should be offset against any gain on the house in priority to the gain on the business assets.

In the tax year 2016/17, the loss would be offset against the general income of £22,500. The claim cannot be restricted in order to obtain relief for the personal allowance of that year. The tax saved would be £(22,500 – 11,500) = £11,000 × 20% = £2,200.

Relief of the terminal loss

The terminal loss can be offset against the trading profit of the business for 2017/18 and the three preceding tax years, starting with the latest year.

The trading profit in the tax year 2017/18 is nil, such that the terminal loss will be relieved in the tax year 2016/17. This would save tax of £(22,500 – 11,500) = £11,000 × 20% = £2,200.

The excess of the trading loss of 2017/18 over the terminal loss is £(21,800 – 17,300) = £4,500. This amount can be offset against general income and capital gains in 2017/18 and 2016/17 as set out above. However, once the terminal loss has been relieved in the tax year 2016/17, Spike's remaining general income of £(22,500 – 17,300) = £5,200 is less than the personal allowance, thus there is no taxable income and, therefore, no further tax saving to be achieved in either of the two relevant years. Accordingly, the remaining loss should be relieved against the capital gains of 2017/18. This would save tax of £4,500 × 10% = £450 if the loss is relieved against the gains on the sale of the business, or £4,500 × 28% = £1,260 if it is relieved against a non-exempt gain arising on the sale of the house.

(b)   **VAT**

Spike should have notified HM Revenue & Customs of the cessation of his business within 30 days of ceasing to make taxable supplies, ie by 30 October 2017.

He may be liable to a penalty if he failed to do so.

Spike should have charged VAT on any machinery and inventory which he sold whilst he was still registered for VAT.

When Spike deregistered, he should have accounted for output tax on all business assets which he still owned in respect of which he had previously recovered input tax. There was no need to account for this output tax if it was less than £1,000.

(c)   **The relocation payment**

The compensation in respect of the sale of the house at short notice at a low price will be regarded as having been derived from employment, so it will be taxable in full.

£8,000 of the payment in respect of the costs of moving house will be exempt; the remaining £(11,500 – 8,000) = £3,500 of the payment will be taxable.

ACCA Strategic Professional – Options

Advanced Taxation (ATX – UK)

Mock Exam 3

(ACCA March/June 2017 Sample questions updated to FA 2017)

Question Paper	
Time allowed	**3 hours 15 minutes**
This paper is divided into two sections	
Section A	**BOTH questions are compulsory and MUST be attempted**
Section B	**BOTH questions are compulsory and MUST be attempted**

DO NOT OPEN THIS PAPER UNTIL YOU ARE READY TO START UNDER EXAMINATION CONDITIONS

Section A – BOTH questions are compulsory and MUST be attempted

1 Pippin (Mar/Jun 17)

Your manager has sent you the notes she prepared following a meeting with Pippin, an established client of your firm who is resident and domiciled in the UK. The notes together with an email from your manager are set out below.

Meeting notes from your manager – dated 8 June 2018

Commencement of 'Pinova' business

Pippin intends to start a new unincorporated business, 'Pinova', on 1 August 2018. He has identified two alternative strategies: strategy A and strategy B.

The budgeted tax-adjusted profit/(loss) of the two strategies are set out below. These figures are before the adjustments necessary in respect of the equipment purchases and employment costs (see below).

	Strategy A		Strategy B	
	Period ending 31 March 2019	Year ending 31 March 2020 and future years	Period ending 31 March 2019	Year ending 31 March 2020 and future years
	£	£	£	£
Profit/(loss)	13,000	60,000	(10,000)	130,000

Equipment purchases and employment costs

The above profit/loss figures need to be adjusted in respect of the following:

(a)   Both strategies will require Pippin to purchase equipment in August 2018 for £8,000.

(b)   Strategy B will require two employees from 1 April 2019. Pippin will pay each of them a gross salary of £2,000 per month. He will also pay them £0.50 per business mile for driving their own cars. He expects each of them to drive 250 business miles per month.

(c)   Strategy A will not require any employees.

Pippin will claim the maximum capital allowances available to him. He will also claim opening years loss relief in respect of the trading loss arising under strategy B.

Cessation of previous business

Pippin's previous unincorporated business ceased trading on 31 December 2017. The taxable profits of the business for its final three tax years were:

	£
2015/16	82,000
2016/17	78,000
2017/18	14,000

Pippin had no other taxable income during these three years.

Receipt of £75,000

Pippin's aunt, Esme, died on 31 January 2018.

On 1 September 2012, Esme's father (Pippin's grandfather) died leaving the whole of his estate to Esme. However, on 1 January 2013 Pippin received £75,000 but cannot remember whether the money came from Esme, personally, or from his grandfather's estate, under a variation of Esme's interest in the will.

On 1 November 2012, Esme had transferred cash of £375,000 to a trust for the benefit of her children.

Shares in Akero Ltd

Pippin owns 16,000 shares in Akero Ltd which have a current market value of £4.50 per share. Pippin subscribed £16,000 for these shares on 4 January 2016. Pippin obtained income tax relief of £4,800 (£16,000 × 30%) under the enterprise investment scheme (EIS) in the tax year 2015/16. He also claimed EIS deferral relief in that year of £16,000 in relation to a chargeable gain on the sale of a painting.

Pippin is considering selling 5,000 of his Akero Ltd shares in order to fund his personal expenditure during the start-up phase of the Pinova business.

Extract from an email from your manager – dated 8 June 2018

Please prepare a memorandum for the client files which addresses the following issues:

(a)   **Additional funds required for the 20-month period from 1 August 2018 to 31 March 2020**

Pippin's taxable income will consist of the profits of the Pinova business and, for the tax year 2019/20 onwards, he expects to receive dividend income of £1,500 per year. His personal expenditure is £4,000 per month.

I want you to complete the table below to calculate the additional funds which Pippin would require during the first 20 months of the business under each of the two strategies (A and B) after putting aside sufficient funds to settle his tax liabilities for the tax years 2018/19 and 2019/20. You should then evaluate the two strategies by reference to the results of your calculations.

Pippin and I calculated his total **pre-tax** cash receipts; you do not need to check them. The only adjustment required to these pre-tax cash receipts is the cost of employing the two employees.

	Strategy A £	Strategy B £
Total pre-tax cash receipts for the 20-month period	61,000	109,500
Cost of employing the two employees	Nil	( )
Pippin's total income tax and national insurance contribution liabilities for the tax years 2018/19 and 2019/20	(_____)	(_____)
Personal expenditure (£4,000 × 20)	(80,000)	(80,000)
Additional funds required	____	____

(b)   **Receipt of £75,000**

Explain, with supporting calculations, the inheritance tax implications for Pippin of the receipt of the £75,000.

(c)   **Sale of shares in Akero Ltd**

Explain the tax liabilities which would result if Pippin were to sell 5,000 of his Akero Ltd shares in the tax year 2018/19.

Tax manager

Required

Prepare the memorandum as requested in the email from your manager. The following marks are available:

(a) Additional funds required for the 20-month period from 1 August 2018 to 31 March 2020 **(20 marks)**
(b) Receipt of £75,000 **(5 marks)**
(c) Sale of shares in Akero Ltd **(6 marks)**

Professional marks will be awarded for the approach taken to problem solving, the clarity of the explanations and calculations, the effectiveness with which the information is communicated, and the overall presentation and style of the memorandum. **(4 marks)**

(Total = 35 marks)

2 Heyer Ltd group (Mar/Jun 17)

Your manager has asked you to take charge of some work in connection with the Heyer Ltd group of companies. A schedule of information from the client files and an email from your manager detailing the work he requires you to do are set out below.

Heyer Ltd group – schedule of information from the client files

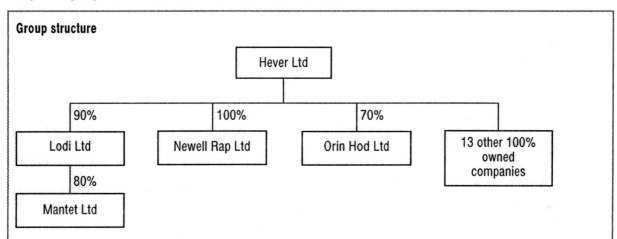

Group structure

General information

- All of the companies are resident in the UK and prepare accounts to 31 December each year.
- The figures given below of taxable total profits (TTP) take account of all possible rollover relief claims.
- None of the companies has received any dividend income from non-group companies.

Specific information

Mantet Ltd

- Mantet Ltd has TTP of between £40,000 and £50,000 every year.

Newell Rap Ltd

- Heyer Ltd acquired Newell Rap Ltd on 1 May 2017.

- Newell Rap Ltd has a capital loss brought forward as at January 2018 of £94,000. This loss arose on a sale of land on 1 February 2015.

Heyer Ltd group – schedule of information from the client files (continued)

Orin Hod Ltd

- The TTP of Orin Hod Ltd exceed £200,000 every year.
- In the year ending 31 December 2018 Orin Hod Ltd will make chargeable gains of £86,000.

Other 100% owned companies

- Each of these companies has TTP of more than £130,000 every year.
- Four of them will have substantial chargeable gains in the year ending 31 December 2018.
- Five of them will have capital losses in the year ending 31 December 2018.

Group restructuring

(a) It is intended that the trade and assets of five group companies (Newell Rap Ltd and four of the other 100% owned companies) will be sold to Lodi Ltd at some point in January 2019.

(b) The assets of the five companies, including the business premises, machinery and equipment will be sold to Lodi Ltd for their market value.

(c) The tax written down value of the main pool of each of the five companies immediately prior to the sale will be zero.

Pink Time Ltd

Heyer Ltd intends to incorporate a new subsidiary, Pink Time Ltd, on 1 September 2018. Pink Time Ltd will have a monthly turnover of £35,000. All of its sales will be to members of the public and will be zero rated for the purposes of value added tax (VAT).

Email from your manager – dated 8 June 2018

Please carry out the following work:

(a) **Group planning**

The group's objective is to minimise the corporation tax payable in instalments by group companies in respect of the year ended 31 December 2018.

I have asked Cox, our tax assistant, to carry out this work and I have provided him with the details of the companies' budgeted results for 2018. There is no group relief available within the group.

Cox has not done this type of work before and he has had very little experience of capital gains groups, so I want you to prepare some guidance for him. The guidance should consist of explanations of:

(i) The circumstances in which a member of the Heyer Ltd group would be required to pay corporation tax in instalments, assuming that the profits threshold should be divided by 18;

(ii) Which companies are members of a capital gains group;

(iii) How Cox should determine the amount of chargeable gains and capital losses to transfer between the group companies in order to achieve the group's objective; and

(iv) The relevance to the group's objective of the **specific information** provided in the schedule of information.

(b) **Group restructuring**

Identify, with reasons, the implications of the proposed group restructuring in relation to chargeable gains, stamp duty land tax and capital allowances, and what will happen to any capital losses belonging to the five companies whose trade and assets are transferred.

(c) **Pink Time Ltd**

Explain whether it will be compulsory for Pink Time Ltd to register for VAT and why the company would benefit from registering.

(d) **Disclosure of transfer pricing**

It has been realised by the management of Heyer Ltd that transfer pricing adjustments should have been made in respect of the year ended 31 December 2014 for three of the companies in the group. The corporation tax liability of the group was understated as a result of this non-disclosure.

I have already explained the interest and penalties which may be charged in respect of this. I want you to list the other matters which need to be considered, by us, as tax advisers to the group, and by the management of the group, in relation to the disclosure or non-disclosure of this information to HM Revenue & Customs (HMRC).

Tax manager

Required

Carry out the work requested in the email from your manager. The following marks are available:

(a)	Group planning	**(11 marks)**
(b)	Group restructuring	**(4 marks)**
(c)	Pink Time Ltd	**(5 marks)**
(d)	Disclosure of transfer pricing	**(5 marks)**
		(Total = 25 marks)

Section B – BOTH questions are compulsory and MUST be attempted

3 Dan and Noah (Mar/Jun 17)

Your client, Dan, requires advice on the inheritance tax implications arising as a result of the recent death of his father, Noah, Dan's own UK residence status, and the potential chargeable gain arising on his proposed disposal of his UK house.

Noah:

- Was resident in the UK from 1 April 1999 until his death on 31 May 2018, following a short illness
- Had a domicile of origin in the country of Skarta and did not acquire a domicile of choice in the UK
- Has one child, Dan

Noah – information for inheritance tax:

- Noah had not made any lifetime gifts.
- Noah left all the assets in his estate upon his death to Dan.

Noah – valuation of assets owned at death on 31 May 2018:

	£
Main residence located in the country of Skarta	242,000
Chattels and cash in the UK	435,000

Inheritance tax and liabilities in the country of Skarta:

- Under the tax system in Skarta, the inheritance tax payable will be £56,080.
- Legal and administration fees of £12,400 will be payable in Skarta in respect of Noah's house.
- There is no double tax treaty between the UK and Skarta.

Dan:

- Is domiciled in the country of Skarta
- Is unmarried, and has no children
- First became resident in the UK on 1 July 2013
- Left the UK on 1 January 2017 to go travelling
- Returned to the UK for the first time on 15 May 2018, when his father was taken ill
- Intends to work part time in the UK throughout the month of July 2018 only
- Will remain in the UK until 5 August 2018, when he intends to move permanently to Skarta

Dan – disposal of his UK house:

- Dan purchased a house in the UK on 1 October 2012 for £286,000, where he lived until 1 January 2017.

- He has not lived in the house since this date.

- He allowed his father, Noah, to live in the house, rent-free, until his father's death.

- He has agreed to sell the UK house on 1 August 2018 for £318,000.

- The house was valued at £297,000 on 5 April 2015.

(a) (i) State, giving reasons, whether or not the house in Skarta will be included in Noah's chargeable estate on death for the purposes of UK inheritance tax. **(3 marks)**

(ii) Assuming that the house in Skarta is subject to inheritance tax in the UK, calculate the value of Dan's inheritance from Noah after all taxes and liabilities have been paid. **(6 marks)**

(b) (i) On the assumption that Dan does not satisfy either of the automatic tests for determining his UK residence status, explain why Dan will **NOT** be resident in the UK for tax purposes in the tax year 2018/19. **(5 marks)**

(ii) Calculate the chargeable gain arising on the disposal of Dan's UK house on 1 August 2018 under the residential property rules applicable to non-UK residents. Dan will not elect to be taxed on the whole of the gain but will elect for the gain to be time-apportioned if it is beneficial to do so. **(6 marks)**

(Total = 20 marks)

4 Achiote Ltd, Borage Ltd and Caraway Ltd (Mar/Jun 17)

The finance director of Achiote Ltd would like your advice on the tax implications of the acquisition of two intangible fixed assets, various transactions involving an overseas subsidiary, and opting to tax a commercial building.

Achiote Ltd:

- Achiote Ltd 100% of the ordinary shares in Borage Ltd and 80% of the ordinary shares in Caraway Inc.
- Achiote Ltd and Borage Ltd are resident in the UK. Caraway Inc is resident in the country of Nuxabar.
- All three companies are trading companies and prepare accounts to 31 March annually.

Borage Ltd – purchase of intangible fixed assets:

- Borage Ltd purchased the goodwill of an unincorporated business for £62,000 on 1 September 2017.
- Borage Ltd will amortise this goodwill in its accounts on a straight-line basis over a five-year period.
- Borage Ltd also purchased a patent from Achiote Ltd for £45,000 on 1 January 2018.
- Achiote Ltd had purchased the patent for £38,000 on 1 January 2015.
- The patent was being amortised in Achiote Ltd's accounts on a straight-line basis over a ten-year period.
- Borage Ltd will continue to amortise the patent over the remainder of its ten-year life.

Achiote Ltd – loan to Caraway Inc:

- Achiote Ltd made a loan of £100,000 to Caraway Inc on 1 April 2017.

- The rate of interest on the loan is 6% per annum, which is 2% below the rate applicable to an equivalent loan from an unrelated party.

- There is no double tax treaty between the UK and Nuxabar.

Achiote Ltd – sale of equipment to, and proposed sale of shares in, Caraway Inc:

- Achiote Ltd acquired its 80% shareholding in Caraway Inc on 1 January 2018 for £258,000.

- Achiote Ltd is now proposing to sell an 8% shareholding in Caraway Inc to an unconnected company on 1 October 2018 for £66,000.

- An item of equipment owned by Achiote Ltd and used in its trade was sold to Caraway Inc on 1 March 2018 for its market value of £21,000.

- The item of equipment had cost Achiote Ltd £32,000 in May 2017.

Achiote Ltd – purchase and rental of a commercial building:

- Achiote Ltd has recently purchased a two-year-old commercial building from an unconnected vendor.

- The building will be rented to an unconnected company, Rye Ltd.

- Rye Ltd is a small local company, which supplies goods to Achiote Ltd but does not charge value added tax (VAT) on these sales.

Required

(a) Explain, with supporting calculations where appropriate, the corporation tax treatment in the year ended 31 March 2018, of the goodwill and the patent acquired by Borage Ltd. **(4 marks)**

(b) Explain the implications of the rate of interest charged by Achiote Ltd on the loan to Caraway Inc by reference to the transfer pricing legislation, and any action which should be taken by Achiote Ltd. **(5 marks)**

(c) Advise Achiote Ltd of the chargeable gains implications arising from (1) the sale of the item of equipment to Caraway Inc; and (2) its proposed sale of the shares in Caraway Inc. **(5 marks)**

(d) (i) On the assumption that Rye Ltd makes only taxable supplies, state **TWO** legitimate reasons why it might not charge VAT on its sales to Achiote Ltd. **(2 marks)**

(ii) Explain whether or not it would be financially beneficial for Achiote Ltd to opt to tax the commercial building, and the implications for Rye Ltd if it chooses to do so. **(4 marks)**

Note. The following indexation factors should be used for this question, where applicable:

January 2015 to January 2018   0.079
May 2017 to March 2018   0.023
January 2018 to October 2018   0.013
March 2018 to October 2018   0.010

(Total = 20 marks)

Answers

DO NOT TURN THIS PAGE UNTIL YOU HAVE
COMPLETED THE MOCK EXAM

A plan of attack

We've already established that you've been told to do it 101 times, so it is of course superfluous to tell you for the 102nd time to **take a good look at the paper before diving into the answers.**

What's the worst thing you could be doing right now if this was the actual exam paper? Wondering how to celebrate the end of the exam in about three hours' time?

Turn back to the paper and let's sort out a **plan of attack**!

First things first

Look through the paper and work out the order in which to attack the questions. You've got **two options**. Option 1 is the option recommended by BPP.

Option 1 (if you're thinking 'Help!')

If you're a bit worried about the paper, do the questions in the order of how well you think you can answer them. If you find the questions in Section B less daunting than the questions in Section A, start with Section B.

There are **two questions** in Section B. **Question 3** has two parts, each broken down into two sub-parts. Most of this question tests technical issues which are new in Advanced Taxation (ATX – UK). Part (a) concerns inheritance tax on an estate which includes overseas assets. Sub-part (i) only has three marks so make sure you address the particular point about the house in Skarta. Layout your computation clearly in sub-part (ii) so the marker can see how you have treated each aspect.

Part (b) is about the determination of UK residence status and the disposal of a UK residential property by a non-UK resident individual. Don't spend too long on sub-part (i). You may want to use bullet points to set out the UK ties. The computations in sub-part (ii) are quite a recent technical change and demonstrate that you need up-to-date knowledge to tackle Advanced Taxation (ATX – UK).

Question 4 has four parts, all relating to corporate taxation. Part (a) is about intangible assets. There are special rules for companies which are new in Advanced Taxation (ATX – UK). Hint – the treatment of goodwill and patents is different.

Part (b) is about transfer pricing, again a new topic in Advanced Taxation (ATX – UK). Start by stating why transfer pricing applies in these circumstances and then deal with its effects.

Part (c) concerns chargeable gains. Where there is a sale of shares by a company you need to consider the substantial shareholding exemption (SSE) but don't assume that it will always apply. This is an important topic in Advanced Taxation (ATX – UK).

Part (d) is about value added tax (VAT). Land and buildings are a new area for Advanced Taxation (ATX – UK) but the aspect of why a trader may not charge VAT is an application of basic principles from Taxation (TX – UK). Stop and think!

Do not spend longer than about 75 minutes on Section B. When you've spent the allocated time on the questions in Section B turn to the **two case-study questions** in Section A.

Read the Section A questions through thoroughly before you launch into them. Once you start make sure you allocate your time to the parts within the questions according to the marks available and that, where possible, you attempt the easy marks first.

Question 1 has three parts. Part (a) is allocated 20 marks so you need to spend about 40 minutes on it. It concerns the tax implications of starting a new business. It is important that you use your calculations to complete the table and don't include any unnecessary explanations. The technical content is mainly from Taxation (TX – UK).

Part (b) is about inheritance tax on a gift which could either have been an inheritance or a lifetime gift. There are reasonably easy marks to be gained here. Most of this question could be answered with brought forward knowledge from Taxation (TX – UK).

Part (c) concerns the enterprise investment scheme (EIS) which is new at Advanced Taxation (ATX – UK). You need to deal with both income tax and capital gains tax implications.

Four marks are available for professional skills in question 1. In order to earn these marks you need to take a sensible approach to solving the problem set in relation to the alternative business structures, provide explanations and calculations that are clear and logical, keep your answer specific rather than general, and adopt a professionally acceptable style.

Question 2 has four parts. Part (a) is about minimising the corporation tax payable in instalments by the group companies by transferring gains and losses around a chargeable gains group. Both aspects should be familiar from Taxation (TX – UK) but you need to take a logical approach and confine your answer to the specific facts given.

Part (b) concerns transfer of trades and assets between group companies. These are mainly new topics in Advanced Taxation (ATX – UK).

Part (c) is about value added tax registration. This should be familiar from Taxation (TX – UK) but, as ever, you need to apply your knowledge to the situation described in the question.

Part (d) is the five mark part on ethics and should yield easy marks.

Lastly, what you mustn't forget is that you have to **answer BOTH questions in Section A and BOTH questions in Section B**.

Option 2 (if you're thinking 'This paper's alright')

It never pays to be overconfident but if you're not quaking in your shoes about the exam then **turn straight to the case-study questions in Section A**.

Once you've done these questions, **move to Section B**. The question you attempt first really depends on what you are most confident at. If you are undecided look at the requirements. It may be easier to obtain more marks if these are broken down into several smaller parts. For example, Question 4 has four parts which are not related to each other so it should be possible to gain reasonable marks on each part.

No matter how many times we remind you...

Always, always **allocate your time** according to the marks for the question in total and then according to the parts of the question. And **always, always follow the requirements** exactly. For example in Question 2(b) you are told in the email from your manager that you need to deal with chargeable gains, stamp duty land tax and capital allowances so you must make sure to cover all these aspects.

You've got spare time at the end of the exam...?

If you have allocated your time properly then you **shouldn't have time on your hands** at the end of the exam. But if you find yourself with five or ten minutes to spare, check over your work to make sure that you have answered all the requirements of the questions and all parts of all requirements.

Forget about it!

And don't worry if you found the exam difficult. More than likely other candidates will too. If this were the real thing you would need to **forget** the exam the minute you leave the exam hall and **think about the next one**. Or, if it's the last one, **celebrate**!

1 Pippin (Mar/Jun 17)

Text references. Employment income is the subject of Chapter 4. Trade profits and national insurance contributions for the self-employed are covered in Chapter 6 and capital allowances are dealt with in Chapter 7. Inheritance tax on potentially exempt transfers is covered in Chapter 16 and variations of wills in Chapter 18. The enterprise investment scheme (EIS) is dealt with in Chapter 2 with EIS deferral relief being dealt with in Chapter 13.

Top tips. In part (a) of the question make sure you follow the structure as set out in the question – the examining team have tried to word the question to help you have a process to follow. Make sure you leave sufficient time to look at parts (b) and (c) of the question as you must complete the whole question. Structure will be important to help the marker follow your answer – in part (a) ensure your supporting calculations are clearly referenced for example by stating which tax year they relate to and in parts (b) and (c) ensure you use sub-headings to make clear the different scenarios you are discussing.

Easy marks. There should have been easy marks available in terms of calculating income tax and national insurance due for each tax year and each strategy in part (a) of the question. Explaining the IHT consequences of a direct gift from Esme should also have provided some core marks. Finally, the tax consequences of investing in EIS shares and then selling them should also be core marks which should have provided you with the opportunity to show your knowledge of this important part of the syllabus.

Examining team's comments. Part (a) concerned a plan to start a new unincorporated business. Candidates were asked to prepare a table of figures in order to determine the individual's cash position for two alternative business strategies after two years of trading. One of the strategies required the individual to take on two employees. The technical content of this part of the question was reasonably straightforward and required candidates to:

- Recognise the availability of the annual investment allowance
- Determine the relief available in respect of a trading loss in the first tax year of trading
- Deal with the tax implications for the employer of paying a mileage allowance to the employees
- Calculate the employer's class 1 contributions in respect of the employees
- Calculate the income tax, class 4 and class 2 liabilities of the individual

Accordingly, in order to do well, candidates needed to concentrate on the detail, be brisk in their approach and avoid any unnecessary narrative. Many candidates were able to do this and there were some very high quality answers to this part of the question. Weaker candidates were less willing to commit themselves to the numbers and instead wrote about the tax implications in more general terms. Some candidates also let themselves down by failing to consider the individual's national insurance contributions position, such that they did not attempt quite a few of the marks on offer. There were few technical problems with this part of the question. The one common error was the implications of the mileage allowance, with most candidates knowing there was a rule regarding the excess over 45p per mile but many thinking it related to the tax deductibility of the payments made as opposed to the class 1 contributions due.

Part (b) concerned inheritance tax and was done reasonably well. Candidates were very comfortable with the basic mechanics of the tax including death within seven years of a potentially exempt transfer (PET), the nil rate band and the availability of taper relief. Weaker candidates did not always relate the facts of the question to the requirement, such that they ignored the chargeable lifetime transfer which was made prior to, but in the same tax year as, the PET. This meant that they wrote in general terms about the availability of the annual exemption and the nil rate band rather than applying the rules to the specific facts of the question.

Part (c) required candidates to explain the tax liabilities on the sale of shares in respect of which income tax relief under the enterprise investment scheme and EIS deferral relief had been claimed. As is so often the case, in order to score well, candidates needed to stop and think. In particular, they needed to identify the three separate implications of the sale of the shares. It was important to do this first because candidates then knew how much needed to be explained in the relatively short amount of time available.

The three implications which needed to be explained were:

- The gain which was deferred when the shares would become chargeable
- An element of the income tax relief obtained when the shares were acquired would be withdrawn
- There would be a chargeable gain on the sale of the shares themselves

Weaker candidates identified one of these points and wrote about it at length rather than identifying all of the points which needed to be made.

Four marks were available for professional skills in this question. On the whole, the performance of candidates in this area was reasonably good.

Marking scheme

			Marks
(a)	Completion of table	1½	
	Strategy A		
	2018/19	3½	
	2019/20	5	
	Strategy B		
	Cost of employees	5½	
	2018/19	3½	
	2019/20	2½	
	Evaluation	2	
	Max		20
(b)	PET and death within seven years	3½	
	Deed of variation	2	
	Max		5
(c)	Gain on shares sold	2	
	Deferred gain	2	
	Capital gains tax liability	1½	
	Income tax	1½	
	Max		6
Problem solving		1	
Clarity of explanations and calculations		1	
Effectiveness of communication		1	
Overall presentation and style		1	
			4
			35

Memorandum

Client	Pippin
Subject	Pinova business
Prepared by	Tax senior
Date	8 June 2018

(a) **Additional funds required for the 20-month period from 1 August 2018 to 31 March 2020**

	Strategy A £	Strategy B £
Total pre-tax cash receipts for the 20-month period	61,000	109,500
Cost of employing the two employees:		
(£48,000 + £3,000 + £1,412)	Nil	(52,412)
Total income tax and national insurance contribution liabilities for the tax years 2018/19 and 2019/20		
(£0 + £16,463)	(16,463)	
(£23,850 – £7,560)		(16,290)
	44,537	40,798
Personal expenditure	(80,000)	(80,000)
Additional funds required	35,463	39,202

Strategy A

2018/19

	£
Budgeted profit	13,000
Less: Capital allowances 100% AIA	(8,000)
Tax adjusted trading profit	5,000
Income tax:	
Covered by the personal allowance	0
Class 4 national insurance contributions (NIC):	
Below the lower profits limit	0
Class 2 NIC:	
Below the small profits threshold	0
Total tax and NIC	0

Tutorial note. Non-payment of class 2 NIC can affect the availability of state benefits, including the state pension. Accordingly, it may be advisable for Pippin to pay the class 2 NIC contributions even if his profit is below the small profits threshold.

2019/2020

	Non-savings income £	Dividend income £	Total £
Trading income	60,000		
Dividends		1,500	
Net income	60,000	1,500	61,500
Less personal allowance	(11,500)		
Taxable income	48,500	1,500	50,000

Income tax:
Trading income

	£	£
£33,500 × 20%	6,700	
£15,000 × 40%	6,000	
		12,700
Dividend income – nil rate band		0
Class 4 NIC		
(£45,000 – £8,164) × 9%	3,315	
(£60,000 – £45,000) × 2%	300	
		3,615
Class 2 NIC		
(£2.85 × 52)		148
Total tax and NIC		16,463

Strategy B

2018/19

	£
Budgeted loss	(10,000)
Less: Capital allowances 100% AIA	(8,000)
Tax adjusted trading loss	(18,000)

Claiming opening years loss relief will result in a repayment of income tax and class 4 NIC of £7,560 (£18,000 × 42%) in respect of 2015/16.

2019/20

	£	£
Budgeted profit		130,000
Less: Cost of employees		
Salaries (£2,000 × 12 × 2)		(48,000)
Mileage allowance (£0.50 × 250 × 12 × 2)		(3,000)
Class 1 NIC:		
Salary (£2,000 × 12)	24,000	
Mileage payments ((£0.50 – £0.45) × 250 × 12)	150	
	24,150	
(£24,150 – £8,146) × 13.8% × 2	4,412	
Less: Employment allowance	(3,000)	
		(1,412)
Tax adjusted trading profit		77,588
Income tax and NIC on profit of £60,000 (per strategy A)		16,463
Income tax and class 4 NIC on excess over £60,000		
(£77,588 – £60,000) × 42%		7,387
Total tax and NIC		23,850

Evaluation of the two strategies

Strategy A requires less additional funding than strategy B over the 20-month period.

However, the annual profit under strategy A will only be £60,000. This will not be sufficient to generate the £48,000 (£4,000 × 12) of post-tax cash receipts required by Pippin.

The post-tax profit under Strategy B will be £53,738 (£130,000 – £52,412 – £23,850), such that there may be sufficient post-tax cash receipts for Pippin's needs.

(b) Receipt of £75,000

The tax implications for Pippin depend on whether the £75,000 was a direct gift from Esme or the result of Esme having made a tax-effective deed of variation of her father's will.

Gift from Esme

The gift would have been a potentially exempt transfer. Esme's death within seven years of the gift would result in an inheritance tax liability for Pippin as follows:

	£
Transfer	75,000
Inheritance tax at 40% (Note)	30,000
Less: Taper relief (5 to 6 years) (£30,000 × 60%)	(18,000)
	12,000

Tutorial note

Esme's annual exemptions and her nil rate band were used by the gift on 1 November 2012.

Deed of variation

A variation whereby £75,000 of Esme's inheritance was transferred to Pippin would not be treated as a gift from Esme to Pippin. Instead, the money would be regarded as having passed to Pippin via his grandfather's will. Accordingly, in these circumstances, there would be no inheritance tax implications for Pippin as a result of the death of Esme.

(c) Sale of shares in Akero Ltd

Capital gains tax

Chargeable gain on the sale of the shares

Pippin will realise a chargeable gain of £17,500 ((£4.50 − £1) × 5,000) if the shares are sold prior to 4 January 2019 at their current market value.

However, if the shares are sold on or after 4 January 2019, the chargeable gain arising on the sale will be exempt.

Chargeable gain deferred in respect of the painting

Regardless of when the shares are sold, the chargeable gain which was deferred on their acquisition will become chargeable. The chargeable gain deferred was £16,000, or £1 per share, such that, on the sale of 5,000 shares, a gain of £5,000 will become chargeable.

Capital gains tax liability

Any chargeable gains realised by Pippin in the tax year 2018/19 will be reduced by his annual exempt amount of £11,300. Any gains not covered by the annual exempt amount will be taxed at 10%, as Pippin has no taxable income.

Income tax

If the shares are sold prior to 4 January 2019 at their current market value, there will be a withdrawal of £1,500 (5,000 × £1 × £0.30) of the income tax relief originally obtained by Pippin. This is because the shares will have been sold for more than their cost.

2 Heyer Ltd group (Mar/Jun 17)

Text references. Corporation tax administration is the subject of Chapter 22. Groups are covered in Chapter 26. Stamp taxes are dealt with in Chapter 19. Value added tax (VAT) registration is dealt with in Chapter 28. Ethics are covered in Chapter 30.

Top tips. Make sure you work logically through this question ensuring you make the time to address each sub requirement. It's important to take time at the start of the question noting the various group relationships and noticing that the transfers in (b) are to Lodi Ltd – a group company rather than an unconnected company.

Easy marks. Parts (c) and (d) should have been the source of some easy VAT and ethics marks provided you attempted them. In part (a) there were also basic marks looking at when companies pay tax in instalments and chargeable gains group planning. In addition to giving the explanations explicitly requested, which involved stating your knowledge, you should also have addressed the request to apply your knowledge specifically to the facts from the question.

Examining team's comments. Part (a) required candidates to prepare guidance for a tax assistant on how to minimise the corporation tax payable in instalments by the group companies by transferring chargeable gains and capital losses between them. This was a slightly unusual requirement. It was vital that candidates spent some time thinking about how they would carry out the assistant's task before they started trying to explain to the assistant how to do it. Candidates needed to think in terms of what needed to be done (objectives), and how it was to be achieved (strategies).

The objectives were:

- Where possible, to reduce the taxable total profits (TTP) of each company below the limit of £1,500,000 (divided by the 18 companies in the group)

- To reduce the TTP of any company required to pay tax in instalments

These objectives can be achieved by:

- Matching gains and losses in a particular company
- Transferring gains from a company with TTP above the threshold to one with TTP below the threshold

As expected, candidates found this task difficult and there was a tendency to fall back on describing the rules in general terms as opposed to trying to address the specific requirement.

Part (b) concerned the proposal to transfer the trades and assets of five of the group companies to another of the group companies and was also challenging. The challenge here was to address all of the issues set out in the manager's email in the time available. Only four points needed to be made but there was only one mark for each point. Having said that this was a challenging question, many candidates made a good job of it. In particular, they kept their answers brief and tried to address all of the issues raised. Weaker candidates focussed on only one or two of the manager's issues which restricted the number of marks which could be obtained. The one common technical error concerned the capital allowances treatment. The point here is that the assets would be automatically transferred at tax written down value because the companies are all under 75% common control both before and after the transfer of the trades.

Part (c) concerned a whether a company making zero rated supplies was required to register for VAT and the benefits of registering. This part was not done particularly well. This was partly due to candidates writing standard answers to the whether or not to register question without focussing on the fact that the company was making zero rated supplies. This meant that the following two points were often missed:

- The company could apply to be exempt from registration even if its supplies exceeded the registration limit

- If the company were to register, there would be no effect on its customers, even though they are members of the public

Part (d) concerned the disclosure of information to HM Revenue & Customs and was done well by the vast majority of candidates.

			Marks
(a)	Requirement to pay by instalments	3½	
	Definition of capital gains group	2	
	Amount to transfer	4	
	Specific information		
	Mantet Ltd	2	
	Newell Rap Ltd	2	
	Orin Hod Ltd	1	
	Other 100% companies	½	
		Max	11
(b)	One mark for each relevant point (maximum of 4 marks)		4
(c)	One mark for each relevant point (maximum of 5 marks)		5
(d)	The need to disclose	4	
	Other matters	3	
		Max	5
			25

(a) **Group planning**

Requirement to pay corporation tax by instalments

In respect of the year ending 31 December 2018, a company in the Heyer Ltd group will be required to pay corporation tax in instalments if its taxable total profits (TTP) exceed £83,333 (£1,500,000/18) and either:

- It had TTP of more than £83,333 in the year ended 31 December 2017; or
- Its TTP for the year ended 31 December 2018 are more than £555,556 (£10,000,000/18).

Tutorial note. Companies which have a corporation tax liability of less than £10,000, are not required to pay tax in instalments. This point is not referred to in the answer as none of the companies falls within this definition.

The Heyer Ltd capital gains group

The Heyer Ltd capital gains group consists of Heyer Ltd, its 75% subsidiaries and their 75% subsidiaries. In addition, Heyer Ltd must have an effective interest of more than 50% in any company which it does not own directly. Accordingly, all of the group companies are in a single capital gains group with the exception of Orin Hod Ltd.

Amount of chargeable gains and capital losses to transfer between group companies

You should aim to:

(i) Reduce the TTP of as many companies as possible to £83,333, such that they are no longer required to pay corporation tax in instalments.

(ii) Reduce the TTP of those companies which are still required to pay corporation tax in instalments, as this will reduce the amount of each instalment.

(iii)   The whole or part of any current period chargeable gain and/or capital loss can be transferred between companies in a capital gains group.

(1)   Gains and losses should be transferred in order to match them against each other.

(2)   Gains should be transferred from a company which has TTP in excess of the £83,333 threshold to a company which has TTP below the threshold.

Relevance of the specific information

Mantet Ltd

Mantet Ltd had TTP for the year ended 31 December 2017 of less than £83,333. Accordingly, it will not be required to pay its corporation tax liability for the year ended 31 December 2018 in instalments unless its TTP for that year are more than £555,556. With this in mind, chargeable gains should be transferred to Mantet Ltd from other companies in the Heyer Ltd capital gains group provided its TTP are kept below £555,556.

Newell Rap Ltd

Newell Rap Ltd's capital losses are pre-entry capital losses because they were realised before Newell Rap Ltd was acquired by Heyer Ltd. These losses cannot be used to relieve gains on assets realised by other members of the Heyer Ltd capital gains group.

Orin Hod Ltd

Orin Hod Ltd's TTP exceed £83,333. However, it is not a member of the Heyer Ltd capital gains group because it is not a 75% subsidiary of Heyer Ltd. Accordingly, it is not possible to reduce its TTP by, for example, transferring its chargeable gains to other companies.

Other 100% owned companies

All of these companies are required to pay corporation tax in instalments.

Current period chargeable gains and capital losses realised by these companies should be transferred to other companies in the Heyer Ltd capital gains group in accordance with the guidance set out above.

(b)   **Group restructuring**

Chargeable gains

Chargeable assets, including the business premises, will be transferred at no gain, no loss automatically, because all of the companies are 75% subsidiaries of Heyer Ltd. Accordingly, no chargeable gains will arise.

Stamp duty land tax (SDLT)

No SDLT will be due in respect of the sale of the business premises because Heyer Ltd owns at least 75% of the ordinary share capital of all of the companies.

Capital allowances

Machinery and equipment will be automatically transferred at tax written down value, rather than market value, because Heyer Ltd controls at least 75% of each of the companies. Accordingly, no balancing charges will arise.

Capital losses

The unused capital losses of Newell Rap Ltd, and any other company whose trade and assets will be transferred, will not be transferred to Lodi Ltd, but current period capital losses can be transferred to companies in the same capital gains group, as set out above.

(c) **Pink Time Ltd**

The taxable supplies of Pink Time Ltd will exceed the registration threshold of £85,000 by the end of November 2018 (£35,000 × 3 = £105,000). However, the company can apply to be exempt from registration because it only makes zero rated supplies.

It would be beneficial for Pink Time Ltd to register for value added tax (VAT) because it would then be able to recover its input tax. The fact that its customers are members of the public is irrelevant because Pink Time Ltd makes zero rated supplies and therefore will not be charging any VAT.

Pink Time Ltd would be in a VAT repayment position if it were to register for VAT because it only makes zero rated supplies. It could improve its cash flow position by making its VAT returns monthly rather than quarterly.

(d) **Disclosure of transfer pricing**

It is more than 12 months since the return filing date, and therefore too late to amend the corporation tax returns. Accordingly, this information must be disclosed to HM Revenue & Customs (HMRC). We should encourage Heyer Ltd to make this disclosure.

The management of the Heyer Ltd group can inform HMRC or may authorise us to do so. However, we must not disclose the error to HMRC without permission.

We cannot continue to act for the companies unless this disclosure is made.

We should notify the group of the following consequences of not providing this information to HMRC:

(i) If they refuse to disclose the error, we will advise HMRC that we no longer act for them. We would not, however, give any reason for our actions.

(ii) Non-disclosure of the error would also amount to tax evasion. This could result in criminal proceedings under both the tax and money laundering legislation.

We should inform our firm's money laundering officer of the situation.

We should ascertain how the non-disclosure occurred in order to determine whether or not there may be other matters which have been omitted from the group companies' corporation tax returns.

3 Noah and Dan (Mar/Jun 17)

Text references. The death estate for inheritance tax (IHT) is covered in Chapter 16 with valuation of assets dealt with in Chapter 17. Overseas aspects of inheritance tax are covered in Chapter 18. UK residence status is covered in Chapter 10 and the overseas aspects of capital gains tax in Chapter 14. Principal private residence relief is dealt with in Chapter 13.

Top tips. In part (a)(i) of this question you would need to ensure you present your answer clearly in terms of deciding Noah's domicile and how that would impact the IHT on the house located in Skarta. Make sure you follow the instructions in the question and include the main residence in Skarta in the death estate in (a)(ii). Part (b)(i) requires text-book knowledge about the sufficient ties tests. Make sure you clearly lay out your argument explaining each of the ties and concluding with how many ties you believe Dan has. The new rules on a non-resident disposing of a UK residential property were tested in (b)(ii) – you must ensure you are familiar with newer additions to the syllabus as they are often tested.

Easy marks. The basic rules about domicile and deemed domicile should have provided easy marks in this question together with the basics of the IHT computation in part (a)(ii). In part (b) of the question the sufficient ties tests should allow you easy marks from stating and applying your text-book knowledge to the scenario. However, you need to know those rules to be able to state them – make sure you learn how to determine an individual's residence status if you don't know this already.

Examining team's comments. Part (a) concerned inheritance tax on assets situated overseas. Candidates performed quite well and displayed a strong knowledge of the rules. However, a minority did not score as many marks as they could have done because they did not follow the instructions in the question sufficiently carefully. In particular, they failed to finish off their answers by calculating the value of the inheritance after deduction of all taxes and liabilities. (**BPP note**. The residence nil rate band was not relevant when this question was originally set so the examining team made no comments on this aspect.)

Part (b) required an explanation of an individual's resident status and a calculation of a chargeable gain on the sale of a property including the relief available in respect of a principal private residence. The majority of candidates had a sound knowledge of the rules in connection with the determination of UK residence. There were just two minor problems; some candidates failed to note that there were only five marks available and simply wrote too much, whilst others did not do enough to apply the rules to the facts of the question. The calculation of the chargeable gain was not done particularly well. The requirement stated that the gain needed to be calculated 'under the residential property rules applicable to non-UK residents'. This required a computation based on the market value of the property as at 5 April 2015 and then a further computation where the gain based on the original cost of the property had to be time apportioned pre and post that date. Unfortunately, many candidates simply calculated a gain in the normal manner.

Candidates who did well in this question:

- Applied their knowledge of the detailed rules to the facts of the question
- Managed their time carefully
- Read the requirements carefully and ensured that they answered the question set

Marking scheme

				Marks
(a)	(i)	Inclusion of house in Skarta in death estate		3
	(ii)	Chargeable estate	2	
		IHT liability	3½	
		Value of Dan's inheritance	2	
		Max		6
(b)	(i)	Need three ties	1	
		Application of ties	4½	
		Max		5
	(ii)	Gain before PPR exemption	3½	
		PPR exemption	4	
		Max		6
				20

(a) (i)   Inheritance tax treatment of the house located in Skarta

An individual who is not domiciled or deemed domiciled in the UK is liable to UK inheritance tax only in respect of assets located in the UK.

An individual is deemed domiciled in the UK if they have been resident in the UK for 17 out of the 20 tax years ending with the tax year in which the transfer is made, and accordingly are liable to UK inheritance tax on their worldwide assets.

Noah became resident in the UK on 1 April 1999, so by the time of his death on 31 May 2018, Noah had been resident in the UK for 19 tax years, so would be deemed domiciled in the UK for inheritance tax purposes. Therefore the house located in Skarta will be included in his chargeable death estate.

(ii) **Value of Dan's inheritance**

Noah – death estate

	£
UK assets	435,000
House in Skarta (W1)	229,900
Chargeable estate	664,900
Residence nil rate band (max)	(100,000)
Nil rate band available on death	(325,000)
Taxable estate	239,900
IHT (£239,900 × 40%)	95,960
Less: Double tax relief – the lower of:	
Overseas tax suffered £56,080	
UK IHT on the house (£229,900 × 95,960/664,900)	(33,180)
IHT payable	62,780

Value of Dan's inheritance after all taxes and liabilities

	£
Value of assets in the estate (£435,000 + £242,000)	677,000
Less: Legal and administration fees in Skarta	(12,400)
IHT suffered (£56,080 + £62,780)	(118,860)
Value of inheritance	545,740

Working: House in Skarta

	£
Value of the house at 31 May 2018	242,000
Less: Legal and administration fees – the lower of:	
The fees incurred £12,400	
Maximum £12,100 (5% × £242,000)	(12,100)
Value to include in the estate	229,900

(b) (i) **Reasons why Dan will be classed as non-UK resident in the tax year 2018/19**

As Dan does not satisfy the criteria under either of the automatic tests for determining his UK residence status, the 'sufficient ties' tests must be considered. These take into account the number of days spent in the UK and the number of 'ties' Dan has to the UK.

As Dan has previously been resident in the UK in at least one of the previous three tax years, and will spend between 46 and 90 days in the UK during 2018/19 (15 May to 5 August 2018), he would be considered to be UK resident in this tax year if he has at least three UK ties.

Dan will satisfy only one tie:

(1)   He spent more than 90 days in the UK in the tax year 2016/17, as he did not leave the UK until 1 January 2017.

Dan will not satisfy the remaining four ties:

(1)   Although he will have owned his house in the UK up to the date of its sale on 1 August 2018 (ie available to him for more than 91 days in 2018/19) he has not spent any nights there in 2018/19.

(2)   He does not have any close family residing in the UK.

(3)   He will not be present in the UK for the same number or more days in 2018/19 than in any other country.

(4)   He will not have substantive work in the UK in 2018/19.

Accordingly, Dan will be classed as non-UK resident in 2018/19.

Tutorial notes

1. A parent (Noah) does not fall within the definition of close family for this purpose.

2. As Dan is planning to move permanently to Skarta on 5 August 2018, he will not be present in the UK for more days in 2018/19 than in any other country.

3. Dan will be working for 31 days in July 2018, which is insufficient to be regarded as 'substantive' (40 days or more).

(ii) **Dan – capital gains tax liability on disposal of his UK house**

Default method – gain arising after 5 April 2015

	£
Proceeds	318,000
Less: Market value at 5 April 2015	(297,000)
Gain	21,000

Straight line time apportionment method (on election)

	£
Proceeds	318,000
Less: Cost	(286,000)
Gain	32,000

Dan will have owned the house from 1 October 2012 to 1 August 2018 ie 70 months.

The period from 6 April 2015 to 1 August 2018 is 40 months.

The post-6 April 2015 gain is £18,286 (£32,000 × 40/70).

Dan should therefore elect to use the straight line time apportionment method as this produces a lower gain.

	£
Gain before principal private residence (PPR) exemption	18,286
Less: PPR exemption (W) £18,286 × 39/40	(17,829)
Chargeable gain	457

Working: PPR exemption

Tax year	Total months	Exempt months	Chargeable months
2015/16 – UK resident	12	12	–
– Actual occupation			
2016/17 – UK resident			
– Actual occupation 6 April to 31 December 2016	9	9	–
– Unoccupied 1 January to 31 January 2017	1	–	1
– Last 18 months 1 February to 5 April 2017	2	2	–
2017/18 – Non-UK resident last 18 months	12	12	–
2018/19 – Non-UK resident last 18 months	4	4	
	40	39	1

Tutorial note. There is no need to consider whether or not Dan qualifies for the PPR exemption in 2017/18 or 2018/19 because the period of Ownership of the property in these two tax years is within the final 18 months of ownership.

4 Achiote Ltd, Borage Ltd and Caraway Ltd (Mar/Jun 17)

Text references. Intangible assets for companies and transfer pricing are covered in Chapter 20. Chattels are covered in Chapter 14, chargeable gains groups in Chapter 26 and the chargeable gains for companies in Chapter 21. Value added tax (VAT) registration and zero rating are dealt with in Chapter 28 and land and buildings in Chapter 29.

Top tips. Each sub requirement in this question tested different topics so it would be key that you ensured you attempted each part of the question. It would also be important that you identified the group relationships existing between the companies in the question as some of the transactions were between group companies thus having special consequences.

Easy marks. The application, or otherwise, of the substantial shareholding exemption is frequently examined in Advanced Taxation (ATX – UK) and should have allowed you easy marks in part (c). In addition the VAT in part (d) contains core topics which you must be able to answer.

Examining team's comments. Part (a) required an explanation of the corporation tax implications of acquiring goodwill and a patent. The goodwill was a minor point and was handled well by the majority of candidates. The patent, however, was not handled so well. Many candidates treated it as a standard asset as opposed to being part of the intangible assets regime. As a result, the inter-group transfer was treated as a no gain, no loss transfer as opposed to a tax neutral transfer. This, in turn, caused problems when calculating the tax deductions available in the future.

Part (b) concerned transfer pricing. This part was not done particularly well because many candidates did not identify sufficient mark-scoring points. It was important to start the explanation at the beginning by identifying why the transfer pricing rules applied. This required a reference to the fact that one of the companies controlled the other and the lack of an arms' length price. Many candidates did not do this but simply took it for granted that the regime applied. Once the relevance of the rules had been established, candidates should then have explained the effect of the rules by reference to the need to increase the company's taxable profit and the amount of the increase. It was this part which most candidates focussed on. It was then necessary to consider any other relevant matters including the availability of the exemption where a group is not large and the possibility of obtaining advance approval of the arrangements from HM Revenue & Customs.

Part (c) concerned the chargeable gains implications of the sale of an item of equipment and of some shares. Candidates needed to concentrate and take care in order to score well. The equipment was being transferred between two companies in a chargeable gains group. However, the company acquiring the property was not resident in the UK, such that the no gain/no loss treatment would not apply to the transaction. In addition, due to the availability of capital allowances, the loss arising on the disposal would not be available. When dealing with the sale of the shares, it was important to recognise that the substantial shareholder exemption would not be available because the vendor would not have owned the shares for a 12-month period in the two years prior to the sale.

Part (d) concerned various aspects of VAT. The aspects of this part relating to the option to tax a commercial building were generally handled well. However, candidates found the other aspect of this part more difficult. Candidates were asked to suggest reasons why a company which made taxable supplies did not charge VAT on sales made to an unconnected party. Stronger candidates stopped for a moment to gather their thoughts and then wrote about the registration limit and/or the making of zero rated supplies. Weaker candidates simply wrote about registration in general and often lengthy terms. Candidates need to be in a rhythm throughout the exam of reading, thinking and then writing.

					Marks
(a)	Goodwill			1	
	Patent			4	
			Max		4
(b)	Transfer pricing – Reason why it applies			1	
	– Implications and action			5	
			Max		5
(c)	Transfer of equipment			2½	
	Sale of shares			3½	
			Max		5
(d)	(i)	Reasons why VAT is not charged			2
	(ii)	Beneficial due to input VAT incurred		1½	
		Implications of option to tax for Rye Ltd		3	
			Max		4
					20

(a) **Goodwill**

No amortisation in respect of goodwill is deductible for corporation tax purposes, so the amortisation charged in the accounts for the year ended 31 March 2018 must be added back for tax purposes.

Patent

As the patent is transferred between two members of a capital gains group, it will be transferred at a price which is tax neutral. The written down value of the patent in Achiote Ltd at the date of its sale to Borage Ltd was £26,600 (£38,000 – (3 × 10% × £38,000)). Accordingly this will be the deemed acquisition price for Borage Ltd. Borage Ltd will continue to amortise the patent over the remainder of its ten-year life. In the year ended 31 March 2018 amortisation charged in its accounts will be £950 (£26,600/7 × 3/12). This amount is allowable for corporation tax purposes.

(b) **Loan to Caraway Inc**

It would appear that an arm's length rate of interest on the loan would be 8% as this is the rate at which Caraway Inc could have obtained an equivalent loan from an unrelated party. As Achiote Ltd controls Caraway Inc, they are connected companies and so the transfer pricing rules apply.

The interest receivable by Achiote Ltd is £2,000 (£100,000 × 2%) less than it would be under an arm's length agreement. This means that Achiote Ltd's non-trading loan relationship income is reduced by this amount, such that less tax is payable in the UK. Therefore, Achiote Ltd must adjust the figures within its corporation tax return to reflect the arm's length price.

As there is no double tax treaty between the UK and Nuxabar, Nuxabar will be regarded as a non-qualifying territory. As a result, the exemption which might otherwise have been available if a group is not large will not be available to the Achiote Ltd group.

Achiote Ltd can seek advance approval from HM Revenue & Customs in respect of any intra-group pricing arrangements, including the rate of interest to be charged on a loan.

(c)   **Transfer of the item of equipment and the sale of shares in Caraway Inc**

Sale of item of equipment

The intra-group transfer of the item of equipment by Achiote Ltd to Caraway Inc will not be treated as a no gain, no loss transfer, because even though Achiote Ltd owns 80% of the company, such that the companies are in a capital gains group, the fact that Caraway Inc is not a UK resident company means that the asset will no longer be within the charge to UK taxation. This is therefore a chargeable disposal for Achiote Ltd at 1 March 2018. Although the equipment has fallen in value, no capital loss will arise as the asset qualified for capital allowances as it was used in Achiote Ltd's trade.

Sale of shares in Caraway Inc

The sale of the 8% holding in Caraway Inc will not be exempt from corporation tax under the substantial shareholding exemption (SSE) rules. This is because Achiote Ltd will only have held its shares in Caraway Inc for nine months prior to the proposed disposal date and so will not meet the criteria to have owned at least 10% of the shares in Caraway Inc for a continuous 12-month period out of the two years prior to disposal. Accordingly, a chargeable gain will arise on the disposal, calculated as follows:

	£
Disposal proceeds	66,000
Less: Cost £258,000 × 8/80	(25,800)
Unindexed gain	40,200
Less: Indexation allowance (0.013 × £25,800)	(335)
Chargeable gain	39,865

Tutorial note. The equipment is not exempt as a wasting asset as it qualified for capital allowances due to being used in a business.

(d)   (i)   **Reasons why Rye Ltd might not charge value added tax (VAT) on its sales to Achiote Ltd**

Rye Ltd is a small company, and its taxable supplies may not yet have reached the registration threshold.

Rye Ltd's taxable supplies have reached the registration threshold, but its supplies to Achiote Ltd are zero rated.

(ii)   **Option to tax the commercial building**

As the building purchased by Achiote Ltd was less than three years old, and a commercial building, it would have been a standard-rated supply. So Achiote Ltd will have incurred a significant amount of input value added tax (VAT) in relation to this expenditure. For this reason, it will be financially beneficial (at least in the short term), for Achiote Ltd to opt to tax the building in order to be able to reclaim this tax. This will also enable Achiote Ltd to recover the input tax in respect of the building's running costs.

However, VAT must then be added to the rent charged by Achiote Ltd to Rye Ltd. The impact of this on Rye Ltd will depend on its size and the nature of its supplies.

(1)   If its taxable supplies are currently below the registration limit, Rye Ltd could voluntarily register for VAT purposes and reclaim the input VAT charged on the rent payments.

(2)   If Rye Ltd's taxable supplies have reached the registration threshold, but its supplies are wholly or partially zero rated, provided it has registered for VAT purposes, the input VAT charged on the rent payments will, again, be reclaimable, and may lead to a (higher) repayment of VAT from HM Revenue and Customs.

Tutorial note. In order to determine whether or not opting to tax the commercial building would be commercially beneficial, longer term implications, such as the impact on the building's future marketability, would also need to be considered. Credit was also available for candidates who made reference to partial exemption.

Tax tables

SUPPLEMENTARY INSTRUCTIONS

1. You should assume that the tax rates and allowances for the tax year 2017/18 and for the financial year to 31 March 2018 will continue to apply for the foreseeable future unless you are instructed otherwise.

2. Calculations and workings need only be made to the nearest £.

3. All apportionments may be made to the nearest month.

4. All workings should be shown.

TAX RATES AND ALLOWANCES

The following tax rates and allowances are to be used in answering the questions.

Income tax

		Normal rates	Dividend rates
Basic rate	£1 – £33,500	20%	7.5%
Higher rate	£33,500 – £150,000	40%	32.5%
Additional rate	£150,001 and over	45%	38.1%

	£
Savings income nil rate band – Basic rate taxpayers	£1,000
– Higher rate taxpayers	£500
Dividend nil rate band	£5,000

A starting rate of 0% applies to savings income where it falls within the first £5,000 of taxable income.

Personal allowance

	£
Personal allowance	11,500
Transferable amount	1,150
Income limit	100,000

Residence status

Days in UK	Previously resident	Not previously resident
Less than 16	Automatically not resident	Automatically not resident
16 to 45	Resident if 4 UK ties (or more)	Automatically not resident
46 to 90	Resident if 3 UK ties (or more)	Resident if 4 UK ties
91 to 120	Resident if 2 UK ties (or more)	Resident if 3 UK ties (or more)
121 to 182	Resident if 1 UK tie (or more)	Resident if 2 UK ties (or more)
183 or more	Automatically resident	Automatically resident

Remittance basis charge

UK resident for:	Charge
7 out of the last 9 years	£30,000
12 out of the last 14 years	£60,000
17 out of the last 20 years	£90,000

Child benefit income tax charge

Where income is between £50,000 and £60,000, the charge is 1% of the amount of child benefit received for every £100 of income over £50,000.

Car benefit percentage

The base level of CO_2 emissions is 95 grams per kilometre.

The percentage rates applying to petrol cars with CO_2 emissions up to this level are:

50 grams or less per kilometre	9%
51 grams to 75 grams per kilometre	13%
76 grams to 94 grams per kilometre	17%
95 grams per kilometre	18%

Car fuel benefit

The base figure for calculating the car fuel benefit is £22,600.

Individual savings accounts (ISAs)

The overall investment limit is £20,000.

Property income

Basic rate restriction applies to 25% of finance costs.

Pension scheme limits

Annual allowance	£40,000
Minimum allowance	£10,000
Threshold income limit	£110,000
Income limit	£150,000
Lifetime allowance	£1,000,000

The maximum contribution that can qualify for tax relief without any earnings is £3,600.

Authorised mileage allowances: cars

Up to 10,000 miles	45p
Over 10,000 miles	25p

Capital allowances: rates of allowance

Plant and machinery

Main pool	18%
Special rate pool	8%

Motor cars

CO_2 emissions up to 75 grams per kilometre	100%
CO_2 emissions between 76 and 130 grams per kilometre	18%
CO_2 emissions over 130 grams per kilometre	8%

Annual investment allowance

Rate of allowance	100%
Expenditure limit	£200,000

Cash basis

Revenue limit	£150,000

Cap on income tax reliefs

Unless otherwise restricted, reliefs are capped at the higher of £50,000 or 25% of income.

Corporation tax

Rate of tax	– Financial year 2017	19%
	– Financial year 2016	20%
	– Financial year 2015	20%
Profit threshold		£1,500,000

Patent box – deduction from net patent profit

Net patent profit x ((main rate – 10%)/main rate)

Value added tax (VAT)

Standard rate	20%
Registration limit	£85,000
Deregistration limit	£83,000

Inheritance tax: nil rate bands and tax rates

	£
6 April 2017 to 5 April 2018	325,000
6 April 2016 to 5 April 2017	325,000
6 April 2015 to 5 April 2016	325,000
6 April 2014 to 5 April 2015	325,000
6 April 2013 to 5 April 2014	325,000
6 April 2012 to 5 April 2013	325,000
6 April 2011 to 5 April 2012	325,000
6 April 2010 to 5 April 2011	325,000
6 April 2009 to 5 April 2010	325,000
6 April 2008 to 5 April 2009	312,000
6 April 2007 to 5 April 2008	300,000
6 April 2006 to 5 April 2007	285,000
6 April 2005 to 5 April 2006	275,000
6 April 2004 to 5 April 2005	263,000
6 April 2003 to 5 April 2004	255,000

Residence nil rate band

6 April 2017 to 5 April 2018	100,000

Rate of tax on excess over nil rate band	– Lifetime rate	20%
	– Death rate	40%

Inheritance tax: taper relief

Years before death	Percentage reduction
Over 3 but less than 4 years	20%
Over 4 but less than 5 years	40%
Over 5 but less than 6 years	60%
Over 6 but less than 7 years	80%

Capital gains tax

	Normal rates	Residential property
Rates of tax Lower rate	10%	18%
Higher rate	20%	28%
Annual exempt amount		£11,300
Entrepreneurs' relief Lifetime limit		£10,000,000
Rate of tax		10%

National insurance contributions (not contracted out rates)

Class 1 employee	£1–£8,164 per year	Nil
	£8,165–£45,000 per year	12%
	£45,001 and above per year	2%
Class 1 employer	£1–£8,164 per year	Nil
	£8,165 and above per year	13.8%
	Employment allowance	£3,000
Class 1A		13.8%
Class 2	£2.85 per week	
	Small profits threshold	£6,025
Class 4	£1–£8,164 per year	Nil
	£8,165–£45,000 per year	9%
	£45,001 and above per year	2%

Rates of interest (assumed)

Official rate of interest	2.50%
Rate of interest on underpaid tax	2.75%
Rate of interest on overpaid tax	0.50%

Stamp duty land tax

Non-residential properties

£150,000 or less	0%
£150,001 to £250,000	2%
£250,001 and above	5%

Residential properties (Note)

£125,000 or less	0%
£125,001 to £250,000	2%
£250,001 to £925,000	5%
£925,001 to £1,500,000	10%
£1,500,001 and above	12%

Note. These rates are increased by 3% in certain circumstances.

Stamp duty

Shares	0.5%

Review Form – Advanced Taxation (ATX – UK) (10/17)

Name: _____   Address: _____

_____

_____

How have you used this Kit?
(Tick one box only)

☐ On its own (book only)

☐ On a BPP in-centre course_____

☐ On a BPP online course

☐ On a course with another college

☐ Other _____

Why did you decide to purchase this Kit?
(Tick one box only)

☐ Have used the complimentary Study Text

☐ Have used other BPP products in the past

☐ Recommendation by friend/colleague

☐ Recommendation by a lecturer at college

☐ Saw advertising

☐ Other _____

During the past six months do you recall seeing/receiving any of the following?
(Tick as many boxes as are relevant)

☐ Our advertisement in *Student Accountant*

☐ Our advertisement in *Pass*

☐ Our advertisement in *PQ*

☐ Our brochure with a letter through the post

☐ Our website www.bpp.com

Which (if any) aspects of our advertising do you find useful?
(Tick as many boxes as are relevant)

☐ Prices and publication dates of new editions

☐ Information on product content

☐ Facility to order books

☐ None of the above

Which BPP products have you used?

Study Text	☐	*Passcards*	☐
Kit	☑	*Other*	☐

Your ratings, comments and suggestions would be appreciated on the following areas.

	Very useful	Useful	Not useful
Passing Advanced Taxation (ATX – UK)	☐	☐	☐
Questions	☐	☐	☐
Top Tips etc in answers	☐	☐	☐
Content and structure of answers	☐	☐	☐
Mock exam answers	☐	☐	☐

Overall opinion of this Kit	*Excellent* ☐	*Good* ☐	*Adequate* ☐	*Poor* ☐

Do you intend to continue using BPP products?   *Yes* ☐   *No* ☐

The BPP author of this edition can be emailed at: accaqueries@bpp.com

Review Form (continued)

TELL US WHAT YOU THINK

Please note any further comments and suggestions/errors below.